Changing Patterns of Communications Control

The Critical Communications Review

Vincent Mosco and Janet Wasko, Series Editors

VOLUME I

*Labor, The Working Class,
and The Media*

Vincent Mosco and Janet Wasko

VOLUME II

*Changing Patterns of
Communications Control*

Vincent Mosco and Janet Wasko

The Critical Communications Review

VOLUME II: CHANGING PATTERNS OF COMMUNICATIONS CONTROL

edited by

Vincent Mosco
Temple University
and
Janet Wasko
California State Polytechnic University, Pomona

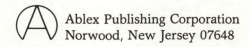
Ablex Publishing Corporation
Norwood, New Jersey 07648

Printed in the United States of America.

Library of Congress Cataloging in Publication Data

(Revised for vol. 2)
Main entry under title:

Critical communication review.

Bibliography: v. 2, p.
Includes indexes.
Contents: v. 1. Labor, the working class and media—
v. 2. Changing patterns of communication control.
1. Communication—Collected works. 2. Mass media—
Collected works. I. Mosco, Vincent. II. Wasko, Janet.
P90.C74   1983   001.5   82-11592
ISBN 0-89391-122-4 (v. 1)
ISBN 0-89391-153-4 (v. 2)

ABLEX Publishing Corporation
355 Chestnut Street
Norwood, New Jersey 07648

Contents

Contributors

Giovanni Cesareo Editor, *Sapere*. Former editor, *IKON*. President, Media/Mente (Italian association studying information and mass communication problems).

Patrice Flichy Researcher, Institut National de l'Audiovisuel, Paris. Author of *Les Industries de l'Imaginaire* (Presses Universitatires de Grenoble, 1980).

Howard Frederick Ohio State University. Author of *Ideology and International Broadcasting: Radio Wars between Cuba and the United States* (to be published by Ablex 1984).

Morten Giersing Associate Professor, Dept. of Comparative Literature, Mass Communication Section, University of Copenhagen. Author of *TV i USA* (Gyldendalske Boghandel, 1982), and articles on literature, literary criticism, and mass communication. Member of Danish Commission on the Media.

Timothy R. Haight Editor, *Telecommunications Policy and the Citizen* (Praeger, 1979) and co-author of *The Mass Media: Aspen Institute Guide to Communications Industry Trends* (Praeger, 1978).

Robert Jacobson Consultant, California Assembly Utilities and Commerce Committee. Author of *The Municipal Control of Cable* (Praeger, 1977).

Noreene Janus Formerly with I.L.E.T. (Mexico City). Co-editor of *Communication and Social Structure: Critical Studies in Mass Media Research* (Praeger, 1981), and numerous articles on transnational advertising.

Armand Mattelart Author of numerous books on communication, including *Multinational Corporations and the Control of Culture* (Humanities Press, 1979), *Mass Media, Ideologies and Revolutionary Movements* (Humanities Press, 1982), and co-editor of *Communication & Class Struggle* (International General, 1979).

Emile McAnany Associate Professor, Dept. of Radio-Television-Film, University of Texas at Austin. Co-editor of *Communication and Social Structure: Critical Studies in Mass Media Research* (Praeger, 1981).

Vincent Mosco Associate Professor of Communications, Temple University. Author of *Broadcasting in the United States* (Ablex, 1979) and *Pushbutton Fantasies: Critical Perspectives on Videotex and Information Technology* (Ablex, 1982).

Graham Murdock Research Fellow, Centre for Mass Communication Research, University of Leicester, England. Co-author of *Mass Media and the Secondary School* (MacMillan, 1973) and *Demonstrations and Communications: A Case Study* (Penguin, 1970), plus numerous articles and papers on the political economy of mass communications.

Manjunath Pendakur Assistant Professor, Dept. of Radio-Television-Film, Northwestern University. Author of numerous articles on the Canadian film industry and international communications.

Jean-Marie Piemme Author of *La Propagande Inavouée* (Presse Universitaires de Grenoble, 1975).

Herbert I. Schiller Professor of Communications, University of California, San Diego. Author of numerous books in the field of communications, including *Who Knows? Information in the Age of the Fortune 500* (Ablex, 1981), *Communications and Cultural Domination* (International Arts & Sciences Press, 1976), *The Mind Managers* (Beacon, 1973); co-editor of *National Sovereignty and International Communications* (Ablex, 1979).

Dallas W. Smythe Professor of Communications, Simon Fraser University. Author of *Dependency Road: Communications, Capitalism, Consciousness, and Canada* (Ablex, 1981). Former Chief Economist, Federal Communications Commission.

Janet Wasko Assistant Professor of Communication Arts, California State Polytechnic University, Pomona. Author of *Movies and Money: Financing the American Film Industry* (Ablex, 1982).

Introduction

Janet Wasko

The world of mass communications and information is changing. But, then, no one ever promised it would remain the same for long. Indeed, change is perhaps inevitable in our technologically-based media/information systems, as in society itself. Yet, recent developments in new information and communications technologies have prompted widespread discussion of a fundamental change—the shift from an industrial society to an information society, based on information as a basic resource. It is further argued that these changes represent a major rupture in advanced capitalism, thus stimulating a revival in the decaying, crises-ridden system.

While new information technologies are making possible increased production of information, other media technologies are providing the potential for wider distribution of information and cultural goods. As a result, "older" established media are undergoing a process of displacement or redefinition of their economic, political, and cultural roles. Most importantly, all of these processes are occurring within a continually changing political and economic climate, with struggles over control and power erupting in local, national, and international arenas.

In order to contribute to this debate from a critical perspective, this volume of *The Critical Communications Review* examines the shifting strategies of control over information and communication resources. The articles explore the consequences of the ongoing restructuring of communication systems, as critical researchers examine the role of information in the revitalization of the capitalist system, in new and evolving forms of social and political control, and in the reshaping of the cultural sphere.

Before introducing each article, a few general trends identified by our authors will be discussed.

MONOPOLY CAPITALISM REVISITED

New technological possibilities for storing, sending, and receiving information and cultural goods have prompted predictions of the revival of a free and open marketplace with abundant consumer choices. Yet, as many of the authors in this volume point out, the development of such technologies and information systems within market economies, or within the capitalist mode of production, in many ways reinforces the inherent tendencies of monopoly capitalism.

The development and control of new communications technologies is concentrated firmly in the hands of the largest transnational corporations and financial institutions, despite a few skirmishes over a piece of the action by smaller companies and entrepreneurs. Historically, entrepreneurial capital has been allowed to take the risks involved in introducing new technological innovations, while larger corporations move in when a market is assured. But, some of the newly emerging technologies (such as satellite communications) must necessarily involve transnational capital, due to the economic costs and the political power necessary to introduce and maintain such systems. With the increased importance of information/telecommunications to the economy as a whole, the participation of companies outside of the sector continues to grow, as large industrial and financial corporations become involved with information/communications technologies, as well as with software production. This is coupled with the trend within the communications/information sector toward diversified activities and cross-media ownership and control, which continues, and thus reinforces another aspect of revitalized monopoly capitalism.

Another common observation by the contributors to this volume concerns the intensified internationalization of information and communications technologies. As technological sophistication advances, so must the quest for additional profits. The transnational marketing of new information systems and products creates new tensions among advanced capitalist countries competing for these markets, and renews the need for military back-up systems in such efforts. As in the past, research/development of new communications contributes to, and is intimately linked with, military activites; thus, new technologies contribute in crucial ways to the rejuvenation of the military-industrial complex and of information imperialism. Questions of national sovereignity, dependence, and development are not only unresolved by these developments, but are especially intensified by the introduction of such new information technologies as direct broadcast satellites, transborder data systems, etc.

PRIVATIZATION, COMMERCIALIZATION AND DEREGULATION

Communication and information production and distribution have traditionally been protected in some way, that is, either subsidized, regulated, or even monopolized by the State as a *public* resource. However, the current political/economic climate finds new communications technologies and established media systems undergoing major changes as the role of the State is gradually transformed.

The increasing trends toward privatization and commercialization of communications and information resources, then, must be seen in light of the steady erosion of the public sector in many advanced capitalist countries. In the U.S., and elsewhere, the spectre of Reaganomics continues to sweep vital social services and public resources into the private sector, where individual consumption is glorified and the myth of freedom of choice reigns supreme. Thus, efforts continue in the U.S. to "unregulate" communications, while publicly-controlled media systems in other countries are increasingly threatened and eroded.

IDEOLOGY FOR AN INFORMATION AGE

These major shifts in political and economic strategies necessitate corresponding ideological reinforcement, another theme discussed by our contributors. The notions of consumer sovereignty, electronic democracy, and pluralist societies dominate liberal discussions of the emerging information age. In addition, the transnational imperative driving the development of new communications technologies further fuels the flaunting of the free flow principle in international arenas.

Thus, the ideology of the information society attempts to prepare the world and its people for the privatized, commoditized world of information.

CONTRADICATIONS AND ALTERNATIVES

The authors in this volume view the changing patterns of communications control not by looking at new developments in media and information distribution or at the technology itself, but by analyzing the social processes involved in the changing world of communications and information. In considering wider political, economic and ideological factors, important critical points, contradictory forces, and alternative strategies emerge in their discussions.

Rather than enhancing the potential for safer, more rewarding and more plentiful job possibilities, the transformation of the workplace by new technologies increasingly leads to unemployment and/or unsatisfying and dangerous labor. (These are also taken up by a few of the authors in Volume I of *The Review*.) Concurrently, unemployment of large numbers of workers is not conducive to the intensified consumption necessary to fuel an information economy based on marketplace principles.

Another critical point is observed on both domestic and international levels where information dependence and unequal information/communication resource distribution may lead to even stronger reactions and struggles by those in dependent positions. Thus, as observed by contributors to Volume I and II of *The Review*, the potential for access to information and alternative uses of information technologies may ultimately accelerate social transformation. Also noted, however, is the need for continuing analysis and critique of the social context in which new technologies are emerging. For such analysis is necessary in order to develop and explore alternative strategies and visions for emancipatory information systems and democratic communications.

This volume of *The Critical Communications Review* contributes to this analysis and promotes such alternative visions.

I. GLOBAL IMPLICATIONS OF CHANGING
COMMUNICATION CONTROL

The first article in this volume presents an analysis of new information/communications technology within the context of international capitalism. In "Informatics and Information Flows: The Underpinnings of Transnational Capitalism," Herb Schiller discusses the vital role of information and telecommunications as the "springboards" for the transformation of the American economy, as well as for the extension of U.S. capitalism internationally.

He reviews some of the new information-based activities, such as transborder data flows, remote sensing, direct satellite broadcasting and database creation and utilization, illustrating how the new information technology further intensifies questions of national sovereignty, dependency, and development. The article also discusses the use of information systems and messages in reinforcing and adding new dimensions of control to military and corporate power centers. In his article, Schiller also discusses the continued attempts by transnational capital to peddle the "frayed" free flow of information principle, upon which rests the defense of the transnational corporate system. He concludes by pointing to a number of embarassing and threatening contradictions facing transnational capitalism in its effort to maintain control over the world's resources, yet in conflict with the needs of most of the world's people.

While Schiller continuously integrates the revitalization of transnational capital via new information technology with military considerations, Dallas Smythe directly confronts the role of communications in increased militarization and the potential consequences for world peace. In his article, Smythe considers not only the U.S., but also the Soviet military-industrial complex (together, the "Exterminist Axis") and their commitment to nuclear weapons, arguing that each cooperates antagonistically with the other in a "reciprocal, spiraling death dance." He further examines the old and new peace movements, observing that the new movement has broadened its base of popular opposition, has made important links to the ecology movement, and (at least in Europe) seems to acknowledge the Extermist Axis and the need for a broad-based internationalist movement. Smythe continues by observing that communications and communication policy are the areas where global contradictions are reflected in their most concentrated form, reminding us that communications—especially as it is produced and used today—plays a vital role in material production.

Noreene Janus presents another global view of the role of new communication technologies in advertising and the creation of global markets. She questions what role new technologies play in expanding transnational systems and how national barriers are attacked. She documents the ways in which transnational corporations are using new technological advances (such as video systems, cable and teletext) to extend global markets through advertising.

Janus looks historically at two distinct periods of transnational advertising, noting that the new communications technologies have changed the organization and impact of global advertising. Major changes are observed in advertising's increased accuracy in the production and the distribution of advertising messages and with increased access to broadcast systems. The article concludes with a discussion of the implications of transnational advertising for the Third World, as Janus reinforces the contention that the new communications infrastructure will not only be a new information age, but also a new commercial age at the global level.

Another general look at the changing world of communications/information technology is offered by Giovanni Cesareo, as he explores the liberal ideology of electronic democracy. He points out that many futurologists start from the technologies themselves, rather than from the social processes in which the new technologies may enter and from which needs emerge. He further argues that the development of new information technologies are not driven by consumer demand, but satisfy corporate strategies and capital's needs.

Cesareo challenges the hypothesis of an electronic democracy evolving with the new information society, basing his critique firmly on an analysis of the mode of production, or the organization of production, distribution and consumption processes. Who will be able to produce information? What relationship will exist between producers and consumers? What will be supplied and demanded? Cesareo questions whether or not the consumer will be able to obtain needed information for the construction of his/her own image of reality. The article concludes by suggesting that alternative discourses or projects may be possible in the process of transformation, creating a new mode of production of information, or, what Cesareo calls, a new "circular communications" based on electronics and telematics.

II. CHANGING CONTROL PATTERNS IN THE U.S., CANADA, AND LATIN AMERICA

Moving from these general and global views, we turn to several articles discussing the impact and implications of new information technology and changing control patterns in individual regions or for specific constituencies. Urgent issues involving the United States, Canada and Latin America are discussed in Part II, followed by several European perspectives in Part III.

The first article in Part II is "High Technology and Pacific Empire: The California Dream Revisited," in which Robert Jacobson dissects the heartland of high technology. California's technology industries, in conjunction with the military, produce a good share of the world's semiconductors, computers, computer services and telecommunications products, in such regions as the Silicon Valley. As a result, California is viewed and used as the testing ground for these new technologies and processes.

In this article, Jacobson contrasts the California dream—the eternal search for a better way of life—with high-tech economics and recent political efforts to preserve the state's indigenous industrial sector. In the process, Jacobson colorfully paints a future California landscape—severe unemployment, a devastated state political system, and "Third-world-like hinterlands," masking a few smaller enclaves for a wealthy elite.

Jacobson suggests, however, that, in order to affect an alternative future encompassing the California dream for all, political power must precede substantive change. He calls on critical communications researchers to point out those aspects of high technology which prevent popular, democratic political power.

Jacobson's Third World scenario for California anticipates the proposals presented in the next article by Tim Haight, which compares the information dependence of Third World countries to the information underclass created by high tech and new information resources in the U.S. Haight calls for a New American Information Order to create information democracy, which is essential in achieving true economic and political democracy.

The article looks to historical and ongoing struggles for a new international information order, noting that international experiences may provide strategies for domestic initiatives. Haight further examines strategies for information independence within the context of changing control structures and policies, observing similarities, and differences in structures of media control, policy making processes in each case, and the political organization of respective groups advocating media change.

"La Guerra Radial: Radio Wars Between Cuba and the U.S." presents a historical and current look at the international ideological battles waged via communication technologies. With shifting political tensions and intensified militarization, often fueled by the quest for further markets for new information/cultural commodities, these ideological battles are becoming more intense.

Howard Frederick presents information from public documents and interviews with Americans and Cubans, as he traces the history of the Cuban-American radio wars during the period after the Cuban Revolution to the present war between Radio Marti and Radio Lincoln. The significance of these radio wars is examined in light of international ideological confrontation, and Frederick concludes with a "modest proposal" for an alternative to the present conflict.

Cultural conflict and dependency is also the theme of the next article by Manjunath Pendakur. Although Canadian media industries continue to be dominated by foreign transnational media firms, recent efforts have been made to "Canadianize" the country's culture and economy. Pendakur situates this struggle for cultural autonomy within larger economic and political contexts, examining the recent history of legislative attempts by Canadian governments to resist cultural domination, and the resulting reactions by foreign media companies, and recent American political administrations. Pendakur concludes by examining the new media technologies in Canada—especially cable—in view of the new matrix of power evolving in both the U.S. and Canada, ultimately framing the continuing quest for Canada's cultural autonomy.

As Pendakur (and most of the other contributors to this volume) observes, the changing world of communications and information must be viewed in terms of international communications systems and global marketing of information and cultural goods. In the next article, Emile McAnany notes that the issues of cultural integrity and communications flow remain important with the growth of new technologies and the export of cultural/ informational software. He goes on to distinguish between different positions in the debate on cultural exchange and cultural dependency, placing emphasis on the importance of examining economic structures of cultural production, or a cultural industries approach. He further emphasizes the use of national case studies as an important research strategy. He uses Brazil as an example that enables him to chart changes that are taking place, and to anticipate consequences, both within Brazil and throughout Latin America.

III. EUROPEAN PERSPECTIVES ON NEW TECHNOLOGY AND CHANGING CONTROL

To introduce Part II of "Changing Patterns of Communication Control," Armand Mattelart and Jean-Marie Piemme offer "Twenty Three Guidelines for a Political Debate on Communications in Europe." The text establishes the general framework necessary for a contemporary analysis of established and new media, as well as the possibilities for alternatives. The authors first acknowledge a change in the very nature of information, arguing that information has become a basic resource with the information industry a leading economic sector. Mattelart and Piemme then discuss the consequences for established media, and for the traditional concept of culture. They remind us again that the notion of an information society masks the political function of the new communications technologies in restructuring the political and cultural apparatuses of the world capitalist system informing a new power bloc.

Mattelart and Piemme further consider the international implications of new technologies, together with the notions of privatization and social creativity. The particular case of Belgium is cited in light of transnational corporate power in that country, as well as Belgium's cultural dependency. The authors offer final guidelines and thoughts on communication alternatives, taking into consideration the new information technologies' effects on the social division of labor, in traditional divisions, and for decentralization.

Patrice Flichy follows with an examination of "Media Control in France," directing his attention to the conflict betwen political and economic rationale. He unfolds the background of communications and information systems in France since the Liberation, outlining the attempts by the new Socialist government to develop new forms of control over communications. Yet, he carefully argues that these new efforts will have to take into acocunt recent developments in the area of new technology and emerging media forms. Flichy provides evidence that, despite these efforts, political logic is being chipped away by economic logic, with the help of the French PTT and the large electronics industry.

A similar scenario is provided for the Scandinavian countries by Morten Giersing in "The Commercialization of Culture: Perspectives and Precautions." Giersing offers perspectives on commercial television and the evolving new forms of media technology for the Nordic region, pointing out commercial influences and contrasting European developments with those in the United States. Giersing then discusses the realistic possibilities for democratic television, in view of recent information technology, and considers economic and political factors. He offers specific suggestions, again, for alternative and emancipitory uses of information technology, together with concrete suggestions for regulatory policies.

In the final article of this volume, Graham Murdock presents an up-to-date summary of the main developments in "The Privatization of British Communications," confirming many of the major trends discussed by previous authors. He focuses on four major communication policy initiatives in Britain: denationalization, the remaking of British Telecom, the commercialization of satellites and of cable industries, and the transformation of public broadcasting (or, the "enterprising BBC"). These policies, Murdock argues, have not promoted competitive capitalism, as predicted, but instead, they intensify and accelerate monopoly capitalism.

The article continues with a discussion of the disappearing public sphere and the emergence of the "Fordism" of consumption. Finally, Murdock joins the other contributors in this volume in pointing to new contradictions which open forms of struggle and potential for public policy, locating them more centrally within the orbit of class struggle and politics. Murdock concludes by arguing that a proletarian public sphere, including a genuinely popular television, emerge from these struggles.

With this second volume of *The Critical Communications Review,* the editors would again like to encourage your comments and reactions to the articles and issues presented in this series. In this way, we hope future editions will continue to reflect critical perspectives and analyses of emerging and important communications and media concerns.

Section I

GLOBAL CONSIDERATIONS

1

Informatics and Information Flows: The Underpinnings of Transnational Capitalism

Herbert I. Schiller

International information flows, and the problems attendant on them, have become central concerns of those who are entrusted with the destinies of the transnational corporate order. The time, energies and attention of the government officials and business executives—though still not too many academics, which says much about where academics are at—are increasingly absorbed with information and communications-related issues.

The Under Secretary of State for Security Assistance, Science and Technology, for example, states flatly:

> For the United States, communications and information technologies are crucial. The U.S. has been the principal source and user of many of the new technologies and associated services. It has been the economic base for the ongoing communications and information revolution and through various means has made available technologies and services around the globe. (Salmon, 1982, p. 3)

More specific still, the Chairman of the Federal Communications Commission (FCC), testifying before a congressional committee in September 1981, described developments this way:

> International telecommunications is a dynamic field with an annual growth rate of at least twenty-five percent—or approximately three times that of domestic communications. The technology is advancing quickly, and this rapid growth strains the ability of the policy maker to find appropriate solutions to the institutional and substantive issues created. The single most important point to be made about international communications is that it cannot be considered in a static

3

limited way. Further, it has become an important expression of the posture of the United States toward the rest of the world, a significant aspect of our foreign policy, and a vital tool in the economic interdependence which is becoming a fact of life for all international policy. The commission realizes that international telecommunications policy is closely aligned to certain political and economic issues, to technology transfer, and to national security matters. As many have observed, the United States is moving beyond an industrial society to an informational society, and telecommunications is the basic instrument by which this transformation is being accomplished. Questions of information flow are taking on a new importance in the business of international relations. Thus, the Commission's involvement in international telecommunications reflects its emphasis on this emerging and important area. (Fowler, 1981)

Chairman Fowler's statement touches on some of the many problems facing the directors of the U.S. transnational corporate economy. They may be summed up in one general proposition: how to maintain, or at least prevent further slippage, of U.S. hegemony in a world of increasing challenge to that domination. It is especially notable that at each pressure point identified by the FCC chairman, a communications issue is present. Information and the communications process have become the pivots of present and future national and international power relationships.[1]

To some, it may seem curious that it has taken so long for high level recognition to be given to communications and information questions. Certainly, a growing international opposition to the U.S.-directed information system has been apparent for many years.

UNESCO meetings as early as 1968 and 1969, however timidly, did raise the issue of world information imbalances. More assertively, the Algiers Non-Aligned (Nations) Summit conferences in 1973 emphasized the need to "Reorganize existing communication channels which are the legacy of the colonial past . . . to take urgent steps to expedite the collective ownership of satellite systems and to involve a code of conduct for directing their use" (Singham and Dinh, 1976).

---

[1] A footnote to this observation is the announcement of the appointment of a new chairman of the Foreign Policy Association (FPA). The FPA is one of the oldest and most distinguished "think tanks" of the American foreign policy establishment. It has generally been assigned the responsibility of identifying significant emerging problems, areas, and issues that could unsettle the American corporate presence abroad and America's international position in general. In February 1982, the Association chose Leonard Marks as its new chairman. Marks, a former director of the United States Information Agency, more recently an executive of the American media combine's World Freedom Association, has been associated closely with corporate and governmental media interests and policy making for thirty years. Media and foreign policy are now joined, symbolicly at least, in his appointment to the FPA's highest position.

After Algiers, a succession of international meetings, revealing profound dissatisfaction with prevailing international communications arrangements were held around the world, most often, though not exclusively, in Third World Countries: Bogotá (1974); Lima (1975); Tunis (1976); New Delhi (1976); Colombo (1976); Nairobi (1976); Paris (1978); Yaoundé (1980); and Acapulco, (1982).

These manifestations of growing discontent, though not completely disregarded, were passed over without much comment in public media in the United States for several years. Beginning with 1976 a big change is observable. The official posture of indifference has been transformed into one of alarmed concern and active self-assertion.

Two convergent developments have produced this shift. It had become evident that the widespread international sentiment against western, especially U.S. information control, threatened to create a powerful opposition force in global politics that might extend to other than media and information matters. At the same time, the American economy was being radically restructured into a service and information-based system. In this still proceeding transformation, information flows and communication processes are decisive in the maintenance and extension of the economy.

These two entirely separate movements, therefore, are bestowing prime importance on the information sector. International efforts to change the world information system were cresting in 1976, and, in the United States, information was becoming the engine as well as the lubricant of the domestic and transnational economy.

When the U.S. media system reached out to preempt the markets and territories of its former allies (Reuters and Agence France Presse, for example), at the end of World War II, the U.S. media combines were acting in their own self-interest. Though constituting a strong and influential part of the U.S. economic machine at that time, the media system still was only a sub-sector of the overall economy. Assertive and influential as it was and remains, it could not expect, with its own resources, to set and direct the *general* policy of the entire system.

But major changes in the American productive system, at home and abroad have been made since 1945. A good part of the industrial base, has been relocated, under transnational corporate direction, outside the country, in areas where either cheap labor, low taxes, new markets or raw materials (are) available. While the old, industrial base of the nation has been narrowed (Congressman Timothy Wirth, in what is perhaps an overstated but not irrelevant comment, argues "We're not just thinking about moving out of manufacturing, we've already done it" [Hirsch, 1981]), new industries, especially those utilizing high technology, microelectronics, genetic engineering, information processing—have grown rapidly.

Simultaneously, the advanced capitalist economy has nurtured the growth of a number of activities which service the needs of past and current capital accumulation. Foremost in this category are banking, insurance, real estate, securities, accounting, legal and professional and communications services. Other services not as directly tied to property manipulative relationships but characteristic also of an advanced capitalist form of development are media, entertainment (sports), sales and transport.

The services as a general overall category now employ 72 percent of the labor force and account for at least two thirds of the gross national product. In world trade, the United States accounts for twenty percent of all services and is the number one exporter in this category. These added a hefty $35 billion surplus to the United States balance of payments in 1981 (Arenson, 1982).

The shift in the domestic economy from industrial production to service activity has given a strong impetus to the communication-information sector. The service industries are enormous producers and users of information. Banking and insurance, for example, require record keeping of billions of transactions. Accordingly, the demand for and utilization of powerful information processing and transmission capabilities are continually stimulated by the expansion of service activities in the society-at-large.

These domestic needs partly explain the emergence of an increasingly influential information industry in the United States over the last two decades. However, the early development and maturation of this sector had other sources. The initiating stimuli and the heavy financial underwriting of the earliest applications of the new information technology were mostly military. Indeed, the communications technology now widely in general use has been conceived, designed, built and installed with its primary objective being the maintenance of economic privilege and advantage and the prevention of the kind of social change that would overturn and eliminate this advantage. The military machine acts, with the assistance of this technology, as the global enforcer of the status quo. The military use of electronics has been especially observable in recent imperialist actions: such as the U.S. Airforce during the hostage situation in Iran, and the British fleet in the Malvinas Islands blockade and intervention.

The electronics industry itself is an outgrowth of military subsidy and encouragement. The early computers and their successors have been developed with the closest consultation between private companies, IBM in particular, and the Pentagon. Government funds financed the outputs. The first communications satellite system was a military effort.

The Department of Defense's utilization of computers is so extensive that it is compelled to finance the development of a standardized computer language—ADA—to overcome its present reliance on more than 1000 computer languages. The dense United States' surveillance networks that encircle the world, rely almost entirely on electronic technologies. Remote sensors (spy satellites) monitor the globe and code-cracking electronic installations, located in many foreign sites, intercept routinely, friendly as well as allegedly adversary country messages in an astonishing volume.

In sum, a great amount of the activity, a good share of the content, and the general thrust of what is now defined as the Information Age, represent military and intelligence transactions.

Thus, with an assured annual multi-billion dollar government (military and bureaucratic) market for computers, programming and satellites, the success of the U.S. information industry—especially the computer, microchip and satellite manufacturing sectors—up to recently, at least, has been guaranteed. For a quarter of a century, IBM, Hughes Aircraft (satellite construction), and a half a dozen other giant U.S. corporations dominated the international information technology market. Though Japanese and some Western European electronics production activities are beginning to weaken the U.S. position, its dominance is by no means at an end.

The hardware of information technology, however, is only one component of modern information domination. Of ever growing importance is the field of computer software—the creation of the programs that enable computers to perform the most elaborate kinds of data handling and decision making. Actually, as the costs of manufacturing the hardware decline, the costs of designing the programming increase. Already, these cost curves have crossed and the programming outlays progressively grow greater. As programming is a field that requires considerable technical education—at the advanced design level, at least—it confers additional opportunity on those possessing the educational infrastructure, for international dominance.

Once the computer base has been installed and the programming created and applied, the sytem can begin to process data. Data processing and transmission are now major economic activities, domestically and in the international market. U.S. companies have acquired a strong position internationally and account for a major share of the world's data processing—a promising source of future profits and a significant contribution to the national balance of payments. A great portion of the data being processed and transmitted internationally is accounted for by the transnational companies. The significance of this will be considered later along. Here, the point to be remembered, is that a large component of the information industry is the actual processing and transmission of data.

One other category of importance is included in the information industry sector. This is a group of activities which constitute database creation and utilization. Information in databases is organized according to some specialization or field, is stored in computers and is available for searching through programs designed to achieve instantaneous and highly precise retrieval. This branch of the information industry includes information packagers, database suppliers and vendors, and information brokers.

Altogether—when hardware and software producers, information packagers and vendors are aggregated, often in one giant combine, sometimes in a number of firms—the information industry assumes an impressive and still growing economic significance, rivaling the most powerful sectors in American industry. Consider the roster of firms, for example, represented on the Board of Directors of the Information Industry Association, a grouping organized as recently as 1968: McGraw-Hill, Dow Jones, Lockheed, Xerox, the Washington Post Co. and Mead Data Central. "Ordinary" members include IBM, Time, Inc., and divisions of the New York Times Co. and Chase Manhattan Bank.

Yet the information industry represents much more than the emergence of a new area of economic activity, important as this would be in itself. The full significance of the information sector is that it is perceived and intended to serve as the springboard for the revitalization of U.S. capitalism, domestically and internationally.

A former high-level Department of Commerce official noted explicitly that "Telecommunications and data processing are the backbone of multinational activity" (Kirchner, 1981).

Similar formulations are heard elsewhere in high decision making echelons and more than wishful thinking stands behind them. Actual developments in recent years confer a kind of fantasy reality on them. W. Michael Blumenthal, formerly Secretary of the Treasury in the Carter administration, now chairman of the Burroughs Corporation, told a National Computer Conference in the Spring of 1981:

> Our urban centers have become, to a great extent, information processors and communicators. . . information has finally made it to center stage. Perhaps one of the seminal contributions of the 20th century to the development of the human race will be the perception and use of information as the central process around which all else revolves, the focal point of all our activities. . . the information industry is the fundamental force behind global interdependence. (Blumenthal, 1981)

Blumenthal's vocabulary assumes a world in which transnational companies carry on their operations creating linkages that he terms "interdependence."

The changing character of the U.S. economy and the continuing shift of labor from industrial to service employments are the practical manifestations of an emerging new, international division of labor. While industrial production is being relocated globally to suit the profitmaking criteria of transnational corporations, the information function and activity are being tightly administered in a few highly developed technological centers, foremost of which are the United States, Japan and some Western European locales.

At least, this is the present pattern *and intention*. How successful this arrangement will be, and whether it will endure as long as the former, industrially-based division of labor did, are highly uncertain matters. The historical presence and increasing social awareness of more than a hundred new nations, emerged from the old colonial empires, indicate primary sources of instability for a remodeled international hierarchical system of differential burdens and benefits. The unwillingness, for example, of these countries, grouped in a loose coalition called the "77", but actually more than a hundred, to accept unreservedly the U.S. view on the Law of the Sea Treaty is one of many instances in which unequal relationships are being resisted tenaciously.[2]

Again, the rivalries *within* the advanced technological bloc of countries—Japan versus the United States, Western Europe versus the United States, Japan versus Western Europe, etc.—are no less indicative of weakness in the newly-constituted global system of concentrated advantage.

Whatever the long-term prospects, the stakes involved in the shifts underway are huge and the problems that the process provides are deep and seemingly intractable. In a study prepared by members of the Canadian Department of Communications, and published as a government document in 1981, the issue of national sovereignty received great prominence.

The study noted that "the information revolution may accelerate the erosion of national sovereignty ['the ability of nationals of a particular country to exercise control over political, economic, social and cultural developments within its boundaries'] by further increasing the dominance of multi-national corporations in the world economy."

What this suggests to the Canadian analysts (Serafini and Andrieu, 1981) is that "countries such as Canada might evolve from a branch plant economy to a 'warehouse economy.' In such an economy, branch plants would have lost to headquarters, not only jobs, but also important decision making functions in such key areas as financial control, administration, research and development, planning and marketing."

Are these concerns well founded? Or, are the Canadians, as well as the Swedes, the French, Latin Americans, Asians and Africans seized by

---

[2] Senator Alan Cranston observed that the policy of the Reagan administration on the Law of the Sea Treaty "has placed the U.S. on the side of a handful of commercial interests and at odds with virtually every other nation in the world" (Nossiter, 1982).

paranoiac visions? A short review of some of the new information-based activities provides more than enough evidence to justify the pervasive ill-ease in the international community. Transborder data flows, remote sensing, direct satellite broadcasting, and database creation and utilization illustrate how the new information technology, when placed at the disposal of the transnational corporations, may and often do undercut national authority, deepen dependency and thwart genuine, autonomous development.

TRANSBORDER DATA FLOWS

By definition international communications historically have crossed borders. What distinguishes earlier flows from those now occurring, and labeled transborder data flows, are the volume and the means of transmission. The amount of data currently moving between some countries is enormous and the rate of growth of such flows is accelerating. The means by which the greatest portion of the flows occur are electronic, not surface transport as in the past. The electronically-transmitted data, therefore, moves rapidly, invisibly, and in great quantity across frontiers. Though a part of the flow is intergovernmental, and a much smaller amount is personal/individual, the great bulk of the message flow is business-originated, and most of this is *intra* -corporate: that is, within the organizational structure of a single corporation and its subsidiaries and branches.

   This latter kind of flow increasingly eludes national circuitry and moves directly from one unit to another within the transnational company. As this data relates to all the basic decisions affecting an economy —raw materials supply, inventory, pricing, labor policy, tax matters, currency holdings and investment plans—a large number of decisions affecting vital national interests are decided in distant centers, by groups with their own priorities, and totally outside the oversight of the national authority. A country's investment planning, monetary and fiscal policy, resource utilization and social programming thereby are made vulnerable to external forces, facilitated by modern information technology (Serafini and Andrieu, 1981).

REMOTE SENSING

If transborder data flows serve to move information into and out of a country without clearance from national authority, remote sensing is a still more powerful means of capturing and removing physical data from a national entity.

Remote sensing is the means by which an earth's surface is "sensed" by an orbiting communications satellite, and the physical features of the terrain mapped minutely. This technology has an incredible capacity for uncovering ordinarily hidden natural resource information as well as revealing physical trouble spots and agricultural and oceanic phenomena.

What is surely a striking international technology, of potential universal benefit, operates presently as the preserve of national power and economic aggrandizement. At the disposal of military intelligence and corporate mining and resource interests, remote sensing confers very special advantages on these power centers and serves to maintain and extend relations or global domination and dependency (Schiller, 1981, esp. ch. 6, "Planetary Resource Flows: A New Dimension of Hegemonic Power on Global Social Utility?").

To date, the efforts of almost the entire international community to establish a genuine international regimen for remote sensing—much like the effort to do same for a Law of the Sea—have been thwarted by the U.S. Government, on behalf of the corporate/military sectors.

DATABASE CONSTRUCTION AND ACCESSIBILITY

One of the vital components in the new information technology is the database. It is a set of data in a specific category or area—chemistry, physics, medicine, sociology, education, health, etc.—which has been stored in some suitably accessible form. The size of a base varies but it may contain millions of records.

This may appear to be no different from precomputer age arrangements. Still with us, but disappearing rapidly, at least in their present form, are traditional libraries with card catalogues, reference books and indexed materials. The databases now being created are stored in computers and are accessible—for a price—for search and instant retrieval of their contents, in a variety of structured ways that are able to provide pinpointed identification of the subject sought.

Most of the databases now in existence have been organized for production, planning and marketing needs of large private corporations (for payrolls, materials flows, property accounting, customer lists, etc.), and for governmental and private administrative units (social security rolls, credit ratings, police records, and health statistics and information).

As computerized database searching becomes the dominant mode of information acquisition, nothing less than the widest participation in the creation of the database would be a prerequisite for meaningful information autonomy, locally, nationally and internationally. In a report issued by the Swedish Data Policy Commission in early 1982, on information technology policy, one of the three fundamental principles agreed upon was that "there must be democratic participation in the creation of systems where those systems affect people. Systems should not be solely the responsibility of management" (Malik, 1982, p. 32).

This means that the user must have the fullest opportunity to know what is and what is not in the database as well as the criteria for data selection (or exclusion) and classification, and how changes may be introduced.

The absence of these guarantees is the source, for example, of the international disquietude over remote sensing and what happens to the data derived thereby.

The French Government-commissioned Nora/Minc report in 1978, dealt directly with these issues. It declared:

> Information is inseparable from its organization and mode of storage. In the long run, it is not only a question of the advantage that may be conferred by familiarity with such and such a set of data. Knowledge will wind up being shaped, as it always has been, by the available stock of information. Leaving to others—i.e., American data banks— the responsibility for organizing the 'collective memory' while being content to plumb it is to accept a form of cultural alienation. Installing data banks is an imperative of national sovereignty. (Nora and Minc, 1980, p. 28)

The French, cognizant of this basic characteristic of modern information systems, have moved diligently to create national databases. An advertisement, promoting an index of the French press, called *France-Actualité,* explains its utility to users:

> Is there a need to research a topic on international politics? Several will think immediately of referring to the *New York Times* and of using the *New York Times Index* to secure accurate information. But international events are also analyzed usefully in the French press, and it goes without saying, from a different perspective. It is very important to have access to information other than Anglo-American exclusively. *France-Actualité* is able to contribute to North American knowledgeability French views of events and in an indirect way, European views as well. (Author's translation)

For most of the world, however, and the less industrially advanced part in particular, databases constructed in the United States are now, and are likely to continue to be, the predominant sources of information, the classifiers of knowledge, and the definers of information categories (Schiller, 1981, ch. 2). But as Nora/Minc emphasize, database creation can only reproduce the dominant social and economic and political assumptions that currently prevail at the site of base construction.

In the United States, as elsewhere, the information sought, the definitions and labeling of the information secured, and the actual data that are collected and organized are dependent on and result from the expressed needs and the ongoing activities of the decision making and influential centers in the economy. Excluded or marginalized groups *inside* the United States find *their* informational needs unattended for the most part. For social groupings and classes *outside* the United States, the problem is still more serious. To the extent that information used outside the U.S. is coming from U.S. databases—as is now the case in most instances—other societies are incorporating, however unintentionally, in their policy-formulation and decision making, the specific social assumptions that are embedded in the U.S. compiled and organized data.

Full knowledgeability and participation in database construction are necessities for all the social strata who are affected by or who use the bases. In international terms this presupposes a code of usage, standards, and criteria which are the results of joint efforts of genuine international participation. Domestically, this requires as wide a representation of interests, social as well as economic, in the process of database organization and construction. Needless to say, neither condition presently exists. With few exceptions, the international community is a passive though paying recipient for U.S. data. In the United States, also with some limited exceptions, the bases are created to suit the needs of the dominant sectors— corporate, bureaucratic governmental and military-police.

DIRECT BROADCAST SATELLITES

On the verso page of a recent issue of *Channels* (February/March 1982), there is a full page ad in color, with a quote from Victor Hugo in center prominence:

> Nothing else in the world...is so powerful as an idea whose time has come.

This still moving statement is then applied in the ad to the following development:

> Direct-to-home broadcasting via satellite...DBS...an idea whose time has come...The proposed DBS system of United States Satellite Broadcasting Company, Inc....opens the next generation of broadcasting to you as a member station on a participating basis...Seize the future. Join us...
>
> United States Satellite
> Broadcasting Company, Inc.

Direct broadcasting from satellites into home receivers is a capability in existence. How soon it actually will be operating in the United States depends largely on the expectations of profitmaking for those who have the resources to introduce the technology on a large enough scale.

What this new technology offers to *audiences* in the United States is difficult to distinguish from what already exists—the transmission of privately financed programs and messages. DBS will have, however, a differential impact on the current ownership structure of TV and data transmission. It *could* lead to shifts in the site of control and rearrangements in the deployment of the technology in general.

At the international level, another, altogether different prospect emerges. To the extent that it is allowed—a strictly political decision—DBS opens national territory to the signals of external message-makers who have the financial resources and technological capability of transmitting images and programming directly into individual homes, thereby circumventing national authority and supervision.

Consequently, the sentiment in the international community is practically unanimous in a preference for what is called "prior consent"—the right of the receiving society, and its national representatives, to decide *in advance* whether to accept the direct broadcast signal. This viewpoint is encapsulated in the recommendation of the Committee of the Canadian Radio-Television and Telecommunications Commission, for application of its own Arctic Inuit (Eskimo) population. It states, that:

> any predominantly native community should have the right to decide
> on the channels to be delivered locally; to eliminate complete chan-
> nels; and, on any particular channel, to eliminate a program or sub-
> stitute one of its own choice. (Green and Simailak, 1981, p. 3)

On the subject of direct broadcasting from satellites, the United States is almost alone in its insistence that there should be no rule of "prior consent" and that to allow such an international standard would be a serious infringement of the free flow of information and even a violation of the U.S. Constitution's protection of the right of free speech, that is, the First Amendment.

The applicability of the U.S. Constitution to the world-at-large, without the world having a say in the matter, is in itself, indicative of current U.S. policy making. More will be said about the free flow of information in what follows.

Actually, the introduction of direct satellite broadcasting on a global scale depends on many technical, economic, and political factors that still have to be taken into account. All that can be said at this time is that the capability of DBS presents still another immeasurable challenge to national sovereignty. Consider for example, the production mounted in early 1982 by the U.S. government, to utilize the Polish martial law crisis to further exacerbate Soviet-Western relations. The overtly provocative hour-and-a-half TV program, "Let Poland Be Poland," was beamed by satellite to more than 50 countries—the costs of transmission being borne by the U.S. government. Yet it remained a national decision in Europe and elsewhere, whether the transmission of the program to local audiences would be allowed. With direct broadcasting from satellites, and no agreement on prior consent, the decision would have been completely in the hands of the U.S. government (or hypothetically, even a private sector initiative).

SPECTRUM SPACE

Connected to the DBS issue is the allocation of orbital slots for the increasing number of communication satellites being thrust into the sky. The already great and continuously expanding volume of international electronic flows of information, depends on submarine cable and communication satellites—increasingly the latter. Yet the number of prime positions available for the location of satellites in geostationary orbit, is not unlimited. At present, "first come, first served" is the rule and de facto operating principle. Not unexpectedly, it is strongly espoused by the United States, which has the technological capability to be "first." While this approach is most agreeable to the Pentagon and the TNCs, a broad front of international sentiment, including the less developed as well as the more industrially advanced countries, is much less enthusiastic.

Closely related to the "orbital slot" allocation issue, is how nations, once they have access to satellites, will share the various radio, television and microwave frequencies that allow information to be beamed to and from the satellites. On frequency use, national needs differ as do the requirements of special user groups *within* the nation. About these questions, there are shifting national and individual group interests. On specific issues, unexpected coalitions of ordinarily adversary participants may be formed.

All the same, the current privileged position of the United States and a few other advanced industrial nations, will be contested with increasing intensity. International conferences involving telecommunications used to be meetings in which a few powerful states, generally in a relaxed setting, agreed, or sometimes disagreed, among themselves, on how to manage world communications. Always it was asserted that the deliberations were technical, could be made only be engineers, and politics were unnecessary and diversionary.

In the 1970s, culminating in the World Administrative Radio Conference in 1979 (WARC), the voices of the hitherto excluded began to be heard, if not seriously listened to. One American consultant notes with some trepidation that "There are at least 20 major international conferences involving telecommunications in the next eight years," and he fears that the freedom of "business to operate as it has in the past is threatened."[3]

It is not an unrealistic assessment.

STEPPED UP BROADCASTING AND ADVERTISING

Computers and communications satellites are being employed in a variety of ways to assist old power centers—military and corporate—achieve an altogether new dimension of control over national and international information flows. At the same time, the informational circuits and messages that predate the electronic age are by no means falling into disuse.

Not receiving as much attention as DBS, *shortwave* radio broadcasting remains another very active form of international communications and it has been intruding in national space for decades. In the current administration, the "information war" receives increased support and shortwave broadcasting by such familiar agencies as the *Voice of America* and *Radio Free Europe* and *Radio Liberty* (the latter two operations having surfaced from CIA administration) enjoys considerable financial largesse. In fact, the battleground is being extended to Cuba. The administration has announced the establishment of a facility called *Radio Martí,* despite the awkardness of using the name of someone with a known antipathy to American imperialism.

INTERNATIONAL ADVERTISING

Remote sensing, DBS, and shortwave broadcasting are each technological means to transmit or receive signals that can elude national control. There are still other means of accomplishing the same end, which rely on the *message* moving through conventional or new communications technologies. One such type of message in particular deserves special attention and consideration. This is the phenomenon of *international advertising,* the creation of marketing messages by and for transnational corporations. This is a field dominated by less than two dozen transnational advertising agencies, mostly U.S.-owned, with franchises or subsidiaries in scores of countries.

Advertising is, of course, most highly developed in the United States itself. Domestically, it plays a crucial role in sustaining monopolies, forming and guiding tastes, maintaining or shifting consumer demand, and creating and reinforcing dominant ideology. Both absolutely and in per

---

[3] Feder (1981) quoting Bertram Cowlan.

capita expenditures, advertising is employed in the United States more than anywhere else on earth.

Though international advertising existed in pre-World War II period, its growth increased phenomenally after 1950. It was at that time and since, that domestic agencies swarmed overseas to follow the migration of private U.S. capital, especially transnational corporate capital (Roncagliolo and Janus, 1979; 1981).

With the prospect of direct broadcasting by satellite looming, the international advertisers and the transnational corporations are licking their chops. Suggestive of things to come, is the sentiment expressed by the chairman of J. Walter Thompson & Co. in Britain (a branch of the huge American agency):

> For the first time, it would seem, we can fulfill the multinational's corporate dream: to establish, at a single moment in time, eyeball-to-eyeball interface with the man in the street on a global scale. What power, what savings, what consistency, what an opportunity. (Newman, 1982)

In 1980, *Advertising Age* predicted that at the beginning of the 21st century, in twenty years, advertising expenditures worldwide would reach $780 billion, a seven fold increase over the $110 billion spent in 1980.

Along with the prediction of growth in volume of ad expenditures, was the still more depressing observation and expectation that "the rest of the world is rapidly emulating many of our advertising practices and by the year 2000 these will be the norm in a number of other countries around the world. In this sense the U.S. may be considered to be a leading indicator of the developments that lie ahead in other parts of the world (Coen, 1980).

This expectation is solidly grounded. It takes into account the worldwide practices of the transnational corporate system to insure the realization of its aims. One of the principal reasons why American advertising is becoming the "norm" in a large number of countries is because it is being heavily promoted to do just that.

The evolution in the broadcasting systems of many European nations, and countries elsewhere, demonstrates this. State broadcasting authorities are being weakened and sometimes replaced, or compelled to share influence with commercial entities. These are introduced or created with the support, political and financial, of the transnationals. Beside money making, the objective of the commercial systems is to overcome the historical reluctance of state broadcasting authorities to permit advertising.

The need of the transnational companies to reach national audiences with their marketing messages, requires *unrestricted* access to the national media. Commercialization of broadcasting enables this to occur. Once the broadcasting system has been withdrawn from public administration, only the transnational companies have the resources to pay the substantial advertising rates. And so it has gone, from place to place.

The Italian situation is exemplary. The *International Herald Tribune* recently carried this report:

> Networks, Italian-style, are the latest development in Italy's commercial television boom, which has put government-run broadcasting on the defensive and created a $90 million-a-year market for American entertainment. . . . This bid for fully independent [commercial] network television is being closely watched in France, Spain and other European countries debating the future of official broadcasting control. (Fitchett, 1982)

Accompanying the spread of transnational corporate advertising is a new pattern of daily living, connected to the products and services heavily promoted. Under the siege of consumerist promotions, national development plans that emphasize other priorities, as well as stressing social equity, are forced to recede and yield place.

How far-reaching this process can be, and how it can escape national control once it has become incorporated into the institutional setting, is suggested in the following account of nutritional changes in the Mexican diet:

> Processed foods are now a staple in the Mexican diet, replacing cheaper and more nutritious traditional foods such as corn and beans. This shift in eating habits over the past 15 years has sparked concern among government and private food experts, who say that choices about what food to eat are increasingly influenced more by advertising than nutritional considerations. This trend, common to all sectors of society, is particularly disquieting in a country where 35 million people are under-nourished, and where one million children a year are born to families who are underfed. (de Cautin, 1981)

Two factors are noted in the shift in the Mexican diet. First, there is the penetration of 130 transnational corporations (99 of them U.S.-based), who have entered the Mexican market by setting up subsidiaries, taking over Mexican companies, or starting joint ventures with Mexican capital.

The second element in the new pattern of nutrition, are the millions of dollars spent on advertising by these corporations to promote their processed and packaged foods. Between 1970 and 1975, for example, consumption of popcorn, potato chips, and other processed foods increased by almost 27 percent. "(Yet) researchers point out that a package of corn chips costs twenty times more than a kilo of more nutritious corn tortillas" (de Cautin, 1981).

As this account indicates, once the penetration of transnational capital occurs, it relies heavily on advertising expenditures in the mass media to persuade local publics of the superiority of the new goods and services offered by the TNCs, as well as the lifestyles associated with them (such as "The Pepsi Generation"). Inevitably and ineluctably, whatever the social need to the contrary, the resources and the energies of the exposed national community are redirected according to the dynamics and imperatives of the transnational corporate system. These are, first, foremost, and exlusively, the search for markets and profits.

This is not an overdrawn appraisal. Consider the following dialogue between a reporter of the *New York Times* and the two chief executives of the Coca-Cola Company ("Talking Business with Goizueta and Keough of Coca-Cola," 1981), one of the most well-known consumer good transnationals:

> *Question:* Are changing demographics working against you and other soft drink companies?
>
> *Mr. Keough:* (President and Chief Operating Officer) We really look at demographics on a worldwide basis. Only 5 percent of the world's population is in the United States. As our business grows, it is inevitable that it is going to grow at a much faster rate abroad.
>
> Around the world, there are huge chunks of population where the demographics are highly favorable. You take the whole continent of Africa and the Pacific Basin from Korea to Austrolasia. In Latin America, where we have a dominant position, the demographics for any consumer product that can be afforded by people there are highly favorable. In Brazil, the median age is under 18.

And Coca-Cola, along with a few hundred other consumer goods transnationals, has the resources to saturate these "attractive" markets with the sales message for its products.

In sum, North American transnational capital, the new information technology, and national mass media systems dependent on TNC advertising financing, are the pillars—along with the never absent armed forces— of the prevailing international economic and information order.

THE TERRAIN OF THE INTERNATIONAL COMMUNICATIONS BATTLE NOW AND FUTURE

The conduits, the content, and the significance of international information flows have been the foci of attention up to this point. Recapitulating, the transnational corporate system and its military shield are heavily reliant on these information flows, and, in fact, are placing great hope on information technology and processes to maintain a system of global advantage. At the same time, it is evident that the entire informational infrastructure that has been created, as well as the messages that it facilitates, contribute greatly, though not necessarily intentionally, to the weakening of national sovereignty wherever the system operates. The substitution for national authority, however, is not some cooperatively designed international order but a powerful transnational corporate coterie intent on its own aggrandizement.

These developments do not take place unopposed or go unremarked. Still, to prevent a full appreciation of the dimensions, impact, and likely consequences of these developments, a rationale is employed to explain and legitimize the transformations underway and the arrangements already in place. Actually, the principles that are called upon to defend the global activities of the transnational companies are a mixture of familiar political, technological, and cultural doctrines offered as a universal ethic.

The basic element in this ethic is the now somewhat frayed doctrine of the free flow of information. United States press organizations and media corporations actively promoted the doctrine in the early post-World War II period, on behalf of their own interests—though claiming, naturally enough, they were representing general social well-being and international peace (Schiller, 1978, ch. 2).

The Associated Press, CBS, Time Inc., and the big U.S. film and TV production companies exploited domestic credulity as they pursued their market expansion overseas, terming their campaigns noble crusades for information liberation and freedom.

Currently, the media industries' interests remain important and continue to offer strong support for the free flow position. But now they are joined and reinforced by the need of the *total* transnational system for an unrestricted flow of *its own* information.

This new situation, which has been noted already, is explained by Phillip H. Power (1980), often a member of United States delegations to UNESCO, and owner and chairman of Suburban Communications Corporation, which publishes forty-two community newspapers in Michigan and Ohio.

> The stakes in the coming battle go far beyond editors and publishers, who so far have been the only ones directly involved. They extend to the great computer and information hardware companies whose foreign sales of billions of dollars are at stake; to the TV networks and movie-makers whose entertainment products range the globe; to the airlines and banks and financial institutions whose need for computer-to-computer data literally defines their business; to the multimillion dollar international advertising industry.

To this list should be added the few thousand U.S. TNCs that also rely on computer-to-computer data for their daily international operations. As for the international advertising industry, it is with few exceptions, strictly a U.S. presence—the top ten U.S. ad agencies dominate the world business of advertising. And since a great part of many TNC businesses depends on reaching the mass audience wherever the operations are undertaken, advertising has become a vital component of the overall system.

It is not unexpected, therefore, to find the free flow of information doctrine being broadened explicitly to include advertising as part of the flow of information which promotes freedom. Leonard S. Matthews, President of the American Association of Advertising Agencies, Inc., makes this connection emphatically. He writes about "the threat to a free flow of information—including commercial information" (1981, p. 18).

The World Press Freedom Committee, too, its membership drawn from some of the largest and most influential North American media combines, hardly is reticent on this point. Meeting in Talloires, France, in May 1981, with other Western media interests, the group declared: "We believe that the free flow of information is essential for mutual understanding and world peace." However, "free flow" cannot exist, according to these private media owners and editors, without a "free press." And a free press, still according to the wisdom of this group, depends on the financial support of advertising. "We acknowledge," the Talloires Declaration states, "the importance of advertising as a consumer service and in providing financial support for a strong and self-sustaining press. Without financial independence, the press cannot be independent."

In this reasoning, a free press (TV and radio broadcasting as well) requires advertising to sustain itself. Internationally as well as domestically, advertising is supplied, for the most part, by transnational corporations. And, since the TNC is the chief support for a free press, those individuals or nations, who fail to recognize the legitimacy and desirability of this linkage, have excluded themselves from the circle of freedom—defined, obligingly enough, by organizations such as the World Press Freedom Committee. Advertising, in this context, and so defined by the transnational system, becomes an indispensable component of freedom.

The Reagan administration endorses unreservedly the TNC interpretation of the free flow principle. In a letter from the White House, addressed to the Speaker of the House of Representatives, the Honorable Thomas P. O'Neill, Jr., in September 1981, the President wrote:

> The United States has long regarded the principle of the free flow of information as a cornerstone of any democratic political order, and an essential instrument for furthering understanding among the peoples of the world and encouraging the growth of free, equitable and enlightened government... We strongly support—and commend the attention of all nations—the declaration issued by independent media leaders of twenty-one nations at the Voices of Freedom Conference, which met at Talloires, France, in May of this year.

The reaffirmed support for a TNC-defined free flow of information, issuing from the highest political level of the U.S. Government, is accompanied with strident attacks on the United Nations and UNESCO (United Nations Educational, Scientific and Cultural Organization), in particular. President Reagan's letter to the Speaker of the House, concluded with this sentence: "We do not feel we can continue to support a UNESCO that turns its back on the high purposes this organization was originally intended to serve."

The objects of the President's (and the media interests') concern are the reservations expressed frequently in votes in UNESCO about the lopsided character of the prevailing international information order. Along with presidential censure of UNESCO, have come congressional initiatives to cut off the U.S. contribution to that organization if it persists in its quest for changes in the international information sphere. For example, the House of Representatives in September 1981, voted in favor of an amendment to the State Department authorization bill, moved by Representative Robin L. Beard, Jr. (R. Tennessee), which read as follows:

> Sec. 104(a) None of the funds authorized to be appropriated by section 102(a) (2) of this Act, or by any other Act for 'International Organizations and Conferences' may be used for payment by the United States of its contribution toward the assessed budget of the United Nations Educational, Scientific, and Cultural Organization, if that organization implements any policy or procedure the effect of which is to license journalists or their publications, to censor or otherwise restrict the free flow of information within or among countries, or to impose mandatory codes of journalistic practice or ethics.

The amendment further instructed the Secretary of State to report annually whether the provisions stated above were being adhered to by UNESCO.

The information issue, important as it is, however, constitutes only one of the precipitating elements that have produced these harsh strictures.

The United Nations and UNESCO have been receiving heavy criticism in the United States from a variety of interests and sources, all of which are distressed with the sentiments and votes of approximately three-quarters of the world's nations and inhabitants. These expressions (and votes) of dissatisfaction with the economic, political and informational structures now prevailing internationally, are viewed—probably accurately—as threats by those who derive advantage from the present arrangements.

Refusing to accept the deceptive doctrines that conceal the interests of the powerful forces at play in the information and economic fields, the Swedes, the French, and the West Germans among other Western Europeans, and the Canadians closer to home, are objecting vigorously to a U.S. TNC-dominated flow of information which threatens their often monopolized industries, their privacy and their national sovereignty. An official Canadian Committee, for example, reported in 1979, that:

> We see communication as one of the fundamental elements of sovereignty, and we are speaking of the sovereignty of the people of a country . . . We urge the Government of Canada to take immediate action to alert the people of Canada to the perilous position of their collective sovereignty that has resulted from the new techniques of telecommunications and informatics. (Consultative Committee on the Implications of Telecommunications for Canadian Sovereignty, 1979)

The director-general of the Swedish Data Inspection Board (Freese, 1978) has stated often that "it seems to be a paradox, but nevertheless the free flow of information . . . has to be regulated by international agreements in order to be kept free."

Dr. Jörg Becker reports (1982) from the German Federal Republic that Western Europe views itself practically as a Third World entity, in its similar information dependency on U.S. computer production, data banks, data processing services and electronic circuitry, in general.

Some United States agencies, governmental and private, are beginning to acknowledge, if not take these manifestations of dissatisfaction seriously. A December 1980 report of the Committee on Government Operations of the U.S. House of Representatives, included this observation:

> Whatever the particular perspective of a country, an increasing number of nations worry that the loss of control over information about internal functions can jeopardize their sovereignty and leave them open to possible disruptions ranging from uncontrolled technical failures to political sabotage. (U.S. Congress. House of Representatives, 1980, pp. 19–23).

More pointedly still, Morris H. Crawford, former executive secretary of the State Department's task force and public advisory group on international information flows, and now a private consultant, states that "a reweighing of past applications of the free flow doctrine is long overdue" and that "U.S. assumptions about free flow need to be reassessed in the context of modern communication technologies and their impact on other members of the interdependent world community. *The U.S. is out of phase in an internatinal reexamination in which we have more at stake than any other country.* Paradoxically, failure to face the reality of changing definitions of free flow tends to strengthen the hands of those who favor stronger controls over all forms of global information exchange" (1980, p. 3).

This assessment notwithstanding, the Reagan Administration, since its installation, has adopted a hard and unqualified free flow position. In the policy paper circulated by the Under Secretary of State for Security

Assistance, Science and Technology, in February 1982, seven basic U.S. objectives respecting international communications and information issues were enunciated. Though priority listing was disavowed, the first principle on the list was free flow:

> To enlarge acceptance of the principle of free international flow of information and ideas, *including applicability of this principle to newly emerging communications and information technologies.* (Salmon, 1982, p. 4)

FREE FLOW AND THE NEW TECHNOLOGY PLOY

How to contain, to say nothing of overcome, the growing opposition to the free flow doctrine, has been a continuing source of difficulty since the early days of the Carter administration (1976–1980). Beginning in that period, the promise of American technological capability once again was enlisted to persuade the dissatisfied countries that their information needs and grievances would be attended to.

Actually, this was an updated replay of the late 1950s and 1960s when the first communications and development siren songs were sung by American theorists and policymakers. As Neville D. Jayaweera (1982) puts it:

> we are witnessing a reversal to the same development-communication paradigm. Except that the tools and the prophets of the 80s are different. In the 60s the tools were radio and TV. In the 80s they will be satellites. In the 60s the prophets came from the behavioural sciences—economics, sociology, etc. In the 80s the prophets are technologists and engineers. But basically the argument is the same— 'Development is something that can be stimulated and engendered through mass communication. The more penetrating, the more widespread, the more efficient the delivery system, the more easily the ultimate development goals can be realized.'

In advancing a technological solution to information dependency conditions, a program under American tutelage, *outside* the increasingly unmanageable UNESCO structure, was envisaged. Yet this plan was thwarted and what resulted was the creation in June 1981, of an International Program for the Development of Communications (IPDC), a grouping organized *within* the UNESCO system.

The inability of United States policy to date, to win sufficient Third World support, or failing that to split the bloc, has reinforced the unilateralist position—expressed often as bilateral negotiation—in high policy-making circles. Though this cannot be taken as a permanent policy stance, unilateralist inclinations manifestly are evident in recent communication initiatives of the Reagan administration.

Attacks, private and governmental, on the UN and UNESCO have multiplied inside the United States. The transnational corporations have grown more outspoken and now advance their interests publicly. Indicative of this trend, a five-page advertisement in color, in *Time* magazine (February 1, 1982), paid for by the Smith Kline Corporation, a medical supplies and pharmaceutical transnational, promoted the communication declaration of the World Press Freedom Committee, the so-called Talloires Declaration. The spread spotlighted what it termed "Danger At The UN," and contributed its bit to the furtherance of public mistrust and suspicion of international organization.

At the United Nations itself, at the end of December 1981, a draft resolution on *Questions Relating to Information* was voted on. The resolution contained, among many matters concerned with the world information situation, an increased budget for the UN Committee on Information —to enable it to cope with the continuously growing number of information issues. The vote showed 147 nations in favor of the resolution and two against (Israel and the United States). There were no abstentions.[4]

How far can unilateralism be pushed? Ultimately, it is confronted with an unresolvable contradiction. The United States transnational corporate system cannot maintain itself in a fervent unilateralist environment. The system requires internationalism—its own brand of internationalism, to be sure. The concept of "interdependence" was created to describe favorably, as well as to conceal, the relationships imposed by international capital on its dependencies.

United States-owned transnational capital needs international communications. If it acts to disrupt international cooperation in information flows too forcefully, it is striking at its own existence. As Dallas Smythe has put it: "Could it be, to plagiarize Mao Zedong, that monopoly capitalism has become, not a paper tiger, but an electronic information tiger?" (1981, p. 312).

Despite the obvious peril to itself, the inability of U.S. transnational capital to have its way politically and economically, has hastened its adoption of unilateralism and arbitrary action. These are petulant, though significant, reactions to a world unwilling to cede national sovereignty and economic independence to huge pools of foreign private capital, backed by political power.

---

[4] How these matters now are viewed by official U.S. policy makers is suggested in a brief account published in the *Chronicle of International Communication* (November 1981, p. 7), itself an organ that reflects official thinking on international communications: "Officials emphasize that these (the recommendations in the Resolution) draw heavily on language and resolutions adopted at the UN in previous years, when, in their thinking, U.S. negotiators acceded to an aggregation of semantic nuances and ideological fine points that now foster Third World control of UN information resources while eroding global press freedom." More crudely put, (Reagan) officials in 1981 are repudiating resolutions and principles agreed to by United States representatives in earlier meetings at the UN.

The impasse which now exists is temporary and fragile. The lack of realism and the inevitable ultimate failure of current American international communications policy is observable in its hostility to and total rejection of principles that reflect overwhelming majority sentiment in the world community.

In space, on land and under the sea, with the exception of the United States and occasionally, but not invariably, a few industrialized Western European states as well, all nations espouse the principle of the "common heritage of mankind." This means that exploitation above and below the earth, in areas not claimed by national states—the sky and oceans, for example—should be for the benefit of all.

This commonsensical and seemingly unexceptional standard, is viewed with alarm by a few U.S. (and perhaps other) transnational corporations. A *New York Times* report gave this overview:

> Some lawyers fear that the direction in which space law is headed is reflected in the Moon Treaty now before the United States Senate for ratification. Communist and developing nations [at least ¾ of the countries in the world] managed to get language included that specifies that exploitation of the moon shall be for the benefit of all mankind. This 'common heritage of mankind' principle, which has also become a stumbling block in negotiations aimed at clarifying the law of the sea related to deep-sea mining, is criticized by many businessmen who believe it may block all profit-seeking ventures and provide for the forced transfer of technology. (Feder, 1981)

Temporary technological advantage may permit American unilateralist action in space and under the seas for a time. Yet it defies the views and violates the rights of the international community. It is hardly a formula for long term stability and peaceful relationships.

On the ideological plane, U.S. policy also makes short term gains. But here as well, its future is in doubt. While castigating violations of individual human rights—mostly in countries which have had social revolutions—the bedrock issue for three billion people in the world is survival and the attendant rights to jobs, health care, and education. On these matters, there is a deafening silence from the American upholders of "rights."

Actually, there is not a total absence of opinion. What there is are guarded statements of opposition to human economic rights.

A United Nations Covenant, setting international standards in economic and social rights, remains unratified by the United States.

> The Administration [Reagan] has not yet taken a formal position on the 1966 International Covenant on Economic, Social and Cultural Rights, which attempted to establish universal rights to such things as secondary education, gainful employment, healthy working conditions and recognized holidays and vacation time. However, officials have said publicly in international forums that the Administration's

view of human rights did not include economic considerations. (Crossette, 1982, p. 3)

What these United States positions add up to is an across-the-board opposition to the most fundamental demands and desires of the large majority of the world's people and nations. It is also probably true that *most people in the United States would support the global majority's views, if* a full explanation and examination of the issues were available to them. Not surprisingly, the forces that are blocking social change and improvement internationally, also are busily at work domestically. The transnational corporate system, which opposes new international economic and informational arrangements and institutions for fear—quite justifiable—that its advantaged positions would be reduced and eventually eliminated, exercises great influence as well over the domestic ideological and informational terrain. As a consequence, the home front is still largely insulated from the powerful international movements for peace and new economic and information relationships.

The new information technologies, however, produce contradictions that embarrass and make life difficult for their main proponents. One, it will be recalled, is the need for international cooperation for secure, long term communications. Another, is that the new instrumentation provides a system of communications that allow people to gain instant knowledge of social movements occurring elsewhere.

It is a fact that the reportage, explanation, and comprehensiveness of the coverage, are largely in the hands of the transnational media monopolies. Despite this, *some* sense, however limited, of what may be going on, gets through.

The transnational corporate system still retains remarkable strength by virtue of its control over capital, technology, the political machinery, and military force. Yet, its vital requirements conflict increasingly with the needs of most of the world's people. Unilateralism cannot long endure as a policy. Control of the information process with attendant opportunity to distort reality also is a waning asset. Transnational corporate capital may not yet be confronting its "high noon." But the sun is rising and the options are diminishing.

REFERENCES

Arenson, K. W. (1982). "Services: Bucking the Slump." *The New York Times* (May 18).

Becker, J. (1982). "Europe and the Third World." *Le Monde Diplomatique* (January).

Blumenthal, W. M. (1981). "Transborder Data Flow and the New Protectionism." Speech delivered before the National Computer Conference, Chicago, IL. *Vital Speeches of the Day* (May 6).

"Channels of Communications." (1982). United States Satellite Broadcasting Company advertisement. (February/March), inside front cover.

Coen, R. J. (1980). "Vast U.S. and Worldwide Ad Expenditures Expected." *Advertising Age* (November 13), 10–16.

Consultative Committee on the Implications of Telecommunications for Canadian Sovereignty. (1979). *Telecommunications and Canada* (The Clyne Report). Ottawa, Canada, 2, 63–64, 75–76.

Crawford, M. H. (1980). "Towards and Information Age Debate." *Chronicle of International Communication* 1(2), 3.

Crossette, B. (1982). "U.S. Casts Doubt on U.S. Rights Accord." *The New York Times* (February 10), 3.

de Cautin, M. (1981). "Mexico: High-Cost Processed Foods Replace Traditional Staples." *Interlink Press Service, No. 9* (December), 10–13.

"Declaration of Independent News Organizations on Freedom of the Press (The Tailloires Declaration)." *The New York Times* (May 18).

Feder, B. J. (1981). "Space Law's Business Impact." *The New York Times* (December 2).

Fitchett, J. (1982). "Private Italian TV Firms Press for Freer Rein." *The International Herald Tribune* (March 15).

Fowler, M. (1981). Statement to Subcommittee on Governmental Information and Individual Rights, Committee on Government Operations. U.S. Congress. House of Representatives. September 22.

Freese, J. (1978). "The Present and Future Swedish Data Policy." *In Data Regulation: European and Third World Realities.* Uxbridge, England: On-Line.

Green, L. and Simailak, D. (1981). "Satellite Communications Reinforcing Cultural Identity in Canada's Northwest Reaches." *Development Communications Report No. 36,* 3.

Hirsch, P. (1981). "Wirth Urges Support for High Tech Firms." *Computerworld* (November).

Jayaweera, N. D. (1982). "Communication Satellites: A Third World Perspective." Paper presented at the Seminar on "New Technologies and the New International Information Order." Bonn-Bad Godesberg, Federal Republic of Germany (March 22–24).

Kirchner, J. (1981). "Panel Told of Barriers to U.S. DP Services Trade." (November 23).

Malik, R. (1982). "Swede: Europe's Tech Policy Politically Based." *Computerworld* (February 22), 32.

Mathews, L. S. (1981). "Designing a Muzzle for Media." *Business Week* (June 15), 18.

Newman, B. (1982). "Satellite Invasion." *The Wall Street Journal* (March 22).

Nora, S., and Minc, A. (1980). "Computerizing Society." *Society* (January/February), 28.

Nossiter, B. (1982). "Official Shifts Role in U.S. Sea Law Delegation." *The New York Times* (March 11).

Power, P. H. (1980). "Threat to Ad Freedom." *Advertising Age* (December 15).

Roncagliolo, R., and Janus, N. (1979). "Advertising, Mass Media and Dependency." *Development Dialogue, 1.*

Roncagliolo, R., and Janus N. (1981). "Advertising and the Democratization of Communication." *Development Dialogue, 2.*

Salmon, W. C. (1982). "International Aspects of Communications and Information." Working paper. U.S. Department of State.

Schiller, H. I. (1978). *Communication and Cultural Domination.* White Plains, NY: International Arts & Sciences Press.

Schiller, H. I. (1982). *Who Knows: Information in the Age of the Fortune 500.* Norwood, NJ: Ablex Publishing Corporation.

Serafini, S., and Andrieu, M. (1981). *The Information Revolution and its Implications for Canada.* Ottawa, Canada: Minister of Supply and Service.

Singham, A. W., and Dinh, T. V. (1976). *From Bandung to Colombo: Conferences of the Non-Aligned Countries, 1955–75.* New York: Third Press.

Smythe, D. (1981). *Dependency Road: Communications, Capitalism, Consciousness, and Canada.* Norwood, NJ: Ablex Publishing Corporation.

"Talking Business with Goizueta and Keough of Coca-Cola." (1981). *The New York Times* (December 1), D-2.

United Nations. General Assembly. (1981). *Questions Relating to Information.* (A/36/819). Agenda Item 6. December 12.

U.S. Congress. House of Representatives. (1980). Committee on Government Operations. *International Information Flow: Forging a New Framework.* H. R. Report No. 96-1535. 19–23. 6th Congress, 2d session. Washington, DC: USGPO.

2

On Thinking the Unthinkable about Nuclear War and its Consequences for the Peace Movement

Dallas W. Smythe

As a basis for analyzing the present peace movement, I begin with a review of the development of nuclear weaponry and the doctrines for its use. There follows an examination of the social context of that antagonistically co-operating linkage of the American and Soviet military-industrial complexes properly to be known as the Exterminist Axis. Some analysis of the "old" and "new" peace movements will be offered in terms which try to deal with their relation to the "hard" and "soft" paths for energy for "peace" and for "war" and the affinity between the "soft paths for energy (for both purposes) and neutralism/nonalignment. Finally a section concerns the role of communications, an institutionalized part of the social order which has a unique and crucial relation to material production and use of the means for both the continuation or destruction of life as it has been known on earth for thousands of centuries.

I. ON NUCLEAR WEAPONS AND THE PROBABILITY OF WAR

The cold war against the Soviet Union really began in 1917 but what is called "Cold War I" began in 1945 and ended in the mid-1960s. In that period, after the U.S.S.R. achieved a nuclear weapons capability in the early 1950s, the Mutual Assured Destruction policy of deterrence seemed to provide a stable "Balance of Terror" in which both the U.S. and the U.S.S.R. acknowledged that a nuclear exchange between them (carried by bombers or intercontinental ballistic missiles) would be so damaging as to be "unacceptable." Nuclear war seemed to be unthinkable because it would be too destructive. In fact each side's population was taken hostage by its adversary in a state of terror—a fact oddly unrecognized by current opponents of "international terrorism."[1] While the old peace movement labored against the soporific effort of the MAD doctrine, and "Detente" (beginning in the 1960s), the military-industrial complex was never deceived by that doctrine. While the argument for MAD was that nuclear weapons were targeted against population centers and that it would be destabilizing to aim them at the opponent's missile sites (because that would imply an intent to launch a first strike to "win"), in fact the U.S. military had been preparing to attack U.S.S.R. armed forced to win beginning in the late 1940s. (I am uninformed whether or not the U.S.S.R. did the same at that time.) And the whole drift of the military-industrial complex has been toward the twin objectives of ever more sophisticated weapons for "counterforce" use and defensive measures to protect the weapons which might be used for either "first strike" or retaliatory strikes.

The Cold War II (from about 1965) has been distinguished from the earlier phase by: (a) the product of the concealed half of "deterrence" has been at least several generations of more sophisticated weapons (with more in the research and development stage) which might give the West the strategic/tactical advantage which would assure "victory." Among these have been the hydra-headed MIRVs, most recently with steerable warheads and increased megatonnage, missiles launched from submerged submarines, Cruise missiles (unmanned, directable, low-flying aircraft carrying nuclear weapons with 1,500 mile range), Neutron warheads (destructive of life but not property), medium range ground-based Pershing II missiles of great accuracy and megatonnage, the MX missile system, a host of "tactical" nuclear weapons with heat-sensing automatic direction, and a vast array of strategic and tactical electronic devices for locating targets, conducting surveillance, jamming opponent's communications, and countering opponent's attempts to jam enemy electronics; (b) development by the Soviet Union of nuclear weapons systems with aggressive capability (nuclear-armed submarines, Backfire bombers, intermediate (SS–20) and tactical range ground-based missile systems, etc.), whereas in Cold War I, Soviet armament appeared to be defensive in character.

The U.S. has taken a very aggressive stance in its policy for the use of these weapons. Under U.S. pressure, NATO decided to deploy 464 Cruise missiles and 108 Pershing missiles capable of hitting targets inside the Soviet Union from Western Europe. They were to be located in England, West Germany, Netherlands, Belgium and Italy. In 1977, the Carter ad-

---

[1] The difference is perhaps that between big and small business, as Chaplin's "M. Verdoux" so well put it.

ministration announced its plan to produce Neutron bombs designed for use in Europe—then in response to public protests tabled its plans—and then began their production. The first public statement by Reagan's Secretary of Defense proposed deploying the Neutron bombs in Europe. This plan was tabled by the White House because of opposition even from NATO governments, although later, according to a Los Angeles Times Service dispatch:

> Weinberger, in an interview published in Washington on Wednesday [February 11], repeated his position. Neutron warheads could 'do quite a lot' to compensate for the Soviet block's advantage in numbers of tanks, Weinberger said. That's one of the reasons the Russians reacted so strongly to this slight [sic] suggestion,' he said in referring to his own support for the weapon. (*Los Angeles Times,* February 15, 1981)

Official U.S. "doctrine" on targeting nuclear weapons had plainly adopted by 1980 a counterforce policy (a first-strike position). In July 1980, the Carter administration revealed Presidential Directive 59. According to the Federation of American Scientists the targeting plan (SIOP):

> has, at least since 1962, contained a range of options. The current SIOP (SIOP-5D), includes some 40,000 designated target installations which not only allows great scope for choice, but actually requires such choices since there are only 9,200 weapons in the SIOP force. These installations cover a variety of target types, divided into four general categories: Soviet nuclear forces, other military targets, political and military leadership facilities, and the Soviet economic industrial base. The Soviet nuclear forces only became a separate target set in August 1950, but the other three categories had all been present in the war plans of the late 1940s. The fact that current planning requires that relatively less emphasis be accorded the destruction of the Soviet economic and industrial base and that greater attention be directed toward improving the effectiveness of our attacks against military targets should not obscure another fact that military targets already account for just one-half the target installations in the SIOP— with the other 20,000 made up of 3,000 targets associated with the Soviet nuclear forces; 2,000 leadership targets; and some 15,000 economic-industrial targets. (1980, p. 4)

As the F.A.S. points out, the explicit targeting of political and military leadership would, in event of its execution, mean the end of any pretense of controlling escalation, and indeed would make it impossible for the Soviets to negotiate war termination!

With the proposed arming of NATO forces with tactical nuclear weapons systems, the U.S. military began talking about the practicability of winning a nuclear war within the European theatre (or the Near East, or Indian Ocean, etc.). And with the prospective deployment of Cruise and Pershing II missiles in Western Europe, their obvious dual purpose character (against targets in Western Europe, *or* against targets deep in the Soviet Union) provided scenarios by which it is alleged a nuclear war could be fought and won in Europe (either including or excluding targets in European Russia). These scenarios conclude that without involving an intercontinental exchange of missiles, the Soviets could be defeated without the United States sustaining any damage. According to both Brzezinski and Vice-President George Bush, such "limited" "theatre" nuclear war is thinkable and winnable (*The New York Sunday Times,* March 30, 1980; *Time,* January 12, 1981, p. 22).

It is manifest that such scenarios are irrational. Their practicality would have to depend upon the continuous functioning of command, control and communications facilities (hereafter C³) by which responsible political and military leadership would have substantially perfect information about the progress of the "theatre" war and perfect ability to direct the firing or non-firing of nuclear weapons. As we will note in section II, this notion is an illusion fostered by the pursuit of sophisticated electronic technique by techno-bureaucrats in the military-industrial complex. Under battle conditions, the C³ system of the U.S. military (and probably of the Soviet's also) is extremely vulnerable to disruption and by its nature is not susceptible to protective "hardening." As E.P. Thompson says:

> In such a hair-trigger situation, the very notion of "political" options becomes increasingly incredible. The persons who decide will not be a harrassed President or First Secretary . . . but a small group of military technicians, whose whole training and rationale is that of war, and who can, by no conceivable argument be said to represent the rational interests of any economic or political formation. Very probably they will act without any 'political' mediation. (1980, p. 10).

Escalation from theatre battlefield nuclear weapons to intermediate range weapons and thence to intercontinental weapons is thus a virtual certainty if "limited" war is attempted. And obviously even a first stage tactical nuclear war in a "theatre" would in reality be an *unlimited* nuclear war for the nations immediately involved. The very discussion of the possibility of winning a theatre war is itself destabilizing, raising as it does the possibility of a preemptive first strike into the opponent's heartland as the only "sure" way of "winning."

PD–59 exacerbates the instability arising from its explicit targeting of Soviet nuclear installations, by adding explicit targeting of Soviet C³ facilities. It is absolutely contradictory to speak of limiting a nuclear exchange (be it within a "theatre" or intercontinental) and at the same time to speak of giving priority to attacking the opponent's C³. If the latter attack is effective, the opponent has been deprived of the means to control the dispatch of his weapons, which means spasm firing. Targeting of C³, as the F.A.S. noted, is to announce a *super*-counterforce policy. "Use it or lose it" is the essence of currently revealed U.S. nuclear policy: a more destabilizing or threatening attitude would only be a clear and unqualified first-strike threat. That ultimate step may be the object of the MX missile system with its greatly enhanced megatonnage and its hoped-for invulnerability to Soviet missiles.

II. THE CONTEXT AND NATURE OF THE EXTERMINIST AXIS

(a) The U.S. Military-Industrial Complex (MIC)

The context of the U.S. MIC is based on a population of nearly 300 million (including the Canadian colony) which has not experienced twentieth century warfare on its own territory; its own Civil War ended 116 years ago, long out of living memory. For Americans in this century wars are events which take place "over there," beyond the Atlantic or Pacific Oceans, and involve issues which make little sense to them, as filtered through the mass media and educational system. Their lives are mostly involved in the pursuit of commodities, the production of which is managed by several hundred giant corporations (transnational corporations). They work at jobs where they are paid and away from those jobs where they market to themselves the commodities they want. They come to want these commodities by observing them and by serving as audiences for the mass media which advertise them. An ideology of possessive individualism permeates the imagery which is built into the commodities and into the advertising. Political candidates and foreign policy (to the extent that such policies are ever formulated as such) have been marketed through the mass media since the 1950s in precisely the same way that commodities are marketed.

The same giant corporations which dominate the markets for consumer goods also are the core of the MIC. Enjoying cost-plus contracts for military goods procurement by the government, they "spin off" into consumer goods marketable innovations based on federally funded military research and development. Practicing oligopolistic pricing of consumer goods, they have avoided the 19th century type cyclical depressions by reducing production while maintaining prices during depression periods. Until the Vietnam War, post-war American capitalism enjoyed substantial material growth while maintaining its "Free World" gendarme policy abroad. The end of that era was signalled by the collapse of the dollar in 1971, and the rise of its former client states in Western Europe and Japan to a condition of relative autonomy.

Were it not for the regular and recently escalated military budgets, the flow of purchasing power to people would have slowed to disastrous levels (because of the retention by the giant corporations of income to maintain profit and dividend levels and reserves for depreciation and undistributed profits). Even so, the rising rate of price inflation accompanies higher levels of unemployment, with resulting tension between ethnic and other disadvantaged groups.

This is in essence the context of the MIC in the U.S. News management by the TNCs and their agents in the military and in the executive and legislative government organs has opportunistically exploited the possibilities of increasing the military budget ever since 1945. A recent example is the treatment of the Iranian hostage affair, which resulted in at least a $30 billion increase in arms expenditures in 1981–82.

Lord Zuckerman is of course correct in saying that it is the technicians in the laboratory—not the military chiefs—who are the individuals responsible for the nuclear arms race in both the U.S. and the U.S.S.R. The technician:

> proposes for this or that arcane reason it would be useful to improve an old or to devise a new nuclear warhead; and if a new warhead, then a new missile; and given a new missile, a new system within which it has to fit. . . . It is he who has succeeded over the years in equating, and so confusing, nuclear destructive power with military strength, as though the former were the single and a sufficient condition of military success. (Zuckerman, 1980)

He is correct that the arguments on which the incremental creep of nuclear weapons is justified politically at each step have exaggerated and falsified the apparent Soviet military threat. He is correct in quoting York:

> 'The guilty men and organizations,' writes York. . . are to be found at all levels of government and in all segments of society: presidents, presidential candidates; governors and mayors, members of Congress, civilian officials and military officers; business executives and labor leaders, famous scientists and run-of-the-mill engineers; writers and editorialists; and just plain folks.' Their motives, he tells us, are various but 'nearly all such individuals' he goes on to say:

> 'have a deep long-term involvement in the arms race. They derive either their incomes, their profits, or their consultant fees from it. But much more important than money as a motivating force are the individuals' own psychic and spiritual needs; the majority of the key individual promoters of the arms race derive a very large part of their self-esteem from their participation in what they believe to be an essential—even a holy—cause. . . . They are inspired by ingenious and clever ideas, challenged by bold statements of real and imaginary military requirements, stimulated to match or exceed technological progress by the other side or even by a rival military service here at

home, and victimized by rumors and phony intelligence. Some have been lured by the siren call of rapid advancement, personal recognition, and unlimited opportunity, and some by promises of capital gains. Some have sought out and even made up problems to fit the solution they have spent much of their lives discovering and developing. (Zuckerman, 1980, pp. 10–11)

But York (and Zuckerman) stop short of identifying the institutional formations which hire, house, and care for these technicians. They are the giant corporations which dominate the American capitalist system. For them the bottom line is profits and capital gains. They have no consciences, being fictitious corporate persons. And their officers hold *their* jobs because they can produce profits and capital gains, and by no means because they are "bad" people.

In short, the U.S. military-industrial complex is integral to the U.S. capitalist system: each depends on the other. And the tentacles of the MIC reach into every region and state in the U.S. and the provinces in Canada, employing people to either produce parts for the weapons, or parts or fuels for the machines with which to produce the weapons parts, or services (such as housing, hotels, taxicabs, lawyers) which are needed by those who make the parts of the weapons, or the teachers, newspaper publishers, and local government officers who work in the communities where the foregoing people work, etc. Note also that the corporate form with its bottom-line rationality employs the great majority of the working population. Encased in the professional/bureaucratic style within corporations and the military itself, it is not much of an exaggeration to suggest that almost the whole population of the U.S. and Canada are involved—one way or another—in the military-industrial complex. After about 100 years of active systemic development, how could it be otherwise?[2]

(b) The Soviet Military-Industrial Complex

In its own way, the Soviet Union is also subject to destablizing pressures. Its economic organization has chronically failed to produce sufficient food and other consumer goods. Since 1965, Soviet military policy has not been primarily reactive and defensive as it had been earlier. The deployment of SS–20 missiles in Eastern Europe, and the Backfire bomber are aggressive. So also the development of an all-ocean navy has aggressive potential.

Possibly the clearest example of the aggressiveness of the Soviet Union concerns its anti-Chinese campaign. In the late 1960s, journal and press articles emphasized the Soviet need to prevent China from acquiring a nuclear capability. President Nixon's top administrative assistant, H.R.

---

[2] This section is a superficial summary of some aspects of Smythe, 1981.

Haldeman, is supported by other evidence in saying that indeed the Soviet Union tried repeatedly to get the U.S. to join it in attacking China. The Soviet had massed divisions of nuclear-equipped soldiers on the frontier at the Usurri River. Their purpose was a "surgical" nuclear strike against China's nuclear plants.

> Then came the Soviet-Chinese border clashes, surprising the rest of the world, which had seen the two countries as one great Communist monolith. And finally word from the Soviets that they could wait no longer for U.S. participation in the attack. If no signal was received from us, they would go ahead on their own.
>
> Kissinger, at first inclined to dismiss a Soviet nuclear attack on China as a fantasy, now realized as the border clashes escalated that war was a serious possibility and told me so. He and Nixon huddled. They decided to send a signal to the Soviets that the U.S. was determined to be a friend of that Eastern nation. (Haldeman, 1978, p. 133)

Such a signal was sent and there followed the reopening of the relations between China and the U.S. and the abatement of the Soviet nuclear threat, at least for the time being.

For years the evidence of the deformed socialism in the Soviet Union has been accumulating: a class struggle (unacknowledged officially) with severe repression of dissent, and the clear ascendancy to power and material privilege of an elite class of technical experts and professionals. Thompson, himself no enemy of socialism or of the U.S.S.R., must be quoted again:

> The arms complex is as clearly the leading sector of Soviet industry as it is in the United States, but this is expressed within bureaucratic modes of operation. There is some spin-off from military technology into civilian industry: civil aircraft, nuclear energy. . . . The military complex and its successes are upheld as a model of organization and of management techniques, and these are exported to other sectors. Moreover, the needs of the military complex—in particular, the imperatives placed upon centralized planning, priority in access to resources, and direction of scientific skills—affect the structure of the economy as a whole, and colour the decisions of the political managers.
>
> At the same time there is a greater direct exposure of the Soviet population to patriotic state propaganda than in most Western democracies: that is, what is (or is attempted to be) accomplished in "The West" by the "free" operation of the media is directly inculcated in Russia by such 'voluntary' organizations as DOSAAF: The Voluntary Society for Cooperation with the Army, Aviation and the Navy, with a membership of 80 million, and with clubs, sports facilities, and military-patriotic or civil defense education organized around factories, farms, and schools. And alongside and supporting all this there are the huge, quasi-autonomous operations of the Security Services, inheriting historic traditions of despotism, supporting military-patri-

otic ideology, and exerting an independent inertia of their own.
(Thompson, 1980, p. 20)

The Soviet's thrust toward exterminism is not as aggressive as that of the
West, but it has the same kind of autonomous techno-bureaucratic inertial
momentum. It has the same kind of incremental growth of weaponry
located in the scientific and engineering establishment with the same kind
of " lead-time" commitment to innovation in weaponry that we find in the
United States. It also supports tendencies in popular culture towards chau-
vinism, xenophobia, and in relation to China, racism (Thompson, 1980, p.
21). When it looks westward, its aging ruling group, for a variety of ethnic,
religious, economic and political reasons, faces what Thompson calls "all
that inflammable human material in Eastern Europe which must be held
perpetually under political, military and ideological controls" (1980, p. 6).

(c) The Exterminist Axis

The danger of nuclear war on a global scale is now very much greater than
in the 1960s because an accelerating readiness to wage it is evident in the
two super powers. Irrationality in military policy is reaching epidemic
proportions in and between them: a condition coming to be known as "Exterminism." The warrant for referring to both super powers as the Exterminist Axis is that each cooperates antagonistically with the other in a
reciprocal, spiraling death dance. The prospects of each new refinement in
nuclear weaponry on one side is the necessary excuse and stimulus for the
other side to match it or go it one better. It is an irreversible ratchet process,
if the relevant populations tolerate it much longer. As Lord Zuckerman
said:

> The men in the nuclear weapons laboratories of both sides have suc-
> ceeded in creating a world with an irrational foundation, on which a
> new set of political realities has in turn had to be built. They have
> become the alchemists of our times, working in secret ways which
> cannot be divulged, casting spells which embrace us all. They may
> never have been in battle, they may never have experienced the dev-
> astation of war; but they know how to devise the means of destruc-
> tion. And the more destructive power there is, so, one must assume
> they imagine the greater the chance of military success. (1980, p. 11)

While it is obvious that the two super powers are not ideologically, militarily, economically, or geopolitically equal, identical or in balance, it is
true that on one level of analysis—their commitment to nuclear weapons—
they are symmetrical. As Thompson says:

> The bomb...is a component in a weapons-*system;* and producing,
> manning and supporting that system is a correspondent social system
> —a distinct organization of labour, research and operation, with dis-

tinctive hierarchies of command, rules of secrecy, prior access to resources and skills and high levels of policing and discipline; a distinctive organization of production, which, while militarist in character employs and is supported by great numbers of civilians (civil servants, scientists, academics) who are subordinated to its discipline and rules. (1980, p. 7)

What is the role of ideology in the Exterminist Axis? On both sides it has the same three functions. It stimulates war preparation. It legitimizes the privileged position of the respective military-industrial complexes. And it polices internal dissent. Substantively, as Thompson says:

The two camps are united ideologically in only one matter: in mutual hostility to any genuine non-alignment, 'neutralism' or 'third way.' For if such a way were possible, it would strike directly at exterminism's legitimacy. (1980, p. 24)

The core of the MIC in both super powers is the bureaucracy of technicians, scientists, and administrators. These bureaucracies are the institutional structures which dominate their respective countries through the power they possess to determine priorities in the use of resources, human and other, and the policies to be employed. The analogy may be helpful of two giant monopoly corporations contesting for control of a world market: they pursue their respective exploitative policies to the brink of mutual destruction, while simultaneously acting like a cartel. SALT and Pugwash meetings are the occasion for each side to probe the intentions, relative strengths and weaknesses of the other. And the outcome of such meetings is a new trade-off of plans for weapons systems innovation, of territorial claims on the second and third world countries. As with all cartels, the participants reserve their rights to use the terms of the "armistice" arrived at in such meetings as the basis to develop further aggressive weapons systems and the "markets" of populations and resources they make possible. The analogy is strengthened by consideration of the long leadtime (with cycles of perhaps 7 to 11 years) which both MICs employ to take a weapons system from the planning stage to full implementation in practice. Of course, such an innovation cycle has long been evident in cartels in the civilian side of the electronics industry. And for a good reason: the civilian innovations are spun off from the military research and development in the same giant TNCs.

It should not surprise us that social systems in which the presently dominant class is technobureaucratic elite (as is true of both the U.S. and the U.S.S.R.) are characterized by capitalist production relations. We should by now know that historically the military has been the leading edge of capitalist technical development, and for obvious reasons including its role in capital accumulation (the seizure, organization into modern empires, and exploitation of precious metals, slaves, and more latterly people produced in the form of "markets"). And we must recall that the Soviet Union took over uncritically capitalist forms and policies for industrial organization. Lenin's *State and Revolution,* with its eager acceptance of scientific management as developed by Frederick Taylor, attests to this. In this sense I disagree in part with E. P. Thompson's argument that the theory of imperialism is not applicable to the Exterminist Axis. That argument is valid only if it be assumed that the Soviet Union in its MIC is *not* operating within capitalist production relations. But if the Soviet MIC is understood properly as operating within capitalist production relations, then analysis of the Exterminist Axis must take account of the rivalry of capitalist systems (such as, the British as against German system as of 1914).

The military (U.S. and Soviet alike) is organized in an authoritarian, downward flow of discipline, with line and staff parameters (which also is the pattern of industrial organization!). The following analysis relates to the U.S. system—I leave it to others more familiar with the Soviet side to show differences or similarities.

Bearing in mind the earlier analysis of the technobureaucratic process which maintains the flow of technical innovations for war, it is evident that the U.S. military in its operational aspect has been committed to: (a) heavy dependence on communications and computer technical equipment (and today these must be perceived as one activity); and (b) an operational doctrine modelled on industrial production of commodities for markets. The consequences of this commitment are: (a) intended mindless destruction of people and resources (the "body count" as the "bottom line" objective, as so instructively displayed in Vietnam); this policy is entirely consistent with a first strike in an early nuclear war, (b) great vulnerability to "inefficiency" arising from the contradictions between the obsessive reliance on super-sophisticated equipment and procedures, and the infinitely complex and dynamic reality of real warfare conditions, affecting both soldiers and their equipment.

General W. C. Westmoreland, former Chief of Staff, United States Army, said in 1969:

> We recognize five functions of an army at war. We have emphasized only three: mobility, firepower and command and control—move, shoot, and communicate. The other two have been neglected: intelligence, and support.

> Large parts of the infantry, ground and air cavalry, and aviation are used in what I will now call 'STANO'—surveillance, target acquisition and night observation—finding the enemy. In this function large areas can be covered continuously by *aerial surveillance systems, un-*

attended ground sensors, radars and other perfected means of finding the enemy.

On the battlefield of the future, enemy forces will be located, tracked and targeted almost instantaneously through the use of *data links, computer assisted intelligence evaluation, and automated fire control.* With first round kill probabilities approaching certainty, and with surveillance devices that can continually track the enemy, the need for large forces to fix the opposition will be less important.

The two preceding paragraphs have the private-sector analogue of market research, with "kill probabilities" equivalent to product sales. He goes on:

The third function [control] includes an improved communication system. This system not only would permit commanders to be continually aware of the entire battlefield panorama down to squad and platoon level, but would permit logistics systems to rely more heavily on air lines of communications.

Today, machines and technology are permitting economy of manpower on the battlefield, as indeed they are in the factory. But the future offers even more possibilities for economy. I am confident the American people expect this country to take full advantage of its technology—to welcome and applaud the developments that will replace wherever possible the man with the machine.

So, like the Executive Vice-President of the XYZ Corporation, the Chief of Staff controls the movements of his product (be it shoes, hamburgers or head count) from factory to consumer by computers in real time. The military provides war industry an almost unlimited purse to apply science to automate war. He goes on:

I foresee a new battlefield array. I see battlefields or combat areas that are under 24-hour real or near-real time surveillance of all types. I see battlefields on which we can destroy anything we locate through instant *communications* and the almost instantaneous application of highly lethal firepower. I see a continuing need for highly mobile combat forces to assist in fixing and destroying the enemy. The changed battlefield will dictate that the supporting logistics system also undergo change. I see the forward end of the logistics system with mobility equal to the supported force. I see the elimination of many intermediate support echelons and the use of inventory-in-motion techniques.

This is scientific management, weighing cost against effectiveness, with maximum possible mechanization and displacement of people in war as in non-war industry. He goes on:

Currently, *we have hundreds of surveillance, target acquisition, night observation and information processing systems either in being, in development or in engineering. These range from field computers to advanced airborne sensors and new night vision devices.* Our problem now is to further our knowledge—exploit our technology, and equally important to incorporate all these devices into an integrated land combat system.

In summary, I see an Army built into and around an integrated area control system that exploits the advanced *technology of communications, sensors, fire direction* and the required *automatic data processing* —a system that is sensitive to the dynamics of the ever-changing battlefield—a system that materially assists the tactical commander in making sound and timely decisions. . . . We are on the threshold for the first time in achieving maximum utilization of both our firepower and our mobility. In order to succeed in this effort, we need the scientific and engineering support of both the military and the industrial communities.[3]

The underlined references to equipment in this quotation are communications systems per se or dependent on and integrated with such systems. The model for the U.S. military is clearly the TNC, "targeting" its customer markets on the basis of intelligence produced by surveys of its potential targets, then applying scientific management, systems theory and the latest automated techniques based on communications/computer engineering to the end of maximizing paying customers (body count).

The technocratic bias of the U.S. MIC has recently been recognized by even the rightist leadership of the Congressional wing of the Complex. Thus an internal critical study within the Air Force concludes that the policy of "pursuing ever-increasing technical complexity and sophistication has made high-technology solutions and combat readiness mutually exclusive." The report says:

Technology is evaluated within an artificial framework derived from the faith in technological revolution, the attrition mind-set and the idea that war is a manipulable, deterministic process subject to central control. This framework considers neither the decisive effort of the human elements nor the central characteristic of actual war. . . . By ignoring the real world, we have evolved a self-reinforcing, yet scientifically unsupportable, faith in the military usefulness of ever-increasing technological complexity. We tend to think of military strength in terms of wonder weapons that are in reality mechanistic solutions.[4]

The evidence to support this conclusion has long been apparent in all branches of the U.S. military and relates to the contradiction between the pursuit of technique for its own sake and the practical necessities of waging war. One example, from the U.S. Army: There are "literally thousands of special purpose computer systems" for battlefield use alone, and the

---

[3] Westmoreland, 1969. Emphasis added.

[4] Franklin C. Spinney, "Defense Facts of Life," quoted by *Washington Post* Service and published in the *Philadelphia Inquirer*, April 5, 1981.

Army in 1980 had under development some 150 automation systems. Adopted because of the incestuous collaboration of military procurement officers and private sector electronics firms, these systems are generally incompatible and hence non-integratable in practical use.[5] Further, the skill requirements to operate and maintain the increasingly sophisticated equipment of the U.S. military is in sharp contradiction to the low skill level, poor morale, and unreliability of the soldiers expected to do the work—again the mirror image of the same problems in "civilian" industry. As the press reported:

> Classified Defense Department documents reveal, for example, that 90 percent of the men and women who maintain and operate the U.S. Army's nuclear weapons in Europe flunked basic tests of their skills last year. . . . The tests were failed by 86 percent of the Army's artillery crewmen, 77 percent of the computer programmers, 89 percent of the track-vehicles mechanics and 82 percent of the Hawk surface-to-air missile crews. . . . Many technical manuals have been converted to comic book formats because U.S. technicians couldn't understand the standard instructions. ("Washington Merry-Go-Round," 1981)

We may conclude this analysis of the MIC by noting that at its western end the Exterminist Axis relies on what Weizenbaum calls "instrumental reason." He acknowledges that computers are fine for dealing with pure abstractions—mathematics and logic, for example, where the programmer understands what the program is about. But he points out that they are invalid for dealing with real world problems where conflict, values and human judgement are involved. There no overall view of reality can be programmed—only the partial, mechanical assumptions about it held by the programmer—and where different programmers change the program, at different times and places, literally no one knows or can know what mix of partial assumptions has been fed into it or what synergistic transformations the computer has made of its own program.

As applied by the military, Weizenbaum says computer programs "embody authoritarianism based on expertise":

> Not only have policy-makers abdicated their decision-making responsibility—though all the while maintaining the illusion that they, the policy-makers are formulating policy questions and answering them —but responsibility has altogether evaporated. Not only does the most senior admiral of the United States Navy, in a rare moment of insight, perceive that he has become 'a slave to these damned computers,' that he cannot help but base his judgements on 'what the computer says,' but no human is responsible at all for the computer's output. The enormous computer systems in the Pentagon and their counterparts elsewhere in our culture have, in a very real sense, no

---

[5] Silvert, 1980. See series of which this article was part, "C³I: Managing Essential Elements of the Battle," *Army,* March 1979–April 1980.

authors. Thus they do not admit of any questions of right or wrong, of justice, or of any theory with which one can agree or disagree. They provide no basis on which 'what the machine says' can be challenged . . . . Computer systems do not admit of exercises of imagination that may ultimately lead to authentic human judgement. (1976, pp. 248, 239–40)

And quoting the head of a computer laboratory at a major U.S. university, he says:

'These systems [sic! no human is responsible] are responsible, in large part, for the maintenance of what peace and stability there is in the world, and at the same time, they are capable of unleashing destruction of a scale that is almost impossible for man to comprehend.' (Weizenbaum, p. 241)

This is the decision-making reality of the Exterminist Axis, U.S. end. What about the Soviet end? The two are the reality with which the peace movement must contend.

III. ON THE OLD AND NEW PEACE MOVEMENTS

The peace movement from 1945 to the mid-1960s made brave and persistent efforts. It contributed significantly to the adoption of the nuclear test-ban treaty and to the avoidance by governments of nuclear war. It has been ineffective in halting or reversing the escalating spiral of terror in nuclear weapons development and deployment.

The potential of doing just that exists in the qualitatively different new peace movement now developing in Europe, in reaction to the advent of tactical nuclear weapons and intermediate range missiles there—if it can be mobilized and brought into action before 1983—the date when the danger of "theatre" nuclear war with the probability of massive first strikes will mature. It is essential therefore to analyze why the old peace movement policy is now largely obsolete (and even counter-productive), and what is qualitatively new about the new peace movement.

For the masses of people in the world, it is unthinkable that there should be nuclear war. Literally, as Bill Livant says:

The refusal to think about nuclear war is *not irrational*. It is only by *not* thinking about nuclear war that we are able to continue thinking about all the other problems of our lives. It is only so that we can find the motivation to continue to think about all the other problems. For if we were to take nuclear war seriously, it would really undermine the basis for thinking about anything in our lives. It is not the case that nuclear war is a big problem only. So is inflation, and yet we do try to think about that. (1981b)[6]

---

[6] I have borrowed freely from Livant in this section of my paper.

This block against thinking about the unthinkable affects all of us—but some more than others. Until the mid-1970s, the chief factor which permitted a small minority to think—and act—against nuclear war was class. The great bulk of the old peace movement (and the leading fraction of the new movement) has consisted of the upper middle class, with a scattering of "defectors" from the ruling class, plus some of their children, and Quakers (of all classes, but mostly upper middle) ethically opposed to all militarism. Only these people, and they for the most part only part-time, were able to think about the unthinkable because these people have the remainder of their human problems sufficiently under control to be able to afford the concern to devote to the issue of nuclear war. Nuclear war was not a concern of working class children or of substantial numbers of their parents.

We now see that one of the major features of the new peace movement is that in Europe, danger of nuclear war has broadened the base of popular opposition. Whereas the old regime of MAD left people immobilized because it seemed not to present an imminent present threat to them, the tactical nuclear weapons (including the notorious neutron bomb), cruise missiles, and intermediate missiles, and the counterpart Russian weapons have begun to shatter the "unthinkability" of thinking about nuclear war for the European working class. Coupled with heightened alarm on the part of the upper middle class and the ruling class and their children, the European Nuclear Disarmament (END) movement has picked up remarkable momentum in 1979 to 1981. Theatre nuclear war now has a clear and threatening meaning for Europeans, a sizeable fraction of whose present population has lived through one or two World Wars in their own territory. The flat refusal by Norway and Denmark to allow nuclear weapons in their countries set a pattern. The Dutch general election in May 1981, signified repudiation of the previous Dutch government decision to accept the missiles which NATO wished to locate there. The Belgian government, at this writing, having tentatively accepted the missiles, is now under great pressure to follow the Dutch empire. Even in West Germany the issue is still not resolved in ways favored by NATO. In Britain the main opposition party and in Greece the governing party are committed to unilateral disarmament and rejection of theatre nuclear weapons. The thrust of this END movement is clear: dismantle both the NATO and Warsaw Pact blocs, neutralize Europe as far as nuclear weapons are concerned. The U.S. and Canadian population, being less immediately threatened and being subject to the selective news management policies of the MIC through the mass media is only starting to mobilize to meet the threat of the Exterminist Axis.

In both Europe and in North America, however, a second and not yet generally recognized qualitative change in the peace movement is on the

horizon, and one with fundamental political possibilities. This change involves what has happened and is happening regarding energy policy. The movement against nuclear energy for "civilian" purposes is closely connected with the ecology movement in both Europe and in North America. *And everybody is thinking about energy,* and we will be forced to think about it more and more as time goes on. The movement against nuclear power must be always linked with the movement against nuclear weapons. The link is a natural one, namely plutonium. Why does the Exterminist Axis favour nuclear power plants? The answer, as Sir Martin Ryle says, is not because of any advantage in the cost of producing electricity (though this is the phoney excuse given):

> There is, of course, such a reason. Amongst the 100-odd unwanted radioactive products in a spent fuel rod there is one—plutonium— which is different; it does not exist in Nature but it is used to manufacture nuclear weapons and in Fast Breeder Reactors. (1981, p. 21)

Ryle cites evidence that the supply of plutonium available is inadequate for the nuclear weapons planned by the U.S., the U.K. and Germany, and concludes that as regards nuclear power industry, "electricity must be seen as a by-product of the plutonium industry."

Therefore:

> On the evidence available it would seem that the future of the Nuclear 'Power' industry depends on a continuing escalation of the nuclear arms race. (pp. 22–23)

To put the matter differently; if a country stopped producing nuclear weapons, the nuclear "power" industry would require massive additional subsidies, or the industry would collapse because its electricity output would have to be priced far above alternative energy sources. Presently (1981) the U.S. government spends 5,000 times as much on nuclear as on solar energy development (Nissen, 1981).

What is becoming clear is that there are two roads or paths for energy: the *hard* (such as nuclear) and the *soft* (solar either directly or indirectly via natural processes). Amory and Hunter Lovins argue that the two paths are mutually exclusive at a very deep level:

> Though each path is only illustrative and embraces an infinite spectrum of variations on a theme, there is a deep structural and conceptual dichotomy between them. Soft and hard *technologies* are not *technically* incompatible: in principle, nuclear power stations and solar collectors can coexist. But soft and hard *paths* are *culturally* incompatible: each path entails a certain evolution of social values and perceptions that makes the other kind of world harder to imagine. The two paths are *institutionally* antagonistic: the policy actions, institutions and perceptions and political commitments required for each (especially for the hard path) would seriously inhibit the other. (Nash, 1979, p. 30)

As Bill Livant (1981b) says, the atomic power industry is collapsing because in all its features: capital costs, centralization, human and environmental damage, it is the hard energy path.[7]

At the other end of the nuclear link, there is a choice of soft or hard paths in war. The Vietnamese War showed that the soft path can prevail over the hard (when nuclear weapons were not used). Soft war is "low technology" war, while hard war is "high technology" war. Wars of liberation are "soft" wars in this sense.

If the policy choices are approached from the point of view that we are dealing with an Exterminist Axis, the ruling class of which is committed to a high technology (that is, hard) policy for both energy and weapons, the forthcoming struggles within the new peace movement will clarify principles and practices which plagued the old. For example, pacifists frequently oppose all "war," refusing to distinguish between nuclear and non-nuclear war. One reader of E. P. Thompson's article in *The Nation* (March 14, 1981) wrote, "I doubt that we can eliminate nuclear weapons unless the war system as a whole is confronted and attacked. . . . I am a strong believer in non-violent aggression [sic]." The contradiction embodied in the last three words betrays the unrealism of the position. And churches and left-wing pacifists find themselves supporting peoples' wars against intolerable conditions, as in Vietnam, Zimbabwe, and El Salvador. We may also find that the old peace movement's high priority advocacy of nuclear arms *control* as a sufficient goal is quite obsolete and counterproductive. The ruling groups at both ends of the Exterminist Axis are quite happy to use such control and negotiations ostensibly aimed at it, as covers for continuing technical development of new nuclear weaponry. Recognition of the reality of the hard as against soft paths in war and civilian energy will clarify strategic and tactical issues for the peace movement. The important point here it that by linking struggle against nuclear weapons to struggle against nuclear power, both arms of the struggle multiply their strengths and the "unthinkable" will be thinkable and the consequences of the thoughts, "do-able" actions.

The third major difference between the new and old peace movements involves what at first glance seem unrelated factors. The "Old Left" faith that the Soviet Union could do no wrong, as carried into the old peace movement, tied it into support of maintenance of the Warsaw Pact and the escalation of the spiral of nuclear terror. The new peace movement in Europe is aimed at eliminating nuclear weapons from its soil and developing a new national autonomy in foreign policy for European countries. END *assumes* that it is correct and necessary to develop links between neutralism in both East and West Europe, and that the initiatives of the Polish

---

[7] Citing Lovins, 1980, p. 54.

people and other peoples in Warsaw Pact countries must be linked with those in the West in a new, broad-based internationalist movement. END assumes that it can only have the credibility which it requires (and which the old peace movement with its links to Soviet propaganda organizations lacked), if it deals with both ends of the Exterminist Axis evenhandedly.

The thrust of the new peace movement in Europe is towards associating neutralist European countries with the Nonaligned Movement. There is an essential basis for this thrust in principle. As Bill Livant puts it:

> Here is where the conception of Western Europe as a 'theater of limited nuclear war' is so important. The emplacement of missiles in Western Europe would dramatically and irrevocably make—forgive me—'gooks' of the English, French, German, Belgian, Dutch, Italian, Greeks, of the peoples who 'cradled' Western civilization. Not a whit different from the Vietnamese, Chinese, Arabs, Black Africans, etc. In the evolution of violence into its most global, comprehensive modern form, these Western peoples would, by such a step, become peoples of the Third World. *Any people which is objectively organized for possible extermination by a superpower in the interest of the defense of that superpower's home base is, it seems to me, a Third World people. Its first and fundamental interest is the elimination of that superpower's power to do this.* (1981a)

Livant presses the point:

> Thompson may indeed be right when he cites Mountbatten, Zuckerman and many others that nuclear war *cannot* be limited to a 'theater.' But my point does not rest on this possible impossibility. Just suppose for a moment that it *can* be 'limited.' What do we mean by 'limited'? For whom is it 'limited'? For the superpower. *Not* for the people in the 'theater.' *For them it is unlimited . . . .* The 'theater' is the garbage dump for the *un*limited-nuclear war—by proxy. (Livant, 1981a)

So the reality of the Exterminist Axis forces us all to connect the struggle in Europe and North America against nuclear weapons with that of peoples in Third World countries from, most obviously, superpower interference with their national sovereign rights (Eritrea, Kampuchea, and Afghanistan, as well as El Salvador, Nicaragua, and Guatemala).

At this point I must come to terms with my own previous views on the Soviet Union—and to some degree most left-liberals in the West share them. We understand that capitalism has fought communism since 1917. We understand that after 1945 capitalism, through its leading formation, the U.S., undertook to contain, and if possible, destroy the Soviet Union by a combination of military threat, economic and cultural offensives. But we have been blocked from parallel critical analysis of the Soviet Union for several reasons. One was that until the mid-1960s the Soviet Union's military preparedness was in fact defensive and reactive to aggressive initiatives from the West, particularly from the United States. And secondly, under the influence of Lenin's theory of imperialism, we saw the superpower confrontation as a holding action by the Soviet Union while anti-imperialist forces around the world wore down and eroded the capitalist system. In that view the arms program of the Soviet Union imposed an unwanted burden on the Warsaw Pact states. But we ignored the fact that as E. P. Thompson says:

> Superpowers which have been locked, for 30 years, in the postures of military confrontation increasingly adopt militaristic characteristics in their economies, their polity, and their culture. What may have originated in reaction becomes direction. (1980, p. 16)

We ignored the deforming effects on the Soviet Union's socialist forces of the technocratic-bureaucratic class, just as we closed our eyes to the fact that Soviet foreign policy was building an imperial structure of investments, markets, and exploitation of Third World countries—the mirror image of that of Western imperialism. In this situation, I agree with Thompson that "To argue from origins, to nominate goodies and baddies is to take refuge from morality in moralism" (1980, p. 16). Indeed, western Marxists in the 1980s are committed to "automatic Marxists'" knee-jerk irrationality unless they reject the notion that the Soviet Union knows best and can do no wrong.

The most critical and decisive problem for the new peace movement, as END has already perceived, is to "engage in delicate and non-provocative work to form alliances between the peace movement in the West and constructive elements in the Communist world . . . which confront the exterminist structures and ideologies of their own nations." END sees this as essential to success because it is absolutely necessary that the anti-exterminist movement be *nonaligned* with either bloc and be seen as such. Otherwise exterminism with its bases in the weapons-system-and-support complex will reassert ideological control and resume its thrust. END is very clear that its movement must *not* be mediated by official or unofficial spokespersons for either bloc. It is building a broad front including churches, Euro-communists, laborers, trade unionists, ecologists and East European dissidents and citizens unmediated by Party structures. It is regenerated internationalism.

IV. ON COMMUNICATIONS AND THE
ANTI-EXTERMINIST STRUGGLE

Communications is the terrain in which the contradictions of the world are reflected in most concentrated form. It is also the terrain in which control of policy has fantastic multiplier consequences for the success of other policy measures. It is the aspect of the technique of the Exterminist Axis which is most vulnerable to deliberate disruption in order to deter aggression—albeit the disruption would be non-violent. To establish this point of view thoroughly would require a book; here I can only summarize the argument.[8]

1. Teleprocessing and other modes of electronic communications depend on the use of the radio spectrum. The radio spectrum has three unique characteristics which distinguishes it from other "resources":
    a. The radio spectrum's original and still its principle use is the act of sharing information between transmitter and receiver, that is, communication. For no other resource is the principal function and transmission *and,* simultaneously, the retention of information or of anything else.
    b. For one nation or class of user to use it, all nations and classes of users must also be able to use it with equipment built to compatible standards. Worldwide cooperation in regulating interference is therefore necessary for the radio spectrum to be used by anyone and everyone.
    c. Because the radio spectrum is used to communicate information and because control of the flow of information is the basis of political power, the control of the use of the radio spectrum lies close to the seat of sovereignty in the nation state. At the same time, the necessary joint decision making by all nations at the world level (the International Telecommunications Union) has for almost a century substantiated the fact that by international and national law, title to the radio spectrum rests not with individuals or nations but in all humanity.
2. Developed capitalism whether in the West or in the deformed Socialist form in the Soviet Union is dependent on telecommunications (and therefore on the radio spectrum to conduct its military, civilian and governmental operations); to the extent that print journalism is used, it in turn is now dependent on electronic technique (and therefore ultimately on the radio spectrum). Weapons systems, the management of news for the propaganda addressed to domestic and foreign targets, and even the production of consumer goods, political candidates and public issues—to the extent that advertising is employed—uses an unpaid form of productive work by audience members attending to television and other mass media: all of these are dependent on the radio spectrum.

---

[8] See Smythe, 1981. Especially the Appendix, "The Electronic Information Tiger, or the Political Economy of the Radio Spectrum and the Third World Interest."

3. The capitalist strength—for war or peaceful activities—lies in its dependence on and skill in using "high technology," as was indicated above in analyzing the MIC. Historically, this strength manifested itself crudely in a policy of "first come, first served" in the allocation of the radio spectrum under the ITU. Third World countries have benefitted from "low technology" (either reliance on pre-capitalist traditional modes of communications, or the simpler electronic techniques—telegraph, telephone, radio telegraph, radio telephone, tape recorders, cassettes). Wars of liberation have relied on such "low technology" (Vietnam, Iran, Algeria). Overall, as Ali Shummo, Minister of Information of the Sudan, said recently, the developed countries "have 90 percent of the spectrum and 10 percent of the population. We have 90 percent of the population and 10 percent of the spectrum."[9] The great bulk of international communications using the radio spectrum either flows to or from the United States. The net flow of communications is from the core to the peripheral countries. The flow of the fruit of other natural resources (labor and materials) is from the periphery to the core. The flow of communications between the industrially developed countries is by no means matched by lateral flows between Third World countries.
4. The "technology" for using the radio spectrum, especially the "high technology" (such as, satellites, automated teleprocessing) is very vulnerable to disruption. Its reliability is at risk from technical faults, natural calamities (including nuclear war), attacks and jamming. Is the Exterminist Axis an electronic information tiger, to paraphase Mao Zedong?
5. Almost two-thirds of the 154 countries which participated in the ITU's 1979 World Administrative Radio Conference were Third World countries, and each of them has one vote, as do the U.S. and the Soviet Union. Varying greatly in size of population, natural resources, cultural character, class formations, terms of government, and degree of commitment to goals of materialistic progress, they share three common interests:
   a. The need for economic planning of their own productive development of their own resources, and trade relations with other Third World countries, while reducing their dependence on the specialization dictated by capitalism, especially by TNCs, through the law of comparative advantage.
   b. The need for capital, preferably by gifts without strings, or long-term loans.
   c. An absolute requirement is that they must own, control and

[9] Quoted by Howkins, 1979, p.12.

operate their own communications systems. Their control of
these systems is as vital to their independence as control of
their military capability. Even more so, because foreign control of communications is a Trojan horse which can immobi-
lize their military and produce dependency directly. Their
communications equipment emphatically need not be "high
technology" stuff (computers and data banks, interactive
television, videotex, etc.). Recall that the overthrow of the
Shah of Iran required no more equipment than cassette tapes,
the telephone and xerox, which together with mosques, festi-
vals (the *takyeh*), meetings (the *doreh*), and the bazaar, did the
trick.

With the coming of formal independence from their previous imperial masters, most of the new counries which entered the ITU between
1945 and the present had little indigenous competence in electronic matters. And their ex-colonial masters have tried to keep them dependent on
the increasingly sophisticated communications equipment which their
governments were pressed to buy from the core countries. With accelerating momentum since the 1960s, the Third World countries have developed
competence in and awareness of the high political significance of communications policy matters. It would be wrong to imply that they are generally as competent or aware in those respects as they would need to be to
resist optimally the cooptation and importuning to which they are subjected in the 1980s. However, their achievements in working together at
the 1979 WARC were substantial and encouraging. Specifically, they have
blunted the monopolistic thrust of the first-come first-served doctrine in
radio frequency allocation, and have initiated the principle of planned
allocation. In doing this they overcome the stern and resourceful opposition of both the western capitalist core, and the Soviet Union (Rutkowski,
1979). Given the dynamics of the present international scene, it is highly
probable that Third World countries will develop their strengths in radio
allocation matters by putting hard-won lessons to work in practice.

The governing of the regulation of the radio spectrum deals with
bundles of contradictions involved in the necessary dependence on use of
the spectrum by all peoples, regardless of their ideological, cultural and
economic systems and interests. Having taken the first steps toward positive planning for the terms on which this common human resource may
be used, it is worth speculating on the directions such positive planning
may take. Two examples are obvious possibilities.

1. Recapture and redirection of economic rent generated by the use
   of the spectrum. The economic rent now siphoned off by private

business from the use of the radio spectrum (conspicuously via television and radio broadcasting) is produced by the use by people of a peculiar form of world property: the spectrum. To recapture all or some of this economic rent and to use it for the development of communication systems appropriate to Third World countries would be manifestly just and wise. The proposal has already been made in the proceedings of the UNESCO International Commission for the Study of Communication Problems. There it was rejected by both the U.S. and the U.S.S.R. (MacBride Commission, 1980, p. 275).

2. Protecting nations from foreign interference in their own affairs. The Third World countries may use their influence to eliminate the military and communications aggressions which continue to violate the rights of peoples to determine their own futures. Consider this scenario. At some future time, the ITU, at Third World nations' insistence, adopts general policies, outlawing the use of the spectrum for aggressive military and propaganda purposes. Potential aggressor countries resist this strongly and serve notice that they will not be bound by such a constraint. Because the ITU as such has no "police" to enforce its policies, what then? Assume that a dictator is toppled in a peripheral Third World country, such as in Central America. The United States begins economic boycott, mass media propaganda, CIA destabilization tactics, perhaps even open intervention militarily. Third World countries through their own collective organizations demand that the aggression be stopped. The United States ignores their demand. The Third World countries then disrupt American use of the radio spectrum in calculated steps: perhaps jamming or otherwise taking over electronic possession of communication satellites on which international teleprocessing of computer data takes place; perhaps jamming military-used radio frequencies, etc. In effect they will have taken such jammed or seized frequencies as hostages, pending cessation of the aggression. End of scenario. What would differentiate this hostage-taking from the type practiced commonly where people are taken hostage would be that:

    a. the radio frequencies and even the equipment jammed or taken over, would be unharmed; one of the unique characteristics of the radio spectrum is that once the interfering signals cease, the spectrum and equipment regains its prior condition of usefulness immediately and completely; and

    b. the sanctions used would be non-violent.

Is this scenario improbable, given the facts of life about the conditions for using the radio spectrum? Maybe not so improbable as those who profit by postponing it will pretend.

It is perhaps easier to appreciate that communications policy and practice is now the area which reflects the world's contradictions in most concentrated form than it is to appreciate a corollary fact. Under the existing conditions of mass production of electronic communications equipment (including computers) and the conditions of their general use, the *substantive* role of communications in material production must be recognized fully. Historically (and the historical lag in changing it is frightening), communications has been attended to almost entirely as part of the "idea" system of society—as a subjective, idealist area of life where vague conceptions such as "ideology" could be discussed as entirely immaterial matters. Today, the evidence is abundant that communications, especially as evident in its mass production and mass use, is a very material force of production. And this is true whether we refer to weaponry or to the production and reproduction of labor power, whether we refer to its use in war or its use in the less lethal forms of (literally) "informing" people, things and social processes.

The available time in which to eliminate the Exterminist Axis is short —a very few years. Let us hurry, carefully.

REFERENCES

Federation of American Scientists. (1980). *Public Interest Report.* (October), 4.

Haldeman, H. R. (1978). *The Ends of Power.* New York: Dell Publishing Company.

Howkins, J. (1979). "The Management of the Spectrum." *Intermedia,* (September),

International Commission for the Study of Communication Problems (The MacBride Commission). (1980). *Many Voices, One World.* Paris: UNESCO.

Livant, B. (1981a). Letter to D. Smythe, March 9.

Livant, B. (1981b). "The Two Faces of the Nuclear Question: Energy and War." Unpublished paper, March 11.

Lovins, A. and H. (1980). *Energy/War: Breaking the Nuclear Link.* San Francisco: CA: Friends of the Earth.

Nash, H. (Ed.). (1979). *The Energy Controversy.*

The Nation. March 14, 1981.

The New York Sunday Times. March 30, 1980.

Nissen, B. (1981). Review of B. Commoner. (1979). *The Politics of Energy.* (New York: Alfred A. Knopf) in *Monthly Review* (February), 50.

Rutkowski, A. M. (1980). "Six Ad-hoc Two: The Third World Speaks its Mind." *Satellite Communications, 4* (March), 22–27.

Ryle, Sir M. (1981). *Towards the Nuclear Holocaust.* London: The Menard Press.

Silvert, Col. W. D., Jr. (1980). "The Goal: A World A/C Network." *Army* (April), 40–42.

Smythe, D. W. (1981). *Dependency Road: Communications, Capitalism, Consciousness, and Canada.* Norwood, NJ: Ablex Publishing Corporation.

Thompson, E. P. (1980). "Notes on Exterminism." *New Left Review* (May-June).

Time. January 12, 1981, 22.

"Washington Merry-Go-Round." (1981). *Philadelphia Welcomat* (March 25).

Weizenbaum, J. (1976). *Computer Power and Human Reason.* San Francisco, CA: W. H. Freeman.

Westmoreland, Gen. W. C. (1969). Address. Sheraton Park Hotel, Washington, D.C. October 14.

Zuckerman, Lord S. (1980). "Science Advisers and Scientific Advisers." *Proceedings of the American Philosophical Society 124* (4), 10–11.

3

Advertising and the Creation of Global Markets: The Role of the New Communication Technologies

Noreene Janus

INTRODUCTION

Information plays a central role in the expansion and consolidation of the transnational corporate system as a whole. In recent years, the development of a broad range of highly sophisticated and efficient information technologies have provided corporate users with a qualitative advance of fluidity in the international flows of vital information. The rapid development of telematics and the creation of giant data processing, storage, and retrieval networks have served the information needs of primarily military establishments and private sector clients. These information networks have become the central nervous systems of transnational corporations, facilitating the optimization of their profits through efficient and synchronous global decision making, timely investments, and appropriate research and development activities.

The centralized and transnational character of these global information systems has serious implications for the world political and economic order—implications that have already begun to cause international disputes. The major reason for conflict is that access to, and control over, these technologies has become decisive in industrial administration and production and national economic and military strength allowing "information-rich" countries increased power over the so-called "information-poor." Discussions of the most important international issues have emphasized that while productivity increases in some of their informatized industries enhancing the competitive position of the advanced industrialized countries on the world market, the information-poor face stagnating employment, productivity and growth levels and a deteriorating position in the world market. Industrial production using information technologies in advanced economies is resulting in a new international division of labor in which the traditional industries are losing comparative advantages to cheap labor. Furthermore, these countries are increasingly alarmed that the use of remote satellites, and other forms of transborder data flow, threatens their national sovereignty. The important economic implications of the new information technologies and the international scope of the applications suggest that the issues must be analyzed within the context of larger trends in the world political and economic order, such as the tendency toward the accumulation of transnational capital and the progressive weakening of state power. The principal questions become: What role do these new information technologies play in the expansion of the transnational system as a whole, and how do they help to break down barriers posed by national sovereignty?

The answers to these questions tend to stress the role of information technology in only some specific types of corporate communication: administration, sales, investments, and the monitoring of raw materials, market conditions, and competitor's activities. There has been surprisingly little attention paid to the use of these new technologies for corporate marketing in the expansion of world consumer markets. This lack is surprising given that the survival of the transnational system depends on the perpetual creation of demand on a global scale. Recent technological advances in video systems, cable television and teletext linked to telecommunications networks (referred to collectively as the "new communication technologies" in this paper) are providing the transnational corporation with new ways to reach and expand world markets through advertising. There have been important changes in the global advertiser's ability to reach world markets, in the relationship between advertising and the mass media, and, perhaps most important, in the ability of sovereign states to control their own media systems. The control of these broadcast channels has become a central issue in many international disputes about the launching of communication satellites, for example. What will the role of the advertisers be and how commercial will the system be? To understand what is at stake, and how the new communication technologies are changing the organization of advertising, one must look briefly at the two rather distinct historical periods of transnational advertising.

Historically, it may be seen that the transnationalization of U.S. manufacturing preceded the international expansion of U.S. marketing. The first big wave of expanding manufacturing firms, during the period from roughly 1945 to 1960, opened their overseas offices before the marketing and communication systems had been formed into coordinated international networks. These early transnationals faced serious international marketing obstacles. They generally contracted a separate local advertising agency in each foreign market where their products were produced or distributed, and they then managed them all from their U.S. headquarters. They suffered from a lack of control over their international image, over variation of the quality of advertising contents, over accounting problems associated with multiple agency relationships, and diverse pricing and audience/media research methods. In short, the means for implementing a coordinated international advertising strategy were unavailable at that time.

STAGE ONE: THE TRANSNATIONALIZATION OF ADVERTISING[1]

During the 1960s and early 1970s, U.S. advertising agencies established the extensive network of offices in Europe, Canada, Latin America, and Asia that forms the basis of transnational advertising today. During roughly the same time period, television became a mass medium in nearly all of the most important consumer markets of the world. Together, the formation of international networks of Madison Avenue advertising agencies and the penetration of television to the households in major consumer markets provided expanding corporations with the necessary communication infrastructure to carry out their global advertising. They were now able to achieve control over their global image, to coordinate the campaigns, to reduce costs, and to obtain centralized advertising know-how from markets all over the world.

In addition, international communication and advertising networks made the "global campaign" possible—one standard message designed at company headquarters and transmitted to all the countries where the product is made or distributed. Since the concept of the global campaign has the appeal of increased efficiency and reduced costs, many major transnational brands and firms (including Revlon, Campbell, Marlboro, Union Carbide, Coca Cola, and Exxon) have, at some period during their histories, used this technique successfully. With television, these advertisers could develop their global campaigns around internationally recognized visual symbols to overcome the major obstacles posed by language diversity and illiteracy.

---

[1] For a discussion of the history of the transnational expansion of U.S. advertising agencies, see Janus, 1980.

Although the first stage of transnational advertising meant a qualitative change in the organization of global advertising, there were still significant probems facing expanding firms as they sought access to the world's consumer markets: (a) Insufficient and imprecise channels of communication and feedback for advertising to specific target populations, due to the underdeveloped state of advertising know-how and communication technology; and (b) national political control over mass media systems in foreign markets limiting advertising access to broadcast channels or limiting the range of product types permitted and media time and space available. The second major stage in the history of transnational advertising—which begins with the development and use of new communication technologies —is characterized by important advances in overcoming these problems.

STAGE TWO: COMMUNICATION TECHNOLOGIES APPLIED TO TRANSNATIONAL ADVERTISING

The second stage of transnational advertising is marked by the use of communication technologies to expand global markets and begins in the late 1970s and early 1980s. Although this stage is just beginning to take shape, it is clear that there will be major changes in two areas: increased accuracy in the production and distribution and feedback systems of advertising, and increased advertiser access to the broadcast systems in foreign countries.

Increased Accuracy in the Production and Distribution of Advertising

The new communication technologies are changing the way that advertising is being created and distributed as well as how audience and media research takes place. Perhaps most important, significant changes are taking place in the way that markets are segmented and specific sectors of the population are reached. While most of these changes have just begun to affect the way advertising is carried out inside the U.S., they indicate probable trends in the organization of international advertising.

1. Advertising Production. Most advertising agencies rely on electronic data processing systems for such routine activities as accounting, inventory, media billing, time summaries, and client profitability profiles and forecasts. Now, however, they have also begun to experiment in, what are known as, the "creative" areas. For example, computers are now being used to write some types of routine content such as real estate advertising. The characteristics of the product are fed into the computer which selects the most important of these and turns out the finished copy. These uses of communication technologies in the production of advertising are still in the experimental stages. They are, however, important indicators of future developments that will help automate other areas of advertising production and link these to electronic distribution systems.

   2.   Advertising Distribution.   In the past, national advertisers in the U.S. have relied on slow and inefficient mechanisms to distribute their advertising campaigns nationally. They have had to edit each spot television announcement separately, and distribute them individually to the television stations in the various regional markets of the U.S. using national mail services or private shippers. In 1979, John Blair and Co. satellite distribution systems began a service which beams advertising spots to Western Union Westar I satellite (*Advertising Age,* April 2, 1979, p. 100). These spot announcements are then picked up by earth stations in the receiving cities and taped for airing in their regular time schedules. In this way, up-to-the-minute commercial schedules are inserted into syndicated series faster and cheaper than by traditional transport systems. Furthermore, the advertiser may monitor the transmission of the spot announcements. This system, a joint project of Ogilvy and Mather advertising agency, General Foods, and Blair, provides national advertisers with distribution efficiency, instant feedback, and lower costs.[2] It will be especially useful for international advertising campaigns.

   3.   Media Ratings and Audience Measures.   Media ratings and audience research techniques have always been speculative and at best rather clumsy. A major problem for advertisers using the new communication technologies is that no satisfactory method has yet been developed for determining their audience ratings. Potentially, however, the new technologies offer new ratings systems with greatly increased accuracy. Interactive cable television, for example, has been used experimentally, linked to telephone lines and computers to record the media viewing behavior of audiences in the home while another part of the system is installed in the supermarket to record the product purchases made by the viewer. In this manner, viewing patterns may, for the first time, be correlated with product purchase data. With such a system, traditional gross media ratings may become obsolete.

   The significance of such computerized media and viewer ratings is that they allow the advertiser to track the individual consumer, thus providing the information required to produce individual or personalized ad-

---

[2] Since only one print is needed for satellite transmission, instead of multiple prints sent by mail to each market, the advertiser may reduce costs considerably. Paramount Pictures is reported to save $500,000 annually with satellite advertising distribution systems (*El Nacional* (Mexico), August 22, 1981, p. 11).

vertising messages. To complete the system, the new communication technologies also offer the means by which such personalized advertising messages may reach the well-defined specific markets that are vitally important to advertisers.

4. Market Segmentation. The new communication technologies will allow advertisers greater accuracy in defining and reaching smaller more specific segments of global markets.[3] The new video technologies—videocassettes and videodiscs—play an important role in their strategies to reach individual households or consumers with what has been called "demassified" or "one-on-one" advertising. But the real breakthrough in reaching these individual markets has come through cable television. With the increased number of available channels provided by cable television, specialized programming reaches smaller more specific audiences. This makes it economically feasible for a tennis ball manufacturer, for example, to advertise on a tennis program which would reach the small limited but highly desirable market with no waste. Advertisers may also use an entire cable channel to promote one specific product category. In the state of Massachusetts, the J. Walter Thompson advertising agency, one of the world's largest, is carrying out a cable "narrowcasting" experiment which involves the use of several local cable channels for advertising on an all-day basis. The viewers choose the channel according to the type of product they are interested in purchasing. Audiences are limited in size —estimated to be no more than .5 per cent of the total viewing audience at any given time—but because they are those who are "ready to buy" they are very valuable to advertisers. Both cable operators and the advertising agency are using the experiment to learn about narrow, highly-targeted broadcasting and the effectiveness of longer advertising formats. The convergence of two powerful forces—more information on media and audiences and the availability of more media channels—is causing advertisers to insist that every medium be thought of as a rifle rather than as a shotgun (*Advertising Age*, October 13, 1980).

5. Media Costs. Media costs have risen spectacularly in the U.S., Europe, and the rapidly expanding markets of the Third World. A study of

---

[3] The apparent contradiction between the search for global sized markets and for small localized or individualized markets is discussed in recent theoretical work about the stages of the transnationalization of capital. R. Trajtenberg and R. Vigorito (1982) describe transnationalization as a historical process with an early and a mature stage. While the mature stage may be characterized by increased rationalization of global production and consumption, the early stage, which includes the present, is characterized by a multiplicity of local markets and a great diversity of production processes developed simultaneously in the various local world markets. These two sizes of markets—global and local—are not contradictory but rather complementary and exist side by side during the early stages of transnationalization.

media cost increases in selected countries has shown that the print media in Saudi Arabia, for example, have increased in cost more than six times the general inflation rates for the year 1980 to 1981. In Japan, television rates have increased five times the general inflation rate of the economy. And, in Belgium, Spain, and Finland the study found that media rate increases were 50 to 100 percent higher than those expected for inflation (Hook, 1981, p. 26). Since media costs are traditionally related to the number of people reached by the channel and the number of channels available, the new technologies with the ability to reach small well-defined audiences through virtually unlimited channels offer substantial cost reductions to the advertisers. A 30 second advertisement on one of the approximately 50 U.S. national cable systems costs about $500 while the three major networks charge an average of $70,000 for 30 seconds on prime time television.

Videodiscs and videocassettes have proven very cost efficient for the production of sales catalogs of the large retail stores. To solve the problem of prohibitively high postage rates for the heavy paper-printed catalogs, Sears, for example, has put its entire 1981 mail order catalog on videodisc. The disc is inexpensive to produce and postage costs are minimal. General Motors is also beginning to use discs for some types of advertising.

Advertisers' access to these new communication technologies has, thus, resulted in increased efficiencies in reaching targeted segments of the market at reduced costs with instant feedback on the impact of their campaigns. This will enhance the competitive position of transnational firms producing consumer products. It will also help the advertising agencies themselves to maintain their competitive lead over local advertising agencies in each market. But the major impact of the new communication technologies on transnational expansion of consumer markets is in the increased control over broadcasting in foreign markets. Here they have proved helpful in reversing many aspects of the 30-year-long relationship between advertisers and the media.

Increased Advertiser Access to Broadcast Media

Ultimate control over the mass media has traditionally been in the hands of the State. In privately-owned systems, the power of the State is expressed through legislation limiting the types and amounts of advertising allowed while in State-owned systems this control extends to include sources of financing. Access to these prized marketing channels has been the subject of constant battle as advertisers pressure for relaxation of existing legislation. The advertisers may ultimately win the battle: the new communication technologies are significantly less regulated than traditional broadcasting.[4] This relative lack of regulation of the new technologies has important implications for the transnational expansion, both inside the U.S. and globally.

1. Access to State-owned Broadcasting. In those countries where broadcasting is still largely State-supported, advertising has been completely banned or strictly limited. Expanding corporations and their advertising agencies have engaged in long struggles to break down these barriers. Broadcasting has been a clear example of the conflict between expanding transnational capital and local states struggling to preserve their national sovereignty. The new communication technologies offer the global firms the means to circumvent existing State control over broadcasting.

Videocassettes are widely used by global advertisers, for example, to penetrate Sweden where broadcast advertising is limited to a few minutes a day. The major breakthrough, however, has come with the use of satellites.

Satellite receiving areas or "footprints" are larger than the geographical limits of most countries making it difficult to subject satellite transmissions to the same sets of legislation that control national mass media. Diverse sets of legislation within the same receiving areas has led to various conflicts in the planned launching of several European national and regional satellites. The issue of whether to allow access by advertisers has become a major source of conflict between countries.[5] Satellites from countries allowing broadcast advertising plan to beam commercial broadcasting into countries where such types of contents are strictly limited.

Successful continent-wide advertising campaigns require that advertisers be allowed unrestricted access to broadcast systems in all receiving countries. Major agencies predict that there will be a big increase in "multinational" campaigns once the satellites are in full operation. The success of the new "Eurobrands" depend on access to Europe-wide advertising channels. Direct mail campaigns by satellite, for example, will be possible for all of Europe once there is an international telephone exchange available.

Over time most state-supported systems have relaxed their regulations limiting the sale of advertising. The threat of foreign-originated commercial broadcast transmissions has recently led Belgium and the Netherlands to allow more time for advertising. Although there are several ways

---

[4] In the U.S. there are few restrictions limiting advertiser access to the new communication technologies which reflects in part technological considerations which make regulation more difficult to implement. This attitude must be understood, however, as a part of the larger trend toward media deregulation.

[5] This conflict over the nature of European satellites is described in G. Fauconnier, 1982.

in which national governments can still exercise their control over the airwaves (limiting the licenses for purchase of Direct Broadcast Satellite receiving equipment, for example) the trend is clear: the new technologies are helping the expanding transnational system to break down remaining State control over broadcasting. As the director of international advertising of the Polaroid Corporation predicts:

> To achieve maximum efficiency the local national TVs, most of which are run by the governments, will have to change somewhere along the line. They'll have to change not only the amount of commercial time but how it's presented; they'll have to change everything in order to compete against the independents and the satellites. (Garson, 1981, p. 7)

And the chairman of Unilever, Europe's largest advertiser, predicts: "National boundaries could, as far as television is concerned, disappear. Reception areas of the satellite might become the new marketing areas" (Chase, 1980, p. 4).

2. Range of Products and Services Allowed. On traditional over-the-air broadcast transmissions, the trend is toward greater regulation limiting the types of products and services that may be advertised. Among the heavily restricted products are drugs and medicines, tobacco, alcohol, and products directed toward children. Other restrictions cover the types of claims made, the national language used, etc. The new forms of communication technologies will not be subject to the same restrictions. A far broader range of products and services will be accepted reflecting the new trend toward "deregulation" and the difficulties enforcing these restrictions on different forms of media. Oracle, the British ITV network's home-video system, will allow the advertising of, among other products and services prohibited on traditional television broadcasting, gambling operations. This decision is justified by the fact that the teletext viewer must call up the data and therefore cannot be unwillingly exposed to the commercials. In the U.S., the use of cable television systems for pornography indicates the unrestricted approach being taken with the new communication technologies.

3. Time and Space Available for Advertising. The most troublesome limitation facing broadcast advertisers is the time available for commercials. While there are also space limitations in print media the restriction is primarily applied to broadcasting due to limited frequency space for channels. These advertising time restrictions vary according to the hour, the medium, and the country.

In virtually all of the new communication technologies, no time limit on advertising will be applied. Commercials of extended length have led to an entirely new concept of advertising called "informercials." No longer will the 30 or 60 second time frame limit what advertisers can convey to their audiences. An entire videocassette or disc is available for commercial messages. As mentioned above, entire channels of cable television have been turned over to advertisers. Other cable channels transmitting traditional types of content (sports, movies, series, etc.) often run commercials of from 5 to 8 minutes. In a survey ("Survey Finds Cable Still Has Doubters," 1980) of advertisers using cable television as an advertising medium, one-fourth of the respondents were found to use commercials longer than the traditional 60 seconds. American Express and L'Oréal are two major firms using cable television to create longer "informercial" advertising. For the advertiser a major advantage of cable television is that the FCC does not regulate advertising time.

4. Advertiser Control Over Media Content. At the same time that advertisers are using the new unregulated communication technologies to broadcast longer advertisements about a broader range of products and services, they are also moving to take control over the general field of media contents. They have now entered the production of what are called "advertiser-created programs" which represents a new stage in the long relation between advertising and the mass media. Instead of limiting themselves to exerting pressure on the production process traditionally in the hands of independent productions houses, networks, and local stations, the advertisers now produce the contents for the new communication technologies themselves. Videocassettes, discs, and cable channels are increasingly being filled with content *entirely* produced by advertisers. The only restriction facing this form of broadcast advertising is viewer resistance.[6]

To avoid viewer rejection of these all-advertising programs, large advertisers are beginning to create media contents which complement the products and services offered.[7] A Ford automobile dealer, for example, may prepare a videocassette or disc on travel tips and landmarks that it would offer free to customers who test drive one of the new automobiles. Kraft Foods might similarly produce a four-volume cassette or disc providing special Christmas recipes which include the use of their food products. Or United Airlines might make a "videobrochure" about the beauty of

---

[6] Some advertising agencies feel that the fact that viewers can skip over or erase advertising on the new technologies will encourage the creation of more appealing and more informative advertising as a means to avoid viewer rejection.

[7] The creation of media contents that complement the commercial messages they contain is not new; what is new is that the production of these complementary media contents is increasingly in the hands of the advertisers themselves rather than production houses or networks.

Hawaii, its history and culture, that would also include United's fares and schedules.

Similarly, to prevent viewers from erasing or skipping over advertising messages in these "advertiser-created programs" programming is being developed with commercials so skillfully intertwined with other information that they cannot be removed or avoided.[8]

5. Advertising Durability. One of the factors which makes traditional broadcast advertising so expensive for advertisers is that costs are calculated on the basis of announcements which run only once. Each commercial announcement gains access to the viewer only at the time it is broadcast. The new communication technologies have begun to change the concept of advertising as a "single-exposure" perishable item. The President of a large transnational advertising agency stressed the durable quality of videocassettes and discs using the important children's market as an example. He suggested that "a company like Sears—already identified commercially with Winnie the Pooh—could publish a series of videodiscs featuring Pooh characters in modern episodes. These episodes would require no intrusive Sears commercials to identify the sponsor and they *could be enjoyed again and again like a set of children's books"* ("New Media Programming View: 'Video Publishing,'" 1980).

Clearly, the coming era of communications by satellite, cable, and computer will be characterized not by increased viewer control and participation in the mass media but by increased persuasion to consume. The new communication technologies will change the way the entire process of advertising is carried out. The significance of the electronic handling of production, distribution and feedback systems is that they form part of a large system that will be able to monitor individual consumers, determine their lifestyles and consumption habits, design personalized advertising, and then deliver it via individual channels. It must be emphasized that the versatility of the advertising process has increased significantly giving the advertiser unlimited options for contents, distribution, and market size. The new communication technologies offer access to specific segments of the market from one person to an entire continent. While these developments are unfolding presently inside the United States they have begun to shape the way that transnational advertisers view their global marketing strategies. As an advertising journal predicts,

> "World commercials" may be coming in TV advertising as satellites open new markets, while elsewhere the new technologies and computers could combine to produce ad messages that would address

---

[8] Keith Reinhard, president of Needham, Harper, and Steers advertising agency, quoted in "New Media Programming View: 'Viedo Publishing,'" 1980, p. 68.

consumers individually in the tone and manner they prefer. (*Advertising Age*, Oct. 20, 1980, p. 2)

THE IMPLICATIONS OF TRANSNATIONAL ADVERTISING FOR THE THIRD WORLD

Third World markets are important to transnational advertisers. The local economies are often growing faster than industrialized economies, the middle classes are expanding quickly, and markets have not yet become saturated with consumer goods. The major thrust of transnational expansion has been in the area of consumer goods producers assembling and distributing to overseas markets. And since consumer goods traditionally require the heaviest advertising expenditures, rapid growth in consumer goods manufacturing and distributing industries generally implies a corresponding boom in advertising expenditures. A three- to fourfold growth of total national advertising expenditures over a ten year period is common in the Third World countries with rapid development and heavily transnationalized economies such as Taiwan, South Korea, and Singapore (see Janus, 1980).

The shift of consumption patterns toward transnational products and the creation of a new consumer culture is not, however, always the harmonious process that the advertising industry and the manufacturers would like it to be. Local populations do not always passively accept new products which are often more expensive, of poorer quality, and different from locally consumed materials and foods. There is a perpetual confrontation between transnational expansion and local cultures (see Janus, 1981). Product acceptance often requires that manufacturers spend large sums on advertising campaigns produced by the transnational agencies who have had decades of experience in overcoming consumer resistance.

It is still premature to assess the role that the new communication technologies will have in the transnational expansion of global consumer markets. We may use present broadcasting patterns, however, as a good indicator. The mass media in Latin American countries, for example, tend to be more dominated by advertising than media anywhere else in the world. Empirical studies show that magazines, newspapers, and television devote from 30 to 50 per cent of their time or space to advertising (Janus, 1981). Furthermore, the largest part of this media advertising is purchased by transnational firms to promote their products. In studies of Latin American women's magazines it has been found that more than 60 per cent of the advertising promotes transnational products while for television the figure is 80 percent (Janus, 1981). What kinds of products do these global advertisers promote on the mass media systems of the world? Contrary to those who claim that advertising is a useful source for all types of product information, a closer look reveals that only some products are advertised: soap, pharmaceuticals, and cosmetics, tobacco, processed foods, and alcoholic beverages are the product groups most heavily advertised. These are also industries which tend to be dominated by transnational capital. *The same firms developing the marketing uses of the new communication technologies control the economies of many Third World countries and dominate their mass media systems.* Given these facts, it is safe to assume that the new communication technologies, as they spread to other countries of Europe, Asia, Latin America, and the Middle East will be at the service of Kraft, Coca Cola, General Foods, Procter and Gamble, Kodak and Anderson Clayton.

These new communication technologies, while still in the initial stages of household penetration in the major consumer markets of the world, are being rapidly installed. In Latin America, several countries plan to have satellite service within the next few years. In August of 1980, Colombia announced its decision to put its own satellite into orbit. Brazil and Venezuela have also announced that they will have satellite service over their territories by 1984 or 1985. And Argentina plans an ambitious project using three satellites to cover the whole expansion of its territory (Schmucler and Mattelart, 1982).

Videocassette recording technology has rapidly made its way into Latin American markets. Sony produces video recording equipment in Brazil for export to other countries within and outside the region. A large number of households in Brazil, Venezuela, and Grand Cayman Island in the Bahamas already have these products. And large areas of many countries, such as Mexico, are already wired to receive cable television.

The expansion of transnational capital, the rapid flow of marketing "know-how" from the headquarters of Madison Avenue advertising agencies to their branch offices around the world, the importance of the perpetual creation of demand for consumer products, and the rapid installation of the new communications infrastructure suggest that the new "information age" will also be a "commercial age" at the global level. The way in which the advertisers plan to use the new communication technologies was clearly revealed when the magazine *Advertising World* announced a few years ago that,

> A New York program bounced off satellite can be "published" as a videodisc thousands of miles away in the jungle somewhere within 24 hours and played on any home TV set with a simple attachment. (October, 1978, p. 20)

Several important questions arise: What measures can local governments take to protect their citizens from externally originated advertising transmitted via satellite? How can legislation keep up with developments in communication technology? How will the transnational corporations use the new technologies to circumvent local government restrictions on the commercial content of broadcasting? The answers to these questions will influence the outcome of efforts to create a New International Information and Communication Order and to preserve national sovereignty in the face of the development of the "Global Consumer" and the "Global Shopping Center."

REFERENCES

Advertising Age. October 20, 1980, 2.

Advertising Age. April 2, 1979, 100.

Advertising World. October 1978, 20.

Chase, D. (1980). "Orr: National Boundaries Could, as Far as Television is Concerned, Disappear." *Advertising Age* (October 20), 4.

"Editorial." (1980). *Advertising Age* (October 13).

El Nacional (Mexico). August 22, 1981, 11.

Fauconnier, G. (1982). "The 'Enfant Terrible' in European Satellite Projects: Lux-Sat." Paper presented to the Tenth Annual Telecommunications Policy and Research Conference. Annapolis, MD, April.

Garson, B. K. (1981). "Polaroid Aims High for Mass Reach in Europe." *Advertising World* (January), 7.

Hook, M. (1981). "Media Inflation." *Advertising World* (July), 26.

Janus, N. (1981). "Advertising and the Mass Media: Transnational Link Between Production and Consumption." *Media, Culture, and Society, 3,* 13–23.

Janus, N. (1980). "The Making of the Global Consumer: Transnational Advertising and the Mass Media in Latin America." Unpublished dissertation, Stanford University.

Kleinsteuber, H. J. (1982). "Direct Broadcasting Satellite (DBS)—Policy of the Federal Republic of Germany." Paper presented to the Tenth Annual Telecommunications Policy and Research Conference, Annapolis, MD, April.

"New Media Programming View: 'Video Publishing.'" (1980). *Advertising Age* (November 24), 68.

Schmucler, H., and Mattelart, A. (1982). *America Latina en la Encrucijada Telematica.* Mexico, D.F.: ILET.

"Survey Finds Cable Still Has Doubters." *Advertising Age* (November 9), 66.

Trajtenberg, R., and Vigorito, R. (1982). *Economia y Politica en la Fase Transnacional: Algunas Interrogantes.* Mexico, D.F.: ILET.

4

Towards An Electronic Democracy?

Giovanni Cesareo

I

"Today a fascinating cultural reversal is underway: the individual is being offered, to an even greater extent, individual access to a totality of information. But the processes by which his access is mediated need to be examined and criticized, which is why our topic is a *subject* and not a futurological scare" (Smith, 1980). Unfortunately, a similar approach, certainly not pessimistic nor catastrophic, to the perspectives opened by new technologies in the universe of mass information and mass knowledge is not now practiced in Europe. As a matter of fact, there is a current trend to predictions and, in some cases, it could be said, to prophecies about the coming social impact of new technologies and about the consequences for the field of mass communication and, more generally, everyday life. These predictions seldom rely on field research because few experiments are yet in being in the different countries. In spite of this, futurologists, professional or amateur, are always very self-confident, especially when they write or speak for mass audiences. Experiments like Prestel (the British videotex) have been developing quite differently from what was forecast, but this does not seem to encourage wisdom amongst futurologists.

The worst vice in these predictions is the reversal of the perspectives with which they operate. Instead of starting from social processes—economic, political, cultural—into which new technologies may enter and from which needs emerge, to analyze the possible relationships between

71

these processes and these needs, on one hand, and the potential of the new technologies, on the other, futurologists often start from the "intrinsic properties" of new technologies just to mechanically draw from them the coming events. As if the solution of a technical problem could automatically bring about the optimal solution of every problem; as if the production and distribution processes of information and knowledge were only, or mostly, conditioned by the "properties" or the availability of technologies. So, futurologists seem to forget that, if under some circumstances new technologies may be the solution, in a different context they may be the problem.

Furthermore, many of those who make predictions seem to disregard that new technologies are not simply driven by the consumers' "demand." Actually, technologies are developing very rapidly, and their development is spurred also (and, sometimes, mostly) by corporations' strategies aimed to increase new equipment production and to place it on the market as well as by the internal logic of technological research which goes on responding to its own problems and to capital's request. So, we find in front of us new technologies which ask for a place inside the market, but new "demand" is not always expected to be there: very often it is to be created (for instance, more sophisticated computers are put on the market while "old" ones are still being tested). That is why it is not so easy to forecast what technologies will be developed first, what interests will be met, and what processes will really come into being.

In a recent report, OECD experts remark that "it is not impossible" to consider family budget a still unexplored market for low-priced information services or for domestic electronic equipment (including domestic computers), "but the evolution which the final consumers' expenses have recorded since the end of the second world war do not allow us to say that consumers' tastes have tended, up to now, towards more qualified information products" (Gassman, 1981, p. 18). This means that, in the future, individual consumers might prefer videorecorders just to be able to store the movies they like best rather than videotex unless they are "persuaded" to act differently (for instance, if some services become available only through telematics). As a matter of fact, some experiments in Europe already show this trend. But even if people should purchase videotex in order to get timetables or to "go" shopping without leaving home, nobody could say, yet, that their information background would be increased. Nevertheless, futurologists proclaim that we shall live in computerized homes and that each and everyone will become a walking encyclopedia.

Another question follows from this. What kind of information—and imagery—will be produced through new technologies? Predictions do not tell us much about this; however, it is a fundamental question. There is a binding relationship between mode of production and products also in the cultural field, and mode of production does not depend only on technology. A mode of production, as for information and knowledge, too, depends on the form of organization of production, distribution and consumption processes, and, therefore, is determined by the relations among different elements which include machines and human intellectual labor, mental practices and work routines, space and time, things and symbols, economic constraints and cultural backgrounds. It is what a Marxist-inspired research group, in Italy, has tried to define as the "form of apparatus" (Cesareo, 1979). So, to answer the question: "will new technologies bring about a new kind of information and knowledge and new forms of cultural consumption," we should consider many more topics than technology. We should guess, at least, *who* will be able to produce information and what relationship will exist between producers and consumers.

"Participation" is a key word in the current predictions, but, once more, "participation" is not necessarily a direct and automatic result of new technologies. On the contrary, we know that at present the trend is to multiply products, channels, terminals, audiences, and, at the same time, to centralize decisions, and to concentrate sources and productive standards. That is why we can say that telematics are likely to increase *distribution* rather than "participation" or "circular communication," and that "there is a clear continuity between the existing and the new" (NUJ, 1980, p. 56) within the present trends. Everything might be transformed and, still, the communication "logic"—and the distribution of power, of course—might persist as it is now.

At this point, it is legitimate to ask whether the current forecasting is aimed to guess the future or, rather, it is a way of seducing people to condition events and behavior anticipating a fascinating picture substantially different from what will be likely to occur.

II

A "liberalist" hypothesis is spreading throughout Europe. It maintains that the Information Society will allow anyone to satisfy, autonomously, his own requirements for information by directly acquiring the available data, and so recomposing "from the bottom" his own image of reality in conformity either with his own needs or his own "tastes." Such a perspective is proposed as a global alternative to the present processes of production and consumption of information and knowledge, in which the one-way communication prevails and the dominant discourses are industrially-produced and offered or imposed on the market "from the top" by mass media and power institutions.

In this perspective, the new ways of recomposing a "subjective" image of reality at the individual level would hinge on electronics and the multiform use of television and cables: and that is why new technologies are proposed as the key to a new civilization founded upon a sort of "electronic democracy."

It is true that this "liberalist" hypothesis can also be considered nothing more than a workable slogan for the interests of the big firms which produce and distribute hardware and software. However, it is worth closer analysis because it can reveal productive and social strategies that will have a great importance on the rebuilding of the information system and, of course, on the forming of collective imagery. With reference to the recent theories about social complexity and the role that communication processes already carry on in the present society, "electronic democracy" seems to give an adequate solution either to the problems of a mass production of knowledge or to those of social reproduction. The liberalist perspective, to cite Luhmann's expression, perceives that a worldwide society "not based on a political and normative integration" has already formed and communication processes are not only a reflection of social and power relationships but are also a constitutive element of the dynamics of reality and of powers. Moreover, the "liberalist" hypothesis seems to be adequate also because it sustains the trend towards "deregulation" (what is the use of regulating, for instance, the relationships between "public" and "private" spheres, since people are able to pick up everywhere whatever information they need?), and might even represent a very good propellent for deregulation.

Actually, this is reminiscent of the old controversy about the opposing theses of "mass manipulation" and of "consumer's sovereignty." Reflections and research have already contributed to overcoming this schematic opposition. They point out, on one hand, the margin of autonomous "productivity" which any form of cultural consumption precludes. On the other hand, they indicate the conditioning which the consumer presently undergoes in response to the arrangements of distribution and to the "courses" inscribed in both the single "message" and the whole of programmed discourses. However, we do not know much yet about information and cultural consumption, its mechanisms, its internal "logic."

But the "liberalist" hypothesis seems to skip all this and give a new and conclusive perspective to the production process of knowledge and learning: "electronic democracy" will give anyone the possibility to find freely and autonomously, starting from his/her inner experience, the "courses" leading from the social processes as such to the recomposition of the image of reality. Are we then leaving behind the "empty space," the "desert" of which Nietzsche spoke? Or, is what is proposed to us only a semiological and sociological mirage?

The suspicion is, at least, legitimate. What rouses the suspicions is that the legs which the "electronic democracy" seem to stand on are the technological "progress" and the "open market." The similarity to the myths of economic liberalism—used again, nowadays, on several sides—is undeniable: and economic liberalism "does not prevent that money flows are split between those which serve to decide and those which only serve to buy" (Lyotard, 1979, p. 16). "Similarly"—Lyotard goes on—"you can imagine parallel flows of knowledge of the same nature using the same channels, some of them to be reserved to the deciders, the others to be used for redeeming the perpetual debt that anyone contracts towards the social tie." May we say that the hypothesis of "electronic democracy" dissolves this image at once?

This is not the only risk that the "liberalist" hypothesis seems to ignore. It is not clear at all, in fact, to what extent the consumer could be enabled to compose his "own" discourse "from the bottom." A recomposition of the image of reality is, more than ever, absolutely necessary, as Habermas defined it, for the "penetration of the social life's universe," or, at least, for any decision and consequent practice: that is also granted by those who think of social complexity in systematic terms and express all their skepticism about the possibility of recomposing—not only "from the bottom," but even "from the top"—a rational and organic image of world and history. That is why we still talk of "synthesis," "linguistic games for complete information," and, finally, of the possible formation of a "collective identity." But the transition from a need for revision—even one at a time and in different contexts—to an autonomous and effective possibility of restructuring cannot be expected to occur only through a large availability of data, the multiplication of terminals and an "easy" access (granted by whom, anyway?) to the databases. Exactly when it ignores different and complex stages which any process of composition of the discourse requires, the hypothesis of "electronic democracy" reveals not only its poverty but also its illusionistic charge. What about the relationships between "technical knowledge" and "critical knowledge," between "subjectivity" and "competence"; what about the problems of "referent," of "simulation," and so on?

But, perhaps, the "liberalist" hypothesis is not contrived at all in order to help a subjective revision of the image of reality "from the bottom," nor to promote a more conscious practice at a mass level. It tends, rather, to increase the people's possibility of feeding their "greedy fruition" of information and imagery through the casual mix of the available fragments, in accordance with a limitless production and a full-market exploitation. Moreover, if we consider that nowadays the conglomerates, controlling information production and the communication channels, tend to homogenize and, at the same time, to segment, to cut, and to stratify the discourse in order to internationalize the audiences and better exploit every possible section of the market, we can easily guess that the "electronic democracy" would not contradict this tendency: on the contrary, it could give it a full support through the incentive of the "greedy fruition."

Furthermore, nothing allows us to expect that discourses composed and programmed "from the top" and aimed at different audiences should be neutralized and finally substituted for by nebulae of fragments: a nebula of fragments can instead make the rays of the compact discourse which pass through it all the more brilliant and resolute.

On the other hand, the "liberalist" hypothesis never pushes beyond the level of consumption. Now, should we assume that data available to consumers will be equivalent to molecules of "reality," a direct product of synthesis of the social experience? Once Laing wrote that the word "data" should be substituted by the word "capta" (taken): there is always a selective process and a space of mediation between the source and the terminal, between the real processes and the information which has been extracted from it. What kind of relationship can exist between a new mode of knowledge production at a mass level and the "electronic democracy" which disregards the problems of the sources and those of collecting and filing information materials (which probably means that everything will be kept as it is at present)?

III

In order to approach the real content of "electronic democracy," we have to begin with the present structure of the sources and the production of data and information material.

What is perfectly clear is that the typology of data that will be collected, computerized, filed, and made available will depend on the sources with which "collectors" will be connected or be able to contact. Presently, among the social sources, the big and centralized ones prevail; and they tend to release information materials, selecting and processing them rather strictly in accordance with their own "logic" and their interests. The outstanding sources are the political and economic institutions, top military officials, the research departments and public relations offices of big firms, and some cultural institutions. Mass media (daily press, specialized and prestigious magazines, television companies) are also considered sources, and more and more as databanks develop it is even clearer that filed and available data have been already selected and manufactured for a determined restructuring of the image of reality. Different sources, especially the atomistic social aggregations, where basic and direct daily experience is being produced, are infrequently, occasionally, or never contacted; and, the selection and the synthesis are still worked out by the "curators." The network of sources is, therefore, restricted and definitely shaped: but the inclusion or the exclusion from it neither depends directly on the social prominence of the source nor on the social meaning of data the source itself could furnish. It depends instead on power structure and on production "economy"; and, by the way, it depends also on technology availability. The most possible of sources for the Third World, for instance, are excluded from the network because of economic and cultural reasons and because the network, increasingly structured on the basis of advanced technology, is conceived and domi- nated by the industrially-developed countries, and, in the first place, by the USA. Similar considerations can also suit a part of the possible sources even in the industrially-developed countries, in relation to the develop- ment hierarchy established among these countries or among the regions within each country.

Why should Information Society automatically modify such a situa- tion? The "liberalist" hypothesis seems to assume that this radical trans- formation will be imposed by the market: by the increase of the "demand" and the consequent increase of the "supply" made possible by the new technologies. We shall try to see, in a moment, whether, where, and when new technologies are fatally destined to increase the "demand." As for the increase of the "supply," it cannot be said that it entails the enlargement of the network of sources. The dominant sources have, up to now, been able to increase their information production constantly; and the informa- tion deluge which we are already drowned in has risen even in light of the concentration of sources. It is rather a matter of examining whether this kind of process has not caused a global pauperization of the contents of available data and a loss of the meaning of information items. The increase in information production has, in fact, mainly occurred through an artifi- cial valuation of small details and through the "thinning" of each in- formation "particle," so that it is very often extremely difficult to recover the process and the context within which single bits have been drawn. Will "electronic democracy" reverse this tendency by itself? Or, will that "loss of contents," which Nora and Minc (1978) hold unavoidable, in the "informatic discourse" be generalized? We should wonder, then, whether the image of fragmentation of "reality," which is often directly attributed to the "pulverization of sources" (?) and, for this reason, is considered un- avoidably connected with the "abundance" of information material, does not result from this typology or from this process. Could we hypothesize that the information "particles" deliberately released by the dominant sources—together with the programmed discourses and the casualness of data obtained from the sources which are not an organic part of the net-work—produce the scattered image in which it seems impossible to grasp the "logic" and the dynamics of the processes that form, at different levels, social experience? It is naive, at least, to affirm that the fragmentariness of the discourse reflects directly the atomization of the world within which we live. As a matter of fact, the composition of a discourse does not occur through the assembling of molecules of "reality," but instead on the basis of data and information that are already selected and processed. So, the fragmented image of reality is not a reflection; it does not necessarily trace "the real": it is produced, anyway, and therefore what counts most is the production process.

There is nothing new in asserting that data have always had a genetic potential which unfolds in relation to other data through the composition of the discourse. Every single datum can be differently combined with others for the composition of different or even alternative discourses. This genetic potential has its own constraints, though: the comparability of data, their typology, what they bear of the process and the context where they have been extracted from, make only some combinations possible and, therefore, condition the composition of the discourses. We can say for any information "particle" just what W. J. Reichmann (1961) said about statistical data: "they cannot be made to demonstrate any conclusion which is not contained within themselves." But here we can see an alternative. On the one hand, processed data are "richer" and are easier to utilize, and they help the composition of the discourse, but they are also more coercive (their generative power is higher, but they already tend to prefigure a narrow range of possible discourses). On the other hand, "raw" data seem to give much more freedom of composition, but have a lower genetic potential, and it requires a very high level of talent to process and utilize information material.

In the international flow of information it is possible to verify, as Schiller noticed (1980), that processed data are considered more precious: who has produced or collected them and is in possession of them exalts his right of property and tends to release them cautiously. "The primary (raw) data is available to all comers. The processed data is handled quite differently" (Schiller, 1980, p. 103). Thus, the countries which are ill-equipped to collect and process data are compelled to face an alternative: either trying to get (to the best of their possibilities) processed data (which may be suitable to their interests and needs, but are always suitable, for sure, to data collectors' and processors' intentions), or being submerged by a tide of "raw" data that they will be almost unable to use. It is easy to surmise how such an alternative becomes more difficult the closer it reaches the individual consumer. And, therefore, we can wonder how "electronic democracy" could change this at a mass consumption level.

IV

One of the benefits that, in the "liberalist" hypothesis, "electronic democracy" should bring about is that "freedom of choice" which the consumer could, eventually, wholly enjoy. But it is clear evident that, apart from any other consideration, the consumer may practice his "freedom of choice" only within the range of the "supply": which means that he/she will be compelled to choose among the information materials which others have produced, collected and made available. That is why, until there will be a structural separation between producers and consumers, the "supply"— obviously controlled by the firms which control production and distribution—will somehow rule the "demand." Once more, consumption is ruled on the side of production, and not vice versa. The rest is what we may call "latent needs": which it is rather difficult to single out and understand from the outside, also because consumers are not accustomed to express themselves in terms of "possible" products.

"Electronic democracy," though, will make consumers able to choose data and information materials on their own, they say. This creates a new sort of self service. Now, it may be fanciful to present the self service as the "consumers' kingdom," but the kitchen is still somewhere else, and it is precisely in the kitchen where dishes are prepared and the menu is made out. Furthermore, it is not obvious that the wider the range of the "supply," the more extensive "freedom of choice" becomes. On the contrary, it may be more difficult (and, as a matter of fact, it is) for the consumer to find his way among too many alternatives: it often happens that, exactly in this situation, the consumer seeks a mediation (advertising, for instance) and let himself be inspired by the offerer's advice, or looks for the most available products.

Collecting, processing, filing, and distribution criteria are still decisive, therefore: but also in this respect, the "liberalist" hypothesis seems to be rather weak, and, somehow, even suspect.

This leads to the problem of access, of course. The "liberalist" hypothesis assumes that the availability of data and information materials, undoubtly improved by telematics, and the "market logic" should give all people equal opportunities. But telematics brings about the possibility to put on the market for direct purchase new services and single products which were, up to now, paid for by consumers through global fees or indirectly through the advertising flows. This means that, though availability of information materials will definitely increase, access will depend, much more than in the past, on consumers' resources: those who will pay more will be able to get more; but, vice versa, those who will pay less will run the risk to be excluded from the channels, since information materials will be more and more distributed only through electronic circuits (this is implicit in the "liberalist" hypothesis; it is one of its foundations).

Besides, the research and the utiization of information materials through the terminals are not so easy, when the common models of telephone directory, travel lists, market prices and weather data are exceeded. The operations become more and more intricate in relation to the needs that should be satisfied, and, that is to say, in relation to the composition of the discourse. What the consumer has to carry on, as soon as the most elementary practices are exceeded, is a real "work of consumption" involving a remarkable ability and a (up to date) cultural background. That is why specialized operators are already expected to manage terminals in some cases. In France, for instance, in the city of Grenoble there is underway a videotex experiment called "Claire." It is a public service, aimed to offer to citizens all the information they require. The terminals will be accessible through local administration employees, who will help citizens to express their requirements and to draw the best from the databank (Lefèvre, 1981). This is likely to be an adequate system. However, it excludes the home use of databanks. Moreover, it adds another level of mediation between consumer and information material, and puts in being a new kind of dealing.

Finally, it will be quite possible that, at least, the dominant sources will refuse to make available data and information, which they determine it is better to keep private ("transparence" is not always so advantageous for profit and power: presently it really seems not to be advantageous at all). In December 1978, the Committee on Data Protection, in Great Britain, argued (see Lindlop Report) that a Data Protection Authority should be established to enforce codes of practice on such matters as "data to be handled," "uses to which they are put" and "disclosure to a third party" (NUJ, 1980, p. 55). Thus, decisive "pieces" could be kept out of that sort of mass puzzle which "electronic democracy" proposes.

No data filing is a neutral operation, especially when the new technologies are applied. Filing is connected, on one hand, with the criteria that guided the data collecting, and, on the other hand, with the consumption forecasting. It is also connected, of course, with the different specific techniques of codification, classification, and processing. Anyone visiting a library, may verify how important a conditioning force is the catalogue. May it be assumed that things are simplified when it is a matter of telematics and databanks? As Paola Manacorda (1980, p. 140) recalls "the conceptual model which allows us to draw information out of an experience is directly reintroduced, in the Information Society, into the machine, through the logic models and the relevant software." And, who is destined to elaborate these models and this software?

Every hypothesis about the future which does not take into account these topics and these problems—and these are still the most elementary ones—can be useful only to conceal that, as Nora and Minc (1978, p. 75) put it, "the differentiation will be based, for the future, more on the ability to research and use knowledge than on the quantity of stored knowledge." This radically contradicts the "liberalist" hypothesis essentially based on the quantity of data and information materials which may be available on the market.

V

Any composition of the discourse presumes, anyway, an operational hypothesis. And since operations take place in a highly technological communication system, the hypothesis must acquire more and more the peculiarities of a "model." But the "liberalist" predictions do not even try to meet this exigency, or, perhaps, take for granted that each consumer will be quite able to elaborate its own "model" starting from the available materials.

We know that, nowadays, the discourses are made up "from the top" and distributed in a programmed way. The integration of different media and the industrialization of the production processes have led to the standardization of these discourses, even in their own diversification aimed at establishing specific audiences (and not in contradiction with the discourses intended for a planetary audience). The products and channels multiplication and the "market logic" lead, on the other hand, to "interlaced" forms of consumption in which the different discourses get mixed up and blended. It is in this extremely complex picture that the tendency of media to impose some "courses of interpretation" and some consumption conditions, in order to improve to the best the impact of the "message," faces the people's possibility to deal with, as Stuart Hall (1975) says, "the meanings within the limits of hegemonic definitions which have been offered them." The "productive valency" of consumption is exerted right at this stage (in the sense that the consumer is able, somehow, to produce his own discourse for his own practice); or, anyway, "systematic distortions" in respect to the "supplier's" intentions are produced. But it is not easy to establish, as recalled above, not even case by case, what is the effective "operational space" which audiences, or the individual consumer, can get for them. The tendency of media is to reduce, as much as possible, this space, giving standards of interpretations and building expectation "courses" to reproduce consumption. It is not easy to trace the consumers' autonomous "deviations."

Now, is it possible to hypothesize that the whole of information and imaginary materials, distributed by the media at international level, set up a sort of "permanent picture" interwoven with "hegemonic definitions" within which the consumer's "operational space" runs the risk to become narrower and narrower? The question is properly important, for instance, as to the present huge melting-pot of the global television programming: do the channels multiplication and the viewer's concrete possibility to shift continuously from one channel to another really neutralize the "picture" or make it more compact just in the interchangeability of the discourses? "Electronic democracy" should make available information "particles" which consumers could utilize on their own: but, still, these "particles" will be utilized within the "picture"; and this counts not only as to the interpretation but also as to the "models" of discourse. On the other hand, there is no doubt that individual consumer and social groups are always dealing meanings in relation to their experience, their social practice, their "competence." Does this dealing allow the consumer to contest the "picture only," or is there any "operational space" also for the composition of autonomous and alternative discourses?

Here arises the problem of how to elaborate autonomous, not subordinate, "models" on consumer's side. The "liberalist" hypothesis would solve it, first of all, predicting the disappearing of the discourses composed "from the top" and referring to the availability of diversified information materials. But, as said above, nothing allows us to presume that dominant sources and media will choose to sell on the market only information "particles": on the contrary, this will be very unlikely to happen. Besides, autonomous and alternative "models" are not there, ready to be used. At least, it will be necessary to experiment with new options and procedures. Will the "market logic" secure proper conditions for these experiments? And will the domestic sphere—definitely privileged by the "liberalist" hypothesis—be the most suitable for them? And what kind of experiments will be allowed by data and information materials which have always been collected and processed by others, under others' control, and only with the purpose of making them "marketable"?

Nobody could say, of course, that such problems can be easily solved, but what is striking in the "liberalist" hypothesis—and not in the "liberalist" hypothesis only, unfortunately—is that it does not even take them in account. However, sometimes the possible solution of a problem brings about new problems. Nora and Minc (1978, p. 53), for instance, hypothesize that "any group, any community should provide for the collection and the processing of the necessary information." Now, this is something that "electronic democracy" based on the "market logic" does not foresee. But, besides, we know that communicative operations limited within the local ambit and separated from the whole, run the permanent risk to be isolated in ghettoes and, often, degraded. If it is true that a local experience cannot be "read" apart from the comparison with other experiences and data of general synthesis, and if it is true, then, that a local discourse must be composed also with data produced elsewhere, many problems still arise beyond a possible decentralization. We can recall, at least, the problem of transparency of the specific criteria of data production; the problem of control of files and distribution circuits; the problem of circulating "models" and operational experience.

VI

If we assume as a perspective the stabilization of the relationship between "system" and "environment" through temporary adjustments of "undersystems," then we can accept the fragmentation of communication processes, the separation between consumers and producers, the complementarity between centrally produced and distributed discourses and, eventually, locally processed information materials. In this case, however, "electronic democracy" reduces itself to a wider distributing system of programmed services and to a new form of consent control. But, in this perspective, after all, would the discourses not be characterized by redundance?

The picture completely changes if we hypothesize that the recomposition of the image of reality can be aimed to the elaboration of new autonomous rules and values, exalting subjective experience, for social reproduction and the formulation of transformation strategies. Every transformation process necessarily proceeds from a "rupture" of the existing balances and, therefore, it is always moved by the arising of dissent which causes and, at the same time, reflects that "rupture." It is developed by alternative discourses, able to turn the social contradictions into "productive" actions and not aimed at removing these contradictions.

In the past, the great movements of "rupture" have been coagulated at a mass level by great perceptions in which the recomposition of the image of reality seemed to be produced abruptly and was extremely simple and synthetic. Nowadays, as told and repeated, such syntheses are, in our complex society, impracticable more than inadequate: they result as an evidence of aphasia.

On the other hand, every process of transformation also entails the elaboration of alternative projects: and this requires that the composition of discourses for the transformation has a cognitive and also a prescriptive value equal to the social complexity we are living in. Does this mean that knowledge must be definitively divided from imagination, or that imagination must, more and more, feed on science? And is the composition of complex images necessarily alternative to the tension towards a global image?

It is by considering such problems and questions, perhaps, that we may start examining the possibility of a new "circular communication" also based on electronics and telematics. We can test, perhaps, the prospect of "a knowledge connected with the identity through projections of concurrent identities" (Habermas, 1976). But the only basis for such a prospect could be—to cite another Habermas' definition—"the consciousness of having equal and general chances for participating to the communication processes" and "to the learning processes creators of rules and values" (p. 94).

Here, once more, appears the exigency of investigating all the levels of production and consumption processes, in order to accomplish a new mode of production of information, new ways of selecting and resuming social experience, to express both the "demand" and the proposals. Here we should try to test new ways of elaborating concurrent, but also general and comparable, "models" of recomposition of the image of reality, connected with the needs and projects of intervention on social processes. But, in this case, is it not essential to start from the sources rather than from the terminals, as it is still too often done, unfortunately, by futurologists, and not only by electronics worshippers?

REFERENCES

Cesareo, G. (1979). "The 'Form of Apparatus' in the Mass Media." *Media, Culture & Society, 1*, 227–87.

Gassman, H. P. (1981). "Un 'Secteur Quaternaire' dans l'Economie?" *L'Observateur de l'OCDE,* No. 113, 18.

Habermas, J. (1976). *Zur Rekonstruction des Historischen Materialismus.* Frankfurt am Main, FRG: Suhrkamp Verlag.

Hall, S. (1975). "The Structured Communication of Events." Paper prepared for the UNESCO Department of Philosophy Conference on Communication Restraints.

Lefevre, B. (1981). "France: Teletext and Videotex." Paper presented to Conference on New Television Prospects, Venice, Italy, March.

Lyotard, J-F. (1979). *La Condition Postmoderne.* Paris: Les Editions de Minuit.

Manacorda, P. M. (1980). "Inform Society." *Ikon* (Milan). New series No. 8/9, 137–45.

Nora, S., and Minc, A. (1978). *L'Informatisation de la Societe.* Paris: Editions du Seuil.

National Union of Journalists (NUJ). (1980). "Journalists & New Technology." Report compiled by members of the ADM Committee on Technology.

Reichmann, W. J. (1961). *Use and Abuse of Statistics.* London: Methuen.

Schiller, H. I. (1980). "Communication Under Control: The Data Banking." *Ikon* (Milan). New series No. 6, 93–109.

Smith, A. (1980). *Goodbye Gutenberg.* New York: Oxford University Press.

Section II

CANADA, U.S. & LATIN AMERICA

5

High Technology and Pacific Empire: The California Dream Revisited

Robert Jacobson

While the rest of the nation was digging itself out from the aching '80s economic debris, with interest rates and a reactionary federal government conspiring to escalate unemployment and business failures, California was confidently plotting a course into the 21st Century, preparing for its destiny in a coming "information age."

The expectation of a bright future built upon technological accomplishment is the essence of the California dream. The dream, widely shared, has not produced glittering rewards for most of California's 23 million inhabitants, but reality in California sinks beneath the cultural murk produced by the state's awesome entertainment machinery. Bedazzled by evidence of their common glory—a magnificent freeway system, the California Water Project bringing priceless water from neighboring states, and towering skylines replacing earthquake memories—Californians too often accept at face value the schemes of wily entrepreneurs and political snake-oil salesmen.[1] Sometimes the salesmen even fool themselves.

California faces real problems requiring forethought and planning. Its economy is one. Although the state's agricultural sector seems reasonably prosperous, its industrial economy is as vulnerable to capital movement as the economies of eastern states facing near destitution. The closure in California of a thousand major and minor plants—throwing hundreds of thousands out of work—has put to rest any doubts on this score.

---

[1] Are spreading anti-nuclear power campaigns and resistance to grandiose water projects symptomatic of a new skepticism—possibly alloyed with post-Proposition 13 antistatism—or just faddish flashes in California's protest plan?

Over the last three decades California's industry has become increasingly dependent on military contracts, a dubious foundation for an economy. Politics shift, continually at the federal level, and with it blows the fate of military contractors. A fortunate byproduct of California's military production *from an economic perspective,* however, has been the growth of an indigenous industrial sector known as the "high technology," or "high-tech," industry.

California's leaders emphasize the need for growth in high-tech businesses. California's future as an industrial force—rather than a mere provider of raw resources and foodstuffs—is staked on semiconductors, computers, computer services, and telecommunications products emerging from picturesque locales such as "Silicon Valley" and Orange County's more prosaic Irvine Industrial Complex.

Spurred on by political ambition and an effective high-tech lobby, California's former Governor Edmund G. (Jerry) Brown, Jr.—a candidate for the U.S. Senate—elaborated ad hoc policies and plans to "save" the industry. These initiatives were short-term, aimed at immediate solutions to long-standing economic problems. Many of these solutions were intended to turn California into an imitator of Japan.

This article deals with the intricate relationship among politics, high-tech economics, and quality of life in California from a critical perspective. It is divided into four parts.

The first part describes the recent outpouring of initiatives proposed to "solve" California's pressing industrial crisis. It is followed by a brief examination of the crisis and its roots in high-tech entrepreneurial spirit.

The third part of this article offers a future scenario the high-tech'ers have conveniently overlooked—the debasing of politics in California, the emergence of severe unemployment problems, and the cleaving of California into wealthy enclaves and Third World-like hinterlands.

This article concludes with a modest suggestion that popular political awareness must precede progressive change, but that it is appropriate for critical communications researchers to point out which applications of high technology retard, and which enhance, democracy.

PART ONE:
". . . A SOMEWHAT INDEPENDENT AND DIVERSE ECONOMIC PATH . . . "[2]

"It seems like everyone wants to jump on the research and development bandwagon these days," according to veteran "Silicon Valley" business

---

[2] From a press release issues April 1, 1982, by the Assembly Speaker's Office to announce legislation creating the "California World Trade Commission."

reporter Daniel A. Beucke (1982), commenting on legislation creating a state corporation to supervise private high-tech R&D. Behind this bill, as so many others, was Governor Jerry Brown, an arch-proponent of high-tech industry and the future for which it stands. The senatorial candidate refuted his previous space-age persona. Now he was a hard-headed realist concerned with the health of American business.

Speaking before the Joint Economic Committee of Congress, for example, Brown recommended that President Reagan "should immediately move to elevate semiconductor and high technology industries to the heart of our trade negotiations with the Japanese . . . to ensure that the Japanese market is as open to our goods as we are to theirs" (Donner, 1982). In his State of the State Address for 1982, Brown proposed an "Investment in People" program (now pending as legislation) to earmark $50 million in state funds for computer-literacy education. The amount was small but significant in a state facing a $2 billion deficit in fiscal year 1983–84.

Brown's scoresheet, though ad hoc, was impressive as political theater, and it inspired action among California's legislators and the state's congressional delegation. Pressed by such newly-muscled industry organizations as the Semiconductor Industry Association and the American Electronics Association (both headquartered in California), legislators introduced bills in the 1982 session of the California Legislature to

- Provide tax breaks for firms contributing computers to schools,
- Restructure the educational curriculum to begin teaching computer literacy, and
- Investigate how the University of California and the California State University can retain engineering faculty attracted by the lurid (but lucrative) world of private industry.

Laws were also passed to upgrade UC Berkeley's microelectronics laboratory, and to make it easier for high-tech industrialists to attract venture capital (by eliminating some capital gains taxes).

In Washington, hordes of high-tech industrialists and investors, with California congressional delegates in tow, pounded the halls, arguing for tax concessions and special trade privileges; and against laws that might reduce the number of students now studying engineering, mathematics, and science in American universities. Citing congressional reports (e.g., Joint Economic Committee, 1982) and participating in public hearings before the National Telecommunications and Information Administration (Kirchner, 1982) and other agencies, the high-tech lobbyists were successful in making their case. One dubious accomplishment was an inordinate shifting of the federal budget to favor "defense"—i.e., production of electronics and computers as weapons of war. (The resulting cost to social programs, like education, is part of the equation only now beginning to be understood by the high-tech'ers: a dearth of engineering faculty and students imperils a glowing high-tech future. More on this below.)

At the local level, high-tech industrialists were busy restructuring the state's geoeconomic environment. When a planning commission in the city of Roseville, a suburb of Sacramento, refused to endorse plans for a new plant sought by a subsidiary of Japan's Nippon Electronics Company (NEC), local NEC representatives flexed their political biceps . . . and within weeks the city council overrode the planning commission's decision (Slater, 1982).

In 1981, Jerry Brown established the California Commission on Industrial Innovation with this warning: 'The information revolution is dramatically restructuring business, the labor force, and society as a whole. We must act together to respond to these changes, or we face inevitable decline as a society" (Office of the Governor, 1981). His words were taken seriously at all levels of government and by corporations, educational institutions, and the public. That the governor's challenge did not indicate how to "respond to . . . changes" seemed not to matter. That he ordained a new "revolution" was enough. Revolution has always been popular, if unreal, in California.[3]

PART TWO:
HIGH TECHNOLOGY TURBULENCE

No decisive figures exist indicating the extent to which high-tech industries —semiconductors, computers, telecommunications, and related services— contribute to California's domestic and trade economies. At least until the California World Trade Commission is established, sectoral activity and trade will continue to be monitored only by the federal government, which measures these essentials by region, not by state.

California's contribution to the national high-tech economy, however, is disproportionate for one state among fifty (see Table 1). California firms manufacture most desk-top computers—nationally estimated at $1 billion annually and expected to grow to $12 billion by 1990—and is a major participant in the multi-billion dollar world computer and computer services markets. Internally, California enterprises, public institutions, and individual subscribers consume over $10 billion in telecommunications services (primarily telephone and data communications).

---

[3] With his 1983 State of the Union Address, President Ronald Reagan, in the words of Robert MacNeil, "took the lead in a parade of many who had gone before." The high-tech evangelists converted even the stubborn septuagenerian.

TABLE I
California Share of U.S. High Technology Industry Jobs
1970–1990

(thousands)

California as Share of United States	1970	1980	1990	California Share of U.S. Growth 1970–1980	1980–1990
Computers	22.9%	27.5%	29.5%	36.4%	33.1%
Communication Equipment	19.6	23.6	26.2	100.0	45.4
Electronic Components	15.2	22.0	22.1	38.0	22.7
Instruments	8.8	14.7	15.1	37.4	20.6
Basic High Technology	15.5%	20.8%	22.4%	39.9%	29.5%
Computer Services[1]	10.7	14.7	16.2	17.6	17.0
Total High Technology	15.2%	20.1%	21.3%	33.7%	23.4%

Source: California Employment Development Department. Center for Continuing Study of the California Economy, 1982.

[1] 10.7 is for 1972, the first year for which data was compiled for this SIC.

California will also absorb the largest share of the *$1.5 trillion* defense budget announced by the Reagan Administration.

California, by any measure, depends on the health of its high-tech industries. Today, in "Silicon Valley" alone, more than 500 firms generate over $100 billion in electronics hardware and services and employ over 150,000 workers (Howard, 1981).

But the slack American economy of the 1980s has diminished the domestic market for high-tech products and services. Like competitors in Japan, Western Europe, and Scandinavia, California's high-tech industrialists must look outward for markets.

According to a report by the National Telecommunications and Information Administration (Leeson, 1981), the leading importers of high-tech goods are:

- Semiconductors—Asia, Western Europe
- Computer—Western Europe, Canada
- Telecommunications—Western Europe, Canada

Significant trade is also conducted in Europe's "gray market," where contraband components and assemblies are shuttled about before reaching their final destination in the Soviet Union or Eastern Europe ("Chips...," 1982). (At least $20 million of this gray market consists of pilfered goods "removed" from Silicon Valley manufacturing sites by executives, engineers, and workers!)

High-tech industrialists therefore fear protectionism. They have lobbied hard in Washington, D.C., to challenge tariff and quota restrictions proposed by old-line industrialists and labor groups (Hagstrom, 1982). Japan, however, has been singled out by the high-tech'ers for anti-"dumping" and other restrictive trade legislation (Madison, 1982; Hume, 1982). There, traditional commercial structures and insurmountable cost differentials have blunted the American export onslaught.

California's wildly entrepreneurial firms, unable to maintain continuous employment of mobile "intellectual capital"—concepts stored in the minds of key engineers and scientists—have been handicapped in their struggle with Japan (Bylinsky, 1981). Consequently, high-tech companies have begun to consolidate. *Fortune* magazine observed that there may be only one solution to the Californians' dilemma:

> The future of the Silicon Valley merchant suppliers...may depend on their getting bigger, either by growing or being acquired by larger corporations....Fairchild is now part of Schlumberger. AMD is owned in part by Siemens....National Semiconductor, fighting to stay independent, now derives 20% to 25% of its volume from selling Japanese computers. Intel is frantically trying to turn itself into a computer manufacturer. (Bylinsky, 1981, p. 56)

Larger institutions will enable greater intra-company storage of intellectual capital. (IBM recently bought into Intel, its primary supplier of chips.) But will corporate conglomerates lose the ability to *innovate* characteristic of small, entrepreneurial ventures?

High-tech industrialists also face the prospect of increasing competition in the domestic market from Japan, Western Europe, Scandinavia, and Asia's "developing economies" (Taiwan, Hong Kong, and Korea).

This situation is particularly acute in California. The state is a convenient staging point for foreign cars, stereo equipment, and information technology, and its proximity to Japan has not been lost on Japan's huge trading companies (*zaibatsu*). "We see California already as part of Japan. Oh, yes. California Prefecture," beamed one Japanese banker in Joel Garreau's *Nine Nations of North America* (1981, p. 279).[4]

This is the California paradox: California is vulnerable to penetration by exports from other powerful economies. The state's response has been a new industrial policy that could tear the fabric of Californian society and bind it inextricably to the fate and dictates of Japan and other aspiring "information societies."

---

[4] The Japanese are the preeminent foreign high-tech presence in California, but they are not alone. West Germany's Siemens, Holland's Phillips, Canada's Bell Northern, and Sweden's Ericsson have all secured beachheads through affiliation with American firms on the West Coast.

Californians stand witness to the most dramatic war between national capitals since World War II.

PART THREE:
"WAR" ON THE HOME FRONT

"If we don't win this battle, you can forget the U.S. as an industrial power."

> Charles Sporck, President
> National Semiconductor Corporation
> (Eckhouse and Johnson, 1982, C1)

Leading the charge toward a new California industrial order is a squadron of the most romantic industrialists to grace American history since the robber barons. Like the robber barons before them, the high-tech'ers want to reshape American society and so bolster their position in the emerging "War of the Pacific Capitals." According to Michael F. Kieschnick, economic adviser to Governor Jerry Brown, the high-tech'ers are:

> the most ideological group of business people I've ever met. They are genuinely excited about their products. They have fierce nationalistic instincts vis-a-vis Japan and a disdain for the older [American] industries and talk of bailing them out. They believe they will transform American business through their products and their management style (Hagstrom, 1982, p. 861).

The high-tech industrialists have a flair for propaganda that finds convenient confirmation in Japanese industrial ideology. The American ideal of "technology as progress," advanced by high-tech industrialists (Blackman, 1978; SRI International, 1982; Hagstrom, 1982) and their political converts ("Business...," 1981), resonates with the near-utopian predictions of Yoneji Masuda, author of *The Information Society as Post-Industrial Society* (1981):

> The first thing to understand is that the information society will be based on different values from the present industrial society, which is characterized by materialism and consumption.

> We are at the threshold of a new age, an information age, in which human creativity and intellectual achievements will flourish. New technology...will make this possible by freeing the individual to pursue his creative interests (Masuda, 1982, Indepth 5).

The aims of the high-tech industrialists in both Japan and America are strikingly similar, clearly recognizable within the context of "present industrial society." The most pressing concerns for the Americans are raising capital, creating and maintaining a skilled workforce, and promoting

free trade (Hagstrom, 1982). The Japanese put more emphasis on automat-
ing the workplace and coordinating technological development on a national scale ("Japan Inc. . . .," 1981; Oshima, 1980; Kurita, 1982). But
capital, workforce, and trade issues are as much the currency of policy
debate in Japan as they are in the United States.[5]

Why should it be any other way? Capital's goals—profits and political control—are without nationality. Homogenization politics within
Japan and America are determined by the same capital interests (Roberts,
1982). With international capital hedging its bets, national managers must
court the favor of investors with peculiar fillips and nuances that give their
firms a temporary competitive edge.

For awhile these stylistic maneuvers, derived from domestic cultural
customs, appeared diverse, even antithetical. But today the "quality circle," a Japanese confection, is finding acceptance in the United States; and
America's very successful R&D methods are being adopted in Japan. A
competition between Japanese and American high-tech firms turns red-
hot, industrial life in Japan and America is becoming the same.

The symptoms of change are particularly acute in California. In its
desperation to retain global leadership, the high-tech industry is preparing
to remold California in its own image.

The destruction of the commonwealth. Superheated high-tech
competition is resulting in overproduction of technology that is neither
state-of-the-art nor standardized. The *San Jose Mercury* (1981) has disparag-
ingly noted that "the object of the game is not just to get rich quick but to
get richer quicker." American high-tech industry is producing unprofitable, low-capacity microcomputers and components—so many "cornflake
machines," according to securities analyst Michael Van Deelen (Richter,
1982). The industry is clearly on the brink of losing its competitive edge
vis-a-vis Japan.[6]

California's panicked high-tech'ers demand special treatment from
the federal and state governments. They insist that public education produce the intellectual capital necessary for innovation which entrepreneurial non-planning has frittered away. At the same time, they support
initiatives like Proposition 13 (an adventure which has devastated the
public sector).

The attack on the public sector has resulted in more than the deterio-
ration of vital infrastructure (roads, harbor facilities, social services, and so
on). It has also perverted the public will: voters in the June 1982 primary

---

[5] For a series of articles highlighting the similarities, see "The Selling of Japan," a
special edition of *The Nation,* February 13, 1982.

[6] Simultaneously, European nations—France is the prime example—threaten American supremacy in the information *services* sector. See Johnson, 1982.

endorsed initiatives further cutting state revenues even though California faces a $2 billion deficit in fiscal year 1982–83. Joel Kotkin and Paul Grabowicz noted a new selfishness in *California Inc.*:

> The middle classes, in effect, have absorbed the values of the business elite. . . . The California dream is not to tear down the class system but rather to stake out one's fortune and enter the realm of the corporate elite. (1982, p. 143)

Bifurcation of the California workforce. Although the high-tech workforce is expected to grow at least twice as fast as the workforce in other industrial sectors, it will amount to only 750,000 by the year 1990 (Center, 1982). This is only a fraction of the millions of Californians who will be looking for work in the 1990s, and who may aspire to careers in the heavily-promoted high-tech field.

Unfortunately, this industry is capital-intensive. The *application* of high technology will ultimately *reduce* work available to California's job seekers (Ferguson and Rogers, 1982). Office automation, for example, may generate unemployment in the service sectors approaching 10 to 20 percent (Economist Intelligence Unit, 1979).

Many potential non-workers are ethnic Californians, largely of Mexican-American descent and skill-deficient. SRI International (1982, p. 59) cautions that unless this large and growing group of students is "brought up to the new standards of technical literacy, . . . there will be drastic social and economic consequences, and a potential alienated ethnic group that will present continuing high unemployment problems." Due to cutbacks in public outlays, however, California schools at all levels are unable to attract and retain essential teachers and faculty.[7]

Workplace life is especially trying for low-wage workers manufacturing high-tech hardware. Abundant industrial toxins are only part of the problem: inflated housing costs are forcing these workers to migrate further and further from work, adding to lost work time, personal commuting costs, and a congested residential environment (Lane, 1981). In Orange County, the 1982 economy showed no growth, and in 1983 will show only moderate growth as workers are forced to move (to adjacent Riverside County and other states) (Lane, 1982). Those who remain face a life of personal insecurity similar to that of Japan's downscale workers (Molony, 1982).

California reality reflects the rabid antiunion philosophy and prac-

---

[7] Unlike their Japanese counterparts (among the *zaibatsu*-employed), California workers cannot rely on private industry for their reeducation. But two school districts in Silicon Valley, "in conjunction with industry," are about to open "the nation's first high school devoted entirely to the study of high technology" [Flinn, 1982]. Silicon Valley's managers are willing to subsidize the technological education of their own children.

tice of high-tech industry. (IBM, the "grandfather" of high-tech, is America's largest unorganized corporation and a major player in state politics and culture.) Most union officials in California consider the high-tech industry "unorganizable." The ease with which manufacturers can shift production among plants and the surface appeal of "high-tech paternalism"—corporate swimming pools and so forth—present formidable obstacles to unionization in Silicon Valley and throughout California (Howard, 1981).

California is witnessing the growth of a quasimigrant labor force circulating among high-tech manufacturers. (This is a California tradition: immigrants, minorities, and women have supplied cheap labor for successive railroad, agribusiness, and textile empires.) In California, as in Japan, superheated competition within the high-tech industry has encouraged capital investment at the expense of human welfare. Both societies are generating powerful disruptive social forces ("The Robot...," 1982).

Transnational corporations and institutions do not share the California dream. For them, California is a testing ground for new technologies and processes. It is here that they first deploy the products of the high-tech industry. How ironic that frantic efforts to preserve and strengthen the high-tech industry may frustrate California society's search for a higher quality of life.

Bringing the Third World home.[8] High-tech has brought about the "corporate village" (Hamelink, 1977). Information is a commodity; communication of information via telecommunications and computers allows transnational corporations and their state surrogates to carry out global "command and control" functions (Hamelink, 1977).

Residence in an "advanced industrial nation" does not necessarily bestow the mantle of technological sophistication (Schiller, 1981). Californians working at remote, isolated computerized workstations or displaced by automated fabricating equipment will have much in common with workers in Europe, Asia, and Latin America. California may be a source of high technology, but it, no less than any Third World nation is subject to the vagaries of "global money" (Samuelson, 1982) made more mobile by high technology.

SRI International (1982) predicts the disintegration of California into regions characterized by varying levels of development and affluence. John Friedmann and Goetz Wolf (1982) have gone a step further and envisioned the complete disappearance of regions in California: a "World City," Los Angeles, will exercise sovereignty in conjunction with World

---

[8] This phrase is borrowed from William W. Goldsmith (1982). Goldsmith fears the importation of "enterprise zones" on the South Asian model. Actually, entire regions in California may be converted into industrial neo-colonies.

Cities in other regions. Within the World City, life will be organized to sustain a managerial elite; outside its boundaries, California will be organized to sustain Los Angeles.

This new alignment of power presages a breakdown of regional allegiances among California's mobile elite, reflected in the cultural life of World-City society. People will come to resemble capital in the fluidity of their attachments to community and relationships. This flightiness is already characteristic of Californian life, especially Southern Californian life. It is an abasement of the California dream.

PART FOUR:
THE SEARCH FOR NEW DIRECTIONS

Mathematician, Ernest Callenbach (1977) captured many Californians' imagination (and hope) with his sketchy but suggestive novel of a utopian West Coast nation, *Ecotopia*. His protagonist, William Weston, an American reporter visiting the newly-independent Ecotopia in the early 2000s, questioned the validity of the Ecotopian ideal:

> While seemingly idealistic, . . . is in fact profoundly pessimistic. . . .
> The way propounded by Ecotopian ideologues leads away from the
> former greatness of America, unified in spirit "from sea to shining
> sea," toward a balkanized continent—a welter of small, second-class
> nations, each with its own petty cultural differentiations. (p. 193)

Weston's worries were misplaced. Using the high technology they have created, California industrialists exercise command and control over production plants in Latin American and Asia, marketing offices in North America and Europe, and R&D activities at research centers throughout the northern hemisphere. Their livelihood *is* the health of transnational corporations ("Multinationals . . .," 1979) and the military forces that protect them.

California should be taking steps, not toward an export-oriented, defense-dependent, Japanese-styled "information society," but toward a more democratic, popularly-determined future. (Lessons can be learned from the Canadian experience, described in Shirley Serafini and Michel Andrieu's *The Information Revolution and its Implications for Canada* [1980].)

High technology exists. Can it be developed in ways that enhance, rather than degrade, quality of life? The answer must be political, rather than technical, because one's concept of life-quality is inevitably shaped by one's experiences and learning—not by a scientific yardstick of "excellence." Political action to harness high technology should be the first order of the day.

There are signs in California that hard political questions are being asked. Maurice Zeitlin's (1982) plans for democratic investment of public capital are gaining credibility. The state's unitary tax laws, which assess corporate holdings on a global basis, signal domestic resistance to transnational corporate predictions (Rennert, 1982). Although it faces determined opposition in the Legislature, a plant-closure bill is making slow progress through the state Assembly.

In the meantime, it is wise to remember Herbert Schiller's (1981a) call to action for critical communications researchers:

> The question to be considered, I believe, is *not* what might happen if a new communications technology should run amok. The issue is much more stark and immediate. It is, how do we check a communications technology that is already running amok, and one which had this tendency to do so built in from the outset? (p. 219)

People cannot do much without the political muscle to enforce their desires, but the public must be alert to the manifold ways that high technology, cunningly employed, can obstruct the path to political power (Dordick, Bradley, and Nanus, 1981).

This is properly a task for critical communications researchers: to demystify modernist, homogenized, internationalized culture based on transnational economics (Lasch, 1982)—the high-tech dream. The California dream is not necessarily a product only for export: as it inspires Californians to search for a better way of life, it can breed progressive collective action. But it is perhaps better perceived in a redwood grove than on a computer video screen.

REFERENCES

Blackman, C. R. (1978). "Telecomputercations: Cause and Effect." *Telecommunications* (November), 145–148.

Buecke, D. A. (1982). "The State Wants to Establish a High-Tech R&D Corporation." *San Jose Mercury* (March 16), 9D.

"Business and Politics: The View from Sacramento." (1981). *San Jose Mercury* (May 17), 1D.

Bylinsky, G. (1981). "Japan's Ominous Chip Victory." *Fortune* (December 14), 52–57.

Callenbach, E. (1977). *Ecotopia.* New York: Bantam Books.

Center for Continuing Study of the California Economy. (1982). *The California Economy: 1970–1990.* Sacramento, CA: Dept. of Economic and Business Development, March.

"Chips: The Human Component." (1982). *San Jose Mercury* (May 4), 6B.

Donner, A. (1982). "Brown: Sanctions against Japan." *Sacramento Union* (February 25), Today Section, 1.

Dordick, H. S., Bradley, H. G., and Nanus, B. (1981). *The Emerging Network Marketplace.* Norwood, NJ: Ablex.

Eckhouse, J., and Johnson, M. (1982). "Electronics Execs Bitter at Japanese." *San Francisco Examiner* (April 27), C1 +.

Economist Intelligence Unit. (1979). *Chips in the 1980s*. London: EIU, Ltd.

Entlin, B., and Buecke, D. A. (1982). "Silicon Valley Plugs into State Politics." *San Jose Mercury* (May 17), 1D +.

Ferguson, T., and Rogers, J. (1982). "The Great Japan Debate." *The Nation* (February 13), 167–171.

Flinn, J. (1982). "Silicon Valley Districts Plan a High-Tech School." *San Francisco Examiner* (February 5), A1.

Friedmann, J., and Wolf, G. (1982). "World City Formation: An Agenda for Research and Action." Graduate School of Architecture & Urban Planning, University of California, Los Angeles (Working Paper No. WCP 3), February.

Garreau, J. (1981). *The Nine Nations of North America*. Boston, MA: Houghton Mifflin Company.

Goldsmith, W. W. (1982). "Bringing the Third World Home." *Working Papers* (March/April), 24–30.

Hagstrom, J. (1982). "High-Tech Leaders Have Their Own Ideas of What Government Can Do For Them." *National Journal* (May 15), 861–865.

Hamelink, C. (1977). *The Corporate Village*. Rome: IDOC International.

Howard, R. (1981). "Second Class in Silicon Valley." *Working Papers* (September/October), 20–31.

Hume, E. (1982). "Plan to Help State Computer Firms Unveiled." *Los Angeles Times* (March 25), part IV, 1.

Ito, Y. (1980). "The 'Johoka Shakai' Approach to the Study of Communication in Japan." *KEIO Communication Review*, No. 1, 13–40.

"Japan Inc. Goes International With High Technology." (1981). *Business Week* (December 14), 40–49.

Johnson, B. (1982). "Critical Programmer Shortage Predicted By '90." *Computerworld* (February 1), 17.

Joint Economic Committee. (1982). *International Competition in Advanced Industrial Sectors: Trade and Development in the Semiconductor Industry*. Washington, DC: USGPO, February 18.

Junkerman, J. (1981). "Japan Worship." *Working Papers* (January/February), 63–66.

Kirchner, J. (1982). "Government Has "Important Role" to Play in Information Revolution." *Computerworld* (June 7), 23.

Kotkin, J., and Grabowicz, P. (1982). *California Inc.* New York: Rawson, Wade.

Kurita, S. (1982). "What To Expect From The 5th-Generation Computer." *Computerworld* (June 14), INDEPTH 14–23.

Lane, L. (1982). "High-Tech Evolution in County Decreases Blue-Collar Demand." *Los Angeles Times* (April 29), part IV, 3.

Lane, L. (1981). "Will California Keep the Silicon Valley Bonanza?" *California Journal* (August), 282–284.

Lasch, C. (1982). "Popular Culture and the Illusion of Choice." *Democracy* 2(3), 88–92.

Leeson, K. (1981). *Trade Issues in Telecommunications and Information, Volume 1: United States Trade in the Merchandise of Information Industries*. Washington, DC: NTIA, April (Report 81–72).

Madison, C. (1982). "Flirting with Reciprocity—New U.S. Trade Policy Makes Some People Nervous." *National Journal* (February 20), 320–324.

Masuda, Y. (1981). *The Information Society as Post-Industrial Society*. Bethesda, MD: World Future Society.

Masuda, Y. (1982). "Yoneji Masuda Talks About the Fifth-Generation Computer." *Computerworld* (June 14), INDEPTH 1-12.

Molony, K. (1982). " 'Contented' Labor: Selective Paternalism." *The Nation* (February 13), 184-185.

"Multinationals and Communications." (1979). *Multinational Business*. No. 2, 1-14.

Office of the Governor. (California). (1981). Press release, November 19.

Oshima, K. (1980). "Technology and Economic Nationalism." *In* O. Hieronymi (Ed.), *The New Economic Nationalism*. London: MacMillan, 201-209.

Rada, J. F. (1981). "The Microelectronics Revolution: Implications for the Third World." *Development Dialogue*, No. 2, 41-67.

Rennert, L. (1982). "Fate of "Unitary" Tax on Multinationals in Hands of Justices." *Sacramento Bee* (May 4), C1.

Richter, P. (1982). "Look Past Glamour, Analysts Tell Potential High-Tech Investors." *Los Angeles Times* (June 1), part IV, 1+.

Roberts, J. G. (1982). "State of Corruption: America and the Making of Japan Inc." *The Nation* (February 13), 171-177.

"The Robot Invasion Begins to Worry Labor." (1982). *Business Week* (March 29), 46-47.

Samuelson, R. J. (1982). "Restless Technology." *National Journal* (March 27), 557.

Schiller, H. I. (1981a). "Information for What Kind of Society?" *Current Research on Peace and Violence*, No. 3, 218-228.

Schiller, H. I. (1981b). *Who Knows? Information in the Age of the Fortune 500*. Norwood, NJ: Ablex.

Serafini, S., and Andrieu, M. (1980). *The Information Revolution and Its Implications for Canada*. Quebec, Canada: Canadian Government Publishing Centre.

Slater, P. (1982). "Roseville Approves Major Plant." *Sacramento Bee* (March 25), A1.

SRI International. (1982). *California's Technological Future: Emerging Economic Opportunities in the 1980s*. Sacramento: Department of Economic and Business Development, March.

White, K. M., and Jacobson, C. R. (1981). *Trade Issues in Telecommunications and Information, Volume 3: Promoting U.S. Trade in Telecommunications and Information Products with Developing Countries*. Washington, DC: NTIA, April Report 81-72.

Zeitlin, M. (1982). "Democratic Investment." *democracy* 2(2), 69-80.

6

The New American Information Order

Timothy R. Haight

National boundaries are not as crucial as boundaries within nations, and consequently, discussion of international phenomena...should be understood at least partly in terms of intranational phenomena (e.g., class interests).

Since Nordenstreng and Varis (1973, p. 404) published the preceding statement, the international debate over information policies has become vastly more visible and intellectually developed. In particular, the relationship between the international information structures and capitalism has grown more distinct, as the following statement by Anthony Smith (1980, p. 73–74)—by no means on the "far left" of the debate—makes clear:

It is impossible, when looking at the evolution of these [international news agencies], to fail to perceive in them the shadow of the structure of the capitalist system itself. For capitalism was an information system, as well as a financial and productive system; its development necessitated bringing one unexploited part of the world after another into a single market in which social classes, companies, transportation methods and stock markets became inextricably combined into a single, complicated and variegated, ever-growing and interdependent system.

Why the profound gap between the level of consciousness of the international policy debate and that within the U.S.? The answer is obvious. As Baran and Sweezy (1966) put it,

The United States dominates and exploits to one extent or another all the countries and territories of the so-called "free world" and correspondingly meets with varying degrees of resistance. The highest form of resistance is revolutionary war aimed at withdrawal from the world capitalist system and the initiation of social and economic reconstruction on a socialist basis. Such warfare has never been absent since the Second World War, and the revolutionary peoples have achieved a series of historic victories. . . . It is no longer mere rhetoric to speak of the world revolution: the term describes what is already a reality and is certain to become increasingly the dominant characteristic of the historical epoch in which we live. (p. 365)

Given this fact, the form of ideology in an international debate is bound to differ from that within the United States. In an international context, certain myths simply cannot be maintained.

But if progressive forces within the United States are not simply to be passive observers—and therefore, perhaps *de facto* opponents—of history, must we not develop as sophisticated an analysis of the role of information in economic exploitation domestically as it is evolving internationally? And, if the objective conditions of the international situation allow analysis of that arena to be more highly developed, may not it be possible to begin a fruitful analysis of the situation in the United States by developing parallels from international analyses? While it is certainly true that in any such analysis our own particular historical conditions must be taken into account, such an approach may have at least heuristic value.

Advocating this intellectual strategy, I do not mean to minimize the many diagnoses of the American situation that have already been produced. The work of authors too numerous to mention here has already illustrated many of the same problems and causes that exist both domestically and internationally. This is particularly true of the work of Schiller (e.g. 1981) whose analysis is regularly applied to both arenas with equal profundity.

In this essay, therefore, I wish to propose a more narrow task. Some issues that have become primary in the international debate have not found domestic parallels. This paper will discuss technology transfer. In the pages that follow, I wish to suggest some parallels which might lead to creative thought about U.S. communications, centered around this issue. In order to do this is more than an intuitive way, I will attempt this analysis in the context of a primitive attempt to develop a theory of the general role of information in capitalism. I do this in all humility, and with due recognition of my status as an amateur economist, but to do otherwise would be to commit the errors Nordenstreng (1980) pointed out in the MacBride report:

> The point is that the problems are too crucial to be left just to some descriptive remarks, and what is more, such a methodological approach leaves the communication problems related to these global problems hanging in a political air without scientifically based solid conceptual links with the totality of social, economic and political realities. (p. 13)

Moreover, I wish to echo Smythe (1977, p. 1) who, when stepping on the same terrain, noted, "The argument presented here...is an attempt to start a debate, not to conclude one."

The fundamental analogy between the domestic and international situations is that what is seen often domestically as relations among classes are mirrored in international class divisions which often fall close to national boundaries. This is not precise, of course, because all nations under capitalism possess their own ruling elites, however subordinate these elites may be in the global system. But because the prime function of many parts of the world under capitalism is to participate in the global market by selling commodities below exchange value and purchasing them above value while allowing better investment opportunities, the parallel roughly holds.

Technology transfer among nations, particularly between countries of the "center" and those of the "periphery," seems to lead to an increasing relative gap between the two sides' level of economic development, often with the developing countries' failing to provide for the basic human needs of some of their populations. While the informational components of this situation do not explain its totality by any means, at least part of the situation can be seen as an informational problem.

Within developed countries, the parallel condition to underdevelopment may be structural unemployment. While the alienation of the worker from the means of production is certainly nothing new, we do hear lately about the prospects of an "information underclass," where "those who do not develop information skills are forced into those aspects of labor that are not as lucrative" (Porat, 1978, p. 44). Porat further has remarked that, "Our present trajectory will produce, by the turn of the century, a new underclass—the information poor."

We usually discuss structural unemployment in the United States as a problem of "retraining" or basic education. What I wish to maintain here is that information has become an increasingly important component of the means of production, and the alienation of the worker from information is necessary for capitalist social relations to continue. In order for firms in the center countries to continue to survive under capitalist competition, they must either erect barriers to competition through monopolistic practices or continue to enjoy higher levels of information use. Very often these two strategies are intertwined. Genuine technology transfer would mean the end of the global capitalist system.

But this level of abstraction is hopelessly high. I can no longer put off presenting some basic theory. Once this has been done, we may return to the comparison of international and domestic contexts.

Capitalism treats information as a commodity. It can be bought or sold. Resources are used in its production. Capitalism also treats labor-power as a commodity. But as Eaton (1966) points out,

> Labour-power is, in fact, a commodity which has the peculiar property of creating when it is used value greater than its own value. . . .
>
> Once this has been understood the secret of profit has been grasped; the source of profit is the difference between the value of the worker's labour-power and the value he produces. (p. 14)

This difference is, of course, surplus value, to Marx the source of all profit.

But what if information is also a commodity which has the peculiar property of creating when it is used value greater than its own value? Some evidence from bourgeois economics would indicate this might be so:

> One of the most interesting economic characteristics of information is that its cost is independent of the scale on which it is used. A given piece of information costs the same to acquire, whether the decision to be based on it is large or small. (Arrow, 1980, p. 310)

What forms can information take in production? One is the degree of skill of the worker. Another is the arrangement of the workers in a division of labor. A third is the knowledge of a new method of production.

What did Marx (1906) say about skill?

> In order to modify the human organism, so that it may acquire skill and handiness in a given branch of industry, and become labour-power of a special kind, a special education or training is requisite, and this, on its part, costs an equivalent in commodities of a greater or less amount. This amount varies according to the more or less complicated character of the labour-power. The expenses of this education (excessively small in the case of ordinary labour-power), enter pro tanto into the total value spent in its production. (p. 191)

The production of skill has value. When the labor is purchased, some amount of the price of the labor-power, which is equal to its value, will be for the value of the training. But what is the relationship between the value of this training and its use-value? That is, how much does the training increase the efficiency of labor, and how is this related to the cost of its production?

Marx (1906) maintains that "in the creation of surplus-value it does not in the least matter, whether the labour appropriated by the capitalist be simple unskilled labour of average quality or more complicated skilled labour." He states:

> All labour of a higher or more complicated character than average labour is expenditure of labour-power of a more costly kind, labour-power whose production has cost more time and labour, and which therefore has a higher value, then unskilled or simple labour-power. This power being of higher value, its consumption is labour of a higher class, labour that creates in equal times proportionally higher values than unskilled labour does. Whatever difference in skill there may be between the labour of a spinner and that of a jeweller, the

> portion of his labour by which the jeweller merely replaces the value
> of his own labour-power, does not in any differ in quality from the
> additional portion by which he creates surplus-value. (p. 220)

Marx seems to be saying that if a worker is trained to be twice as productive, the worker would be paid twice as much. But if the worker's wages are pegged to productivity, how are they related to the cost of training? Moreover, the increased productivity of the worker goes on indefinitely. This is unlike productivity achieved by introducing new machinery into the production process. There, a little of the value of the machinery is supposed to be used up in each production run. The sometimes arbitrary nature of depreciation schedules may call this into question fundamentally, but with particular reference to information, how is it used up? If information about a method of production is the same regardless of how many times it is used, none of it is used up in each production run. Skill seems to be capital equipment that does not depreciate.

Although Marx (1906, pp. 368–404) does not employ the term "information," he discusses at length the problem of skilled labor. He concludes that gains in wages are pegged to gains in productivity due to skill. He does this, however, in the context of a long discussion of the historical development of production. An historical battle took place. Production went through a transition from handicraft to cooperation to manufacture to manufacture employing machinery. In that historical process, the control of information—and therefore the determination of its value—was wrested from the craftworker and appropriated by the capitalists. Once this was done, the capitalist could grade the value of skilled labor in proportion to the amount of time the skilled worker's operation took in an organized process of manufacture. Once this was in turn accomplished, the contribution of the training to the value of the produced commodity due to the particular quality of information became zero, thus allowing the surplus to be completely appropriated by the capitalist.

The battles that took place on this terrain are quite similar to those going on today as skilled workers are replaced by computers operated by secretaries:

> Although it adapts the detail operations to the various degrees of maturity, strength, and development of the living instruments of labour, thus conducing to exploitation of women and children, yet this tendency as a whole is wrecked on the habits and the resistance of the male labourers. Although the splitting up of handicrafts lowers the cost of forming the workman, and thereby lowers his value, yet for the more difficult detail work, a longer apprenticeship is necessary, and even where it would be superfluous, is jealously insisted upon by the workmen . . . . Since handicraft skill is the foundation of manufacture, and since the mechanism of manufacture as a whole possesses no framework, apart from the labourers themselves, capital is con-

stantly compelled to wrestle with the insubordination of the work-men. . . . And had we not the testimony of contemporary writers, the simple facts that, during the period between the 16th century and the epoch of Modern Industry, capital failed to become the master of the whole disposable working-time of the manufacturing labourers, that manufactures are short-lived and change their locality from one country to another with the emigrating or immigrating workmen, these facts would speak volumes. (Marx, 1906, pp. 403–404)

This discussion of skill points up two important aspects of information. First, it can create exchange-value—depending on who gets to define the value in trained labour-power. It does appear to be a commodity that can increase the value of other commodities. But the second point is that capitalism must not allow it to do so. Capitalism must so totally appropriate information that its multiplicative quality disappears. That bourgeois economists are beginning to realize that the economic aspects of information are challenging neoclassical theory is an indication that something is happening historically that is upsetting this appropriation. But until we can examine the role of information in the crisis of capitalism, we must first continue with our study of its role in production.

Arrow (1980) has written that

> Specialization in information gathering is one instance, in my view the most important instance, of the economic benefits of organization. The basic gain in all such cases is that a group working together can produce more in total than the sum of their products working individually. This surplus cannot be achieved if all individuals perform the same tasks, for then they might as well be working separately. It is achieved only by specialization of function, by a suitable sharing of duties. This is precisely the division of labor among individuals whose importance was so much stressed by Adam Smith.
>
> Of all forms of division of labor, the division of information gathering is perhaps the most fundamental. Indeed, the chief gain from other forms of specialisation is that the individual worker can acquire the skills for a particular task more effectively if the range of the task is restricted: in other words, the efficiency gain is owing to the lower cost of information permitted by specialization. (pp. 309–310)

Marx (1906) was very much aware of the economies of cooperation. He wrote:

> The special productive power of the combined working day [hiring many workers together at the same time—TH] is, under all circumstances, the social productive power of labour, or the productive power of social labour. This power is due to co-operation itself. When the labourer co-operates systematically with others, he strips off the fetters of his individuality, and develops the capabilities of his species. (p. 361)

But labor in cooperation could only be achieved by "their assemblage in one place" (Marx, 1906, p. 361). This meant that somebody had to pay them and pay for the raw materials which they would transform before the finished goods were sold. This required capital. The capitalist, however, had more interests than merely serving as the coordinator of a cooperative:

> The control exercised by the capitalist is not only a special function, due to the nature of the social labour-process, and peculiar to that process, but it is, at the same time, a function of the exploitation of a social labour-process, and is consequently rooted in the unavoidable antagonism between the exploiter and the living and labouring raw material he exploits. (Marx, 1906, p. 363)

The capitalist, then, goes about organizing labor into the pattern of cooperation he desires. He realizes the profit from the information cost-savings that cooperation generates. This does not have to happen, as the success of labor unions in pegging wage increases to productivity during some periods illustrates. In that case, productivity rises in the total process are treated as if they were due to training or as if the act of labor cooperating was their own property. But this is only won through struggle. As Marx (1906) saw it in *Capital,* the capitalist's appropriation of cooperation meant that

> The productive power developed by the labourer when working in co-operation, is the productive power of capital. This power is developed gratuitously, whenever the workmen are placed under given conditions, and it is capital that places them under such conditions. Because this power costs capital nothing, and because, on the other hand, the labourer himself does not develop it before his labour belongs to capital, it appears as a power with which capital is endowed by Nature—a productive power that is immanent in capital. (pp. 365–366)

When Marx uses the word "appears," he is not assuming the pose of the humble scientist wishing to qualify his judgment. He means "made to appear," through the functioning of the relations of production. Because the workers are recruited separately into the cooperative-production process, "the connexion existing between their various labours appears to them, ideally, in the shape of a preconceived plan of the capitalist" (Marx, 1906, p. 364). Speaking ideally, one can see this "plan" as "information." It is the pattern of organization. It came from an idea about how to organize a productive process. But to so view information is to deny that that pattern is really a lot of workers informing themselves about their environment and communicating with each other.

It is true, however, that the knowledge of how to cooperate is a resource. In the form of the services of a management consultant, it is a commodity. But like raw materials, it needs to be touched by labor to produce anything. This is the essence of the labor theory of value, that labor adds the life without which transformation of reality is not possible. But the interesting thing about such knowledge, in its turn, is that it can multiply the productivity of labor. The entity who controls how this multiplication will take place can arrange to profit from it. Determining the pattern of cooperation, or the nature of the division of labor, not only realizes economies of information exchange but also builds in the relations of production. And this is fundamentally a battle over control of information. As Marx (1906) wrote,

> Intelligence in production expands in one direction, because it vanishes in many others. What is lost by the detail labourers, is concentrated in the capital that employs them. It is a result of the division of labour in manufactures, that the labourer is brought face to face with the intellectual potencies of the material process of production, as the property of another, and as a ruling power. This separation begins in simple co-operation, where the capitalist represents to the single workman, the oneness and the will of the associated labour. It is developed in manufacture which cuts down the labourer into a detail labourer. It is completed in modern industry, which makes science a productive force distinct from labour and presses it into the service of capital. (pp. 396–397)

Examining the process by which this occurs is instructive not only to reveal the workings of capitalist ideology but also to provide us with a way of looking at the "information age."

Marx begins his examination by comparing a division of labor with a division of manufacture. When several capitalists are involved, perhaps a cattle-breeder, a tanner, and a shoemaker, what we have is the exchange of commodities. The cattle-breeder sells to the tanner, and so on. Surplus values are realized as each semi-finished product is sold. It then becomes the raw material for another application of labor. In a factory, however, one person on the assembly line does not sell the product to the next person down the line. Both workers get wages, and the capitalist sells the product of the whole series of operations. Marx (1906) makes the distinction:

> Division of labour within the workshop implies the undisputed authority of the capitalist over men, that are but parts of a mechanism that belongs to him. The division of labour within the society brings into contact independent commodity-producers, who acknowledge no other authority but that of competition. . . . The same bourgeois mind which praises division of labour in the workshop, lifelong annexation of the labourer to a partial operation, and his complete subjection to capital, as being an organization of labour that increases its productiveness—that same bourgeois mind denounces with equal vigor every conscious attempt to socially control and regulate the process of production, as an inroad upon such sacred things as the rights of property, freedom and unrestricted play for the bent of the individual capitalist. It is very characteristic that the enthusiastic

apologists of the factory system have nothing more damning to urge against a general organization of the labour of society, than that it would turn all society into one immense factory. (p. 391)

By such remarkably irrational processes is ideology maintained!

In addition to the savings due to productivity, the division of labor allows the capitalist to define the skill for each task. As a result, the capitalist can provide on-the-job training rather than relying on apprenticeship programs or the like. Thus, the problem of having to account for prior training in setting wages disappears.

The consequence of this, for labor, is receiving no training save for the narrow task performed in production. Marx (1906, p. 397) quotes Ferguson, who wrote, "Ignorance is the mother of industry as well as of superstition." And to illustrate the point, Marx quotes Adam Smith:

> The understandings of the greater part of men," says Adam Smith, "are necessarily formed by their ordinary employments. The man whose whole life is spent in performing a few simple operations. . . has no occasion to exert his understanding. . . . He generally becomes as stupid and ignorant as it is possible for a human creature to become. (pp. 397–398)

Marx mentions that Smith recommended, "education of the people by the State, but prudently, and in homeopathic doses," and he quotes Smith's French translator as recommending against public education. We begin to approach the problem of structural unemployment and technology transfer.

But while information may have its most basic relationship to production in the question of the skill of the worker versus the division of labor, the greatest impact of knowledge on production is usually said to be in the developing new manufacturing technology. Habermas (1971), for example, wrote:

> The institutional pressure to augment the productivity of labor through the introduction of new technology has always existed under capitalism. But innovations depended on sporadic inventions, which, while economically motivated, were still fortuitous in character. This changed as technical development entered into a feedback relation with the progress of the modern sciences. With the advent of large-scale industrial research, science, technology, and industrial utilization were fused into a system. Since then, industrial research has been linked up with research under government contract, which primarily promotes scientific and technical progress in the military sector. From there information flows back into the sectors of civilian production. Thus technology and science become a leading productive force, rendering inoperative the conditions for Marx's labor theory of value. (p. 104)

One need not agree to obsolesce the labor theory of value to agree with Habermas that knowledge has had a tremendous effect on the production of wealth. But to go further with the question requires a more detailed analysis of the role of information in productive technology, the third manifestation of information in production.

In the same way that Marx saw the productive power of cooperation under capitalism as "developed gratuitously," so Marx (1906, p. 423) sees the productive component of technology due to information as "gratuitous service." With the examination of the division of labor, however, Marx was conscious of the ideological nature of that definition. But in the case of capital machinery, the definition appears to be his own.

He wrote:

> We saw that the productive forces resulting from co-operation and division of labour cost capital nothing. They are natural forces of social labour. So also physical forces, like steam, water, &c., when appropriated to productive processes, cost nothing. But just as a man requires lungs to breathe with, so he requires something that is work of man's hand, in order to consume physical forces productively. A water-wheel is necessary to exploit the force of water, and a steam engine to exploit the elasticity of steam. Once discovered, the law of the deviation of the magnetic needle in the field of an electric current, or the law of magnetisation of iron, around which an electric current circulates, cost never a penny. But the exploitation of these laws for the purposes of telegraphy, &c., necessitates a costly and expensive apparatus. (Marx, 1906, p. 422)

In a footnote to this passage, Marx (1906, p. 422) adds, "Science, generally speaking, costs the capitalist nothing, a fact that by no means hinders him from exploiting it. The science of others is as much annexed by capital as the labour of others."

Knowledge of the amounts of money spent on research and development, either directly by industry or indirectly by the State, brings into question how seriously we can consider science to cost the capitalist nothing. In addition, we have all the institutions of intellectual property: patents, copyright, and secrecy (together with the cost of keeping it, from shredders to encryption). But before dealing with this objection directly, we should share a little more familiarity with how Marx did deal with the issue of capital equipment. As mentioned above, he assumed that the continuing growth of scientific knowledge would mean the continuing development of very expensive pieces of capital machinery. For Marx's capitalist, "doing more with less," seems to have meant doing more with less labor. Since these expensive machines would have to be manufactured, a great deal of labor would be expended in their construction. Like any other commodity, then, the capital equipment's value would be measured by the amount of labor that went into it. Each time the machine were used, it would give up a little of its value "by wear and tear." When it had worn out, all of its value would be gone. The amount of wear and tear on the machine would be the amount of labor the machine transferred to the article it helped make. Marx (1906) describes the process:

> After making allowance, both in the case of the machine and of the tool, for their average daily cost, that is for the value they transmit to the product by their average daily wear and tear, and for their consumption of auxiliary substances, such as oil, coal, and so on, they each do their work gratuitously, just like the forces furnished by nature without the help of man. The greater the productive power of the machinery compared with that of the tool, the greater is the extent of its gratuitous service compared with that of the tool. In Modern Industry man succeeded for the first time in making the product of his past labour work on a large scale gratuitously, like the forces of nature. (pp. 423–424)

Marx assumed that large capital equipment wore out slower than tools, so when he compares them, above, he is saying that the slower a piece of capital equipment wears out, the more it works for free. Its cost— or the labor value transferred to the product—is equal to the depreciation of its physical form. The labor involved in discovering the scientific law, or even in designing the machine (except as it is part of the machine's price and disguised as a cost of manufacture) is not included. And how could it be, for information is not used up when it is transferred?

What happens if the design of the machine produces more wealth, multiplies the effect of labor, vastly out of proportion to the physical cost of the piece of capital equipment?

What happens to the tendency of profits to fall, and what happens to the role that technological innovation plays in competition under capitalism?

Very briefly, capitalist competition tends to follow the following pattern. To compete, a capitalist installs a new system of production. This must increase productivity to be competitive. Usually this means purchasing more efficient capital equipment. If the method is more productive, the capitalist will be able to sell his goods at a price above the exchange value of the labor involved until his competitors make similar productivity gains. Then he must innovate again. If this process of constant innovation involves increasing expenses for plant, equipment and raw materials and relatively less for labor, the amount of surplus value will decline relative to the capital and raw material expenses. Thus, over the entire economy, the rate of profit will tend to fall.

Within the economy, however, firms will compete. Successful competition by innovation and increasing productivity will keep a particular firm's profits from experiencing the effect of the general tendency of falling profits.

Innovating by using scientific knowledge which is not costly in place of expensive capital equipment would put the user in the position of more productivity for less capital expense. Over time, this firm or industry would experience a higher rate of profit than one with a higher proportion of capital investment. The result would be a flow of investment capital into those firms or industries with a better utilization of the information portion of capital equipment. In the same way, if employing information workers to make communications within the firm more efficient would result in more productivity at a cost below that of replacing capital equipment, over time investment capital would flow to those firms. Information-intensive firms using scientific knowledge efficiently, or using information workers to improve efficiency, would grow. As these firms grew, the workers using information would tend to replace the workers in production. Thus the evolution of the information economy can be seen as a result of capitalism's need to simultaneously cheapen the value of productive labor and avoid the tendency for profits to fall. This in turn is based on the peculiar property of information to be a commodity that is not used up as it is used.

The implications of this analysis may be fairly extensive. We have been told that we have become an "information economy (Porat, 1978, p. 4)," but—particularly from a Marxist point of view—we have not been told why. Simply put, competition to extract surplus value requires innovation without excessive investment in capital equipment or raw materials. Thus, within the limits of historical conditions capitalist competition tends to seek out information-intensive solutions.

From this general tendency a number of corollary tendencies can be predicted. First, the knowledge-producing industries of the most information-intensive economies would increasingly specialize in searching for even more information-intensive methods of production and circulation. This would primarily involve such fields as basic research which could lead to major breakthroughs and to such applied fields as computer science and electrical engineering. It would also mean an increase in the social sciences, to the extent that social scientific knowledge could be applied to making the division of labor ever more efficient. This would lead to national specialization in branches of knowledge and of approaches, such as behaviorism.

Large firms would benefit the most from new information, because they would be able to purchase the information at the going price but use it on a grand scale. This would be limited by the cost of the channels of communication within the firm. If the cost of channels of communication were declining, however, this would result in increased firm size. Furthermore, only large firms or those receiving extraordinary benefits from doing their own research and development (such as the pharmaceutical industry) would be able to afford a private research and development program. This is because the results of R&D cannot be predicted accurately in advance. A certain spreading of risk is therefore necessary, either among the operations of a large firm or over the society through socialized payment for R&D, perhaps by state-supported universities or defense research.

Increased concentration of industry would again be expected because of the large firms' use of the research results their sole support of the process allowed them to keep secret or to patent. The demand for research, however, would mean that some would be socialized. While this would spread the risk of financing the uncertain activity, it would speed innovation and competition to the extent it were successful. Leading firms would retaliate against this competition by using their superior capital resources to merge with innovative small firms using socialized research or to drive them out of the market by sheer economic force.

The relationship between competition and the production of knowledge would likely be complex and vary considerably with historical circumstances. In a period when the control of capital could control the application of scientific knowledge, we would tend to see the socialization of the knowledge-producing industries to minimize costs. As capital became more dispersed—as, for example, when certain economies ravaged by war again became independent sources of capital—we might see the leading firms pressing for the privatization of knowledge production.

The control of information by the vesting of property rights would become more central to production, and litigation in this area would increase. This would become particularly problematic in the international arena due to the substitution of compulsory licensing agreements for international patenting. The result would be an increasing dependence on secrecy instead of patenting.

To the extent that decreasing costs of communication channels and increasing knowledge of the behavior of organizations made it possible, increasing productivity by reorganizing the division of labor, either within a firm or within an industrial sector, would become a favored tactic.

The composition of the labor force would also change, with an increase in system designers and low-level information workers, a decrease in workers trained to handle expensive capital equipment that became outmoded, and a decrease in employment relative to output overall.

Less information-intensive production would be exported to areas of the world with a cheaper labor supply. Part of the surplus produced abroad, however, would pay for information occupations in the center countries based on the world distribution of the products. This would occur because investment capital would flow to firms specializing in circulation to the extent that information technology increased productivity in these areas to the point where profits exceeded the falling rate in production. The information-intensive economies would become increasingly centers of circulation.

Some very severe contradictions would develop, one being that the need for the growth of scientific knowledge would demand the free circulation of this information, while the desire to restrict competitive innovation through information control would restrict it.

In addition, the instability of the business cycle would increase. Since a larger number of workers would be involved in circulation, their jobs would fluctuate with investment decisions much like those of the producers of capital equipment. An increasingly large structure of nonproductive workers would depend on the trade cycle of production. To the extent that knowledge production were socialized through State expenditures, financial pressures on the State could increase. The inability to accurately estimate the output of the information workers in the State would require that their wage levels were set by other means. O'Connor (1973, pp. 18–23) has mentioned this as a contribution to fiscal crisis.

It is tempting to continue to speculate on the theoretical consequences of a basic trend toward information-intensiveness, as one may list virtually all of the problems that various writers have associated with our present information economy. The contribution of this paper, however, is that the characteristics of information are discussed with reference to the labor theory of value. Unlike Habermas, my emphasis on the importance of information, and on its characteristic of being able to create value greater than its own value, does not fundamentally question the labor theory of value. (This also distinguishes my position from that of Bell, 1980, p. 168). The fact that the proportion of labor-power to overall wealth produced constantly falls was Marx's basic prediction. The concept of exchange value based on labor still holds, because it is the ratio of exchange among the amounts of labor in each commodity that is important, not the ratio of the exchange-value of a good to its use-value.

In the same way that natural forces such as water power can be appropriated by a system of relations of production defining private property, so can information be appropriated. As a society becomes more information-intensive, however, the contradiction between the need to treat information as a commodity and its increasingly immaterial nature becomes more problematic. This, in turn, is a result of the antithesis between "informing" as a human activity like labor and "information" as a set of symbols recorded on a material medium that can be treated like land.

This fundamental antithesis can be the source of wide-ranging speculation. Perhaps the appropriation of information turns out to require the property relations that turn "from forms of development of the forces of production. . . into their fetters" (Marx, cited by Eaton, 1966, p. 19).

Marx was certainly aware of the basic importance of communication systems. Anticipating Innis (1951), he wrote:

> The foundation of every division of labour that is well developed, and brought about by the exchange of commodities, is the separation between town and country. It may be said, that the whole economical history of society is summed up in the movement of this antithesis. . . .

> Just as a certain number of simultaneously employed labourers are the material pre-requisites for division of labour in manufacture, so are the number and density of the population, which here correspond to the agglomeration in one workshop, a necessary condition for the division of labour in society. Nevertheless, this density is more or less relative. A relatively thinly populated country, with well-developed means of communication, has a denser population than a more numerously populated country, with a badly-developed means of communication; and in this sense the Northern States of the American Union, for instance, are more thickly populated than India.

But these speculations must be left for another time. The final task of this chapter is to return to its beginning and to show, now that the trend toward information-intensiveness in capitalism has been analysed, how it operates in the international and national arenas with respect to technology transfer, remote sensing, transborder data flow and their domestic counterparts.

Put briefly, if increasing information-intensivity is the best way to innovate, and if innovation is the basis of competition, then allowing information to circulate freely is inviting competition. Technology transfer, therefore, is only in the interest of the developed countries to the extent that either the relative technology gap is not closed or the transfer is necessary to keep a country from going socialist.

In terms of the United States, technology transfer between classes seems to be following this pattern. Capitalism seems to need a large group of information workers with very general information-processing skills and a small number of highly trained engineers. The drive to increase productivity, particularly through robotization of production and computerization of office work, may mean a lower demand for labor overall, particularly to the extent that the U.S.' traditional branch-plant strategy continues. Thus if that child cannot become an engineer, she may not be needed at all. Given the other pressures on the national budget, cuts in funding to education will reduce the socialization of education, forcing the reproduction of labor to come increasingly out of wages. Simply put, the success of a child's education will depend more in the future on the extra resources the family is willing to expend, if it can. The consequence will be less upward social mobility. In addition, there is a possibility that an increasing percentage of the technical elite in the U.S. will immigrate here from abroad. According to Lusignan (1982), about fifty percent of the engineers now at work in Silicon Valley's computer industry are from out of the country. The transnationalization of capital and improved international communications may also mean that technical elites do not have to be national. The necessary innovation may be appropriated from abroad, if national policies do not obstruct the flow.

The question of technology transfer is a major item on the agenda of both the new international economic and information orders. We have not yet drawn the same general picture of information here. We are still talking about the mass media, or the telephone company, or education. We need a theoretical analysis that cuts across issue-areas, and we need a call for a New American Information Order. The closest to such a call that any U.S. group has yet come is the Willow Declaration, now being circulated by the Washington Chapter of the Union for Democratic Communications (1981). The declaration reads:

> We are a group of artists, educators, researchers, film and video producers, electronic technicians, social scientists and writers united in our support for democratic communications. The economic, cultural and spiritual welfare of humanity is increasingly tied to the structure for production and distribution of information. Most communications today is one-way, from the centers of power to passive audiences of consumers. We need a new information order here in the U.S. to give the power of voice to the unheard and the disenfranchised. We strongly support freedom of the press, but we see that in our own country, this freedom now exists mainly for huge corporations to make profits, to promote socially useless consumption and to impose corporate ideology and agendas. As workers who produce, study and transmit information, we pledge to change this reality. We will work to preserve and encourage face-to-face communication: people can speak best for themselves without the intervention of professionalism or technological mediation. We support that technology which enhances human power and which is designed and controlled by the communities which use it. We support the participation of workers and non-professionals in media production and the use of media for trade union and community organizing. We support the development of community channels for programs, news flow and data exchange. We support popular access to and control of media and communications systems. We support the internationally guaranteed right to reply and criticize and deplore the fact that this right is being attacked now in the U.S. by efforts in Congress to eliminate the Fairness Doctrine and public interest broadcast regulations. While these laws have been underutilized and difficult to apply, they have been the principal tools for forcing even token public debate. We who live and work in the U.S. pledge outselves to struggle for the democratization of communications within our communities, our places of work, and

our political institutions. We support the further inquiry by international organizations such as UNESCO into the social relations of the electronic environment. We hope that these discussions will continue and will resonate among and between nations and peoples.

REFERENCES

Arrow, K. J. (1980). "The Economics of Information." *In* M. L. Dertouzos and J. Moses (Eds.), *The Computer Age: A Twenty-Year View.* Cambridge, MA: MIT Press.

Baran, P. A., and Sweezy, P. M. (1966). *Monopoly Capital.* New York: Modern Reader Paperbacks.

Bell, D. (1980). "The Social Framework of the Information Society." *In* M. L. Dertouzos and J. Moses (Eds.), *The Computer Age: A Twenty-Year View.* Cambridge, MA: MIT Press.

Eaton, J. (1966). *Political Economy* (U.S. edition). New York: International Publishers.

Habermas, J. (1971). *Toward a Rational Society.* London: Heinemann.

Innis, H. A. (1951). *The Bias of Communication.* Toronto, Canada: University of Toronto Press.

Lusignan, B. (1982). Remarks at a panel on "Developing Telecommunications Infrastructures in the Third World." Tenth Annual Telecommunications Policy Research Conference. Annapolis, MD. April 26.

Marx, K. 1906. *Capital.* Volume 1. New York: The Modern Library.

Nordenstreng, K. (1980). "The Paradigm of a Totality." *In* C. Hamelink (Ed.), *Communication in the Eighties: A Reader on the "MacBride Report."* Rome, Italy: IDOC International.

Nordenstreng, K., and Varis, T. (1973). "The Nonhomogeneity of the National State and the International Flow of Communication." *In* G. Gerbner, L. Gross, and W. Melody (Eds.), *Communication Technology and Social Policy.* New York: John Wiley and Sons.

O'Connor, J. (1973). *The Fiscal Crisis of the State.* New York: St. Martin's Press.

Porat, M. U. (1978). "Communication Policy in an Information Society." *In* G. Robinson (Ed.), *Communications for Tomorrow.* New York: Praeger Special Studies.

Schiller, H. I. (1981). *Who Knows: Information in the Age of the Fortune 500.* Norwood, NJ: Ablex Publishing Corporation.

Smith, A. (1980). *The Geopolitics of Information.* New York: Oxford University Press.

Smythe, D. (1977). "Communications: Blindspot of Western Marxism." *Canadian Journal of Political and Social Theory, 1*(3), 1–27.

Union for Democratic Communications. (1981). "The Willow Declaration." Unpublished.

7

La Guerra Radiofonica: Radio War Between Cuba and the United States

Howard H. Frederick

Radio broadcasting plays an important role in contemporary international relations.[1] Interstate commmunication through external radio services at times has had a great impact on the course of international events. Today, throughout the world's radio spectrum, ardent opponents battle for the hearts and minds of attentive publics. This international "war of ideas"[2] shows no sign of abating. Indeed, over 80 countries daily broadcast some 22 thousand hours of international programming to over 250 million listeners (Frost, 1982, p. 32).

In few regions of the world is this war as intense as it is in the Americas between ideological rivals Cuba and the United States. These two countries are very close geographically but poles apart politically. Separated by only 140 kilometers across the Florida Straits, Cuba and the United States daily engage in this war of ideas. Their radio confrontation is the quintessential conflict between capitalism and communism, between imperialism and revolution, between freedom and liberation.

There are many weapons in this battle. Foremost are the two government-run official external radio services: La Voz de los Estados Unidos de America (Voice of America, hereafter VOA), broadcasting to Cuba and the

---

[1] This article was completed in January, 1983.

[2] For further reading in the field of international broadcasting and the war of ideas, see particularly: Arbatov, 1973; Abshire, 1976; Hale, 1975; Browne, 1982; Nason, 1977; Bumpus, 1980; Gordon et al., 1963; Barghoorn, 1964; Panfilov, 1967; Rolo, 1943; Lerner, 1951.

rest of Latin America in Spanish; and Radio Havana Cuba (hereafter RHC), broadcasting in English to the United States. In addition, clandestine and pirate radio stations have operated illegally on Caribbean islands and in the United States, where the Federal Communication Commission makes no effort to close them down.

Both Cuba and the United States are about to bring out the biggest guns in this two-and-a-half decades war. In 1983, the United States hopes to launch Radio Marti "to break the Cuban government's control of information in Cuba...[and to] tell the truth to the Cuban people" (Allen, 1981). Not to be outdone, the Cuban government is "prepared to give a suitable response...[to] their subversive station" (Castro Ruz, 1982). Cuba is constructing a 500,000 watt station to reach the entire North American continent "to answer every aggression" (Prado, 1982).

This article will trace the history of the Cuban-American "radio war" through its inception soon after the Cuban Revolution to the present battle over Radio Marti. It concludes with a discussion of what this radio war signifies in the context of international ideological confrontation, and with a modest proposal for an alternative to the present radio confrontation. It relies on public documents and interviews with Cuban and American participants in the radio war. This article in no way pretends to be exhaustive; nor are all the documents and statements that the author has gathered necessarily truthful and accurate. Time, distance, and ideological differences tend to cloud the memories of past events.

Yet the outlines of an intense conflict of opposing belief systems unmistakably emerge. International radio serves as one conduit for this conflict. Though nonviolent in the physical sense, the Cuban-American radio war involves tremendous manpower and physical resources, at times inflicts "damage" on the opponent, and, short of armed conflict, serves as a way for the two antagonists to express their enmity.

THE BATTLE IS ENGAGED: RADIO SWAN

As he began to consolidate his control over the island during the first two years after the 1959 revolution, Fidel Castro became increasingly concerned about what he regarded as attempts to sabotage the Cuban people's morale through foreign radio broadcasts.

In particular, he saw the broadcasts from Radio Swan as a U.S. attempt to combat the Cuban revolution. Radio Swan's mediumwave transmitter was located on a barren island 170 kilometers off the coast of

Honduras.[3] Owned by the Gibraltar Steamship Company, Swan's three-tower array blanketed the Caribbean area and delivered a powerful signal to the entire Cuban archipelago. Swan operated at at least 50 kilowatts on 1160 KHz, the same frequency as KSL in Salt Lake City. Coro reports that the Swan transmitter was eventually sold to Venezuela as a one million watt transmitter, thus belieing reports that it was only 50,000 watts (Coro, 1982).

The President of Gibraltar Steamship Corporation was Thomas Dudley Cabot, of Weston, Massachusetts. Cabor was a banker, former President of United Fruit and, in 1951, director of the State Department's Office of International Security Affairs. Gibraltar officials admitted that the corporation had not owned a steamship for ten years (Wise & Ross, 1964, pp. 328 ff.). But in May 1960, the firm announced that it had leased land on Swan Island to operate a radio station. Strictly a commercial venture, the station was to broadcast music, soap operas and news from studios in New York. The Federal Communication Commission, which is required to license all stations operating from U.S. territory, stated that it did not know who owned the island. Such responses raised suspicions about Swan's real ownership and mission.

Meanwhile, World Wide Broadcasting station WRUL (which still operates a shortwave transmitter in Scituate, Massachusetts) announced it would cooperate with Radio Swan. Its programs featured Miss Pepita Rivera, a Cuban exile billed as "Havana Rose." World Wide said Swan would tape and rebroadcast WRUL's programs (Wise & Ross, 1964, p. 318).

One figure involved in Radio Swan was E. Howard Hunt, later convicted in the Watergate break-in. Hunt disclosed in 1973 that David Atlee Phillips bragged about Swan's achievements in CIA director Allen Dulles's office. Hunt assured the leaders of the counter-revolutionary exiles in Florida that as soon as the invasion at the Bay of Pigs started, Radio Swan and other stations would start a massive series of radio broadcasts urging the people and army to throw out Castro and come to terms (Hunt, 1973, p. 164).

---

[3] Swan Island had been claimed by the United States since 1863 when then-Secretary of State Seward awarded a certificate to the New York Guano Company. In 1856, the U.S. government had enacted a law allowing the President to issue a certificate to any American citizen who discovered phosphates on an unclaimed island. In the 1920's, Honduras attempted to assert its sovereign claim on the island, but it was thwarted by United Fruit Company, which harvested coconuts there. In the 1970's, Honduras pressed its claim for sovereignty over the Swan Island. The U.S. secured the right to maintain a weather station and radio beacon there. Radio Swan reappeared in 1975 broadcasting from San Pedro Suly, the second largest city in Honduras. It continues to transmit propaganda against Cuba and to laud Chile.

In 1960, Phillips located an available 50 kilowatt transmitter in Germany that belong to the U.S. Army. With the help of the Navy, the transmitter was quickly installed on Swan Island. With studios in Miami, Swan was to be a "black" station, that is, its location and its financing were to be a secret. Staffed by Cuban exiles, its commercial format displayed the "rough" edges that would have characterized a legitimate anti-Castro station. Different Cuban exile groups purchased time on the CIA station to promote their particular viewpoints (Wyden, 1979, pp. 22–23; 118).

On April 17, 1961, Radio Swan broadcast the following message: "Alert, alert—look well at the rainbow. The fish will rise very soon. . .the sky is blue. . .the fish is red. Look well at the rainbow" (Wise & Ross, 1964, p. 56). These were coded messages informing counter-revolutionaries in Cuba that the CIA–planned Bay of Pigs invasion was about to start. While the Cuban people fought back the invasion, Swan was saying that "a general uprising on a large scale [has been carried out]" and that "the militia in which Castro placed his confidence appears to be possessed by a state of panic." "An army of liberation is in the island of Cuba to fight with you against the Communist tyranny. . . . Listen for instructions on the radio, comply with them and communicate your actions by radio. To victory, Cubans" (Wise & Ross, 1964, p. 57).

Interestingly, Wyden (1979, p. 209) believes that these messages meant nothing to the Cuban underground. "They were gibberish composed in David Phillip's propaganda shop to build an ambiance of conspiracy."

During the invasion, Swan was on the air 24 hours a day. Even when it was clear that the invasion had failed, Swan continued to broadcast appeals to nonexistent battalions. It ordered various detachments not to surrender and claimed that "help is on the way." After being captured, many mercenaries who heard these broadcasts were bitter at what they felt was misleading information by Swan.

Swan's ties to the CIA have never been conclusively proven. Wise and Ross (1964, p. 335) write that "because it became operationally involved in the Bay of Pigs, [Swan] never enjoyed more than the thinnest of covers." Marchetti and Marks (1974, p. 135) also reach a similar conclusion.

Ultimately, Radio Swan changed its name to Radio Americas (although still broadcasting from Swan Island), and the Gibraltar Steamship Corporation became the Vanguard Service Corporation. But its mission remained the same: to destabilize Cuba.

> It called on Cubans to burn cane fields and to carry matches to be ready for sabotage at all times. It instructed them to go into offices and telephone booths and take the receivers off and hooks to tie up

communications. And it urged the people of Cuba to smash as many bottles as possible. The CIA's reported plan was to curtail the island's beer supply by creating a bottle shortage. (Wise and Ross, 1964, p. 336)

EARLY HISTORY OF RADIO HAVANA CUBA

In 1960, Cuban radio and TV charged that the Swan broadcasts were "a new agression of imperialistic North America" ("Cuba Sees 'Agression,'" 1960). Fidel Castro charged before the United Nations that Radio Swan had been "placed at the disposal of war criminals and subversive groups that are still being sheltered by this country [the United States]" (Kneitel, 1961).

To combat Swan's influence and to broadcast the message of the Cuban revolution to the Caribbean, Central and South America, Castro first turned to the extensive mediumwave facilities he had inherited from the Batista regime. In 1956, UNESCO reported that Cuba was operating 135 radio transmitters (UNESCO, 1956, p. 102). He entrusted Antonio Nunez Jimenez to launch the radio attack on Swan (Stanbury, 1961, p. 53). Jimenez owned station CMBN, La Voz del INRA, and was director of the Instituto Nacional de Reforma Agraria (INRA), established in 1959 to undertake land reform. La Voz del INRA stepped up its power to jam Swan's freqency on 1160 KHz. It also broadcast longer each day than Swan. Under the direction of Adrian Garcia Hernandez, La Voz del INRA adopted a popular commercial format with Cuban music, news, radio plays, and even advertising. There were occasional propaganda messages and many long speeches by Fidel Castro.

Similarly, other mediumwave stations began regional propagandizing. On 860 KHz, CMBL combatted Dominican dictator Trujillo's Radio Caribe, which had been rebroadcasting the programs of the Cuban Freedom Committee. CMGS (Radio Varadero) tried to project its signal to the eastern United States but was often blocked by a Canadian station.

Only one shortwave transmitter was available in Cuba, COBL (Radio Aeropuerto) broadcasting from Jose Marti airport near Havana on 9833 KHz. It could not be heard well in the United States because of interference from teletype and the one hundred kilowatt signal of Radio Budapest on the same frequency (Stanbury, 1961). It soon became apparent to Castro that these shortwave and mediumwave stations could not provide a voice strong enough to have an impact on the region.

In early 1960, the Cuban government announced its intention to establish an international shortwave radio service. A proposed transmission schedule was filed with the International Telecommunication Union in Geneva that summer (Blustein et al., 1971). The station was constructed in late 1960 and early 1961 at Cayo la Rosa near Havana. Swiss transmitters manufactured by Brown Boveri were brought in (Phillips, 1961). The new Cuban station had 120 kilowatts of broadcasting power (Redding, 1971, p. 40).

The first public reference to what was to become Cuba's strongest overseas voice was a reference made by Fidel Castro at the burial of victims of an airport attack by rebel Cuban Air Force pilots: "Do you think they can hide their act before the world? No. Cuba already has a radio station transmitting to all of Latin America. Innumerable brothers in Latin America and the whole world are listening to it" (Perez Herrero, 1982, p. 8). Radio Havana Cuba had begun experimental broadcasts in February 1961 and was identified on the air at that time.

Radio Havana Cuba's birth in early 1961 came at a fortunate moment for the Cuban revolution. In April of that year, a CIA–trained force landed at the Bay of Pigs to try to overthrow the Castro government. During the two months prior to the aborted invasion, Radio Havana Cuba "confronted the slanderous campaign against the Cuba revolution and denounced Washington's preparations to invade our country" (Malmierca, 1977).

One powerful personality loomed over RHC's birth: Ernesto "Che" Guevara, the Argentine medical doctor who joined Castro's revolution in Mexico and later became an active exporter and eventually martyr of the Cuban revolutionary cause. Guevara knew how great a role broadcasting could play in creating and perpetuating revolution. He had helped to create Radio Rebelde (Rebel Radio) in the Sierra Maestra mountains of eastern Cuba. Radio Rebelde was successful in attracting a large audience with its clandestine broadcasts while Castro and his troops fought a guerrilla war against the Cuban dictator (Martinez Victores, 1979). Guevara felt that the most effective propaganda medium was radio because:

> It could reach the reason and emotions of people. . . . Without a doubt, radio ought to be directed by the fundamental principle of popular propaganda—the truth. It is better to say the truth, though it be small in impact, than to tell a grand lie made of tinsel. Above all, radio should give live news of battles, all types of encounters, assassinations, practical teachings to the civilian populations, and from time to time discourses from the leaders of the revolution. (Guevara, 1978, pp. 148–149)

Radio Havana Cuba's propagandistic goals have never been kept secret. Its purpose was "providing continuity in the work of enlightenment, broadcasting the truth, [and] acting as a spokesman for the Revolution and its ideas." It was to be a "faithful reflection of revolutionary Cuba's process." It would "hit hard at the imperialists, the people's enemies," and offer "its fraternal hand to all those who in one way or another fight for their rights and for emancipation, those who hope to free themselves from exploitation and imperialism" (Malmierca, 1977, p. 8). "The essence of RHC's work has been and will always be to unmask imperialism and to alert the peoples of the danger of disunion on the face of its brutal assault" (Perez Herrero, 1982, p. 9).

In other words, Radio Havana Cuba is an avowed, unashamed combatant in the international "war of ideas."

> What we are dealing with is a struggle between two conceptions: information as an ideological-cultural instrument of the imperialist system versus information as a medium for social development, as a mechanism to affirm the identity of the peoples and as an instrument at the service of their cause. (Perez Herrero, 1982, p. 15)

Needless to say, U.S. commentators saw a less charitable purpose in RHC's mission. Its message urged Latin American peoples to overthrow their governments and "to follow the example of the Cuban revolution and throw off the yoke of Yankee imperialism" (Phillips, 1961, p. 13). The *New York Times* radio and TV critic Jack Gould said that RHC "follows essentially the political line of Moscow radio and Peiping radio" (Gould, 1961, p. 79).

In the beginning, RHC's broadcasts were in Spanish and were repeated many times. In mid-evening there were also broadcasts in English. Later, broadcasts were transmitted in French, Portuguese, Arabic, Guarani, Quechua and Creole. By 1963, 188 hours were transmitted per week (Burks, 1964, p. 42). By the end of the year RHC's weekly programming had reached 267 hours (Organization of American States, 1963, p. 20).

Radio Havana Cuba's transmissions had an immediate and large-scale impact. In late 1962, a UPI dispatch said that "it was made known in the United States official circles that a formula is being sought to counteract the propaganda emanating daily from Radio Havana." Nicaraguan dictator Anastasio Somoza is supposed to have said indignantly that he could hear accusations against him "in my own home as if [Radio Havana Cuba] were installed in Managua" (Malmierca, 1977, p. 5).

RHC's Creole broadcasts were one of the few voices raised against the Haitian dictatorship:

> Every night they gather around any available radio, often small cheap transistors, to listen to a fellow countryman who sympathizes with their tribulations . . . the news blackout that hangs over the Haitians is effective except for one great loophole, the communist radio broadcasts from Havana which the population avidly soaks up. (Malmierca, 1977, p. 9)

During the uprising in the Dominican Republic in 1965, RHC broadcast 24 hours per day to provide Latin America and the world with information about the Dominican resistance to the landing of U.S. Marines. The last message released by the constitutionally elected Dominican government over Santo Domingo Radio and Television was picked up by RHC and retransmitted several times while the fighting lasted. The message urged resistance to the invaders of their "brother country" (Malmierca, 1977, pp. 9–10).

By 1963, Cuba held fourth place among Communist international broadcasters in hours per week beamed abroad ("Reds Add 700 Hours," 1963). By 1965, Cuba was broadcasting an estimated 160 hours per week to Latin America (Cozean et al., 1968, p. 22). Programming emphasized the coordination of revolutionary action programs. Relatively simple broadcasts were beamed in Creole to Haiti; guerrilla warfare manuals were read over the air.

More sophisticated programs were beamed to Venezuela and to Chile. Venezuela charged that RHC had fomented riots and had caused enormous damage through sabotage to its oil installations. According to an official report of the Organization of American States, which earlier had expelled Cuba, daily transmissions by RHC encouraged insurgency by the Armed Forces of National Liberation (FALN). Regular broadcasts gave instruction to cadre of the Venezuelan Community Party (PCV) and messages from the FALN to the people (Marryott, 1965, p. 24).

Chile was the object of daily broadcasts in which Castro attacked President Eduardo Frei and his Christian Democratic government as "bourgeois reformists." These special programs to Chile and Venezuela were discontinued in 1969 when, according to the *New York Times,* Radio Havana Cuba's "shrill and abrasive tone" was eliminated due to "signs of Soviet influence" ("Cuba Tones Down Overseas Radio," 1969). Yet its interest in the Chilean political process did not abate. When President Salvador Allende was assassinated and his Popular Unity government overthrown, RHC extended its coverage to 24 hours daily over frequencies throughout Latin America. "In this way all the information on the resistance to fascism and the impressive wave of world solidarity with this brother people was relayed...to Chile and to other Latin American countries" (Malmierca, 1977, p. 13). One correspondent remembers Fidel Castro's emotional description on Radio Havana Cuba of the overthrow of Allende. A weeping Castro told of how Allende in self-protection had fired the submachine gun Castro himself had given him (Esrati, 1978).

During the summer of 1963, Cuba began the first electronic jamming in the hemisphere. Reportedly, the Russians had provided the jamming device to shield Soviet advisors in Cuba from the Russian-language broadcasts of WBT-AM Charlotte, North Carolina. WBT had begun transmitting mediumwave programs prepared by the then-CIA-financed Radio Liberty (Redding, 1971, p. 41).

A year later Cuba began jamming Spanish-language broadcasts from United States mediumwave stations. The noise, sounding much like a whirring buzz saw, jammed VOA transmitters in the Florida Keys, Radio Swan, WGBS Miami (which broadcast news to Cuba), WMIE Miami and WKWF in Key West ("Cuba Said to 'Jam'," 1964). Since 1962, WGBS, WKWF, WWL New Orleans, Radio Caribe from the Dominican Republic, and Radio Americas on Swan Island all had been transmitting programs prepared by the Cuban Freedom Committee founded in Washington by Representative Roman Pucinski (D. Ill.), who believed that Cubans had been "brainwashed with . . . a hate-America campaign." The Cuban Freedom Committee produced programs intended to respond with the "unadulterated truth" (U.S. Outlets Answer, 1962).

The Cuban Freedom Committee's slogan, "Sin Libertad La Vida Nada Vale" (Without Liberty Life is Worth Nothing), was the basis of its program content. Programs were prepared with news, commentary, interviews with Cuban refugees and music. Cuban radio was monitored continuously and replies to Cuban broadcasts were made throughout a program called "La Verdad Responde" (The Truth Answers). Broadcasts were even designed for the Cuban woman. "Programa Para El Hogar" (Program for the Home) discussed the problems affecting families living under Communism. The purpose was "to expose the Communist system so that their listeners will know how to combat it most effectively. [It stressed] that the strongest force for liberation is the Cuban family, and success depend[ed] on the spiritual moral resistance of each member." Most of the Cuban Freedom Committee programs were in Spanish, but some of the news spots on Radio Americas were in English for the West Indies, and in Cantonese for the once-large Chinese population in Cuba (Cuban Freedom Committee, c1962).

Later in the 1960s Radio Havana Cuba provided a unique service to U.S. anti-war activists. From January 8, 1968, to January 8, 1976, RHC broadcast more than 2,500 programs of the Voice of Vietnam in English (Cozean et al., p. 19). As RHC Director Alfredo Vinas (1982) has said, "when the Voice of Vietnam was sent out over our international signal, we felt as ours the suffering and victories of the fighting Vietnamese and their leader Ho Chi Minh."

The Voice of Vietnam followed the example of vitriolic Radio Free Dixie, which used Cuba's mediumwave facilities to exhort revolution among American blacks. Dedicated to "gallant freedom fighters," Radio Free Dixie was organized by Robert Williams, an American Black leader under indictment for kidnapping in North Carolina (Szulc, 1962). Williams urged Black Americans to burn American cities:

> Black men, organize, find arms and form underground and secret
> defense forces! The most effective anti-lynch law and force for justice

is the power of one gas bomb, the switchblade, the razor, the lye-can and the bullet. Mr. Charlie's days are numbered. It is he who is going to be annihilated. Our cause is just. We are not alone. (Cozean et al., 1968, p. 25)

These broadcasts lasted three hours daily until 1965.

Radio Havana Cuba's greatest competition in the region were and continue to be the Spanish-language broadcasts of the Voice of America (see p. 132). Cuban opinion leaders admit that they tune in to the VOA frequently to listen to the news and commentaries (Mas Martin, 1979; Benitez, 1982). Cuban sources indicate that RHC is listened to as much or more than VOA in Central America. Pedro Joaquin Chamorro, assassinated Director of Nicaragua's opposition newspaper *La Prensa*, once declared that "by nine o'clock in the morning everybody in Nicaragua knows what Radio Havana Cuba said the night before. The Voice of America is rarely mentioned" (Malmierca, 1977, p. 11).

But United States Information Agency (USIA) research found that during the late 1960s, more people listened to VOA than to RHC. Six percent of a sample of 3,053 adult and student, rural and urban dwellers in three Central American countries listened to RHC several times a week. In comparison, eight percent listened to VOA several times a week. VOA received many more pluses than Radio Havana on "complete news," "truthfulness," and "impartiality" (United States Information Agency, 1968).

Yet during the same time period, the *Miami Herald* reported that "the Rockefeller mission learned that all over Central America and the Caribbean, Cuban radio propaganda wins out over the Voice of America during prime time." Rockefeller told President Nixon that the VOA "must see to it that its programs are more attractive than those of Radio Havana Cuba" (Malmierca, 1977, p. 11).

RADIO HAVANA CUBA TODAY

In 1982, Radio Havana Cuba was broadcasting 53 hours daily in eight languages (up from 46½ hours in 1979). The English program is 90 minutes long, and it is broadcast 15 hours and 40 minutes a day (12 hours and 40 minutes to America, 2½ hours to Europe, and 1 hour for Africa). The French program is transmitted 6 hours and 20 minutes daily (30 minutes to America, 2 hours and 10 minutes to Europe, and 3 hours and 40 minutes to the Mediterranean and Africa). Portuguese is broadcast 3 hours to the Americas and 2 hours to the Mediterranean and Africa. Quechua, intended for the 16 million Andean Indians of Peru, Bolivia, and Chile, is broadcast 1 hour and 50 minutes daily. Creole for Haiti and the surrounding islands is transmitted 2 hours daily. Arabic is sent to the Middle East 2 hours daily. Guarani, spoken by Paraguayan peasants, is broadcast 1 hour daily.

The bulk of RHC's broadcast time is in Spanish (12 hours and 50 minutes to the Americas, 6 hours and 15 minutes to the Mediterranean and Africa). RHC utilizes 20 frequencies in the 16, 19, 25, 31, 41, and 49 meter bands (Radio Habana Cuba, 1982). From midnight to 6 AM, RHC transmits on mediumwave (AM) for Central America and the Gulf region. The Soviet Union retransmits RHC's signal in Arabic and French to the Middle East.[4]

Twenty-seven percent of Radio Havana Cuba's broadcast is music. Another 27 percent is news. Forty percent of its air day is general programming. The rest is taken up with announcements, identification and sign-off. There are 31 newscasts each day ranging from three to twenty minutes in length (Hernandez, 1979). There are 5 commentaries on weekdays, 2 on Saturday, and 1 on Sunday (Prado, 1982). Every day's broadcast leads off with "Today in History," a short remembrance of some historical event in Cuba's history. After the newscast and editorial, there follows a variety of programs, including "Spotlight on Latin America," "From the Land of Music," "Voices of Revolution," "The Cuban Story," "Latin American Songs," "Socialism: The New World," "Marxist Review," "Philately in Cuba," and "Sports Round-Up."

Radio Havana Cuba has a General Administration (Direccion General) headed by a General Director (Alfredo Vinas in 1982) and three General Vice Directors who oversee programming, information and overseas correspondence, and international relations, respectively. Beneath the General Administration are various Divisions (Direcciones) divided in turn into Departments and Sections. For example, the Programming Administration has a Production Department, a Section for Music, and so on (Prado, 1982).

Though there are very few members of the Communist Party employed by Radio Havana Cuba, the ideological credentials of its personnel are sterling. According to Barreras (1977), 100 percent of its 166 workers have fulfilled their individual emulation contracts and 94 percent have finished with "indices suscritos." They have worked more than 11,000 voluntary hours. In the Socialist Emulation of Cuba they have been awarded "punteros, Moncadistas, Heroic Traditions and the Centro Promotor."[5]

---

[4] RHC General Vice Director Jose Prado reports that in exchange for Cuba's retransmission of Radio Moscow, the Soviet Union and Cuba trade allocated frequencies so that RHC can reach Europe, the Middle East and Africa. The Cuban State Radio Committee, and not Radio Havana Cuba, makes this arrangement. (Prado, 1982).

[5] The Socialist Emulation system in Cuba is a productivity campaign that pits fellow workers in friendly competition (thus emulation) to reach higher work outputs. The Punteros etc. are titles or levels of worker achievement.

Newsgathering at Radio Havana Cuba is done by a central bureau which receives Associated Press,[6] EFE (Spain), TASS (Soviet Union), Reuters (U.K.), ANSA (Italy), and Prensa Latina (Cuba). The news is processed by the central news staff and routed in Spanish to the language services. Eighty to ninety percent of the news received is processed in some way —either rewritten, put into archives, or passed on as is. Language departments are free to adapt the news to their particular audiences. For example, the English service to North America emphasizes news of particular interest to listeners in Canada and the United States.

Cuba has clearly defined information policies which originate within the Cuban Council of State and Ministers and the Communist Party of Cuba. Cuba was one of the first developing country to articulate its cultural and informational policies (see Otero, 1972). The State and Party issue general guidelines on information. "Our station interprets and applies these policy guidelines. . . But *we*, not the government, conform our information to these guidelines. *We* decide what information to offer" (Prado, 1982). "We are not rabbits. These are not guidelines that change every moment. We share a political line and we interpret this line creatively" (Martinez Pirez, 1982).

What are the special objectives of the English service to North America? "First, we should give them [North Americans] perspectives about Latin America and about Cuba. Second, we must give U.S. and Canadian citizens news about events not reported by local U.S. stations." Toward this latter goal, RHC receives numerous North American publications including: *The (New York) Guardian, The New York Times, Akwasasne Notes, Daily Worker, WIN, NACLA Report, Covert Action.* Also the Prensa Latina office at the United Nations relays news of U.S. affairs directly to Cuban newsrooms (Santisteban, 1982).

Radio Havana Cuba personnel have no accurate way of estimating their audience in the United States. According to RHC General Vice Director Jose Prado (1982), thousands of letters arrive from the U.S. each year. Given the unreliability of communications between the two countries, Prado wonders whether additional letters are not lost en route. There is a twice weekly program called "Post Office Box 7026" on which RHC's International Correspondence Division reads listeners' letters over the air and answers questions. Based on these letters, RHC Vice Director Hernandez (1979) believes that most of the North American audience is young.

A review of the sparse literature on the subject of the American shortwave audience might be helpful at this point. This much-neglected audience has been the subject of only a handful of measurement studies.

---

[6] By the terms of the U.S. economic blockade of Cuba, no financial transactions may take place between parties in the United States and Cuba. Associated Press and Prensa Latina exchange their wire services in Mexico.

In 1941, a nationwide survey of 2,902 respondents found that seven per-cent of the sample had listened to shortwave from Europe during the pre-vious week (Childs, 1942). In 1961, Smith surveyed a Midwest American community of 17,000. Only five out of 204 households listened to short-wave broadcasts regularly "for content" at least once a month. His study indicates that U.S. shortwave listenership is limited and that listeners only expose themselves to foreign broadcasts that reinforce already held values, beliefs and interests (Smith, 1962).

Eight years later, Smith described a national survey which indicated an American audience of approximately two million adults, half of whom had listened at least once a week for the past year. Respondents who had a high interest in current events ranked Radio Havana Cuba second as the most listened to station (Smith 1969/70).

Two surveys by the Gallup Corporation give us more precise data about the American audience for Radio Havana Cuba. In a 1975 study commissioned by Radio Canada International, eleven percent of the sam-ple of 3,118 persons claimed to own a shortwave receiver. Thus, total American shortwave receiver ownership could be estimated at something over 22 million. Radio Havana Cuba ranked fifth in popularity behind Radio Canada International, BBC, Deutsche Welle (The Voice of West Ger-many), and Radio Moscow (Radio Canada International, c1975). (See Table 1). Thus, approximately 200,000 Americans listened to Radio Havana Cuba weekly. About 1.3 million Americans listened to RHC at least once a month.

In 1977, the Gallup Corporation carried out a survey for the British Broadcasting Corporation of approximately 6,000 adults in the United States. Seven percent of the sample claimed to have shortwave receivers. Thus, the total potential American audience in this study would be about 15 million. About 180,000 Americans listened to RHC weekly and 400,000 listened monthly in this study (BBC External Broadcasting Audience Re-search, 1978). (See Table 2).

TABLE 1
American Shortwave Owners
Listening to Station's English Broadcasts, 1975

	At least monthly		At least weekly	
	Percent	Number	Percent	Number
Radio Canada Intl	15.2%	3.3 mill.	4.5%	0.9 mill.
BBC	13.3	2.9	4.7	1.03
Deutsche Welle	6.4	1.4	2.2	0.48
Radio Moscow	6.1	1.34	1.9	0.41
Radio Havana Cuba	5.9	1.3	1.2	0.2

Source: Radio Canada International, "Shortwave Radio Listening in the United States, Sur-vey II," (N.p., n.d.). Number calculated by the present author.

TABLE 2
American Shortwave Owners
Listening to Station's English Broadcasts, 1977

	At least monthly		At least weekly	
	Percent	Number	Percent	Number
BBC	10.1%	1.5 mill.	3.8%	0.57 mill.
Radio Canada Intl	9.7	1.4	2.9	0.43
Radio Havana Cuba	2.7	0.4	1.2	0.18

Source: BBC External Broadcasting Audience Research. Survey in the United States: October/November 1977, (N.p., May 1978). Number calculated by the present author.

But RHC English service head Guillermo Santisteban is not convinced. He quotes a UNESCO calculation which says that for every letter there are 10,000 listeners in the audience. He distrusts the VOA and BBC-commissioned studies, for whoever pays for the study always comes out on top. "Suppose Gallup had done a study on Nicaragua during Somoza. During that time we had only one or two letters, but afterwards we learned that almost everyone was listening to us" (Santisteban, 1982).

Radio Havana Cuba's role in the international war of ideas is the subject of much commentary and criticism. Its role in the ideological struggle (as perceived by the Cubans) is best illustrated in a resolution in the mass media which was adopted by the First Congress of the Cuban Communist Party in 1965:

> Overseas radio broadcasts are highly important to our Revolution. As the ideological struggle against imperialism sharpens, they represent a powerful weapon against enemy campaigns and diversionist efforts in the international arena.

> Together with this role in the ideological struggle, overseas radio transmission permits the dissemination of our culture and cultural expression of the brother peoples of the socialist camp, of Latin America and the Caribbean and other countries of the so-called Third World.

> These transmissions should stress publicizing our objectives, achievments and the daily advances of our people in the task of building socialism, spreading Leninist concepts and strengthening links to listeners in all continents. (Malmierca, 1977, pp. 16–17)

HISTORY OF VOICE OF AMERICA'S SPANISH SERVICE

Before there was a Voice of America, Latin America was the scene of one of the first engagements of "radio warfare" between Nazi Germany and the United States. Radio Zeesen, the Nazi External Service, broadcast 12 hours daily to Latin America. Zeesen had once paid Mexicans the dubious

honor of calling them "fellow Nordics." More important, Nazis had infil-
trated Latin America's broadcasting industry and had promoted "canned
programs" which had been "commercialized" in Germany to give them
local flavor (Whitton & Herz, 1942, pp. 23; 31–32). The U.S. made little
attempt to counter either the signal strength or the political impact of the
Nazi propaganda until August 1940, when Nelson Rockefeller became
Coordinator of Commercial and Cultural Affairs between the American
Republics, later renamed Coordinator of Inter-American Affairs (Hale,
1975, p. 101). President Roosevelt organized a coalition of broadcasters to
set up a government shortwave service to Latin America. By July 1941,
WRUL in Massachusetts was broadcasting 50 kilowatts to Latin America.
It was put on the air with $200,000 in contributions from the National
Broadcasting Company (NBC), the Columbia Broadcasting System (CBS),
Westinghouse Corporation and others "to counteract the deluge of short-
wave propaganda emanating from Europe" ("Latin Serenade," 1941).

After World War II, the Voice of America, founded in February 1942,
struggled to stay alive and could find no resources to pursue Latin American programming. In 1958, the VOA was broadcasting only 30 minutes a
day, repeated once, to Latin America—in English! This constituted less
than one percent of VOA broadcast schedule ("Voice of America's $17
Million Pitch," 1958).

The Cuban revolution changed all this. Suddenly, right on its door-
step, the United States found an ideological rival for the hearts and minds
of Latin Americans. On March 21, 1960, a scant fifteen months after Castro's entrance into Havana, the VOA resumed Spanish-language broadcasts "edited with an eye toward Cuba" (Phillips, 1960). In April 1960,
Congress authorized the United States Information Agency (USIA), VOA's
parent agency, to use $100,000 of money previously authorized for other
purposes for a short-term increase in Spanish-language broadcasts "to cul-
tivate friendship with the people of Cuba and to offset anti-American
broadcasts in that country" ("Fund Bill Approved," 1960). Spanish-language broadcasts were beamed six hours per day via shortwave transmitters in Greenville, North Carolina.

At the same time in Washington, the Central Intelligence Agency
(CIA) stepped up plans to direct broadcasts to Cuba from an obscure, barren piece of Caribbean island located off the coast of Honduras. Operated
under the name of the Gibraltar Steamship Corporation, Radio Swan,
named after the island on which it stood, went on the air in summer 1960
(see p. 120).

In February 1961, the VOA announced a series of anti-Castro broadcasts to the Caribbean and Central and South America. Among the first
programs was a one-hour documentary called "Anatomy of a Broken
Promise." It included five prominent anti-Castro exiles and recited a list of

broken promises for free elections and a free press ("U.S. Plans Broadcasts," 1961). But before VOA's programming could gain any accumulated effect, one event singularly devasted U.S. propaganda efforts in the region: the Bay of Pigs invasion.

Some hours after anti-Castro insurgents landed on the beaches of Cuba on April 17, 1961, cots were moved into the Latin American service of the Voice of America. With their broadcast day increased from two hours (one hour of original material, one hour of repeat) to nineteen, the Spanish Branch's sixteen employees would need to catch up on their sleep between duties. For five days they broadcast news, commentaries, features, music and extensive coverage of the United Nations debate. When the debate ended, the schedule was cut to 11 hours daily. News and commentary stressed official pronouncements. Speculation regarding the CIA's role in the invasion was scrupulously avoided.

When the invasion failed and the CIA's role became apparent, the VOA had to retract its previous statements. Then-VOA Director Edward R. Murrow expressed some of the anxiety when he said the VOA was forced to carry the "whole story—Castro's announcement, the self-labelled 'invasion,' the writhing in Washington, the agonies in the United Nations, and even the agonizing reappraisal which a critical aftermath spilled over the Administration" (Kenworthy, 1961).

The Voice of America, and with it the Latin American Division, had been caught off guard. With the expectation of future problems in the region, President Kennedy sought to expand the Spanish-language services of the VOA. He added $3 million to the USIA's budget to expand the Latin American service from six hours daily, all in Spanish, to 22 hours daily in Spanish and Portuguese. He pointed out that the Communists already were broadcasting 134 hours per week in Spanish and Portuguese and "that broadcasts from Havana are encouraging new revolution in the hemisphere" (Raymond, 1962).

By 1962, this expansion had been completed. Early in the year, intelligence sources noticed an increased Soviet military presence in Cuba. President Kennedy called up 150,000 troops. Senators wanted to earmark them for Cuba. The VOA commented that the Soviets had a "lust for power and a disregard for truth" (Raymond, 1962). Radio Swan stepped up its broadcasts. The Cuban Freedom Committee placed hours of anti-Castro programs on Florida and Gulf radio stations aimed at Cuba.

In July 1962, Russian arms and men began arriving in Cuba. Included were medium- and long-range intercontinental ballistic missiles. Overflights by U–2 reconnaissance aircraft showed more than thirty missiles. On October 22, President Kennedy broadcast over the VOA and other national media that he was declaring a naval quarantine of Cuba in an attempt to force the Soviets to withdraw the weapons. The world waited for possible nuclear confrontation.[7]

Kennedy and his Press Secretary Pierre Salinger called on VOA to broadcast the message to all of Latin America. At the time, the Voice of America was broadcasting only via shortwave to Cuba and the Americas. Any effective radio propaganda campaign needed to be conducted on the mediumwave (AM) band as well. Cuba could be saturated much more densely with American mediumwave signals, which could be picked up on many more receivers in Cuba. Before the VOA could set up its own mobile AM transmitters, Salinger devised a plan whereby a powerful network of American commercial AM stations from Florida and the Gulf could flood the Cuban AM band with American reports.

Ten stations immediately volunteered their services and were connected through telephone line patches to the Voice of America in Washington. They included WCKR (10 kilowatts at night), WGBS (10 kilowatts at night), WMIE (10 kilowatts at night), all from Miami; WSB Atlanta (50 kilowatts); WGN Chicago; WWL New Orleans (50 kilowatts); WCKY Cincinnati (50 kilowatts); WRUL Scituate, Massachusetts; WGEL (now KGEI) Belmont, California. These latter two were shortwave stations ("Commercial Stations Magnify Voice," 1962).

An eleventh station should be mentioned in the service of U.S. government broadcasting to Cuba: Radio Americas, the successor to Radio Swan. Its new owner, the Vanguard Company of Miami, reportedly was operating under the direction of the CIA ("Eleventh Station," 1962).

Meanwhile, the VOA tripled its Spanish-language programming via shortwave to 24 hours daily. The number of frequencies also increased from five to eleven. It even broadcast 30 minutes a day in Russian for the Soviet technicians assigned there. The Voice then moved to transmit its signal via mediumwave. Two mobile 50 kilowatt transmitters, each housed in two twenty-foot truck trailers and driven by diesel generators, were moved into the Florida Keys, one at Marathon, the other at Tortuga. They were connected via landlines to Washington ("Voice of America to Demobilize," 1962).[8] The government transmitters were on 1040 KHz at Tortuga and on 1180 KHz at Marathon. The Tortuga transmitter was on the same frequency as WHO(AM) in Des Moines, Iowa, a 50 kilowatt clear channel station serving the entire mid-section of the country. The WHO manage-

---

[7] In an ironic sidelight, just two hours after the Kennedy announcement, Radio Moscow in its Spanish language broadcasts was accusing the United States of building a secret nuclear intercontinental missile base in the jungles of Paraguay! (Hartman, 1962).

[8] Coro believes that the Tortuga transmitter was in fact at Sugar Loaf Key. His transcriptions of the Voice of America for 1962 show an identification stating "This is the Voice of America transmitter at Sugar Loaf Key signing off" (Coro, 1982).

ment complained of interference with the Tortuga transmitter and eventually got the government to shut it down.

But the Marathon transmitter was never shut down, became the VOA's Cuba-directed transmitter, and has remained to this day the only U.S.-based mediumwave governmental international signal, with a directional antenna at 1180 KHz. For many years, WHAM(AM) of Rochester, New York (also on 1180 KHz) complained in the same way as WHO, but to no avail. This transmitter, now called "Radio Marathon,"[9] "has been interfering with WHAM illegally for 19 years . . . in violation of Federal Communications Commission (FCC) allocations and international treaties" (Rust, 1981). Radio Marathon can be heard throughout Cuba and the Caribbean, and WHAM complains that Cuban jamming of that frequency interferes with its signal. The violation of international treaties referred to is the fact that Radio Marathon was not reported to the International Frequency Registration Board, part of the International Telecommunication Union in Geneva, until 1981. It was nineteen years old when the United States finally got around to declaring it to that international body.

But to return to the Cuban missile crisis, across the Atlantic, the VOA, together with Radio Free Europe and other stations, mounted an eight-and-one-half-hour barrage explaining the U.S. position on Cuba. This massive assault used 4,331,000 watts to try to break through Soviet jamming ("'Voice' Reports Success," 1962). The AM barrage aimed at Cuba lasted through November 1962, and cost the ten stations involved $175–225,000 in lost air time, for which each received special commendation from President Kennedy ("Voice of America Helpers," 1962). By December 17, the VOA also had cut its broadcasts aimed at Cuba from 24 hours to one third that much ("Voice Disbands," 1962).

This intense radio propaganda blast at and about Cuba caused considerable consternation in the VOA. These stations' broadcasts reached millions of American ears. The VOA is forbidden by its Charter from broadcasting its programs within the United States. This is supposed to prevent an American presidential administration from using governmental radio channels to propagandize.

But the controversy persisted. Former VOA Chief and USIA Director George Allen said that the overkill barrage aimed at Castro "actually did more harm than good . . . and nothing could have helped him [Castro] more" ("Brickbats and Roses for USIA," 1963). Castro, he said, was able to

---

[9] "Radio Marathon" is a misnomer because it has never since its inception in 1962 originated its own programming. It was and still is a relay or repeater station receiving its audio feed via landlines from the VOA studios in Washington. Some Cubans speak of a Radio Marathon in Miami. They refer to the VOA studies in Miami which in turn routes its material to Washington for broadcast.

claim sympathy as "the target for the largest concentration of propaganda effort unleashed against an individual since Stalin tried to purge Tito in 1948" (Hale, 1975, p. 101).

After the missile crisis, the Cuban-American radio war continued in more moderate fashion. Cuba broadcast Radio Free Dixie and the Voice of Vietnam along with its regular Radio Havana Cuba broadcasts. Some of the personnel from Radio Americas moved under the Voice of America around 1963. VOA's Cuba-directed programming format was known as "Cita Con Cuba" (Rendezvous With Cuba). It broadcast morning and evening programs of news, features, Cuban music and vitriolic commentary. One Cuban author described these broadcasts as encouraging "counter-revolutionary elements [to make] campaigns tending to distort the work of the Cuban revolution" (Fernandez Moya, 1977, p. 248). In 1968, a program called "El Show de la Nueva Ola" (New Wave Show) began. It urged youth to create listeners clubs which, one Cuban believed, would be "converted into antisocial group."

"Cita Con Cuba," staffed primarily by Cuban exiles, continued broadcasting five hours daily from Marathon Key until 1973. On April 1, 1973, it was reduced to a half-hour in the evening and a next-morning repeat. On July 1, 1974, the half-hour repeat was dropped and the time was given to the popular VOA Latin American program "Buenos Dias, America." The Nixon administration had concluded that it would be more productive and persuasive "to incorporate the materials carried in that program into the general flow of programming in Spanish to the Hemisphere." At the same time, for budgetary reasons the VOA reduced its Spanish-language broadcasts to Latin America by two hours daily. The "Cita Con Cuba" slot became part of the new two-and-one-half hour evening magazine show called "Buenas Noches, America." Items formerly carried in "Cita Con Cuba" continued within the general service to Latin America. One reason given for the phase out was lack of news to warrant its continuation (U.S., Congress, House, 1981a, p. 23). In testimony before Congress, U.S. Undersecretary of State Thomas Enders said the reason for dropping the program was because it "was not consistent with the VOA mission" (U.S., Congress, House, 1982a, p. 567).

THE SPANISH SERVICE OF
THE VOICE OF AMERICA TODAY

Today the Spanish branch of the Voice of America is one of 41 languages broadcast daily. The weekly 1983 VOA schedule for all languages lists

981¾ hours, carried over 33 transmitters in the United States and 74 transmitters overseas (U.S., Congress, House, 1982a, p. 116). VOA broadcasts reach an estimated 70 to 80 million listeners each week (Straus, 1978).

VOA ranks third among international broadcasters in weekly worldwide transmissions. The leading services are the Union of Soviet Socialist Republics, with 2,020 hours per week; the People's Republic of China with 1,390; Federal Republic of Germany with 798; Great Britain with 712. However, if Radio Free Europe (555) and Radio Liberty (462) are added to VOA's transmissions, total hours of U.S. governmental broadcasts (1,845) are second only to the Soviet Union (Browne, 1982, p. 358).

Despite this favorable worldwide figure, the United States lags behind Communist nations and other Western countries in broadcasting efforts to Latin America and the Caribbean. Religious station HCJB, the Voice of the Andes, leads the list with 427 hours per week, followed by Cuba, 280; BBC, 186; Soviet Union, 133; Federal Germany, 98; Voice of America, 84; China, 67; Albania, 56; South Korea, 56; and Democratic Germany, 54 (U.S., Congress, House, 1982b, p. 4).

The actual total 1981 VOA budget was $95,987,721 and the estimated 1983 budget is $117,390,000. There were 2,266 people in the VOA, including 54 in the American Republic Division (Spanish and Portuguese to Latin America) in Washington and a correspondent each in Mexico City and Rio de Janeiro. The estimated 1983 budget for the American Republics Division is $2,156,285 for the domestic staff and programming and $307,000 for the overseas bureaus (U.S., Congress, House, 1982a, pp. 116, 120, 124–125, 131–132).

Broadcasts to Latin America were transmitted directly from U.S. facilities in Greenville, North Carolina; Delano, California; Bethany, Ohio; and Marathon, Florida. In addition, broadcasts to the Caribbean basin were also originating from temporary mediumwave facilities in Antigua beginning April 1982. These Antigua facilities are on a U.S. naval base and operate at 1580 KHz with a 3 tower array with an azimuth oriented toward Georgetown, Grenada (Coro, 1982). These Antigua facilities soon will be replaced by a modern automated station. Three additional identical mediumwave stations were to be constructed at Grand Turk and Grand Cayman islands. Alternatively, one of the facilities on Grand Cayman might be placed in Jamaica on a time sharing basis. The existing station at Marathon will be modernized and automated. The Marathon relay station employs six technicians and is slated for a $263,625 budget in 1983. The Antigua relay budget will increase from $12,000 in 1981 to $123,000 in 1983. The Cayman, Turk, and possible Jamaica transmitters are scheduled for about $70,000 each in the 1983 budget (U.S. Congress, House, 1982a, pp. 116, 134).

The Voice of America's Spanish branch broadcasts 38½ hours weekly (5½ hours daily—2½ hours in the morning and 3 hours in the evening). Thus the Spanish branch is fifth largest in hours of transmission with the VOA, after English, Russian, Chinese and Arabic.

The Spanish-language service reaches an estimated 3.6 million listeners in eighteen Latin American countries. While there are no statistics on the audience in Cuba, former Spanish branch Chief Guy Farmer (1979) believes it to be substantial. From letters and from visitors' reports, he believes that many people, especially youth, listen to the Voice. According to Cuban officials, many Cuban leaders start their day with the news from the Voice of America (Mas Martin, 1979; Benitez, 1982).

The morning show, "Buenos Dias, America" (6:30–9:00 AM EST), has been hosted for the last two decades by Jose Perez "Pepe" Del Rio, whose congenial personality has made the show so popular that it is even re-broadcast on many stations in the hemisphere. "Buenos Dias, America" is a radio magazine show with news, music, interviews, special reports, sports, human interest features, scientific reports, historical news and frequent reports from numerous special correspondents in the United States and Latin America.

The evening show, "Buenas Noches, America" (7:00–10:00 PM EST), also utilizes the magazine format. The first hour consists of the standard fifteen minutes of news plus two regular segments, "Noticiero Grafico" (Voice in the News/Actualities) and "Escenario Norteamericano" (U.S. Scene). The next two hours feature rotating emcees presenting news, commentaries, analyses and special features. The evening show is generally more formal than the morning program.

News is the single largest portion of the day's programming and accounts for 25 percent of all broadcast time. Originating from the Central VOA Newsroom, news is broadcast for ten minutes on the hour and five minutes on the half hour during the morning and evening broadcasts. The news is updated occasionally but remains essentially the same throughout each show. "Virtually every part of our broadcast is news-related," stated former Spanish branch Chief Guy Farmer (1979). "Every survey we have made indicates that the main reason people listen to our shortwave Spanish broadcasts is our news."

The VOA newsroom is one of the most sophisticated in the world. One correspondent specializes in Latin American events, but the news is first written in English and then is sent to the various language branches for translation. Occasionally, the Spanish branch will suggest a news item to be included, but the news gathering process is centralized in the main newsroom for all the language services. Thus, one-quarter of the Spanish branch's broadcast time, namely the news, is essentially out of its hands.

The integrity of the VOA newsroom has been a subject of concern for many years. The present VOA Charter, which mandates objective news, was wrestled from Congress in 1976 largely through the efforts of the indefatigable former News Chief Bernard Kamenske. Regarding truth in VOA news: "We report facts: we collect only facts." Asked what ideological position the VOA newsroom might ever espouse, Kamenske stated: "Our only ideology is the irrepressible idealism of the American people. Where we violate that, we have no right to call ourselves the *voice* of America" (Kamenske, 1979).

Supporters of this concept are disturbed by what they see as efforts to make the Voice a global mouthpiece for Administration efforts to rally international support for stronger anti-Soviet policies. Their fears were intensified in 1982 with the highly controversial appointment of Philip Nicolaides, a former Houston radio commentator and contributing editor of *Conservative Digest,* to be VOA Deputy Program Director for Commentaries and News Analysis. The appointment was hailed as a turning point in VOA history by conservatives who agreed with his well-publicized conception of the Voice of America as the nation's first line of defense in the East-West struggle. But Nicolaides was soon ousted and it is not clear where this internal VOA conflict will result (see Marder, 1981b; "Voice Aides," 1981; Goshko, 1982; Fenyvesi, 1981; Bethell, 1982; Friendly, 1982; Grey, 1982).

The VOA is forbidden to broadcast programs that deal exclusively with the affairs of Cuba except as they relate to international foreign policy. Indeed, the author's previous content analysis study of two week's news on the Voice of America (in Spanish) in 1979 substantiates that point. There was only one news item in the sample that treated Cuba (Frederick, 1981).

But the Voice reported that it continued to carry Cuba-oriented materials outside of the news:

> Among the program materials used in the regular Spanish-language programming in the first half of 1980, for example, were interviews with Cuban political prisoners Huber Matos and Emilio Rivero and with a broad cross-section of Cuban refugees in Costa Rica, Peru, Key West, Miami, Elgin Air Force Base, Fort Chaffee, and Indiantown Gap, Pennsylvania. Developments involving Cubans in Angola and Ethiopia are reported to Cuba, as developments in Cuba are reported to Africa. News analyses, commentaries, editorial opinion packages, and special reports and documentaries appear regularly and on special occasions.

> Evidence through the years—the latest coming from the recent influx of refugees—suggests that Cuban listeners have indeed used VOA Spanish as a chief source of information about the outside world, about the United States, and about developments in and concerning their own country. It is not the *form* that has been important to them,

but the *substance* of the broadcasts. And it has been, from the VOA point of view, just as important to keep the rest of the Hemisphere informed regarding Cuban developments as Cuba itself. Creating a separate broadcast "for Cubans only" would in no way increase the supply or availability of appropriate broadcast materials, but could rather be interpreted as a special propaganda campaign, less credible and even dismissable. (Voice of America, 1980)

Any description of the Spanish branch would be incomplete without mentioning the extensive rebroadcasting and local radio placement of VOA programs in Latin America. For years the VOA has had the policy of feeding free programs, often the "back half" (after the news and commentary), to local stations in Latin America. These are taken by 40 percent of all radio stations in 17 countries (Hale, 1975, p. 102). Some stations, quite to the consternation of the VOA, even run commercials among the programs!

In addition, the Spanish branch transmits a daily one-and-a-half hour Correspondent Feed to United States Information Agency offices. These are placed 3,000 times daily on more than a thousand stations during prime time. In Colombia, for example, 200 of 280 stations carry VOA correspondent reports and/or package programs (at least once weekly). VOA research indicates that "there may be a twenty- or thirty-to-one multiplier factor in listenership through local placement" (Farmer, 1979).

The Spanish branch receives about one thousand letters each month. Much of it is directed to the "Club de Oyentes" (Listeners' Club), which responds over the air. According to Farmer (1979), the Branch received 40 letters from Cuba in January 1979 and 52 letters from Cuba in March 1979.

THE NEWEST BATTLE:
RADIO MARTI VS. "RADIO LINCOLN"

By late 1981, officials of the International Communication Agency (ICA, in 1982 renamed the United States Information Agency) were telling Congress of the need to hone the Agency into a "cutting edge" of foreign policy implementation. At the heart of this move was a campaign known as "Project Truth," authorized in outline by President Reagan and the National Security Council in August 1981.

The goals of "Project Truth" were to refute "misleading Soviet propaganda and disinformation" and to "underline the Soviet threat" to world stability and security. At the same time, Project Truth intended to emphasize the commitment of the United States to project peace "from a position of strength" ("Memo Outlining 'Project Truth' Campaign," 1981).

ICA Director Charles Z. Wick directed an interagency committee to coordinate Project Truth. Wick had no illusions about the challenge he faces. He told the National Council of Community World Affairs Organizations: "We are at war . . . We are in a war of ideas with the Soviet Union" (Marder, 1981a).

Within this new political climate but separate from ICA, the Reagan administration announced in September 1981 plans to launch a "Radio Free Cuba," known as Radio Marti. National Security Advisor Richard V. Allen asserted that Cuba's

> leaders have kept the Cuban people ignorant of [Cuba's] campaign of international violence by systematic manipulation of information. . . . The Administration has decided to break the Cuban government's control of information to Cuba. . . . Radio Marti will tell the truth to the Cuban people about their government's mismanagement and its promotion of subversion and international terrorism. (Allen, 1981)

The decision to name the station after Jose Marti (ho-ZAY mar-TEE) was not without some irony, for Marti was one of the most outspoken anti-imperialist and anti-American writers in the late nineteenth century. Poet, revolutionary, journalist and articulate representative of Cuban middle-class radical nationalism, Marti believed that an independent Cuba would pose a threat to U.S. interests in the Caribbean. He tirelessly publicized and raised money among Cubans in the United States for the Cuban independence struggle against Spain. He returned to Cuba to join the fight against Spain and died in a skirmish in 1895.

Marti's name is venerated by Cubans on both sides of the Florida Straits, but, as every Cuban knows, he deeply distrusted the U.S. On the day before his death he wrote to a friend:

> I am in daily danger of giving my life for my country and duty. It is my duty—inasmuch as I realize it and have the spirit to fulfill it—to prevent, by the independence of Cuba, the United States from spreading over the West Indies and falling, with added weight, upon other lands of Our America. All I have done up to now, and shall do hereafter, is to that end. . . . I have lived inside the monster and know its entrails—and my weapon is only the slingshot of David". (Marti, 1970)

Fernandez Retamar (1982), Director of the Center for Marti Studies, told a group of Americans: "Only a government that has demonstrated such repeated evidence of its ignorance can commit such a stupidity of taking the very name of the greatest anti-imperialist we have had. Even the *Washington Post* editorialized its disapproval of the choice of Marti's name ("Cuban Liberty," 1982).

To be fair, though, Jose Marti was a philosopher and political writer whose views often transcend simple anti-Americanism and reach a level of general horror against hegemony. The Presidential Commission on Broadcasting to Cuba has rightly pointed out that Marti "was passionately dedicated to the truth, to democracy and freedom, and to the independence of Cuba from foreign dominance from whatever source. . . . He is perhaps the only such symbol to all Cubans" (Presidential Commission on Broadcasting to Cuba, 1982, pp. 1–2). As Cuban-American National Foundation Director Frank Calzon pointed out in Congressional testimony, Marti's support of democratic principles puts him at odds with the present regime in Cuba. Marti once wrote:

> The continuous, frank and almost brutal debate of open political life strengthens in man the habit of expressing his opinion and listening to that of others. There is great benefit in living in a country where active coexistence of diverse beliefs prevents a timorous and indecisive state to which reason dissents and where a single and unquestionable dogma prevails. (Calzon, 1982)

Though the concept of a surrogate Cuban domestic radio service had its origins in "Cita Con Cuba" (see p. 137), the Radio Marti concept seems to have had its beginning before the Reagan election victory. Perhaps the first mention was in the so-called "Santa Fe Report" of the Council for Inter-American Security. It called for the

> establishment of a Radio Free Cuba, under open U.S. government sponsorship, which will beam objective information to the Cuban people that, among other things, details the costs of Havana's unholy alliance with Moscow. If propaganda fails, *a war of national liberation against Castro must be launched.* [Emphasis added.] (Committee of Santa Fe, Council for Inter-American Security, 1980, p. 46)

Later in 1980, the Campaign for a Democratic Majority, headed by Senators Henry M. Jackson and Daniel P. Moynihan, published a study advocating "a Radio Free Cuba of the intelligence, imagination, and skill of Radio Free Europe" (Thomas, 1980, p. 13).

In the spring of 1981, a member of Reagan's transition team floated the idea of a special broadcasting service to Cuba as part of an aggressive foreign policy approach. Kenneth L. Adelman (1981, p. 932) proposed that the VOA broadcast special programs for Cubans that would include "the casualty rates of Cuban troops in Africa and their discontent at being there, and the declining fortunes of Cubans at home." He also suggested broadcasting reports about Cuban refugees in Florida, about the economic difficulties on the island, and World Bank statistics showing a net decline in Cuba's per capita income since 1960. "Twenty years after the revolution," Adelman wrote, "stringent rationing continues, the economy is declining and unemployment is on the rise. In sum, there is grist enough for a public diplomacy campaign toward Cuba, should policy makers adopt a more confrontational approach."

In June 1981, Senator Jesse Helms proposed to the Senate Foreign Relations Committee that "any program of the United States Government

involving radio broadcasts to Cuba...shall be designated as 'Radio Free
Cuba'" (Gwertzman, 1981). The Inter-American Press Association, which
expelled Cuba in the early 1960s (see Gardner, 1965), brought pressure to
bear on the U.S. At its 37th General Assembly in Rio de Janeiro in October
1981, IAPA passed a resolution "to encourage free journalists...to make
every effort to bring about the end of the news blackout for the people of
Cuba, and support any means that would help achieve that objective."
The conservative Heritage Foundation stated that "direct radio broadcasts
to Cuba, independent of the Voice of America, should be increased to
24-hour service" ("Removing Soviet Influence from Cuba," 1981).

These moves led to a July 1981 meeting at the State Department
where representatives of various concerned agencies examined the various
options available for a stepped up radio broadcasting offensive aimed at
Cuba. In September 1981, National Security Advisor Richard V. Allen announced Administration intent to launch Radio Marti "to break the Cuban
government's control of information in Cuba ... (and to) tell the truth to
the Cuban people" (Allen, 1981).

On September 22, 1981, President Reagan signed Executive Order
12323 creating the Presidential Commission on Broadcasting to Cuba
(Presidential Commission, 1981). The Executive Order directed the Commission to examine such issues as possible program content, information
gathering, writing and editing needs, staffing requirements, legal structure
for a broadcasting organization, proposed legislation, budgets, and the
location, structure and function of possible broadcasting facilities.

The Commission had a decided conservative and anti-Castro com-
plexion. It was headed by F. Clifton White, a public relations specialist in
Connecticut. White ran Senator Barry Goldwater's presidential campaign
in 1964 and also was a senior advisor to the Reagan campaign. Another
Commission member is USIA Director Charles Z. Wick. A lawyer and
former Hollywood music promoter, Wick once told Congress that Communist agents were influencing U.S. media. He raised $15 million for the
Reagan campaign and was a close personal friend of the President (Bumiller, 1982).

Two Cuban-Americans served on the Commission. Jorge Luis Mas
Canosa was president and chief executive officer of Church and Tower of
Florida, Inc., a Miami-based firm of engineering contractors. He lobbied
hard for the Radio Free Cuba idea. Known to be a close advisor to Senator
Paula Hawkins (D. Fla), Mas only became a U.S. citizen in 1981 when it
became essential for his appointment as a commissioner (Silva & Melton,
1982). The other Cuban-American was Dr. Tirso del Junco, Chairman of
the California Republican Party.

The most conservative credentials on the Commission came from
personalities long-known as supporters of right-wing causes in the U.S.

One was Joseph Coors, President and Vice Chairman of Joseph Coors Brewers, whose nomination to the Federal Communication Commission never reached the floor of Congress because of advance opposition. Coors helped launch the Heritage Foundation with $300,000 and has donated yearly about $2.5 million to conservative causes. Another Commission member was millionaire recluse Richard Mellon Scaife. Scaife's philanthropies have supported scores of conservative organizations including the Heritage Foundation and Georgetown Center for Strategic and International Studies. Scaife once owned Forum World Features, exposed in 1975 as a CIA-sponsored operation (Rothmyer, 1981).

Experienced communication professionals included: Herbert Schmertz, Mobil Oil's vice president for public affairs, who developed the company's aggressive campaign of op-ed-like newspaper ads and newscast-like TV commercials; William B. Bayer, outspoken conservative political editor and news commentator for WINZ(AM) Miami; and George Jacobs, noted broadcast engineer, who has long served both the Voice of America and Radio Free Europe/Radio Liberty.

Rounding out the Commission was former Senator Richard F. Stone, who told the House Foreign Affairs Committee that it is "our moral duty" to give the Cuban people freedom of information. The Commission's staff was headed by career foreign service officer George Landau and included Yale Newman, former director of the American Republics Division of the Voice of America.

In addition to the Commission, a non-profit entity called Radio Broadcasting to Cuba, Inc. was created. It would serve the same role for Radio Marti that the Board for International Broadcasting did for Radio Free Europe/Radio Liberty. Its three Board members were Midge Dector Podhoretz of the Committee for a Free World; Robert Walter Zimmerman, former Foreign Service Officer; and William P. Stedman, Jr., retired ambassador. Such an entity would allow the station to receive private funds before it is authorized by Congress.

The goals of Radio Marti, as explained in the enacting legislation (H.R. 5427) stated that:

> It is the policy of the United States to support the right of the people of Cuba "to seek, receive, and impart information and ideas through any media and regardless of frontiers," in accordance with Article 19 of the Universal Declaration of Human Rights. (U.S., Congress, House, 1982b, p. 1)

Its specific goals were to provide an alternate, reliable source of information concerning Cuba's domestic and international policies and actions which, according to the Commission, the Cuban people were lacking; to provide the information necessary for the Cuban people to make informed judgments on these policies and actions and to try to hold their government more accountable; to provide news and analysis that is not manipulated by the state but is objective, accurate, credible, relevant and timely (Presidential Commission on Broadcasting to Cuba, 1982, p. 3).

The Reagan Administration disavowed any belligerent or propagandistic role for Radio Marti. The station intended to exert pressure over the long term, not to incite disaffection on the short run. In testimony before the House Foreign Affairs Committee, Assistant Secretary of State for Inter-American Affairs Thomas Enders (1982, pp. 4–5) stated "it would be immoral, irresponsible to set a people against a government that monopolizes the means of coercion." Conditions in Cuba were "provocation enough," he said. Radio Marti's role was to "give Cubans the means they now lack to know what kind of society has been imposed on them." Enders compared Radio Marti to the operation of Radio Free Europe (RFE), which he said had changed the political climate in Poland over the long run.

Nevertheless, Enders declared that Radio Marti would not broadcast propaganda: "We will not succeed in attracting an audience in Cuba if we offer them propaganda. If there are false reports, the listeners will react. If false reports continue, they will turn off. . . . So it must be a creature of no political tendency, of no action group, of no vested interest." On the contrary, Enders said he expected that Radio Marti would have to work years, as did Radio Free Europe, to earn its audience.

Plans were to use one 50 kilowatt transmitter located at Saddlebunch military reservation in Florida. Another transmitter of greater power was to be located later somewhere in the Caribbean, perhaps on Cayman, Turk, Jamaica, or Antigua. Technical studies by the Federal Communication Commission and the Department of Defense indicated the best frequency for Radio Marti to be 1040 KHz (later changed to 1180 in the 98th Congress). The Presidential Commission also recommended consideration of additional frequencies in order to make Cuban jamming of Radio Marti broadcast more difficult.

Although Congress had not yet voted the funds for Radio Marti, the U.S. Navy began construction of four 250-foot transmitting antennas for the station 12 miles north of Key West, Florida (Martinez & Ducassi, 1982; Martinez, 1982; Fruhling, 1982; "U.S. Is Said to Build Antennas," 1982; Weintraub, 1982). According to Department of Defense plans, the transmitter was to serve a dual function: as Radio Marti's transmitter and for a classified Defense function. The latter activity could presumably allow the Department of Defense to seize Radio Marti's facility in times of crisis, such as during the Cuban missile crisis (see p. 134). According to a House Appropriations Committee internal document, when the Radio Marti proposal ran into lengthy delays in Congress, the Secretary of Defense directed the Navy to proceed with construction because the Defense Department could not wait any longer to get a facility for its 'classified' function.

During all of the legislative battle, the Presidential Commission continued to plan its programming strategy for Radio Marti. Of the 168 staff positions recommended, 148 were program-related. Personnel would be drawn from the ranks of professional broadcasters and newspersons with special emphasis on Hispanic, including Cuban, backgrounds. The station was to begin with 14 hours a day (9 hours plus 5 hours of repeats) of news commentaries, and entertainment programming. News would include information about Cuban domestic and international affairs which was unreported or underreported in the Cuban mass media. For example, news of casualties and costs in Cuba's Angola and Ethiopia interventions were intended "to enable the Cuban people to have the means by which they can hold their own government to some degree accountable. . . . The Cuban people are deprived of the means of . . . influencing policies of their government" (Enders, 1982).

One of the greatest tasks Radio Marti had was to gather timely and reliable information about events inside Cuba. After all, Radio Marti's predecessor, Cita Con Cuba, was cancelled for lack of reliable information (U.S., Congress, House, 1981a).

According to Presidential Commission, the station would follow the standards of the U.S. professional press. The station's information "journalistically will be responsible, will be comprehensive, and will be verifiable" (Serafino et al., 1982, pp. 10–11). The standards cited in the Interim Report of the Presidential Commission on Broadcasting to Cuba were:

> The news must be accurate, objective, timely, interesting and relevant to the concerns of Cuban listeners. Materials made available for newscasts should be thoroughly verified by news personnel as to facts and sources, as well as to avoid any suggestin (sic) of bias or sensationalism. Confirmation by two independent sources is required when facts appear to be in doubt. Clear attribution to the source is required when the information content clearly constitutes opinion or can be considered partial or self-serving. (Presidential Commission on Broadcasting to Cuba, 1982, pp. 1–2)

Radio Marti's programming plan stated that the news department would subscribe to six wire services—Associated Press, United Press International, Foreign Broadcasts Information Service (a Commerce Department monitoring service), Reuters, EFE from Spain, and Caribbean News Agency. However, only two of these news agencies had correspondents in Cuba. Reportedly, Radio Marti had contacted the European offices of news agencies who had correspondents within Cuba to inquire whether their staff might be willing to cooperate. One Cuban sources claims that at least one news agency categorically refused to cooperate (Ramirez Corria, 1982). Associated Press had no representaiton in Cuba, though it exchanged its news wire with the Cuban Prensa Latina agency in Mexico City. FBIS had monitoring posts in South Florida, where it picked up Cuban broadcasts. Caribbean News Agency concentrated strictly on English-speaking Caribbean countries and rarely carried news on Cuba.

Popular entertainment programs would attract the listener and draw him to newscasts and commentaries. Romance-filled "radionovelas" (soap operas) from Mexico, Venezuela, and Colombia, unavailable in Cuba, might be popular on Radio Marti. Among the other suggested programs were: recorded excerpts of Castro's past speeches on political and economic pledges he has not kept; political satire programs on contemporary Cuban life; a radio drama series on the history of the Cuban family covering several generations. The New York Yankees and Los Angeles Dodgers franchises offered their Spanish-language broadcasts free of charge to the government. Popular Mexican music, now available from many Miami stations, could also draw a substantial youth audience. According to the Presidential Commission, "entertainment features. . . should help expose Cuban listeners to the spontaneity, creativity and diversity of free societies (Presidential Commission on Broadcasting to Cuba, 1982, p. 4.)

All of this caused a great deal of concern in Cuba about the intrusion of Marti's signal. Cuba prepared both domestic and international responses. On the domestic side, Cuban radio and TV expanded local and national public affairs and news coverage. The daily "Revista de la Manana," a daily morning magazine-format show, expanded to six hours. Such expansion was due in part to the competition from Radio Marti to provide more "hard news."

But the most dramatic Cuban response for North Americans would be the launching of a new 500 kilowatt superstation, dubbed by some Cubans "Radio Lincoln," which could reach the entire United States. This new station would not only produce interference with U.S. stations operating on that frequency but would generate adjacent channel interference up to four channels from its frequency. Its programs were to include proper south-of-the-border music, news of minority struggles in the U.S., baseball, and, of course, Communist commentaries on U.S. "adventurism" overseas and repression at home. Much of the programming would be in English and receivable on ordinary AM radios. Hispanic-Americans might find programs directed at them in Spanish on immigration issues, farm labor struggles, Central American news, and musical-cultural programs. Black Americans and poor whites might also hear programs designed to create dissatisfaction in them.

Cuban communication experts were quick to point out that such a station is an enormous drain on their scarce resources. They preferred not to engage in an escalated radio war. But Radio Marti was seen as such an overt act of aggression that it demanded a considered response of high production quality and a high investment in equipment and electrical energy.

Yet this Cuban concern about an escalated radio war is belied by the fact that Cuba announced plans for two 500 kilowatt superstations in 1979, long before Radio Marti was conceived. Cuba seems to have used Radio Marti as an excuse for something it intended to do all along.

THE INTERFERENCE WAR

Intimately connected with the growing radio war was the so-called "interference war." This refers to the growing amount of unacceptable signal disruption caused by radio transmitters that operate on the same or nearby frequencies. Interfering channels, known as incompatibilities, make it difficult or impossible for listeners to comprehend messages. For U.S. commercial broadcasters this is doubly vexing because the lost signal quality and reach also means lost advertising revenue. To put this rather technical discussion into perspective, a brief overview of AM or mediumwave signal propagation is in order.

AM radio allocations are subject to international agreements established through the International Telecommunications Union (ITU) in Geneva and supplemented by regional agreements. By international agreement the AM channels extend from 535 KHz to 1605 KHz. Each AM radio station is allocated a 10 KHz bandwidth, thus allowing 107 AM channels. At the 1981 ITU Conference in Region 2, a proposal was rejected that would have put the Western Hemisphere on a 9 KHz spacing, the standard which the rest of the world uses. (See "Ray of Hope," 1981; "AM Future on the Table," 1981.)

Radio waves are propagated outward from the transmitting tower. Normally they radiate in a perfect circle, but a directional antenna can conform the waves to desired contours. The AM wave travels both through the ground and the sky. In practice, AM ground waves can cover a radius of 15 to 120 kilometers from the transmitter depending on transmitter power, the frequency of the channel, the conductivity of the soil, the amount of interference present, and other factors. Sky waves of AM stations reach far beyond this radius and can be heard by receivers located 200 to 2500 kilometers from the transmitter. Sky waves depend on the ionosphere and are most reliable at night when the sun does not distort the ionosphere.

Because Cuba and the United States are so close (140 kilometers separates them), for years the two nations coordinated their frequency assignments to minimize mutual interference. Cuban and American radio systems grew up side by side. Indeed, some of Cuba's radio infrastructure was designed and built by U.S. broadcasters (Lopez, 1981). By the 1940s, both systems were thriving and increasingly interfering with one another and with other Caribbean and North American countries.

In 1950, under the pre-revolutionary government, Cuba agreed to a U.S. plan called the North American Regional Broadcast Agreement (NARBA). Signatories were the United States, Canada, Mexico, Cuba, the Bahamas, and the Dominican Republic (which never ratified it). NARBA divided the 107 channels of the AM band into local, regional, and clear channels, and specified power limits for each. The U.S. received 24 unduplicated clear channels and 19 shared clear channels; Canada received 6 and 4, respectively; Mexico, 7 and 5; Bahamas, 1 and 0. Cuba ended up with one unduplicated and one shared (with Canada) clear channel to service the entire 700-mile long island (Head, 1976, p. 41).

At the time NARBA was first signed, according to Coro (1982), the Cuban delegates were neither capable engineers nor skilled negotiators. "The possibility of expansion of Cuban radio in 1959 [the year of the Cuban revolution] was next to zero." This was because Cuba accepted an interference standard (26 decibels between the desired and undesired stations, or a 20:1 ratio) that put it at a disadvantage. At a 20:1 ratio, if there was a 50 kilowatt station in Nashville, the Cuban station on the same frequency could broadcast only 250 watts at night. "So the development of Cuban radio broadcasting was blocked by the presence of a very large number of U.S. stations radiating high intensity signals to here."

Despite its status as a treaty signatory, Cuba did not abide by the terms of NARBA. Exactly when Cuba began ignoring NARBA is uncertain. Some claim that Castro never really abided by its terms, while others say that it has only been since 1980 that interference has become a significant problem. In addition to unintentional interference, Cuba has been deliberately jamming a Miami station (WQBA) for 13 years. This station broadcasts in Spanish the viewpoint of the Cuban exile community in Florida.[10] In 1980, Cuba gave the required one year's notice of its intent to withdraw from NARBA, an action that took effect in November 1981.

Canada and Mexico also have felt the same domination of U.S. signals. As a result, Cuba, Canada, and Mexico have announced their intention to abrogate the NARBA agreement. Of course, bilateral negotiations have continued on all sides, for there is a built-in incentive to reach agreement. No one wins when an interference war escalates.

---

[10] The details of Cuban interference, intentional and unintentional, have been discussed in several sets of Congressional hearings during 1981. See the hearings before: House Committee on Foreign Affairs, Subcommittee on International Operations (June 1981 and June 1982); House Committee on Government Affairs, Subcommittee on Government Information and Individual Rights (October 1981); and House Committee on Energy and Commerce, Subcommittee on Telecommunications (May 1982).

Mutual benefit was the apparent goal that even arch-antagonists Cuba and the United States seemed to have chosen until late 1981, when the two issues—Radio Marti and interference—collided. Bilateral meetings had been working amicably to resolve these problems. But the announcement of Radio Marti in September 1981, and the clash over frequency changes at the ITU Regional Administration Radio Conference on Medium Frequency (MF) Broadcasting in the Western Hemisphere (also known as the "Rio Conference") wrecked these good faith efforts.

In 1979, as part of its preparations for the "Rio Conference," Cuba had submitted to the ITU a list of 188 operating and planned stations. Under the abrogated NARBA agreement, Cuba could operate as many as 174 AM stations, although only 75–80 were on the air at that time. Thus, the number of on-air stations would have more than doubled. Power levels would have increased substantially too. Two were to be huge 500 kilowatt superstations that could be heard as far away as Alaska and Hawaii. Further aggravating was the fact that Cuba does not use directional antennas.

A National Association of Broadcasters (1982) study predicted that over 200 U.S. AM radio stations in 34 states and the District of Columbia would experience interference and reduced listening areas under the proposed Cuban inventory. Formerly clear channels would lose their entire nightime coverage. Thirty-seven clear channels would lose large portions of their service areas. In particular, the two 500 kilowatt stations, operating on 1040 KHz and 1160 KHz as indicated by the Cubans, would drastically reduce the service area of the two U.S. "clear channel" stations on those frequencies (WHO, Des Moines, and KSL, Salt Lake, respectively).

Whether Cuba actually intended to implement all these changes was questionable. One factor weighing against such plans is the amount of electricity required for these stations. According to engineer Michael Rau of the National Association of Broadcasters, the input power for a radio station is approximately twice that of the output. The proposed and operating radio stations listed by the Cubans would require a total of 5.4 megawatts of power (Serafino et al., 1982, p. 51).

Yet the determination on the part of the Cubans to go through with this plan seemed to be there, at least in public. Cuban Deputy Foreign Minister Ricardo Alarcon told the *Washington Post* that Cuba would respond with stepped-up transmissions that would block commercial programming in the United States (Dickey, 1982). An internal Congressional memorandum predicted that Cuba would definitely jam Radio Marti if and when it goes on the air and that Cuba has the capability to carry out its threat to jam U.S. radio broadcasts.

Florida broadcasters have complained for years about Cuban interference. The South Florida Radio Broadcasters Association reported that at least 20 stations in the state were experiencing Cuban-caused interference ("AM Future on the Table in Rio," 1981). In an internal International Communication Agency memorandum it was noted that Cuban jamming of Radio Marti alone would affect radio stations in Mexico, Central America, and northern South America. But, it goes on, the United States will be seen as responsible since it originated the signal (Case, 1982). Some received FCC permission to increase their power as a countermeasure. Others have been stymied because a power increase would damage the signal of another United States station or because of the high cost of instituting such a change. Technically, the U.S. also violated the NARBA treaty with these power increase authorizations.

To be fair, Cuban broadcasters also experienced considerable interference from U.S. and other Caribbean radio stations. The protection ratio was not sufficient to safeguard full utilization of many assigned Cuban frequencies. For example, WCAU from Philadelphia drowned out a Cuban station in Santi Spiritus. KMOX from St. Louis made this frequency unusable to the Cubans. According to Coro (1982), the U.S. AM system is so well engineered that it "solves some of its incompatibilities between its own stations (especially nightime). . . by beaming its signals to the south (to Cuba) so as to be able to accomodate more stations in the U.S.

One American reporter described the Cuban side of the story:

> as the dial spins down the AM band [in Havana], WTOP from Washington announces beach traffic conditions on the Bay Bridge. . . . Half a dozen other American commercial stations came in clearly. . . . A Southern evangelical preacher brings me the message of Moses and the Burning Bush. Then Miami's WGBS reminds the radio audience of how Americans loved "My Favorite Martian." ("WTOP Fades," 1982)

In summer, 1981, U.S.-Cuban negotiations briefly appeared on the verge of breaking the impasse. Both sides offered technical solutions to many of the incompatibilities. During the second bilateral meeting in Washington in August (the first had been in Havana in April), the *New York Times* leaked a report that the U.S. was planning a "Radio Free Cuba" (Gwertzman, 1982, p. A7). Not even that perturbed the Cuban negotiators.

But just before the Rio Conference, Richard Allen's announcement left the Cubans no room for graceful maneuvering. The Cubans submitted a list of changes to their original inventory, changes that seemed to be detrimental to U.S. stations and beneficial to other Caribbean broadcasters.

The U.S. delegation successfully argued against the Cuban proposal and it was rejected. In the last week of the conference, the Cuban delegation walked out, denouncing the United States because of the plans for Radio Marti, U.S. operation of Radio Marathon (which the Cubans termed "illegal"), and the successful U.S. effort to prevent Cuba from making the 48 changes.

The U.S. delegation reportedly was surprised at the Cuban move, since neither Radio Marti nor Radio Marathon had arisen previously as issues. The Cubans claimed that they had three meetings with U.S. delegates at which the U.S. demonstrated no interest in eliminating or limiting Radio Marathon broadcasts; the U.S. delegates at the conference were quoted as saying that the issue was never raised ("Cuban Walkout," 1981).

Clearly, the interference issue is a two-way street. The choice is stark: mutual accomodation or chaos. There is a built-in incentive for neighbors to resolve these differences. But the Radio Marti proposal inflamed the underlying mutual distrust to the point where bilateral negotiations were broken off.

As a result of the walkout and withdrawal from NARBA, Cuba was no longer bound by any AM broadcasting agreement, and could operate in whatever manner it chose. At the same time, other countries were not required to protect Cuban radio stations from interference. Cuba notified the ITU that it intended to make the 48 unilateral changes which were blocked by the United States at Rio ("Lingering Cuban Problem," 1982).

The Cubans apparently began implementing some of the changes included in the 1979 plan during 1980 and 1981, but more changes have occurred since the Rio conference. The clear channel station operating at 1160 KHz (KSL Salt Lake) began experiencing measurable interference from a Cuban station. And when in late summer 1982 it appeared that Congress might soon pass the Radio Marti bill, Cuba let go an electronic volley that WHO General Manager called the "first firing of a radio war." Cuba broadcast on five frequencies for four hours on August 29, 1982. Officials from WHO in Des Moines said they had calls from listeners in Texas, Missouri, Tennessee and Iowa saying the WHO signal was being wiped out or affected by the Cuban broadcast. Another two volleys were put on clear channel frequencies assigned to WMAQ (Chicago) and KSL (Salt Lake). Two other frequencies disrupted were regional channels used by a variety of lower-powered stations across the United States ("Cuba Accused of Waging 'Radio War'," (1982).

AN EVALUATION AND A MODEST PROPOSAL

> If Mao was correct in saying that "power grows out of the barrel of a gun," ideology is the force that triggers the gun. (Cherne, 1979, p. 47)

Our age has seen a period of intense ideological conflict. Exacerbated by global confrontations and aided by instantaneous communication, the ancient battle of opposing human belief systems has grown in scale to become one of the most intense means of conflict today. Nations devote huge resources to promote their particular views of the world and to win over people of other nations—all in the name of ideology.

Today's two major opposing ideologies, capitalism and communism, each have systematized sets of ideals rooted in seemingly rational, commonly intelligible, "self-evident" (at least to the espouser) patterns of thinking and viewing the world. Each puts forward certain material and moral goals for its society. Each emphasizes values to guide individual lives. Each provides systems to satisfy basic human needs and to accumulate resources for future prosperity. Irreconcilable though they may be, capitalism and communism both may rightly claim to be champions of human achievement in this century, for both have elevated the standard of living in societies in which they have held sway.

In this paper we have been concerned with only part of the Cuban-American conflict: the Cuban-American radio war. The gatherers and transmitters of ideological information between the two systems serve a vital function. They both reflect and create the ideological content of their respective systems. As receptors and emitters of ideology, Radio Havana Cuba, the Voice of America, Radio Marti, "Radio Lincoln," and all of the commercial, priate and clandestine stations in the Caribbean area are but small reflections of the broader conflict that goes on around them. All of them claim to adhere to the highest standards of truth and objectivity. Here lies the crux of the issue.

Within the newsroom and board room of these radio stations real men and women with conscious and unconscious biases shift daily through the deluge of incoming messages. Their task is to select some and to reject others for further transmission to their audiences. All producers of messages operate within a fundamentally ideological context which compels them to select certain events or opinions as important and to reject, or simply not to recognize, others. There is no such thing as nonideological newsgathering. Neither the so-called "free press" nor the so-call "controlled press" can claim to have a hold on objectivity. No journalist can escape the fact that "all news are views; . . . all editorial choice patterns . . . have an ideological basis" (Gerbner, 1964, p. 495). As delegated representatives of opposing belief systems, these radio stations reflect the ebb and flow of tensions within and between the systems that created them.

But beyond ideology, the astute observer should try to ascertain what the unstated goals of this radio war might be. Fears have been expressed that the true intent of Radio Marti, for example, is to destabilize Cuba. As Professor LeoGrande noted in his Congressional testimony:

> We should not fail to mention the possibility, however remote, that
> Radio Marti may be part of a wider effort aimed at overthrowing the

Cuban government by force of arms. . . . Given the Reagan Administration's obvious preoccupation with and animosity towards Cuba,
and its stated intention to restore covert action to the arsenal of
foreign policy instruments, one cannot dismiss the possibility that
Radio Marti is intended to play the same role as Radio Swan was two
decades ago. (LeoGrande, 1982)

To be sure, no one in the Reagan administration has stated these
goals in so many words, though members of the highest levels of government have in the past implied that this was the purpose of such a station
(see Committee of Santa Fe, 1980). In public statements, the administration
has disavowed any belligerent or propaganda role for Radio Marti. As
Assistant Secretary of State for Inter-American Affairs Thomas O. Enders
stated, "it would be immoral, irresponsible to set a people against a government that monopolizes the means of coercion." Conditions in Cuba are
"provocation enough." Radio Marti would "give Cubans the means they
now lack to know what kind of society has been imposed on them"
(Enders, 1982).

But in private conversations, administration officials have had quite
another thing to say about Radio Marti's goals. According to a source close
to WHO-AM (Des Moines), Jim Duncan, a member of the Special Advisory
Staff to the Deputy Under-Secretary of Defense for Policy, Fred Ikle, told
WHO officials that the establishment of Radio Marti was "an international
game of chicken, and the U.S. *will not* blink." He told them that by setting
up Radio Marti the U.S. will be "drawing a line across which Castro will
know he cannot step across without paying for it." Cuban interference, he
added, would be a violation of international law, and the U.S. would then
have the legal justification for going in and *"surgically removing"* their
transmitters. Kenneth R. Giddens, former head of the Voice of America
and now a consultant helping to set up Radio Marti, told WHO it should be
"proud to be on the front lines" of this effort, which was characterized as
a battle for freedom.

The model by which the Administration is operating is to create a
Radio Free Cuba in the image of Radio Free Europe/Radio Liberty, that is,
to effect changes in the Cuban government over the long run. In reality,
though, Radio Free Europe, Radio Liberty and Radio Free Asia (now
defunct) were set up in the 1950s precisely to "liberate" the peoples of
Eastern Europe, the Soviet Union and China. Their CIA financing was
kept secret until 1971 (see Price, 1972; Adelman, 1981; Marchetti & Marks,
1974).

In the 1950s, these stations operated as voices of an aggressive foreign policy in an attempt to destabilize the governments at which they
were directed. When "liberation" proved unfeasible, these operations
conformed their messages to the new U.S. policy objectives, long-term
"liberalization" of these governments. Their programming was intended

to provide an alternative "home service" for these peoples, which would provide news and entertainment banned in their homeland. Through "cross-reporting" techniques, news of liberalizations or improvements in living standards (by Western criteria) were relayed from one "enslaved" nation to the other, and thus created discontent. If Hungarian workers achieved a more liberal labor agreement, Polish workers would then push for similar concessions, it was thought.

Since 1974, Radio Free Europe and Radio Liberty have operated under the oversight of and funding from an independent government monitoring agency, the federally-chartered Board for International Broadcasting, Inc. This gives these stations a measure for autonomy from the Executive branch. Radio Liberty broadcasts to the Soviet Union and targets "the narrow but politically important Soviet dissident community" (Adelman, 1981, p. 930). Radio Free Europe broadcasts to the other nations of Eastern Europe. It tries to appeal to the entire population of these countries. According to Adelman, "55 percent of adults in Poland and Romania —and a third to a half in Hungary, Czechoslovakia and Bulgaria—tuned into RFE at least once a week. During a crisis, the listenership may soar to a staggering 80 percent of those over 14 years old."

Radio Free Europe is credited by the Reagan Administration and others with important assistance to the opposition in Eastern Europe, particularly Poland, during the past decades. This view is corroborated by a recent European report:

> Knowledgeable observers of Eastern Europe and the communist leadership are certain that events in Poland would have taken a different course if the populace in Silesia, Warsaw and Poland had not been kept constantly informed by Western radio stations (including the VOA, RFE, and BBC and *Deutsche Welle*) about the developments in Gdansk and Szczecin. (Stamm, 1980, p. 31)

This, then, is the model that the current administration has regarding broadcasts to Cuba. But the analogy of the current situation in Eastern Europe (particularly Poland) and Cuba is faulty. Further, the model is based on a discredited, though appealing, theory of communication.

The analogy with Poland simply does not hold up. Communism was imposed on Poland against the will of its people. Cubans, on the other hand, brought about a revolution against a hated dictatorship without outside intervention. Even during the worst of economic and social times in Cuba, the Cuban government has enjoyed a legitimacy and support never equalled in Poland. The Solidarity movement and Polish nationalist sentiments in general are directed against the Soviet Union, and thus serve to undermine the Polish government's link with its main outside supporter. Cuban nationalism, on the contrary, is anti-U.S., which strengthens its links with its outside supporter. No institution in Cuba can rival the historic importance of the Polish Catholic Church as an institutional and ideological rival to the regime. Finally, while Polish government has exacerbated tensions by responding to popular disaffection with empty promises, the Cuban government has acted pragmatically to defuse discontent with real reforms, honest explanations, and sincere efforts to the extent of its capabilities.

In addition, the analogy with Radio Free Europe/Radio Liberty is based on an outmoded communication theory. The "hypodermic model" of communication and persuasion posits that the communicator need merely fill his electronic syringe with carefully crafted messages and inject them into the target population to achieve a particular communication effect. Most international propaganda and communication research in the pre-1945 era was based on this model. In the post-World World War II era, communication researchers began to see that mass communication does not take place in such a linear, cause-and-effect environment. Other factors mediate the intended response. The audience is not a passive recipient but rather processes incoming information. The particular social and cultural circumstances of the recipient, the attitudes and opinions he might have regarding the message, the particular environment in which he hears the message, the way in which the message comes to him: All of these factors suggest that the viewer, reader or listener selects or rejects, internalizes or acts upon available messages based on complex psychological and social processes.

For example, people typically avoid messages that are dissonant with existing beliefs and would cause some internal tension ("cognitive dissonance"). Alternatively, people actively seek out or readily accept information that confirms existing beliefs or opinions. In international propaganda, it seems that the recepient would not actively seek out information that diverges from pre-existing beliefs or ideologies. Instead, he would seek out and listen to information that confirms or reinforces his beliefs. Radio Marti, as a voice of the United States government, probably would not be widely listened to in Cuba. Cubans already listen to U.S. radio. By and large, they have a faith and trust in their own government, and they do not find the news coming from present U.S. stations to be credible on Cuban affairs.

Indeed, as U.S. diplomats stationed in Havana have pointed out, Radio Marti could well have precisely the opposite effect intended ("U.S. Diplomats in Cuba Dissent," 1981). Historically, Fidel Castro's most effective political appeal has been to rally nationalist sentiment to resist attacks and threats from the United States. The defeat of the CIA-backed mercenaries at the Bay of Pigs in 1962 is still used by Castro as a propaganda tool. In Cuba today one sees billboards proclaiming "Use the Spirit of the Bay of Pigs to Graduate from the Ninth Grade" or "Use the Spirit of the Bay of Pigs to Harvest a Bumper Sugar Crop." The U.S. economic blockade is used constantly in Cuba's propaganda overseas to support its image of the North American "warmonger." Obviously, negative and propagandistic programming on Radio Marti might simply serve to stimulate Cuban nationalism and to enhance the Cuban regime's legitimacy.

If Radio Marti does succeed in creating discontent in Cuba, there could be substantial costs to the United States. One of the Cuban government's most effective mechanisms for managing discontent has been simply to export it to the United States. According to the Congressional Research Service, the total costs associated with the influx of 125,000 Cubans during 1980–81 was over $739 million, or $5,914 per emigrant (Jones, 1982).

For those people, the present author included, who are working to bring Cuba and the United States closer together, what is needed is not a radio voice that pits confronting ideologies against each other. *What we need is a radio service that acts as an interpreter or arbitrator of opposing ideologies,* one that affirms the legitimacy of both systems and works for greater understanding between Cuban and American people.

What we need is a *Radio Romero,* a broadcast voice of reconciliation and coexistence named after the life and work of the great assassinated Salvadoran Archbishop Oscar Romero.

Romero stood for human rights and for the dignity of the people in the face of incorrigible governments. He fought valiantly to overcome injustice and condemned the violence of all sides. No better symbol of peace and hope could be found for such an endeavor.

Radio Romero would broadcast from international waters in the Gulf from a ship equipped with 100 kilowatt transmitter on the AM band. Its message would be a progressive voice in support of peaceful and democratic change in the Americas. Its youth-oriented format of popular music and progressive news would capture the minds of attentive publics in Cuba, Florida, the U.S. Gulf states, Mexico, and Central America.

Radio Romero's success is based on the firm belief that the majority of the Cuban and U.S. audience has a disposition to peace rather than to war, to conciliation rather than to confrontation, to coexistence rather than tension. If this is true, then such a broadcast voice can indeed have an impact: To reinforce the striving of the Caribbean and North American peoples for peace, justice and security.

REFERENCES

Abshire, D. M. (1976). "International Broadcasting: A New Dimension in Western Diplomacy." Beverly Hills, CA: Sage Publications, (The Washington Papers, Vol. 4, no. 35.)

Adelman, K. L. (1981). "Speaking of America: Public Diplomacy in Our Time." *Foreign Affairs 59*, 932.

Allen, R. V. (1981). Statement by Richard V. Allen, The White House, September 23, Washington, DC.

"AM Future on the Table at Rio." (1981). *Broadcasting* (November 9), 38.

Arbatov, G. (1973). *The War of Ideas in Contemporary International Relations: The Imperialist Doctrine, Methods and Organization of Foreign Propaganda.* Moscow: Progress Publishers.

BBC External Broadcasting Audience Research. (1978). *Survey in the United States: October/ November 1977.* Gallup Corporation.

Barghoorn, F. (1964). *Soviet Foreign Propaganda.* Princeton, NJ: Princeton University Press.

Barreras, A. (1977). "Radio Habana Cuba y Su Lucha Contra el Mentira." [RHC and Its Struggle Against Lies]. *Trabajadores* [Workers] (September 6), 8.

Benitez, J. (1982). Interview with Jose Benitez, Union of Cuban Journalists, May 6, Havana.

Bethell, T. (1982). "Propaganda Warts: What the Voice of America Makes of America." *Harper's* (May), 19–25.

Blustein, H. I., Anderson, L. C., Betters, E. C., Lane, D., Leonard, J. A., and Townsend, C. (1971). "Area Handbook for Cuba." American University, Foreign Area Studies Division. Washington, DC: Government Printing Office.

"Brickbats and Roses for USIA." (1963). *Broadcasting* (August 12), 46.

Browne, D. R. (1982). *International Broadcasting: The Limits of the Limitless Medium.* New York: Praeger Publishers.

Bumiller, E. (1982). "The Wick Whirlwind: Reagan's ICA Chief Brings Hollywood Hustle to Washington." *Washington Post* (May 11), B9.

Bumpus, B. (1980). *International Broadcasting.* Paris: UNESCO. (Documents of the International Commission for the Study of Communication Problems, no. 60.)

Burks, D. D. (1964). "Cuba Under Castro." New York: Foreign Policy Association. (Headline Series, No. 165). *Quoted by* Marryott, R. F. (1965). "Cuba-Venezuela: A Triumph Over Subversion," M.A. Thesis, The American University, Washington, DC, p. 24.

Calzon, F. (1982). Testimony by Frank Calzon, Executive Director of the Cuban-American National Foundation Before the House Committee on Foreign Affairs, March 3, Washington, DC.

Case, A. (1981). *Jamming of Medium Wave in the Caribbean.* Washington, DC: International Communication Agency. Memorandum Mr. Haratunian, Deputy Director, Voice of America, June 1981. *Quoted by* Rep. Thomas Leach, *Congressional Record—House,* August 3, 1982, p. H5018.

Castro Ruz, F. (1982). "Speech Before the Union of Cuban Youth, April 4." *In* T. O. Enders, "Statement by Assistant Secretary of State Thomas Enders Before the House Subcommittee on Telecommunications, May 10, 1982." Washington, DC: Department of State.

Cherne, L. (1979). "Ideology and the Balance of Power." *The Annals of the American Association of Political and Social Science 442* (March), 46–56.

Childs, H. L. (1942). "America's Short-Wave Audience." *In* H. L. Childs and J. B. Whitton (Eds.), *Propaganda by Short-Wave.* Princeton, NJ: Princeton University Press.

"Commercial Stations Magnify Voice: Ten Outlets Carry President's Speech." *Broadcasting* (October 29), 34.

Committee of Santa Fe, Council for Inter-American Security. (1980). "A New Inter-American Policy for the Eighties." Washington, DC: Council for Inter-American Security.

Coro Antich, A. (1982). Interview with Professor Arnaldo Coro Antich of the Cuban Institute of Radio and TV Broadcasting and the Institute of Foreign Affairs, May 5, Havana, Cuba.

Cozean, J. D., Krymis, K., Hitt, D., and Arensberg, M. (1968). *Cuban Guerrilla Training Centers and Radio Havana: A Selected Bibliography.* Washington, DC: The American University, Center for Research in Social Systems.

"Cuba Accused of Waging 'Radio War.'" (1982). *Washington Post* (September 2), E14.

"Cuba Said to 'Jam' 6 U.S. Stations." (1964). *New York Times* (April 14), 14.

"Cuba Sees 'Agression,' Charges Swan Island Broadcasts 'Piracy' by U.S." (1960). *New York Times* (September 15), 12.

"Cuba Tones Down Overseas Radio." (1969). *New York Times* (August 24), 25.

Cuban Freedom Committee. (c 1962). *Powerful Voices of the Cuban Freedom Committee Cover Cuba and Latin America.* Washington, DC: Cuban Freedom Committee.

"Cuban Liberty, American License." (1982). *Washington Post* (July 4), Editorial.

"Cuban Walkout Finishes Off Hope of AM Conference Success in Rio." (1981). *Broadcasting* (December 21), 30.

Dickey, C. (1982). "Cuba Vows War of the Airwaves to Counter U.S. 'Radio Marti'." *Washington Post* (August 18), A16.

"Eleventh Station." (1962). *Broadcasting* (October 29), 5.

Enders, T. O. (1982). "Statement by Assistant Secretary of State Thomas Enders Before the House Subcommittee on Telecommunications, May 10, 1982." Washington, DC: Department of State.

Esrati, S. (1978). "Listening to the World." *New York Times* (January 19), C9.

Farmer, G. (1979). Interview with Guy Farmer, Chief of Spanish Branch, American Republics Division, Voice of America, April 27, Washington.

Fenyvesi, C. (1981). "I Hear America Mumbling: Why the Voice of America Won't Win Any Emmys This Year." *Washington Post Magazine* (July 19), 21 ff.

Fernandez Moya, R. (1977). "La Propaganda y La Guerra [Propaganda and War]." Editorial Arte y Literatura, Havana, Cuba.

Frederick, H. H. (1981). "Ideology in International Broadcasting: Radio Warfare Between the Voice of America and Radio Havana Cuba." *Potomac Review: Journal of History and Politics 21* (Spring/Summer), 39–59.

Friendly, J. (1982). "Voice of America to Broadcast More Opinion." *New York Times* (July 11), 4.

Frost, J. M., (Ed.) (1982). *World Radio TV Handbook.* New York: Billboard Publications, Inc.

Fruhling, J. (1982). "Congressmen Suspicious of Navy's Radio Station." *Des Moines Register* (June 16).

"Fund Bill Approved; Aids Urban Renewal." (1960). *New York Times* (April 8), 20.

Gardner, M. (1965). "The Evolution of the Inter American Press Association." *Journalism Quarterly 42,* 547–556.

Gerbner, G. (1964). "Ideological Perspectives and Political Tendencies in News Reporting." *Journalism Quarterly 41,* 495–508; 516.

Gordon, G. N., Falk, I., and Hodapp, W. (1963). *The Idea Invaders.* New York: Hastings House.

Goshko, J. M. (1982). "Controversial Nicolaides is Leaving Post at VOA." *Washington Post* (January 20).

Gould, J. (1961). "Radio-TV: New Short-Wave Voice of Fidel Castro." *New York Times* (April 19), 79.

Grey, R. (1982). "Inside the Voice of America." *Columbia Journalism Review* (May/June), 23–30.

Guevara, E. 'Che' (1978). "La Guerra de Guerrillas [Guerrilla Warfare]." Editorial de Ciencias Sociales, Havana, Cuba.

Gwertzman, B. (1981). "U.S. Considering Special Radio Broadcasts to Cuba." *New York Times* (August 27), A7.

Hale, J. A. (1975). *Radio Power: Propaganda and International Broadcasting.* Philadelphia, PA: Temple University Press.

Hartman, R. T. (1962). "Propaganda Falls Short in Moscow." *Washington Post* (October 25), A6.

Head, S. W. (1976). *Broadcasting in America: A Survey of Television and Radio,* 3rd ed. Boston: Houghton Mifflin Company.

Hernandez, A. (1979). Interview with Angel Hernandez, Vice Director, Radio Havana Cuba, April 9, Havana, Cuba.

Hunt, E. H. (1973). *Give Us This Day.* New Rochelle, NY: Arlington House.

Jones, C. J. (1982). Report by Charlotte J. Jones, Analyst in Social Legislation, Education and Public Welfare Division, Congressional Research Service, to Representative Thomas Harkin, August 6.

Kamenske, B. H. (1979). Interview with Bernard H. Kamenske, Chief of News, Voice of America, April 27, Washington.

Kenworthy, E. W. (1961). "Murrow Decries Alabama Strife." *New York Times* (May 26), 25.

Kneitel, T. (1961). "Radio Swan: The Thorn in Castro's Side." *Popular Electronics* (March).

"Latin Serenade: U.S. Giants All Set to Go to Town on Hemisphere Shortwave." (1941). *Business Week* (July 19), 32.

LeoGrande, W. (1982). Testimony of William LeoGrande, Director of Political Science, The American University, Before the House Committee on Foreign Affairs, March 4.

Lerner, D. (1951). *Sykewar.* New York: George W. Stewart.

"Lingering Cuban Problem." (1982). *Broadcasting* (January 25), 84.

Lopez, O. L. (1981). *La Radio en Cuba: Estudio de su Desarrollo en La Sociedad Neocolonial [Radio in Cuba: A Study of its Development in a Neocolonial Society].* Havana: Editorial Letras Cubana.

Malmierca, I. (1978). Speech Delivered by Isidoro Malmierca, Member of the Secretariat of the Central Committee of the Communist Party of Cuba, on the Anniversary of the Founding of Radio Havana Cuba. *In XV Anniversary of Radio Havana Cuba.* Department of Revolutionary Orientation of the Central Committee of the Communist Party of Cuba, Havana.

Marchetti, V. and Marks, J. D. (1974). *The CIA and the Cult of Intelligence.* New York: Knopf.

Marder, M. (1981a). "Administration Moving to Sharpen Tone of U.S. Information Programs Abroad." *Washington Post* (November 10), A10.

Marder, M. (1981b). "Propaganda Role Urged for Voice of America." *Washington Post* (November 13), A1.

Marti, J. (1970). "Carta a Manuel Mercado [Letter to Manuel Mercado]." *In* F. Retamar (Ed.), *Marti.* Montevideo, Uruguay: Biblioteca de Marcha.

Martinez, G. (1982). "Transmitter Near Key West Intended for Radio Marti?" *Miami Herald* (June 16).

Martinez, G. and Ducassi, J. (1982). "Radio Marti Towers Provoke Suspicions." *Miami Herald* (June 16), 1A.

Martinez Pirez, P. (1982). Interview with Pedro Martinez Pirez, Director of Information, Radio Havana Cuba, May 4, Havana, Cuba.

Martinez Victores, R. (1979). *7RR: La Historia de Radio Rebelde [7RR: The History of Rebel Radio].* Havana, Cuba: Editorial de Ciencias Sociales.

Marryott, R. F. (1965). "Cuba-Venezuela: A Triumph Over Subversion." Master's thesis, The American University, Washington, DC.

Mas Martin, L. (1979). Interview with Luis Mas Martin, Director of Radio Rebelde, Havana, Cuba, April 7, Havana, Cuba.

"Memo Outlining 'Project Truth' Campaign." (1981). *Washington Post* (November 10), A11.

Nason, J. O. H. (1977). "International Broadcasting as an Instrument of Foreign Policy." *Millenium 6* (London), 128–145.

National Association of Broadcasters (1982). "Cuban Interference to United States AM Broadcast Stations." Washington, DC: National Association of Broadcasters.

Organization of American States. (1963). *Report Submitted by the Special Committee to Study Resolutions II.1 and VIII of the Eighth Meeting of Consultation of Ministers of Foreign Affairs.* Washington, DC: Pan American Union.

Otero, L. (1972). *Cultural Policy in Cuba.* Paris: UNESCO.

Panfilov, A. F. (1967). *U.S. Radio in Psychological Warfare.* Moscow: International Relations Publishers.

Perez Herrero, A. (1982). Statement by Antonio Perez Herrero, Substitute Member of the Political Bureau and Member of the Secretariat of the Central Committee of the Communist Party of Cuba, During the Celebration of the Twentieth Anniversary of the Founding of Radio Havana Cuba. *In XXth Anniversary of Radio Havana Cuba.* Havana: Editora Politica.

Phillips, R. H. (1960). "American Flyer Downed by Cuba." *New York Times* (March 22), 1.

Phillips, R. H. (1961). "Cuba Completing New Radio Voice." *New York Times* (February 13), 13.

Prado, J. (1982). Interview with Jose Prado, General Vice Director, Radio Havana Cuba, May 4, Havana, Cuba.

Presidential Commission on Broadcasting to Cuba. (1981). Executive Order 12323, September 22. *In Weekly Compilation of Presidential Documents 17* (39, 1981), 1019.

Presidential Commission on Broadcasting to Cuba. (1982). *Interim Report: May 24, 1982.* Washington, DC: Department of State.

Price, J. R. (1972). *Radio Free Europe—A Survey and Analysis.* Congressional Research Service, March 22, Washington.

Radio Canada International. (1975). *Shortwave Radio Listening in the United States, Survey II, 1975.* New York: Gallup Corporation.

Radio Habana Cuba (1982). "Frecuencias y Horarios de Transmisiones: En Vigor desde de 2 de Noviembre de 1981 Hasta el 28 de Febrero de 1982 [Frequencies and Transmission Schedule: In Effect from November 2, 1981 to February 28, 1982]." Havana, Cuba: Radio Havana Cuba.

Ramirez Corria, M. (1982). Interview with Mariana Ramirez Corria, Cuban Institute of Radio-TV Broadcasting, May 6, Havana, Cuba.

"Ray of Hope from 9 KHz Meeting." (1981). *Broadcasting* (July 13), 24.

Raymond, J. (1962). "Three Senators Urge a Cuba Warning in Call-Up Plan." *New York Times* (September 13), 1.

Redding, J. (1971). "'Castro-ating' the Media: The Consolidation and Utilization of Cuban Broadcasting by Fidel Castro." *Educational Broadcasting Review 5.*

"Reds Add 700 Hours of Radio Propaganda." (1963). *Broadcasting* (February 18), 112.

"Removing Soviet Influence from Cuba." (1981). *National Security Record 35*(3). Washington, DC: The Heritage Foundation.

Retamar, F. (1982). Interview with Fernandez Retamar, Director, Center for Marti Studies, May 6, Havana, Cuba.

Rolo, C. J. (1943). *Radio Goes to War.* London: Faber and Faber.

Rothmyer, K. (1981). "The Mystery Angel of the New Right." *Washington Post* (July 12), C1.

Rust, W. F., Jr. (1981). Letter of William F. Rust, Jr., Rust Communications Group, Inc., owner of WHAM, to Sol Taishoff, Editor of *Broadcasting,* November 3. *Published in* "Radio Station WHO: 'The Voice of the Middle West,' Des Moines, Iowa," Materials submitted to the House Subcommittee on Telecommunications, May 10, 1982, 117.

Santisteban, G. (1982). Interview with Guillermo Santisteban, Chief, English Language Division, Radio Havana Cuba, May 4, Havana, Cuba.

Serafino, N. M., Smith, M. S., and Siddall, D. R. (1982). *Radio Marti.* Congressional Research Service, Washington. (Report Prepared in Response to an Inquiry from the Senate Committee on Foreign Relations, June 28).

Silva, H. and Melton, E. (1982). "Radio Marti Leader Finally Becomes U.S. Citizen." *Miami Herald* (January 31), 2B.

Smith, D. D. (1962). "Is There a U.S. Audience for International Broadcasts?" *Journalism Quarterly 39,* 86–87.

Smith, D. D. (1969/70). "America's Short-Wave Audience: Twenty-Five Years Later." *Public Opinion Quarterly 33,* 537–545.

Stamm, R. (1980). "Foreign Broadcasts to Eastern Europe." *Swiss Review of World Affairs* (December), 31.

Stanbury, C. M. (1961). "Castro's Radio Voice." *Popular Electronics* (March), 53.

Straus, R. P. (1978). "When U.S. 'Tells It Like It Is' on Broadcasts Overseas." *U.S. News and World Report* (June 12), 55.

Szulc, T. (1962). "Radio Free Dixie in Havana Praises Negro 'Revolt' in South." *New York Times* (October 8), 1.

Thomas, H. (1980). *Coping with Cuba.* Washington, DC: Campaign for a Democratic Majority.

UNESCO (1956). *World Communications: Press, Radio, Film, Television.* (3rd ed.). Paris: UNESCO.

U.S. Congress. House of Representatives. (1981a). *International Broadcasting: Direct Broadcast Satellites.* Hearings Before a Subcommittee of the Committee on Government Operations. October 23, 97th Cong., 1st sess. Washington, DC: Government Printing Office.

U.S. Congress. House of Representatives. (1981b). *International Shortwave Broadcasting and Direct Broadcast Satellites: Voice of America, Radio Free Europe/Radio Liberty, Radio Marti.* Twentieth Report by the Committee on Government Operations, H. Rept. 97–398, 97th Cong., 1st sess. Washington, DC: Government Printing Office.

U.S. Congress. House of Representatives. (1982a). *Departments of Commerce, Justice, and State, The Judiciary, and Related Agencies Appropriations for 1983, Part 6.* Hearings Before the Subcommittee on the Departments of Commerce, Justice, and State, The Judiciary, and Related Agencies of the Committee on Appropriations, 97th Cong., 2nd sess. Washington, DC: Government Printing Office.

U.S. Congress. House of Representatives. (1982b). *Radio Broadcasting to Cuba Act, Report Together With Dissenting and Additional Views.* H. Rept. 97–479, 97th Cong., 2nd sess. Washington, DC: Government Printing Office.

"U.S. Diplomats in Cuba Dissent on Radio Plan." (1981). *New York Times* (October 29), A3.

"U.S. Is Said to Build Antennas for Radio to Transmit to Cuba." (1982). *New York Times* (June 17).

"U.S. Outlets Answer Cuban Propaganda." (1962). *Broadcasting* (June 4), 70.

"U.S. Plans Broadcasts." (1961). *New York Times* (February 13), 13.

United States Information Agency. (1968). *VOA and Radio Havana Audiences in Central America.* Washington, DC: United States Information Agency, Office of Research and Assessment. (Doc. E-7-68, February 29, 1968; declassified following June 22, 1973.)

Vinas, A. (1982). "Palabras Pronunciadas por Alfredo Vinas, Director General de Radio Habana Cuba, en el Acto de Celebracion del 20 Anniversario de la Fundacion de Radio Habana Cuba" [Words Spoken by Alfredo Vinas, Director General of Radio Havana Cuba at the Celebration of the Twentieth Anniversary of the Founding of Radio Havana Cuba]. *In XX Anniversario de Radio Habana Cuba.* Havana, Cuba:

Editora Politica.

"Voice Aides Try to Underscore 'Integrity' of News Product." (1981). *Washington Post* (December 22).

"Voice Disbands Remaining Crisis Hookup: Some Cuban Exiles Charge Censorship of News." (1962). *Broadcasting* (December 17), 60.

Voice of America. (1980). *VOA Broadcasting to Cuba.* Washington, DC: Voice of America. (Information leaflet.)

"Voice of America Helpers Figuring Up the Cost." (1962). *Broadcasting* (November 26), 58.

"Voice of America to Demobilize Ten Commercial Stations." (1962). *Broadcasting* (November 12), 42.

"Voice of America's $17 Million Pitch for Truth." (1958). *Broadcasting* (January 6), 40.

"'Voice' Reports Success Over Jamming in Europe." (1962). *New York Times* (October 26), 20.

"WTOP Fades, WSM Twangs in Havana." (1982). *Washington Post* (August 18), A16.

Weintraub, B. (1982). "Dispute Over Broadcasts to Cuba Intensifies." *New York Times* (June 27).

Whitton, J. B. and Herz, J. H. (1942). "Radio in International Politics." *In* H. L. Childs and J. B. Whitton (Eds.), *Propaganda by Short Wave.* Princeton, NJ: Princeton University Press.

Wise, D. and Ross, T. B. (1964). *The Invisible Government.* New York: Random House.

Wyden, P. (1979). *Bay of Pigs: The Untold Story.* New York: Simon and Schuster.

8

United States-Canada Relations: Cultural Dependence and Conflict *

Manjunath Pendakur

Prime Minister Pierre Trudeau's crusade to Canadianize his country's culture and economy at the expense of the United States is bogging down in political and financial quicksand. It is a crusade that, in the course of gaining easy victories over American broadcasting and publishing and battering our energy companies, has managed to exacerbate Ottawa's bitter conflict with the Western provinces, force sorely needed Canadian investment money into the United States, depress the Canadian dollar to a 50-year low and bring the American Congress to the brink of retaliation that would give Canada a taste of its own restrictive medicine.

The stinging commentary produced above in part which makes "Canadianization" policies sound apocalyptic was written by Walter H. Annenberg the owner and publisher of *TV Guide,* a widely circulated magazine in the U.S. and Canada (Annenberg, 1981). Many such reports appearing in the U.S. media in the past year have placed the burden of the conflicts between the two countries on Trudeau's "extreme nationalism," a characterization that does not explain the domestic power processes in Canada and their implication for U.S.-Canada relations.[1]

Given the overwhelming presence of U.S. direct investment and know-how in Canada, and the fact that it is an important link in the imperialist chain (NATO, NORAD, etc.), how can we explain the "belligerent"

* My sincere thanks are due to Professors Nathan Godfried and Chuck Kleinhans for their critiques of this paper. Any shortcomings, however, are mine.

[1] For such a typical article see "A Canadian Kick in the Shins," *Chicago Tribune,* November 2, 1980.

position of the Canadian state vis-a-vis American capital in the last decade culminating in policies which are dubbed in the U.S. press as "nationalistic," and "ungrateful." The two countries have found themselves at odds with each other over a wide range of issues—the National Energy Program, the Foreign Investment Review Agency, acid rain, fishing rights, trade in magazines, advertising, cable television, and motion pictures. This paper analyzes conflicts related to Canada's cultural policies since 1975, locating that analysis in the broad context of Canada's political economy as a dependent state. It is argued that in its expanded role as the chief arbiter among various factions of national and international capital, even a dependent state can challenge the hegemony of the dominant state. When, how, and in what shape the challenge will come about depends on the specific array of forces that come together to influence national policy. It is further argued as Canadian domestic capital expands into U.S. markets, it will become a limiting factor to Canada's pursuit of an independent course to cultural autonomy.

DEPENDENCE AND POWER

Dependency essentially amounts to an asymmetrical relationship in power between the countries involved. While Canada's historical development as a rich dependency of the U.S. is well documented (Levit, 1970), it may be worth noting a few important aspects of that relationship here.

Since the turn of the century, Canada has been the chief locus of U.S. external investment accounting for a consistent 25 percent. In the aftermath of World War II when the U.S. emerged as a new Super Power, its investment worldwide expanded enormously, and Canada's share of that investment has remained consistent. The book value of U.S. direct investment in Canada today is estimated to be nearly $40 billion. This amounts to about 80 percent of all foreign investment in the country (Canada, 1982, p. 2). One consequence of the size and age of U.S. direct investment, according to Joan Gherson, an economist with the Foreign Investment Review Agency in Canada, is its ability to grow from earnings generated in the country. She concluded that in recent years retailed earnings of foreign subsidiaries have been the principal source of additions to foreign direct investment (*Canada,* 1982, p. 7).

Another important consequence of foreign direct investment is that it generally is invested in the most lucrative and key sections of the economy. For instance, 78 percent of Canada's oil and gas production and 46 percent of manufacturing are controlled by subsidiaries of foreign corporations. American firms dominate the production, refining, and marketing of Canada's oil and gas. Chemicals, auto industry, and electrical products and a great deal more are controlled by U.S. investors.

The appetite for foreign capital in the Canadian economy seems voracious. W. D. Mulholland, the Chairman and Chief Executive Officer of the Bank of Montreal, the third largest bank in the country, was reported to have said that Canada's economy in the 1980s will require the equivalent of $700–750 billion new investment—in constant U.S. dollars—during the remainder of the decade (*Canada,* 1982, p. 6).

While that forecast suggests the possibility of increasing control of the Canadian economy by foreign capital, it is not without opposition in the country. Consider for instance the following statement by Gorse Howarth, Commissioner of the Foreign Investment Review Agency, where he articulates a number of problems associated with the transnational corporations' control of the Canadian economy:

> Make no mistake about it, most Canadians recognize and acknowledge the signal contribution that foreign investment, including U.S. investment has made to Canada . . . But we are also aware of the costs associated with at least some of that investment . . . I am, of course, referring to situations where a substantial proportion of foreign-controlled Canadian businesses are in effect restricted to servicing the Canadian market, are not permitted to take advantage of export opportunities, do not have any research and development program nor any reasonable measure of autonomy in decision-making and technological innovation . . . Canadians are understandably quite sensitive to the behavior of foreign-controlled corporations whenever it affects their chances of getting high-skilled employment, their ability to participate directly in the development and benefits of industry and, especially, their ability to determine their own economic destiny. Public opinion polls have consistently shown strong popular support for measures designed to remedy problems of this sort. (*Canada,* 1982, p. 4)

Not having complete control over the economic destiny of Canada by Canadians is best explained by Prime Minister Trudeau's oft-quoted statement:

> Living next to the United States is in someways like sleeping with an elephant. No matter how friendly and even-tempered is the beast, one is affected by every twitch and grunt.[2]

What Trudeau is referring to are decisions made by Wall Street and Washington which often affect Canada's economic development deeply. The current policies in Washington to maintain high interest rates contributing to a recessionary trend spillover into the whole international system, not just Canada.

---

[2] Quoted in *TV Guide,* November 7, 1981, p. 32.

The hegemonic position held by U.S. capital in Canada produces its own contradictions which often lead to government policies that attempt to protect the interests of certain sections of indigenous capital. The current interstate conflicts between the U.S. and Canada, if seen in such a light, become better understandable.

The Canadian federal government, in proposing a certain degree of national control over Canada's energy resources, which came to be known as the National Energy Program in 1980, was an outcome of such contradictions within Canada. The Western Provinces have always demanded more control over their resources from Ottawa which reached a new height in the aftermath of the OPEC price increases starting in 1974. Alberta demanded a higher price for its oil and gas and essentially succeeded in that effort in 1980. The indigenous big capital found allies in the Alberta government and the opposing block was formed by an alliance of the manufacturing capital in Ontario consisting of foreign as well as indigenous interests. In such a conflict, the federal government had no choice but to give in to Alberta's demands and, playing the role of a mediator in the larger national interest, articulated a new energy policy which embodies an economic strategy that asserts greater participation and control by certain sections of indigenous capital.[3]

Consistent with the Liberal Party's policies of national unity and Canada for all Canadians, the National Energy Program in fact alters the power of U.S. oil transnationals in Canada. That policy has three basic goals: to achieve energy self-sufficiency, to provide Canadians with the opportunity to participate in the growth of the energy industry, and to ensure an equitable distribution of energy revenues among all Canadians. To accomplish the second objective, the proposed policy provides for a system of incentives for indigenous capital and discriminates against foreign capital. The government's target is to achieve 50 percent Canadian ownership of oil and gas production by 1990.

Various agencies of the U.S. government have reacted to these issues. Canada has been put on the defensive by threats of retaliation from Washington.

While there are nearly two dozen separate reciprocity bills circulating in the Congress at the present time, it does not, however, mean that the American capitalists, the Congress, and the Reagan administration are all unified in opposing Canada's new economic policy. The Reagan administration opposes any legislation that would force the U.S. to confront a single nation and demand reciprocal access for U.S. goods and investment on a sector, industry, or balance-of-trade basis (*The Financial Post*, April 3, 1982). The preferred route of the U.S. administration is to negotiate a new

---

[3] For a detailed analysis of Canada's current economic policies, see Laxer, 1981.

set of multilateral rules to lower investment barriers, similar to those that have been worked out under the General Agreement on Tariffs & Trade (GATT) on world trade in goods.

At the GATT ministerial conference held last November in Geneva, the U.S. could not convince the 88 member nations present to lower trade barriers, eliminate "unfair" government export subsidies given world-wide recession and social havoc. The U.S., however, was reported to have won an agreement in the GATT to study the possibility of liberalization of trade in services in this decade despite opposition from the Third World, particularly Brazil and India (*New York Times,* November 29, 1982).

American capitalists are equally divided with respect to retaliation against Canada. Many petitions have been filed by various corporations to oppose Canada's policies, particularly, the National Energy Program and the Foreign Investment Review Act. While some U.S. corporations have urged the administration and the Congress to retaliate, most others, including Mobil Oil Corporation, Getty Oil Company, Pacific Power and Light Co., and the American Stock Exchange have advocated full and open-door access to Canadian firms investing in the U.S.[4]

Many Canadian firms with investments in the U.S. have also pressured the Congress and the administration to keep the U.S. markets open to them. That list includes some impressive names—Noranda Mines Ltd., Cominco Ltd., Dome Petroleum Ltd., and Hiram Walker Resources Ltd. They have strongly argued that the "Canadianization" policies are harmful to Canada. One such opponent is G.S. Fletcher, president of Regal Resources, who expressed his bitter opposition to the Trudeau government's policies in the following manner:

> The federal government in Canada neither wants nor listens to the opinions of the oil industry and we are unfortunately powerless when dealing with the current regime. We can only work for and hope for a change of government in Canada which will lead to some economic sanity. (*The Financial Post.* January 16, 1982)

What needs to be kept in mind, however, is that such Canadian policies do not attempt to overthrow foreign ownership and control of the Canadian economy. They are merely attempts at restructuring those relations in order to provide for greater participation for certain indigenous capitalists. In other words, these continuing conflicts remain cast within the general framework of American hegemony in Canada. Also, a mirror image of such developments in economic strategy pursued by Canada at the present time can be observed in the cultural policy arena.

---

[4] *The Financial Post* (Canada), January 16, 1982. Also see, "Stop Worrying About the Canadian Invasion," *Fortune,* October 19, 1981.

CULTURAL DEPENDENCE AND CONFLICT

With the integration of American capital into the Canadian economy, the imperial relation is secured, made compatible with liberal democracy, and maintained more fundamentally within Canadian civil society itself via mass education, mass media of books, advertising, film, television, etc. As one American observer, Horace Sutton wrote in his 1950 book entitled, *Footloose in Canada,* what Canadians have come to accept as normal is the fellowship of consumption and the "freedom" to choose to consume:

> Visitors from the United States will find that Canadians have adopted American commerce and culture. They brush their teeth with Pepsodent, fill their noses with Vicks, do their wash with Oxydol, laugh with Bob Hope, cry with 'Our Gal Sunday,' and most any summer afternoon any one on the street can give you the score of the Yankee-Indians game in Cleveland.[5]

There are many among Canadians who oppose such integration into the U.S. continental economy and culture. Their anxiety over the loss of Canada's cultural sovereignty is documented in numerous studies including four Royal Commission Reports, a Committee Report, and a Senate Report.[6] A common theme underlying all these reports is the presence of foreign content in Canadian mass media outlets and the initiatives that the federal government should undertake to alter that situation in favor of Canadian content. Consider the following statement which sums up historically the regulatory role of the government of Canada:

> It is equally clear that we could have cheaper radio and television service if Canadian stations became outlets of American networks. However, if the less costly method is chosen, is it possible, to have a Canadian nation at all? The Canadian answer, irrespective of party or race, has been uniformly the same for nearly a century. We are prepared, by measures of assistance, financial aid and conscious stimulation, to compensate for our disabilities of geography, sparse population, and vast distances, and we have accepted this as a legitimate role of government in Canada. (Royal Commission on Broadcasting, 1957)

I shall return to the nature of government intervention later. Now, it is important to note that merely four years after introducing television in Canada, the Canadian government had already realized that American media companies had economies of scale in their favor and Canadian-owned media companies would be dependent on government support one way or another.

---

[5] Quoted in Smith, 1981, p. 1.

[6] See *Royal Commission on Broadcasting,* 1929; *Royal Commission on National Development in the Arts, Letters, and Sciences,* 1965; Canada Senate, 1970b.

With the emergence of satellite, cable and pay-television delivery systems which have aggravated Canada's dependence on imported programming, the government appointed the Federal Cultural Policy Review Committee in 1980 to examine current federal cultural policies and programs, to receive briefs and hold public hearings, to study the needs and opportunities that lie ahead, and to recommend future directions (Federal Cultural Policy Review Committee, 1981). While its White Paper on Cultural Policy was scheduled for publication sometime in 1982, the Committee made some telling observations on the situation in Canadian media industries in 1981 which reinforce the all too well-known fact of cultural domination by foreign transnational media firms in Canada.

The committee found that more than 80 percent of sound recordings purchased in Canada originated outside the country and 97 percent of new feature films available for distribution in Canada were of foreign origin. Domestic production of books in Canada accounted for only 28 percent of total Canadian book market and the Committee remarked that foreign firms occupying that market had an adverse impact on Canadian economy and culture by limiting:

> the capacity of Canadian publishers to offer editorial and other developmental support to promising new novelists, poets and play wrights. Book publishers, especially smaller firms, are hindered by a distribution system which puts them at a disadvantage to foreign suppliers. (Federal Cultural Policy Review Committee, 1981, pp. 9–11)

The Committee's observation with respect to underdevelopment in Canadian book publishing can be extended to the Canadian feature film and television industries as well. While Canada produced nearly 500 feature films between 1968 and 1978, available data indicate that many of these films have never been shown on Canadian screens (Canadian Film Development Corporation, 1968–78). Of the 64,236 film exhibitions that took place in Canadian cinemas in 1978, only 3.4 percent were of Canadian films (Federal Cultural Policy Review Committee, p. 11). In a market dominated by the eight leading vertically-integrated U.S. film producing and distributing companies (the Majors), opportunities for investment and creative expression in film were practically nonexistent to Canadians until 1968 when the Canadian Film Development Corporation was created by the government with a mandate to develop the film industry in the country (Pendakur, 1981).

In television, English Canadians spend 75 percent of their viewing time watching non-Canadian programs, and the French Canadians 39 percent of their viewing time (Fox, 1981, p. 11).

In such a situation of dependence on foreign cultural product, the nature of intervention made by the Canadian government on behalf of indigenous media industries has been to shore up certain sections of Canadian capital, ensure its profitability, and, in the process of doing so, hope that Canadian talent will have the opportunity to express itself in various media. This approach to the whole problem of cultural dependence was made clear in the 1973 Green Paper on Communications Policy issued by the Department of Communications:

> The problem for Canadians is not primarily one of excluding foreign programming and sources of information but rather of ensuring access and exposure to such Canadian material as may be available, and ensuring that available Canadian material is comprehensive and of excellent quality.

The critical terms of this position are the "open door" for foreign programming, access and exposure to Canadian material and the production of high quality content in Canada. The primary contradiction of market preemption is not dealt with directly, but what is assumed is that the availability of "high quality" Canadian content will somehow, in the long run, check Canada's integration into a continental culture. Furthermore, faced with a marketplace that does not provide equal opportunities for Canadian capital and talent, the government has had to spend substantial sums of money to subsidize cultural industries.

Table 1 lists the many cultural programs or agencies that the government of Canada supports which cost the Canadian taxpayers a sum of $927 million in 1980. More than half of that amount or $577.5 million was spent on the nationally-owned Canadian Broadcasting Corporation alone. These are direct expenditures on culture by Canada's taxpayers. If one considers indirect government subsidies such as the Capital Cost Allowance Program, a 100 percent tax write-off scheme for investors in feature film and video production, Canadians spend many more millions of dollars on supporting cultural production in the country. It appears that they are willing to pay a hefty price for having the "choice" to consume foreign cultural materials.

Even such a cautious approach to ensure profitability to certain sections of indigenous capital as a measure to check the power of international capital in Canada has produced international conflicts between Canada and the U.S. to which I will now turn.

THE BATTLE GROUND

Although a complete treatment of all the conflicts that have occurred between Canada and the U.S. prior to 1975 cannot be covered in an essay, it should be noted that such battles must be seen on a historic continuum.

TABLE 1
Net Expenditures on Culture, 1980-81, Federal Agencies and Programs

Agency or Program	Net Expenditure (Canadian $ million)	Percent of Total
Canada Council	44.7	4.8
Canadian Broadcasting Corporation	577.5	62.3
Canadian Radio-Television and Telecommunications Commission	10.9	.7
National Arts Center	10.9	1.2
National Film Board	40.3	4.4
National Library of Canada	21.2	2.3
National Museums of Canada	60.2	6.5
Public Archives of Canada	21.2	2.3
Social Sciences and Humanities Research Council	42.1	4.5
Arts and Culture Branch, Department of Communications	20.7	2.2
*Citizenship Branch, Department of Secretary of State	25.3	2.7
*Parks Canada	52.0	5.6
Total	927.0	100.0

Source: Federal Cultural Policy Review Committee, *Speaking of Our Culture, Discussion Guide,* 1980.
*Estimates only

One researcher has documented 27 cases of known conflicts between 1947–1971 which range from banking to the magazine industry (Leyton-Brown, 1976). Among the conflicts in the last decade, however, Canada's policies in broadcasting and periodical publishing industries have been marked with high intensity and tension on both sides of the border.

Central to the conflicts between the U.S. and Canada is Bill C–58, an amendment to the Canadian Income Tax Act that was passed on July 16, 1976, by Parliament. It disallowed as a deduction against taxable income the costs incurred for advertising placed on a U.S. periodical or broadcasting station by a Canadian corporation if that advertising was directed primarily at Canadian audiences. A Canadian company's advertising expenses in a U.S. magazine or broadcasting outlet aimed at U.S. audiences were allowed as tax deductions. The primary goal of this legislation was to direct revenues to Canadian-owned magazine and broadcasting companies and away from the U.S. This policy has been the source of much ire among the U.S. border television stations and the U.S. magazine industry which have lobbied the Congress. Several diplomatic moves have been made by the Carter and Reagan administrations. The repercussions of that

1976 legislation are still being heard in both the countries, and, in fact, the lobbying activities on both sides of the border have only intensified given the "Canadianization" policy of the Trudeau government in the last five years.

A brief history of how that legislation came about illustrates the way Canadian governments have handled the problem of cultural domination by American media firms in the country.

Canadian periodical publishers had sought financial support from the government at least since 1920 and had intensified their efforts in the fifties when they were faced with a shrinking market for their magazines. The share of the Canadian market obtained by all U.S. magazines, including special editions, had risen from 67 percent in 1948 to 80 percent in 1954 (Litvak and Maule, 1978, p. 20). While *Time* and *Reader's Digest*, both American publications increased their share of advertising revenues in Canada from 18 percent to 37 percent in the same period, only a few Canadian-owned magazines—*Canadian Home Journal, Canadian Homes and Gardens, Chatelaine, MacLean's, Liberty, Saturday Night, La Revue Moderne, La Revue Populaire,* and *Le Samedi* barely survived (Litvak and Maule, 1978, p. 20).

These Canadian publishers and their lobby, the Canadian Periodical Publishers Association, pressured the Canadian government for intervention in the magazine industry, the result of which was the Royal Commission on Publication in 1960. Maclean-Hunter, a major publisher of business periodicals in Canada which published a fledgling general interest magazine *MacLean's*, spearheaded the attack on *Time* and *Reader's Digest* in the Commission's hearings. They argued for removal of special tax treatment for those two magazines which basically treated them as "Canadian" magazines and, furthermore, demanded protection for Canadian magazines in the interest of Canadian cultural sovereignty (Royal Commission on Publications, 1960).

The Commission concurred with the Canadian publishers and concluded their report that "a nation's domestic advertising expenses should be devoted to the support of its own media of communications" (Royal Commission on Publications, 1961, p. 76), and that "a genuinely Canadian periodical press can only exist by assuring for Canadian publishers, under equitable conditions, a fair share of domestic advertising" (Royal Commission on Publications, 1961, p. 74). The Commission went on to recommend that:

> a) The deduction from income by a tax payer of expenditures incurred for advertising directed at the Canadian market in a foreign periodical, wherever published, be disallowed, and b) the entry into Canada from abroad of a periodical containing Canadian domestic

advertising be excluded under Schedule C of the Customs Act. (Royal Commission on Publications, 1961, p. 74)

Canadian publishers had to wait until the 1965 budget when the government introduced these two measures recommended by the Commission. *Time* and *Reader's Digest,* however, successfully blocked the first measure with the help of the Johnson administration. The U.S. government was reported to have linked the magazine industry issue with the passage of the auto pact which the Canadian government placed high on its political agenda at the time.[7] Consequently, the two U.S. magazines emerged victorious from the 1965 budgetary provisions aimed against their market control.

The Canadian government came under increased pressure from the Canadian Periodical Publishers Association in the following years to deal with the stagnation in that industry. *Time's* circulation had risen from 215,000 in 1960 to 440,000 in 1969; and that of *Reader's Digest* from 1,068,000 to 1,448,000 in the same period (Canada Senate, 1970b, p. 157). The special Senate Committee, established in 1968 to study the ownership and control of the mass media in Canada and to report on the extent and nature of their impact and influence on the Canadian public, observed:

> If *Time* and *Reader's Digest* are allowed to maintain their present competitive advantage, it will become increasingly difficult for existing magazines to survive, and for new ones to be launched. (Canada Senate, 1970b, p. 164)

The Senate Committee recommended that the exemptions granted *Time* and *Reader's Digest* under Section 12A of the Income Tax Act be repealed, and it required both magazines to sell 75 percent of their stock in their Canadian subsidiaries to Canadian residents and have Canadian residents make up at least 75 percent of their officers and directors.

Maclean-Hunter, which had supported such legislation in 1960, reversed its position in its submissions to the Senate Committee in 1970 (Canada Senate, 1970a, p. 159). Among other reasons for the change, it had begun acquiring cable franchises in the U.S., and, perhaps, feared that any U.S. retaliation against Canada in response to *Time* and *Reader's Digest* might affect their investments in the U.S.

The Senate Committee recognized that its proposals might invite retaliation from the U.S., but it argued that national interest should not be subordinated to the business concerns of a group made up of two foreign publishers and a section of Canada's magazine industry. In balancing these various interests, the Committee chose to recommend a policy that

---

[7] Gordon, 1966, p. 97. Also see Newman, 1968, pp. 255–26.

would not only satisfy a larger section of the Canadian publishing industry, but meet the general goal of strengthening Canadian capital and identity.

The Special Senate Committees' recommendations finally were taken up by the federal government in 1975 when Bill C–58 was introduced embodying those recommendations. An impressive array of forces lined up for and against that legislation.

This legislation had the support of the private broadcasters represented by their powerful lobby, the Canadian Association of Broadcasters (CAB), and the Canadian Radio-Television Commission (CRTC), a government agency which regulates the broadcasting industry in Canada.

The Canadian Periodical Publishers Association, which had lobbied the government previously for such legislation, Maclean-Hunter Ltd., and the owners of *Content, Chatelaine,* and *Saturday Night* magazines, all representing Canadian capital supported this legislation. It found opponents from within and outside Canada—*Time, Reader's Digest,* the Writer's Union, which was afraid of losing existing jobs in those two American periodicals in case they decided to pull out of Canada, and finally, the Association of Canadian Advertisers (ACA) which represented the interests of major corporate advertisers in the country.

The members of ACA, 220 companies in all, are the major producers and sellers of goods and services in Canada. An estimated $50 billion worth of goods and services are produced and sold by these companies, and they also represent nearly 75 percent of all national advertising placed in Canada (ACA, n.d.). Slightly more than half of these companies are subsidiaries of transnational companies with their head offices in such countries as England, France, Germany, Switzerland, and the U.S. They formed a formidable block of opposition to the proposed legislation.

ACA's opposition to the bill had both economic and ideological reasons. That group feared that costs of advertising would go up if the bill passed, and it maintained that Canada should keep its doors open for international commerce:

> Whenever arbitrary government legislation is brought in, it interferes with free flow of commerce. That was our philosophical basis to opposition to ill C–58.[8]

ACA fought the bill vigorously by explaining its position to the Parliamentary Committee.[9]

The frustrating experience of the CRTC may have provided the Parliamentary Committee with reason to pass this piece of legislation. Since

---

[8] James, 1981. Mr. James stated that the costs of advertising in Canada did not rise as badly as his association predicted.

[9] See ACA, 1975. Also see, ACA, 1976.

its inception in 1968 (under the terms of the Broadcasting Act), the CRTC has tried to ensure the viability of Canadian-owned broadcasting companies. The CRTC had to balance their comparative disadvantage in scale against the assurance that Canada's cultural interests were served by producing programs at home.[10]

Because most Canadians lived within 100 miles of the U.S. border, they had been receiving American television signals from the U.S.-owned stations even before television was introduced in Canada.[11] The introduction of cable technology in the 1960s had improved the quality of American signals available to Canadians. Section 3(c) of the Broadcasting Act of 1968 stated that "the right of persons to receive programs...is questioned," thus making it illegal to restrict American television signals in Canada. The CRTC, in turn, had introduced some imaginative policies to strengthen Canadian-owned broadcasting organizations.

In 1971, the CRTC decided to permit cable franchise holders to delete commercials from all stations not licensed in Canada and insert in their place Canadian commercials sold by Canadian broadcasters. It had also introduced simulcasting, a policy of substituting a Canadian signal for a U.S. signal when a common show was being aired. Both of these measures were found to have increased the revenue flow to Canadian-owned television stations (Donner and Lazar, 1979, p. ii).

Additionally, the CRTC had been urging the government since 1971 to amend Section 19.1 of the Income Tax Act so that it would be unattractive to Canadian corporations to advertise on U.S licensed broadcast outlets.

The commercial deletion and simulcasting policies of the CRTC were strongly opposed by affected U.S. broadcasters. Principal among these were broadcasters from Buffalo, N.Y. who reached Canada's largest market, Toronto, and, KVOS-TV in Bellingham, Wash. which primarily aimed its signal at another important Canadian market, Vancouver, B.C. These American broadcasters claimed that CRTC policies were not only illegal but immoral. The CRTC made its position clear in the following statement issued in 1973:

> The objective of the Commission's commercial deletion policy is to restore the principle of local license and strengthen the Canadian television service. Revenues and other benefits derived from the implementation of the policy are intended to strengthen broadcasters. (Donner and Lazar, 1979, p. 37)

---

[10] A typical cost of an hour-long U.S. produced television show such as "Kojak" is about $200-300,000 whereas Canadian networks pay approximately $10-15,000 for the same. See *Variety,* April 21, 1982, p. 54.

[11] For example, WBEN-TV Buffalo started broadcasting in 1948 and its signals reached Toronto. Canadian Broadcasting Corporation started telecasting in 1952. See Wolfe, 1975, p. 34.

U.S. broadcasters brought other pressures on the CRTC such as a lawsuit in 1974 by the Buffalo stations in the Federal Court of Appeal in Ottawa where it was argued that the CRTC had no authority under the Broadcasting Act to delete commercials. The three judges hearing the appeal upheld the CRTC policy unanimously. Justice Arthur Furlow, who presided in the case declared in an individual opinion:

> U.S. broadcasters have no right to have their signals received in Canada in any form, whether altered or unaltered. Nor have they any right to require that the license (of a Canadian cable firm) conform to their requirements and demands. (Donner and Lazar, 1979, p. 38)

American broadcasters brought diplomatic pressure on the Canadian government as well. At their urging, the then Under Secretary of State for Economic Affairs, William Casey, was reported to have written the Department of External Affairs in Ottawa (Donner and Lazar, 1979, p. 38). On April 25, 1974, the subcommittee on inter-American affairs of the Committee on Foreign Affairs of the House of Representatives met to discuss U.S.-Canadian broadcasting relations. The meeting was called by New York Representative Thaddeus J. Dulski, whose Congressional district included Buffalo. He spoke of peaceful relations between the two countries, and of the economic piracy by Canadian cable operators which was disturbing those relations. Powerful senators, Warren Magnuson of the Senate Appropriations Committee and Henry M. Jackson of the Senate Armed Services Committee, both of whom represented Washington state, sent a written statement to the meeting praising the Bellingham broadcaster's contribution to Canadian society and urging that the CRTC reconsider its policies. In the following year, 18 U.S. senators were reported to have written a letter to the then Secretary of State, Henry Kissinger, asking him to intervene in the matter.

Neither the CRTC nor the Canadian government buckled under all that pressure. As much was at stake for Canada. In 1975, gross Canadian-placed advertising on the U.S. border television stations amounted to approximately $21.5 million (Donner and Lazar, 1979, p. ii). Due to the passage of Bill C–58 in 1976 those revenue outflows declined sharply.

The Buffalo stations in 1975 attracted about $9.5 million, KVOS-TV (Bellingham) about $6.7 million, and the other U.S. broadcasters about $5.3 million in U.S. funds from Canadian advertisers. By 1977, the estimated decline in the revenues of the Buffalo stations were $5.1 million that of KVOS-TV to about $3.4 million (U.S.), while the others incurred loss of revenues from Canada amounting to about $2 million (Donner and Lazar, 1979, p. ii). Dave Mintz of KVOS-TV testified to the Congressional Committee that "elimination of our commercials. . . would frankly, put us out of business."

Despite the lobby efforts, legal and diplomatic maneuvers of the U.S. broadcasters, the CRTC and the Canadian government did not back down and, furthermore, passed Bill C–58 in 1976.

What seems like a bold move on the part of Canada opposing U.S. economic and political power was indeed a limited move to protect Canadian investment in broadcasting and magazine industries. The CRTC had realized it was not only the survival of the existing licenses that were in question if the outflow of advertising dollars were not stopped, but that no new licenses could be issued in television broadcasting as well. It was amply demonstrated to the Commission when a newly licensed network, Global-TV in Ontario had reached near bankruptcy for lack of advertising dollars while the conflict between the two countries was raging in 1974–75. Global-TV had attempted to utilize mostly independently-produced Canadian programming in its first two months of existence but had failed to attract sufficient advertising dollars (Babe, 1974, p. 85). It appears that the CRTC, which was obligated under the Broadcasting Act to ensure that more Canadian content would be available to Canadians, had no choice but to stand firm against the pressure from the U.S. It also had the support of the private broadcasters, the periodical publishers, and some cable franchisees as well.

The overall impact of Bill C–58 in terms of creating opportunities for indigenous capital, and new jobs in the periodicals industry for Canadians has been found to be positive (see Litwak and Maule, 1979, pp. 4–11). The debates and the tension between the two countries, however, have continued. Whether or not the Canadian government will maintain its present position on Bill C–58 in the future, is difficult to tell. It will largely depend on the new matrix of forces that are being shaped in the Canadian magazine, newspaper, cable and television industries as well as in their U.S. counterpart industries.

NEW MATRIX OF POWER

While various sections of Canadian capitalists were lobbying the Canadian government along with the support of the CRTC for Bill C–58, some major Canadian cable companies had started investing in the U.S. (and European) cable television industry. It is quite likely that these cable operators with an international character to their companies may, in the future, become an opposing block to policies such as Bill C–58, and, consequently, find themselves aligned with the very international capital that they were opposed to in the '70s. I will consider here three of those major Canadian corporations which have expanded internationally and suggest what possible shape the new matrix of power might take in the near future given their pattern of operations now.

Maclean-Hunter Ltd.—a diversified communications company, active in periodical publishing, radio and television broadcasting, business forms, book distribution, commercial printing, radiopaging, and a number of other communication and information services—had begun to invest internationally in the early 1970s. By 1980, its U.S. cable holdings included Suburban Cablevision, 89 percent owned with 89,500 subscribers; Wayne Cablevision in Detroit, 90 percent owned with 11,700 subscribers; and, Metro Cablevision, 100 percent owned with 3,700 subscribers in the city of East Detroit (Maclean-Hunter, Ltd., 1980, p. 20).

Maclean-Hunter declared in its 1980 annual report the extent and growing importance of its international operations:

> The Company's foreign operations have continued to expand. Businesses in the United States and United Kingdom, which accounted for 17.4% of total revenues in 1979, accounted for 27.3% of revenues in 1980.

The Company further stated that:

> operating income contributed by operations outside of Canada grew from 7% of total operating income in 1976 to 28% in 1980. Net assets employed in our foreign operations now exceed net assets employed by our Canadian operations.

Another major Canadian cable firm, Canadian Cablesystems Ltd., has expanded rapidly into the international market in a short period of time to become one of the largest cable operations in the world. It entered the U.S. market in 1979 by buying a 66.7 percent interest in Syracuse Cable Systems, which has the potential to service 65,000 homes.[12] It won two more franchises in 1981, including Minneapolis, another major market with 56,000 homes (Canadian Cablesystems, Ltd., 1981). The 1981 annual report of Canadian Cablesystems made clear the international character of its investments:

> Cablesystems is no longer solely a Canadian company. While one of its primary obligations continues to be the strengthening of the national fabric, your company now has responsibilities to those communities we serve elsewhere in North America and abroad.

It further went on to declare, "Our objective is to have as many subscribers in the U.S. as we have in Canada." With cable saturation reaching 90 percent in some major markets of Canada and the potential for growth

---

[12] Syracuse is one among the top 100 U.S. cable markets. See Canadian Cablesystems, Ltd., 1980.

in the U.S. being very high, these Canadian companies were well poised to enter that market. An article in the business periodical, *Barron's,* commented about the Canadian presence in the U.S. cable market in the following manner:

> Maclean-Hunter which entered the U.S. market in 1975, now derives half of its cable revenues from stateside operations. . . . expects that proportion to climb to 60% by 1985. Cablesystems, which is relatively a new entry in the sweepstakes predicts that it will get 10% of its revenues from the U.S. by the end of 1981 and nearly 60% by 1985. (Goldenberg, 1980)

Canadian Cablesystems changed its name to Rogers Cablesystems in order to mask its nationality because it was facing some difficulties with U.S. competitors who were only too eager to point out to municipalities that it was "unAmerican" to franchise a Canadian-owned company in the U.S.[13] The Federal Communications Commission, however, has held since 1976 that there is no evidence that foreign ownership of cable franchises is harmful to the public.

Rogers Cablesystems is further entangled with U.S. investments since its dramatic acquisition of United Artists-Columbia cable franchise in the U.S. in 1981. A sum of $152 million was reported to have been paid by Rogers Cablesystems which increased its total cable subscribers in Canada, U.S., and Ireland to 2 million thus making it one of the largest cable companies in the world (*Advertising Age,* October 5, 1981).

Selkirk Communications, another Canadian communications company with newspaper and broadcast properties in Canada, has also entered the U.S. cable market beginning with a franchise in Ft. Lauderdale, Florida (Goldenberg, 1980).

It is highly unlikely that these and other Canadian companies with such international operations will be able to argue strongly for a protected market in Canada, while at the same time asking for open access to the U.S. cable and other markets. They might align themselves more closely with certain sections of international capital such as the National Association of Broadcasters (NAB) to pressure the Canadian government to repeal the 1976 amendment to the Income Tax Act.

The NAB and the 15 individual broadcasters who have been affected by Bill C-58 took up their issue with the U.S. Special Trade Representative in July 1980, and urged the Carter administration to pass a "mirror" law to restrict expansion of Canadian capital into the U.S. (see Office of U.S. Trade Representative, 1980). Among the many trade barriers demanded by them were import restrictions such as duties and taxes against Cana-

---

[13] *Globe and Mail* (Toronto), January 7, 1981. Also see Goldenberg, 1980.

dian feature films and records entering the U.S. (see *Variety,* July 16, 1980, p. 1). Senators Daniel P. Moynihan of New York and John Heinz of Pennsylvania appeared before the Special Trade Representative to demand such a course. The Carter administration's position, submitted to the Congress in September 1980 following the Special Trade Representative's inquiry, was that the Canadian law was unreasonable and that it would send a request to the Congress for "mirror" legislation. The elections were, however, high on the agenda of that administration and the Congress at the time, and consequently, no action was taken.

The U.S. broadcasters and their allies in the Congress have returned to lobby the Special Trade Representative and the Reagan administration. President Reagan was reported to have been considering the manner in which the U.S. should attempt to persuade Canada to repeal the Income Tax amendment passed in 1976. He was further reported to have said that the "mirror" legislation being considered was "not to erect new barriers to trade, but rather to encourage the Canadians to eliminate their unreasonable and restrictive trade practice" (*Broadcasting,* November 16, 1981).

While the NAB supports punishing the Canadians, others do not. For instance, Jack Valenti, the President of the Motion Picture Association of America/Motion Picture Export Association of America, has expressed his opposition to such a policy.[14] His member companies, who are the leading producers and distributors of film and television programs in the world, and for whom Canada is the largest unrestricted market, see it against their interest if the existing frictions between the two countries are intensified by a "mirror" law (n. 14, *supra*). It might, in fact, force Canada to impose some of the restrictions on U.S. distribution of films, television programs, and recorded music which many indigenous producers have been asking for nearly a half century.

It is still unclear as to how the major Canadian communications companies such as Rogers Cablesystems would line up. Smaller firms such as British Columbia Television and City-TV have expressed opposition to any U.S. intervention (n. 14, *supra*).

The Canadian Association of Broadcasters, which represents the interests of private broadcasters in Canada, has expressed its support for Bill C–58 in several documents it has presented to the Canadian government. It stated clearly that the Canadian government should not give in to any pressure from the U.S. government out of fear of retaliation because to do so, in their view, would be to concede that Canada's cultural sovereignty is of less importance than its desire to attract U.S. investment dollars.[15]

---

[14] Section 301, Committee of the Office of the Special Representative for Trade Negotiations, Washington, D.C., Docket No. 301-15.

[15] The Canadian Association of Broadcasters, 1979b. Also see Canadian Association of Broadcasters, 1979a.

When Canada and the U.S. do consider Bill C-58, and the many other economic and cultural issues that were discussed in this paper, at GATT or some other forum, it will be a testing ground of Canada's historic attempt to pursue "Canadianization" of its economic and cultural spheres, however limited they might be. Whether or not the imperial power would tolerate that limited resistance will largely depend on the new matrix of power in both the countries. As two decades of Canada's struggle to create Canadian content and opportunities for Canadians to express themselves on Canadian media outlets have only partially succeeded, the present interstate conflicts resulting from Bill C-58 (and other issues) may place Canada at a crossroads where new and innovative options may have to be considered to deal with the problem of creating an autonomous culture.

REFERENCES

"A Canadian Kick in the Shins." (1980). *Chicago Tribune* (November 2), editorial.
Advertising Age. October 5, 1981, s-7.
Annenberg, W. H. (1981). "Canadian Unfairness Doctrine." *TV Guide* (November 7).
Association of Canadian Advertisers (ACA). (n.d.). "Opening Statement By ACA to Standing Committee. Committee on Banking, Trade and Commerce, C-58." Ottawa, Canada: ACA.
Association of Canadian Advertisers (ACA). (1976). "Position of the Association of Canadian Advertisers (ACA) In Relation to Bill C-58." Ottawa, Canada: ACA.
Association of Canadian Advertisers (ACA). (1975). "Introductory Remarks by the Association of Canadian Advertisers at the Standing Committee on Broadcasting, Films, and Assistance to the Arts." Ottawa, Canada: ACA.
Babe, R. E. (1979). *Canadian Television Broadcasting Structure, Performance and Regulation.* Hull, Canada: Minister of Supply and Services.
Broadcasting. November 16, 1981.
Canada Today/D'Aujord'hui. (1982). Vol. I. Washington, D.C.: Canadian Embassy.
Canada Senate. (1970a). *Hearings of the Special Senate Committee on Mass Media.* Vol. I. Ottawa, Canada.
Canada Senate. (1970b). *Report of the Special Senate Committee on Mass Media.* Vol. I. Ottawa, Canada.
Canadian Association of Broadcasters. (1979a). "The Future of the Communications System." Presentation to the Consultative Committee on the Implications of Telecommunications for Canadian Sovereignty. January 8.
Canadian Association of Broadcasters. (1979b). *The Clyne Committee Report, Analysis of Recommendations.* (July 13).
Canadian Cablesystems, Ltd. (1981). *Second Quarter Report.* (April 24).
Canadian Cablesystems, Ltd. (1980). *Annual Report.*
Canadian Film Development Corporation. (1968-78). *Annual Reports.*
Donner, A., and Lazar, F. (1979). *The Impact of the 1976 Income Tax Amendment on the U.S. and Canadian TV Broadcasts.* Ottawa, Canada: Department of Communications.
Federal Cultural Policy Review Committee. (1981). *Speaking of Our Culture, Discussion Guide.* Ottawa, Canada.
The Financial Post (Canada). April 3, 1982.

The Financial Post (Canada). January 16, 1982.

Fox, F. (1981). "Canadian Broadcasting in the Eighties: Pointing the Way to a Strategy." Notes for an address to the Annual Meeting of the Canadian Association of Broadcasters. Quebec City, Canada. April 6.

Globe and Mail (Toronto). January 7, 1981.

Goldenberg, S. (1980). "Canadian Cable." *Barron's* (December 29).

Gordon W. (1966). *A Choice for Canada.* Toronto, Canada: McClelland and Stewart.

James, R. (1981). Interview with Rolf James, Secretary, Association of Canadian Advertisers, Toronto, Canada, June 17.

Laxer, J. (1981). *Canada's Economic Strategy.* Toronto, Canada: McClelland and Stewart.

Levit, K. (1970). *Silent Surrender. The American Empire in Canada.* New York: Liveright.

Leyton–Brown, D. (1976). "The Multinational Enterprise and Conflict in Canadian-American Relations." *In* A. B. Fox, et al. (Eds.), *Canada and the United States: Transnational and Transgovernmental Relations.* New York: Columbia University Press.

Litwak, J. A., and Maule, C. J. (1978). "The Impact of Bill C–58 on English Language Periodicals in Canada." *Arts and Culture Report.* Ottawa, Canada: Secretary of State.

MacLean-Hunter, Ltd. (1980). *Annual Report.*

Newman, P. C. (1968). *The Distemper of Our Times.* Toronto, Canada: McClelland and Stewart.

Office of the U.S. Trade Representative. (1980). "In the matter of a Complaint of KVOS Television Corporation, et al., against Section 19 (1) of the Canadian Income Tax Act, Section 301." Docket No. 301-15, Committee of the Office of Special Representative for Trade Negotiations. July 9, 1980.

Pendakur, M. (1981). "Cultural Dependency in Canada's Feature Film Industry." *Journal of Communication 1*(3).

Royal Commission on Broadcasting. (1957). *Report.* Ottawa, Canada.

Royal Commission on Broadcasting. (1929). *Report.* Ottawa, Canada.

Royal Commission on National Development in the Arts, Letters, and Sciences. (1965). *Report.* Ottawa, Canada.

Royal Commission on Publications. (1961). *Report.* Ottawa, Canada.

Royal Commission on Publications. (1960). *Hearings.* Ottawa, Canada.

Smith, D. (1981). "Culture and the Canadian Entrepreneur" *InSearch/En Quete, 8,* 1.

"Stop Worrying About the Canadian Invasion." (1981). *Fortune* (October 19).

Variety. April 21, 1982, 54.

Variety. July 16, 1980, 1.

Wolfe, M. (1975). "The Desperate (and Sometimes Ridiculous) Battle to Save Canadian Television." *Saturday Night* (September).

9

The Logic of Cultural Industries in Latin America: The Television Industry in Brazil

Emile G. McAnany

INTRODUCTION

For over a decade, there has been serious discussion of the various forms of Latin American dependency on the Central Powers, and most especially the United States (Cardoso, 1971; Cardoso and Faletto, 1979; dos Santos, 1974). Somewhat later, the discussion drew a special focus on the cultural aspect of dependency emphasizing the mass communication media (Mattelart, 1973; Schiller, 1976; Beltran, 1976; Beltran and Fox, 1979; Sarti, 1981). The publication of a preliminary study of worldwide export and import of television programming (Nordenstreng and Varis 1974) contributed to the beginning of what has become a full-scaled debate over the "free" and "balanced" flow of communications materials between advanced and less developed countries of the world (UNESCO, 1980). There have been a number of responses to the charges of cultural imperialism or cultural dependency. These defenses have not denied the existence of a problem of imbalance in the exchange of communication materials, but they do differ from their opponents in the explanation of its underlying causes, its possible effects and competent policy responses in the face of the one-sided flow.

Those who are subject to the flow [objects of the flow] contend that the mass media (and most especially, television and film) are inappropriate to local cultural values and undermine the indigenous culture. For example, the Brazilian Minister of Communications sums up a common attitude in Latin America when he said some years ago "Culture and values foreign to Brazilians are practically being imposed on our young people, especially the younger children. Our commercial television is becoming a privileged vehicle for cultural imports, a basic factor in our losing what is most characteristic in our creations" (*O Estado de Sao Paulo,* Nov. 28, 1974 (cited by Mattos, 1982a, p. 74)). Beltrán and Fox de Cardona (1979), two Latin American communication scholars, observed after a survey of research on foreign communication content that "U.S. programming distributed either through Latin American media (such as the case of television shows) or that which is directly distributed to the audiences (such as films and magazines) operates under an unrestrained mercantile maximization and tends to play a more commercial than political role in their type of distortion of society. This type of program-ming is encouraged by the commercial structure of the media, and in particular by US advertising companies and clients in that it fosters con-sumerism" (p. 59). There are numerous other sources which denounce the impact of foreign, and particularly U.S., imports on Latin American cultures.

Countercritics to charges of cultural or media imperialism have responded in the latter part of the decade. Lee (1980), for example, believes that the dependency thesis put forward by Schiller (1976), Nordenstreng and Varis (1974), Salinas and Paldán (1979) and Murdock and Golding (1977) is too simplistic and reductionist and fails to explain the variant cases like Canada (developed but media dependent) and Taiwan (develop-ing but media self-sufficient). He admits, however, that the media depen-dency analysis seems to hold better for Latin America. Tunstall (1977) has made a strong case for Anglo-American influence on world-wide media development but thinks that that influence is on the wane. Katz (1979) argues that U.S. television is popular in the Third World more for reasons of limited economic means for producing local programs (what he calls "pull" or demand reasons) than for aggressive selling of such products by the U.S. ("push" or supply reasons). Finally, Straubhaar (1981) in a long and carefully researched study of Brazilian television tries to demonstrate that U.S. influence is waning and cultural dependency relationships as well.

What this paper will argue is that a better understanding of the issue may be available from the perspective of cultural industries and a world economic market rather than from an imperialism or dependency per-spective alone. Further, it is suggested that from the former perspective there is a close and necessary relationship between media products in a variety of areas (like television, film, and musical records) and the cultural content and potential impact of these products. Instead of seeing a simple solution to the problem of the cultural imbalance in mass communication media through a few national cultural policies or communication policies as the MacBride Commission Report (UNESCO, 1980) seems to suggest, a longer term solution is called for that will require a more decisive rearrangement of forces that go to make up the cultural industries of Latin America.

LATIN AMERICA AND CULTURAL INDUSTRIES

The use of the term "cultural industries" in the context of the discussion on mass media in Latin America has a series of implications that need to be understood from the outset. We mean to emphasize by the term "cultural industry" not only that the content of the media are value-laden and carry meaning for their audiences (thus cultural) but that the creation, production, distribution and consumption of the products involves a process that has been rationalized in a Western, industrial model and that the market economy has a decisive influence on the nature of the resultant cultural industry. This also implies a close and logical relationship between the economic structure that produces the product, and the content and presumed impact of that product. It is not argued that this relationship can be easily demonstrated at present with the empirical evidence at hand. Rather, an outline of the argument will first be made with areas and types of evidence available from various sources identified, then an examination of the case of Brazilian mass media will be made in order to see to what extent it illuminates the suggested approach.

We do not wish to launch on a long and often futile discussion of the meaning of culture within the scope of this paper, but several distinctions may be useful in order to clarify the following exposition. Hall (1980), for example, refers to two relevant paradigms of European cultural studies. The culturalists adopt a more anthropological approach to culture as *"both* the meanings and values which arise amongst distinctive social groups and classes. . . *and* as the lived traditions and practices, through which those 'understandings' are expressed and in which they are embodied" (p. 63). The structuralists focus on the more abstract categories of thought, and even the relationships among those categories, which though not observable and concrete in the same way as culture in the "culturalist" paradigm, still have a profound influence on the conscious explanation of the way societies are structured and operate. In both paradigms culture is not only related to lived practices, beliefs, values, and norms, but the "meaning" these have for people. The system of meanings that make up a culture then account for the understanding of the reality of a given environment that different groups share. This understanding, in turn, may explain why some (for example, Enzenberger, 1964, and Schiller, 1976) refer to the cultural industries as "consciousness industries," stressing the meaning generated and reinforced by such mass media institutions.[1] Underlying some disagreements about the cultural impact of mass communication products, of course, are a set of assumptions about the meaning of culture as well as a disagreement about the usefulness of different methodological approaches.

An important consideration to a discussion of cultural industries is the distinction between the cultural industry and whatever other form of cultural production a society might undertake. How creative artists manage to survive within a given system of production may in part depend upon the different cultural policies their governments may design (for a discussion of film in two European countries cf. Sainsbury, 1980, and Donner, 1980). In this paper, we concentrate our attention on some of the more easily distinguishable forms of our mass culture such as television, film, and musical records since the production in these areas have been thoroughly industrialized.

It is not a new theme to stress the consumption-oriented nature of cultural products in much the same framework as other consumer goods. Horkheimer and Adorno of the Frankfurt School as well as Hannah Arendt (1961) in the U.S. all have reminded us of the production and consumption aspect of much of Western culture. What is new within the last twenty years is not so much a change in some of the approaches suggested by these critics, but the rapid expansion of the cultural consumer market both within the United States and Western Europe and its spread to segments of the Third World as well. The growth of criticism about Third World penetration arises in the 1970s (the whole UNESCO debate about communication begins seriously about 1972–73) because it is in that decade that the full impact of the international cultural market begins to be felt in many Third World countries. But even Western Europe, part of the core and not the periphery, has begun to feel the strain on certain of their own cultural industries (Council of Europe, 1980). The penetration of societies in Latin America, Asia, or Africa is not primarily due, as some seem to argue, to the expansion of the technological infrastructure of distribution (such as satellites, telecommunications, computers), but the mechanism of industrial production and market distribution that is more basic than the

---

[1] As with many arguments about the meaning of culture in studies of communication, so there are many disagreements over the meaning of ideology in this context. In this paper that term is not used in order to avoid the confusion of meanings advanced in the debate. Hall (1980) makes some clarifications on this score.

technological innovation as such.[2]

Cultural production in this sense has three aspects: first, the artistic processes of creation and presentation in its industrial forms have tended to be removed from direct interaction of artists with audiences (in theater, live musical performance, etc.) and have been placed in a product (such as a film, television program, record) that is sold to audiences for their personal (often, at home) consumption; second, the product enters a system of distribution and exchange that is either entirely or partially under the influence of capitalist market forces in a national and international context; third, the influence of the industrial production processes as well as the competitive market both have significant indirect influence upon the nature of the content.

There is a danger here of misunderstanding. Am I saying that there is a simple, one-way economic explanation of why we have the kind of television, film or musical products that we do in a wide variety of countries? Not at all. I am saying that an aspect of the cultural phenomenon called the mass media is overlooked if we do not take into consideration: (a) the historical development of an industrial, rationalized production process to create the products of these media (along with the technologies basic to their production), mirrored very much in the production process of other industries; (b) the market mechanisms that would sell the product for a price that would allow costs to be covered and a profit to be generated. We will come to example and counterexample later. I am not saying this system is inherent in the very technology itself as some have argued. I am saying that even in a situation where market forces do not directly enter (such as a state-controlled television system) there is still an indirect influence on things like production costs and international distribution, to name but two obvious examples.

A final question arises at a more abstract level. Does this approach have a view of society that is unitary or deterministic? I will argue that at a minimum society's economic, cultural and political spheres all interact and essentially tend to reinforce one another.[3] In the present case, even with Brazil as a special focus, I argue that the interaction of the economic

---

[2] The emphasis on the hardware innovation on its consequences has been more favored by American writers who have often been on technological bandwagons with early, naive predictions about social benefits (McLuhan seems to have been the master of this style), but recent French writing also emphasizes the centrality of technological innovation but without the same social optimism (Flichy, 1979).

[3] This does not preclude contradictions among those spheres on occasion, but unlike Bell (1975), I do not see the three spheres as operating independently. Lee (1980) takes Bell's position and divides off the three spheres and thereby loses any holistic approach to television within the total social structure of a country.

with the cultural spheres is most important to examine and that the political sphere (the role of the state in particular in the formation of policies for cultural industries), though important, would take a lower level of significance. It is, however, an approach that sees all three spheres as essential for the understanding of the problems posed by cultural dependency in Latin America.

CULTURAL INDUSTRIES, IMPERIALISM OR DEPENDENCY: NATURE OF THE EVIDENCE

The theoretical differences among a variety of approaches to the study of the mass communication media in Latin America may be broadly divided on the basis of the particular assumptions regarding the evidence on the discrepancy of communication flow among countries. The first recognizes the imbalance but insists that it is temporary and will work itself out if Latin American countries will simply let the market forces operate (Read, 1976; Pool, 1977). The second sees the need for some intervention by the state to adjust the imbalance but rejects any wider interpretation of communication as part of a national or international social structure (Katz and Wedell, 1977; Tunstall, 1977; Lee, 1980). The third sees communication in Latin America and elsewhere as only a part of a larger social and international order working against the independent development of the region in cultural, social, or economic terms. This latter group is a heterogeneous one but would include three approaches that could be designated as cultural imperialism, cultural dependency and cultural industries. It includes a wide variety of views concerning the precise nature of the problem, and the evidence relevant to its solution is indicated in a recent review by Sarti (1981).

There is an abundant literature concerning the problem of communication flow and dependency (Beltrán and Fox, 1979; UNESCO, 1980; Sarti, 1981). For the present purpose, we will review only a portion of the evidence with a set of categories that has emerged among a variety of groups concerned with the problem. The imbalance in communication is seen in: (a) export-import patterns of communication hardware and software; (b) foreign media ownership patterns; (c) imitation of core media systems and professional practices; and, (d) cultural impacts of mass media on audiences. The following paragraphs will briefly outline what arguments and evidence have been developed in each category by both proponents and critics of the various positions noted above.[4]

---

[4] The area of information and new information technologies is left aside in this paper because a comprehensive discussion of information within a framework of culture is difficult. This is a critical area for study, however, and a number of people have called attention to it recently (Cruise-O'Brien and Helleiner, 1981; Smith, 1980, Jacobson, 1979, Schiller, 1981).

Export-Import of cultural products:[5] Much of the so-called "new international information order debate" was preceded by a less acrimonious period of research on the import-export of television programs. In the early 1970s, UNESCO sponsored a preliminary mapping of the patterns of international exchange of programs. Nordenstreng and Varis (1974) found in their survey that the vast majority of television programs were exported by the U.S. (approximately 150,000 hours per year) to Western Europe, Latin America and the Far East; the three Western European powers of the UK, France and West Germany were distant competitors (all three accounting for only about 32,000 hours per year) while most others accounted for little by comparison. Some of their figures presenting percentages of imported programs in comparison with nationally made television seemed shocking, even suspect, at the time. Subsequent research from a point-of-view less sympathetic to the imperialism thesis have shown minor changes and broad confirmation (cf. Lee, 1980, for example, and Straubhaar, 1981; Read, 1976; Katz and Wedell, 1977).

Generally, when faced with the fact that there is a large importation of foreign television programs by Third World countries (or even by some countries of Western Europe or Canada), there are several varieties of reaction. Read (1976) and Pool (1977) would argue that this is a temporary phenomenon and that like many other products, television has a natural "life cycle" over the course of which local cultural industries will produce their own programs which local people will prefer over the foreign commodity. Pool adds the proposition that cultural assimilation is a constant and universal process that has always gone on. He means, presumably, that it is not harmful, and that it is perhaps inevitable or both. The evidence for the product life cycle is not strong as Lee (1980) explains: "If general American multinational enterprise expansion fits rather neatly, it is because manufacturing industries depend upon transferable technology to produce standardized products. When it comes to producing cultural products such as television programs, other countries (industrialized or underdeveloped) do not offer competitive advantages. Such factors as low labor cost, raw material supply and the coercive power of the state are extremely important to manufacturing products but not to cultural products. Producing cultural products demands, instead, a constant supply of talent, markets, and a supportive media infrastructure (pp. 80–81)." Straubhaar (1981) attempts to show, that in the case of Brazil, such a theory may be working since U.S. imports in television seem somewhat less popular in the late 1970s. He does admit that the absolute number of U.S. imports is going up, however. More on this below.

---

[5] Since we are using television as a primary example of cultural industries, we will call upon the evidence in this field, but we will make some references to film and recorded music as well.

Those who argue on the basis of cultural imperialism seem to be taking a somewhat similar approach in that they place a major emphasis on whether the material is made in the core countries or locally. Beltrán and Fox (1979) seem to make this argument, as does Beltrán (1976) when he outlines the variety of the impacts of U.S. television programming on Latin American audiences. Lee (1980) argues in a somewhat similar vein but from a different perspective. Having narrowed the field from cultural to media imperialism, he goes on to admit that the nature of the programming and the power of the U.S. to undersell most local products is the basis for the kind of domination through the marketplace that exists in most countries. He tempers his criticism constantly because of avowed aims to criticize the Marxist position and to take a middle path. Katz (1979) and Katz and Wedell (1977) argue similarly: local programs can not be produced to compete with cheap U.S. imports because there is a shortage of local funding, and local television networks insist on trying to provide too many hours each day for their audiences.

Those who argue from a dependency position would question both the product "life cycle" theory and even the arguments of cultural or media imperialism. Sarti (1981), for example, argues that for Latin America the forces should not be on all countries as a general category, nor on the simple external threat of domination by the U.S. nor, finally, on the mere fact of importation. Rather, one needs to analyse each country in the light of its own historical circumstances and look within the country to the various classes whose interests are served or undermined by media, whether they be foreign or locally produced. Salinas and Paldán (1979) make a similar point in their analysis of cultural dependency as a part of dependent development in Latin America. They also strongly invoke the notion of class struggle to suggest that certain classes will react against media content that is clearly alienating. Each of these authors pay little direct attention to the threat of foreign imports as such, but place the problem within the larger question of social structure of the particular country.

Currently, there seems to be a pause in the effort to collect more evidence about the importation of foreign cultural materials in Latin America, and, indeed, elsewhere. The reason is that the various positions have been outlined, preliminary evidence provided, and no more purpose seems to be served by further adding to the point of domination of U.S. material in the television area. But this attitude may overlook several important considerations. First, despite some reassuring general arguments about the waning of U.S. influence and the lessening of imports (Tunstall, 1977; Lee, 1980; and, Straubhaar, 1981), there are no convincing data to indicate a long-term trend. The MacBride Commission Report for UNESCO (1980) may have created some sensitivity among nations on the point, but no sharp improvement can be found. Second, there are two contrary indications that would argue for a more careful monitoring of cultural imports. The major push toward increased earnings from exports is currently on the minds of all countries and the U.S. is presently promoting the export of its main economic products in the services and information area. In a recent article in the *New York Times* (February 7, 1982), this emphasis on the export of our service economy has received the very highest priority by the Reagan administration. Among other things, cultural products (included in this sector) will be an area for special promotion. Third, the burgeoning market for hardware in the new technologies underpinning our own cultural market (such as videocassettes, cable television and other home entertainment video equipment) will be part of a major thrust in Latin America in the 1980s (*Chronicle*, 1981). As cable television and videocassette players are pushed into Latin American markets, the demand for some cultural materials will increase rather than decline. In this sense, importing of foreign materials will perhaps reach a growth period in the mid-1980s.

The cultural industries approach does not exclude imperialism or dependency, but, by placing an emphasis on the economic base and the nature of the industrial production and marketing system, it recognizes that more careful study of the development of cultural industries in individual countries is crucial for an understanding of the role the media will play. As markets change, and some Latin American countries like Brazil and Mexico emerge with their own cultural industries, we need to monitor and interpret these changes constantly.

Foreign media ownership patterns: The arguments advanced about foreign media ownership, especially concerning television in Latin America, seem to come to the comforting conclusion, at least for Latin Americans, that after a brief period in the 1960s when U.S. networks established a number of their own stations in Latin America, these institutions sold their direct ownership interests as unprofitable ventures (Lee, 1980). Even critics of media imperialism in Latin America like Beltrán and Fox (1979) admit that "the 1970s have witnessed a decrease of North American direct investment in Latin American media, especially in television, due to a growing apprehension of possible political intervention" (pp. 35–36). Even for the less direct form of control of technical service contracts to Latin American TV stations, these authors admit there has been a reduction of U.S. presence.

Straubhaar (1981) dwells at length on the controversial contract that Time-Life had with the now-dominant Brazilian television giant TV-Globo. He argues that Globo broke the contract in 1971 and thereafter developed its media empire on its own. Several quotes will provide an idea of his argument:

> The structural problems which lingered in TV Tupi [an early rival to TV Globo] invited competition from other stations and networks, some of whom looked to the US for viable commercial models to borrow and adapt (p. 47). TV Globo eventually emerged dominant because it absorbed the most successful of the programming ideas and was even more efficiently advertiser-oriented [than rivals]. TV Globo organized a true national network, modeled after the US commercial networks, which could provide nation-wide advertising opportunities (p. 81). I feel that TV Globo's extraordinary success from 1966–1970 depended on a complex interaction of people, resources and ideas: Brazilian businessmen like Marihno, Brazilian programmers like Walter Clark and Jose Bonifacio, and managers like Wallach and Jose Arce [non-Brazilians] who decided to become Brazilians; equipment and salaries from Marihno's money, Time-Life money and re-investment of TV Globo's earnings; and Brazilian ideas about programming to the Brazilian mass audience reinforced and supported by America ideas about commercialization and network management. While there was a definite dependence by TV Globo from 1966–1970 on foreign factors listed above, the Brazilian inputs were very strong and tended to quickly diminish dependence on foreign money, ideas and expertise (p. 168).

This latter argument is important because Straubhaar is writing to counter arguments made by those using an imperialism or from what Sarti (1981) calls, a nationalistic dependency perspective. It is primarily focused on foreign control or influence in Latin American cultural industries. If it can be shown that foreign ownership declined, or that even foreign imports are less popular, then the problem has largely been solved. Sarti argues that a genuine cultural dependency approach would look primarily *within* for its form of dependency and not focus only on an external enemy. The cultural industry approach would examine carefully the nature and growth of these industries regardless of ownership to see to what extent they follow the same model of commercial development and structural features as the dominant model in the U.S.

Some have argued that Brazil and Mexico are emerging as semi-peripheral powers and may even move into a core power status eventually, perhaps replacing ailing powers such as Britain. We would see this argument as perhaps premature, but meriting close monitoring. Within the cultural and ideological sphere as well as the economic structure of the cultural industries, careful studies of the formation and development of these industries is merited. Straubhaar has provided us with important evidence concerning one such cultural industry and others are called for.[6]

---

[6] Televisa, Mexico's emerging cultural conglomerate, is worth careful study. Thus far few published studies have appeared in English though Mahan (1982) is making a beginning; also, cf. Gutierrez and Schement, 1981.

What one must conclude is that the ownership is not the essential question to be asked unless the perspective is narrowly conceived in nationalist terms. Rather, the question is what the prevailing model is for cultural industrialization in a given country and what implications this has for its various classes.

Imitation of core media institutions and professionalism: From the discussion in the last section, it may be easy to understand the argument here. The media institutions of many peripheral countries have tended to imitate the structure of central powers like Britain and France in Asia and Africa and the U.S. in Latin America. Again the particular nature of the perspective taken makes a difference in how such imitation is interpreted. Lee (1980) makes his own position quite clear when he says: "The American commercial television system can find its foremost influence in the United Kingdom, Latin America and the Philippines. . .and Canada. . . It should be noted that institutionalization of media commercialism can be more clearly considered as a part of 'media imperialism' *only insofar as its primary source of pressures is exogenous.* If the primary source of pressure is endogenous [as in Lee's case study of Taiwan], evidence for 'media imperialism' may be necessarily weakened" (p. 91, my emphasis).

Whether and how much "influence" was exerted by a given U.S. company (as Straubhaar tries to do in the TV Globo–Time-Life connection is not at stake here so much as is the nature of the local institution once established and how its basic goals are worked out in its activities. Here, the descriptive division among broadcasting systems as either commercial, public-authority (e.g. the UK or France) and government controlled (such as USSR, Cuba) as proposed by Lee (p. 88) and others may be irrelevant. There is a certain usefulness in seeing how broadcasting serves several goals—whether those of public service, central government dissemination of information, or commercial purposes—but the nature, and especially the practices, of such institutions may not be captured with such categories. Nor may it be useful simply to note, as Lee does, that increasingly even state-owned television systems are turning to advertising as a means of support. Much closer scrutiny of how this affects communication services in those countries where commercial systems are not the norm is called for at this time of large-scale change. More critical, perhaps, is to see whether countries carry the logic of the commercial system to its conclusion or stay in the middle position where neither model really works.

Here even a dependency and imperialist perspective may break down. Rather than look upon the core powers as a monolith and the peripheral countries as victims, a cultural industry approach would suggest we also examine the "dependency" position of many of the core powers vis-à-vis the dominant cultural (if no longer the economic) power of the United States. Lee argues that such examples as Canada (a developed country but media dependent) weaken the case for dependency, but they do so only if we understand dependency in a simplistic manner. Sarti (1981) has suggested that each Latin American country be examined separately in its own particular circumstances and in the light of the particular class structures prevailing at a given time. I would agree but add that, in addition to Latin America, we may also examine other cases of cultural dependency that may be developing in the European powers themselves.

Guback in several studies (1971, 1974, for example) has clearly shown the variety of ways in which long established film industries of Western Europe were economically losing control to U.S. financial and film interests during the 1960s and 1970s. In 1980, these same European countries held a seminar on "The State's Role vis-à-vis the Culture Industries" (Council of Europe, 1980) in which the central concern was how the radio, television, film, record, and publishing industries of Western Europe could resist a growing outside threat from transnationals (primarily U.S. TNCs). Much of the material was strangely reminiscent of the dependency and imperialism arguments advanced for Third World countries who are struggling to establish their own cultural industries.

Why this example is provided is not only that it enlarges the analysis beyond Latin America, but indicates two other conclusions as well: (a) the fact that a given country can establish its own cultural industry (as perhaps Brazil) may be no guarantee that the threat of external influence will not surface at a later date; (b) the successful model of the U.S. forces others to compete on the same terms if they want to survive in the international and even their own national markets.[7]

We will not detail the arguments concerning two other matters that are often brought up in the context of imitation: professional training and norms for communication institutions and the growth of advertising support for all media world wide. Both are important in a Latin America context, especially the latter, but each deserves and has received more extensive treatment (Cruise-O'Brien, 1976; Golding, 1977 on professionalism; Janus and Roncagliolo, 1979; Fejes, 1980; Janus, 1981; Mattos (1982b) for advertising in Latin America).

Cultural impacts of media upon people: An underlying assumption, sometimes stated, of the debate over the flow of communication ma-

---

[7] In the case of musical recordings, for example, Vignolle (1980) argues for the vitality of small local French production companies and the strength of a national tradition despite dominance of local market shares in France by transnationals (none French). But later in his paper he admits that the popularity of French vocal music (the top share of the market at 40% in 1978) was steadily losing out to English vocals of all things (p. 8). This is a telling admission from a country where national culture is an important part of political life and ideology.

terials among nations is that alien messages will have a negative effect on audiences by undermining their cultural values. The statement of the Brazilian Minister of Communications cited above is a case in point: "Our commercial television is becoming a privileged vehicle for cultural imports, a basic factor in our losing what is most characteristic in our creations" (Mattos 1982a, p. 74). There are several responses to the argument, depending again on one's perspective. For Pool (1977) there is no major problem because the process of cultural assimilation has always gone on, and the implication is that, even if communication flow did not balance itself according to market forces, audiences essentially elect to watch the programs they like best. A middle ground is taken by Lee who, though admitting patterns of media imperialism, says that there is no conclusive evidence for its influence upon people (pp. 103, 108). He says of the evidence so far gathered that "while anecdotes and scattered research are available, it is obviously difficult to gauge the exact pattern and magnitude of alien media 'invasion' (p. 108)." Lee seems to argue for witholding judgment until much more work is done. We cannot help but think that this judgment could be made about all of the effects research promoted by various public and private agencies in the U.S. concerning television violence. The conclusion is that there is no conclusion, and there will not be one if we expect a final, persuasive form of evidence that all sides will accept. This does not mean that more research within given countries is not called for on the cultural impact of mass media, only that the role of research in making policy, for example, be clearly understood and that the lack of a final conclusion not deter action.

The third response to the cultural impact argument from an imperialism or dependency perspective is twofold. The first comes from a more concrete and empirically-oriented methodology and is well represented by Beltrán's (1976) summary of much effects research in Latin America to that time. He cites studies of content (which presume but do not measure impacts on audiences), in-depth qualitative studies of children's responses to televised material and surveys of adults' responses to popular television soap operas. Some would argue with the methodologies of the individual studies, others with the conclusions Beltrán makes for those studies about the alienating effects of both indigenous and foreign material. The second response of this group is cast at a more abstract level and may be identified with studies of ideology whether these be more culturalist or structuralist (using Hall's (1980) distinction). A quote from a footnote in the UNESCO MacBride Commission Report (1980) may state one form of the argument. According to Hugo Gutierrez:

> The cultural industry is not a mere ideological apparatus . . . that does
> not create ideology but is limited to promoting and disseminating it.

The cultural industry does in fact also create ideology . . . Clearly, if
the principle underlying activities of the cultural industry is commercialization, all the productions of art, science, literature and cultural
in general which it mediates are necessarily affected . . . Clearly, too,
the cultural industry plays a major role in moulding the mentalities of
its consumers, exercises an increasingly marked influence upon the
psychic economy. (p. 160, footnote)[8]

Another distinction that may help in the understanding of the argument about "effects" is one among the three effects most often cited:
alienation, consumer orientation and class discrimination. Briefly, the
more common national argument among Latin Americans concerns the
danger of citizens of a given country losing their national (and sometimes
ethnic) identifies because they are exposed to Hollywood's view of the
world through *Dallas* or *Kojak*. The second involves a concern that the
commercial nature of the media will have the effect of generating a con-
sumerism that is either exaggerated (Lerner's (1964) rising frustrations
argument) or inappropriate (Wells, 1972; Sauvant, 1979). The third focus is
much more in a classic Marxist paradigm where alienation of the working
class is accomplished among other means through the bourgeois mass
media (Salinas and Paldán, 1979; Sarti, 1981). These are by no means the
only kinds of effects that are discussed in the Latin American context of
dependency but the three categories distinguish a large body of the literature.

BRAZIL AS A CASE OF CULTURAL INDUSTRIAL DEVELOPMENT

The case of Brazil is an intriguing one. It has many of the characteristics of
other dependent economies with large foreign debts, a dual economy with
a large rural population sharing little in the rapid growth of the modern
sector and an authoritarian central government that has kept itself in
power for almost twenty years. On the other hand, Brazil along with Mexico in Latin America in the past two decades has managed rapid growth
within a stable political situation and provided increased economic improvement for at least some of its population. It has adopted a much more
technocratic than a merely repressive approach to its state capitalism and
it has created a modern industrial base that is promising future growth in
terms of world trade.

---

[8] Also found in the preparatory documents for the MacBride Commission, #77 *Cultural Industry* by Hugo Gutierrez. Paris: UNESCO, n.d.

In addition to the economic growth in the past 15 years, there are a series of cultural factors that suggest that Brazil is experiencing significant changes there as well. As we have noted, Straubhaar (1981) shows that Brazil has emerged as a serious television industry which is not only producing a number of popular television series (the *telenovelas*) for its large internal market (20 million television sets for its 120 million people in 1980), but is beginning to aggressively market these homemade series in some 50 countries. Added to this, Mattos (1982a) shows that the Brazilian military government over the past sixteen years (1964–1980) has put into place a series of laws and institutions that have reinforced a technically competent and rapidly expanding television system. Johnson (1982) also provides evidence that the same technocratic state capitalism has created an economic and legal base for a local film industry that has grown rapidly in terms of income (188 percent growth from 1974 to 1978) and even begun to export films to other countries (exports expected to rise 500 percent between 1981 and 1982, and from $1 million to about $5 million in sales). Finally, Mattos (1982b) indicates that the hegemony of U.S. transnational advertising agencies may be slackening considerably in Brazil, due, apparently, to an aggressive state policy of "buying Brazilian" through the large state enterprise system that currently dominates the economy, and, consequently, the advertising industry.

Does all this mean that, indeed, the dependency model is inadequate to explain Brazil and is an inappropriate paradigm for other Third World countries as well? The following section will argue that, properly understood, the dependency model may still provide a useful guide to comprehending both the economic, political, and even the cultural reality of Brazil and other Latin American countries, but also that, as Sarti (1981) has argued, each country must be examined within its own specific historical circumstances. Brazil certainly has a set of circumstances that would merit individual study and may offer (along with Mexico) a good case to apply a cultural industry approach in order to chart the changes that are taking place and to anticipate the consequences both within Brazil and throughout Latin America.

The following pages will draw upon the previously cited recent work on the Brazilian cultural industries and use it to illustrate some of the more general arguments concerning the relations among economic, cultural and political factors outlined at the beginning of this paper.

The technological base: Although I stated that I did not believe that technological innovation as such was of singular importance in dependent countries (since all of these technologies are imported), it is clear that the development of a cultural industry in any country is closely related to the use of a series of technologies. In Brazil, the history of television's development over the past two decades was influenced by a number of technical factors that were crucial. Both Mattos (1982a) and Straubhaar (1981) point out that these factors greatly affected the growth and direction of Brazilian television. The combined list from their works includes: (a) national production of television sets; (b) lower relative cost of sets; (c) use of videotape in the early 1960s; (d) creation of a dubbing facility in Brazil in the early 1960s; (e) improved television transmitting equipment; (f) improved microwave links in the late 1960s; (g) credit buying law in 1968; (h) use of Intelsat satellite for major world events; and (i) introduction of a color system in mid-1970s.

It would take more space than is available here to spell out the implications of these developments for the growth and direction of Brazilian television. But several observations are called for. We find that Brazilian television has followed a clear U.S. commercial model during the past 20 years, and has done so successfully. This could not have happened without the introduction of many of the technologies listed above. For example, the whole growth of television is intimately related to the growth of the advertising industry and the growth of the consumer goods market that took place in the 1960s and 1970s. The rapid investment of the consumer goods manufacturers in television for the latter's growth was essential, but this in turn depended on the size of the television market and the number and kinds of people who were watching. A rapid expansion of sets was critical to this growth. Straubhaar (p. 48) shows that there was a doubling of the number of sets for a 12 year period from 1964 to 1976, and Mattos (1982b) shows that these sets were concentrated in cities (a 75 percent penetration by 1980). The relative lower cost of a set was due, in part, to local production, but, also, to relative gains in disposible income for some classes and to an important 1968 law that allowed credit buying of a set over 36 months. The use of dubbing and videotape in the early 1960's allowed Brazil to enter fully upon almost a decade of major importation of U.S. programs and allowed a number of television stations to grow and to organize into groups. Even if such a deluge of imports could raise the question of cultural values by a minister of communication, it allowed a large audience to be formed in its tastes. The microwave links, however, may have been the most telling of the innovations because it allowed TV Globo to first conceive of a national network and to begin to sell advertising on a national basis. This was an enticement not only for local, but especially the transnational businesses to invest heavily in television from the beginning of the 1970s. The rapid increase in television advertising (Mattos 1982b) shows a 700 percent growth in television expenditures from 1969–1978 and accounts almost entirely for the large advertising growth in general. Finally, the addition of color and the use of satellite transmission internationally (World Soccer Cup events being but one attraction) are additional factors that reinforce a commercially prosperous system by the mid-1970s.

The role of the state: Mattos (1982a) argues that the military coup of 1964 and the subsequent establishment of a strong state capitalism influenced the direction of television in Brazil. He summarizes his position as follows:

> In Brazil the short and long-term responses of the military regime were geared toward accelerating order, progress, security and modernization, including strong state participation in the economy, friendliness to multinational investment, and development of basic conditions for national integration through a telecommunications system. The military regime contributed directly and indirectly to the development of Brazilian television, which benefited from the social, political and economic situation of the period between 1964 and 1980. (p. 93)

The government's role in television's growth was indirect for the most part but crucial to the competing groups that had emerged by 1964. Among other things, it promoted many of the technical improvements mentioned above (the national microwave network was begun early as a defense measure but also served admirably for commercial purposes). It also created over a dozen years a series of state institutions that promoted in their different ways both the television (Mattos, 1982a, p. 42) and film (Johnson, 1982) industries. The role is distinct in the two for a variety of reasons. In television, the military government saw an important instrument for promoting its ideas about national security and modernization, but it chose to work indirectly to promote the technical base, the legal control on content (through censorship, especially 1969–1978), and the fostering of a series of financial conditions to help the commercial networks grow. Straubhaar (1981) discusses the indirect role of the government in Globo's growth (pp. 125, 159). In film, according to Johnson, the government has taken a much more direct role, assuming important aspects of finance, distribution and exhibition of Brazilian films. In addition, it has enacted over the past 13 years a series of legal requirements for showing Brazilian films (from 63 days per year in 1969 to 140 days a year in 1979) that have had the effect of increasing the market share of national films from 13.8 percent of audiences in 1971 to 29.2 percent in 1978 (and increasing income from $13 to $38 million from 1974 to 1978). The state organization, Embrafilme, is also responsible for distribution of about one-third of all Brazilian films nationally (second only to the major foreign distributor in income) as well as export where for many years it has had minimal success until 1981 when it first reached the $1 million mark and hoped to move up to $5 million by 1982.

Clearly, the cultural industries of film and television are very different in nature in most countries and have different structures. In a commercial television system that operates according to market forces as is the case in Brazil, advertising and the consumer market are important to growth, but also to the nature of programming. In film, a relatively expensive product is sold directly to consumers over a period of months or even years. The financing and distributions mechanisms are critical in both film and television, but the money is upfront in television whereas in film it only comes in much later from box office receipts. Lacking a corporate structure as it exists in Hollywood, the Brazilian film industry (if it can be so termed at this time) needed the government to step in to provide the impetus toward growth.

Advertising and television growth. The series of critical circumstances that existed in Brazil during the last twenty years helped to account for the growth of a major cultural industry in television. But clearly the most important of these circumstances was the rapid economic expansion in the late 1960s and the accompanying growth of advertising expenditure as a natural part of that system's apparatus. Mattos (1982b) and Fejes (1980) have both demonstrated the significant growth of the advertising industry. From 1968 to 1979, for example, Brazilian expenditures on all forms of measured advertising rose from $233 million to $1,582 million (an increase of 600 percent) and, as we have noted, television advertising received a major portion of this increase (going from $100 million to $684 million during the same period). It is not difficult to understand that with the influx of such wealth into the television industry there would be an unprecedented growth in all directions. But that growth was uneven and TV Globo, which by the later 1960s had not only originated a national network but dominated the ratings in major markets (Straubhaar, p. 180), grew from another competitor among several to the fourth largest network in the world (after ABC, CBS and NBC in the U.S.) but also a close imitation of those networks as a cultural conglomerate. Thus, Mattos (1982a) points out that by 1979 TV Globo, in addition to its major television production operations, owned and operated 5 stations in major markets, had 36 affiliated stations, owned a major newspaper, 17 radio stations, a publishing company, a record company, a telecommunications industry, an entertainment promotion business, an art gallery, a cable television company, and a corporate foundation.

However the system developed and to whatever extent Globo or others were influenced by different foreign companies, the nature of the basic model is clearly similar to that which the U.S. has developed. Straubhaar argues for a strong Brazilian contribution to the growth of the system but admits that '''dependence on technology and advertising revenues for finance do keep the industry itself firmly linked to the international capitalist system'' (p. 223). The basic commercial nature of Globo and its rivals is important to understand. Globo's real success was its ability to create a national network for attracting national advertising expenditures and creating programming (at first largely imported but later based on local *telenovelas*) that attracted large audiences which were what advertisers wanted. With important early financing from a $6 million loan from Time-Life, a tightly-controlled central administration and a programming policy based on audience research and large numbers, Globo was able to outdistance its rivals and enter the international market as well. In 1977, TV Globo was at Cannes to sell some of its better products to other countries and by 1979 was able to boast that it exported to 50 countries (Mattos 1982a, p. 21).

One more aspect of the operation of television in Brazil needs underlining. Investment in advertising by the consumer market found a natural outlet in television not only because more people were buying sets in the 1970s, but also because the consumer market itself was growing. To what extent this was stimulated by outside transnational advertisers or local Brazilian counterparts is perhaps less important in a cultural industry than in a cultural imperialism framework. What Brazilian television advertised was, in many ways, similar to what U.S. television advertised (Valdez, 1981), consumer products that large audiences could purchase. Mattos (1982b) points out that in 1980 the top twenty products on television were a majority of small consumer items like toiletries, food, drugs, cigarettes, beer, shoes, whose purchase falls within both the necessities and the minor luxuries of a significant number of viewers.

Some contradictions in the system: It is tempting to see the Brazilian case as a clear counter-argument to the dependency paradigm in much the same way as Lee (1980) argues for Taiwan. But two things would caution against such a hasty conclusion. First, the evidence is preliminary and calls for study over a longer period of time. Second, as Sarti (1981) points out, one must be careful not to generalize a single case to all countries, but to look on a case by case basis. Brazil is a rapidly industrializing state that is, perhaps, escaping some of the more blatant forms of dependency. But even today, most would argue, it is still dependent in many ways on external financial sources and technologies. If countries like Brazil, Mexico and, perhaps, some OPEC countries are seen to move toward a semiperipheral status, there are still many cases of genuinely dependent economies and cultures which do not have the endowments of Brazil and may never emerge as Brazil has done.

There are in the case of Brazil itself several contradictions in the system that need to be called to the attention of scholars of cultural industries. First, Brazil is a case of strong state capitalism where state enterprises make up a significant portion of the national economy (about 75 percent of net assets of the 200 largest nonfinancial enterprises and almost 50 percent of the net profits according to Mattos (1982b)). The military government has techno-economic reasons for promoting, either directly or indirectly, the cultural industries of film and television (they help the economy), but it is also clear there are political interests at stake about the contents of industry products. In a clash of values, there is always the danger of contradiction. The government may wish for home-made products so as not to undermine Brazilian cultural values, but it is doubtful that this goal will predominate to the detriment of the television industry (still very much in need of imports). In film, for example, the *pornochanchada* (soft porn films) are a consequence of higher national film quotas (quota quickies) and are tolerated for economic reasons by a military government that puts morality high in its list of national values (Johnson, 1982).

The existence of censorship and commercial values in the cultural industries of Brazil has not caused major contradictions to date, but the underlying logic of commercial television would dictate the dominance of profit over patriotism. Straubhaar says: "TV Globo's executives have argued that they utilize their relative independence to be as creative as possible and to emphasize education and culture as much as possible within the limits of what will be commercially successful" (p. 193). If the government is to play a major role in the promotion of culture and education, it must at some point come into conflict with the prevailing values of the cultural industries. It is a standing contradiction in capitalism according to Bell (1975) who says of the U.S. system: "the breakup of the traditional bourgeois value system, in fact, was brought about by the bourgeois economic system—by the free market, to be precise. This is the source of the contradiction of capitalism in American life" (p. 55). He clarifies this point in another paragraph: "Changes in cultural ideas have an immanence and autonomy because they develop from an internal logic at work within a cultural tradition. . . But change in cultural practices and life-style necessarily interact with social structure since works of art . . . are bought and sold in the market" (p. 55). Some similar contradicitons will await the rising new cultures in a number of other countries as well.

This brings into focus another problem for the analysis of cultural industries. If the commercial system of television is to sell consumer products to audiences, then the question of impact needs to be raised briefly. Straubhaar quotes two Brazilian critics of television and society, Fernando Cardoso, a leading dependency theorist, and Marco Antonio Dias, a former communications professor at the University of Brasilia. They both agree that the purpose of television is not to provide information and entertainment to audiences but to sell consumer products to them. They disagree, however, as to whether the long term result will be an elite or a mass consumption society. Cardoso argues that the Brazilian economy is geared to dualist development and the consumption patterns will be those of the elite class (relatively speaking) and will exclude the lower classes. Dias, on the other hand, argues that the vast majority of Brazilians will be drawn into the consumer society through the promotion of television (among other things). The argument may not be easily resolved in the short run, but, at present, Cardoso's position is clearly more tenable. Looking at TV set distribution in 1980, we find that the 20 million sets covered about 55 percent of the population with a 75 percent penetration in urban areas. If we look at population figures for 1980, we can conclude that even in 1980 only about 17 percent of rural families owned sets (about 32 million people were without sets in this area) and that among the urban population, there were about 20 million people excluded. It is this large segment of both urban and rural populations that is often overlooked in the concentration on Brazil's growth as a cultural industrial state. Not only are these people not able to buy a television set but they are obviously not the audience for whom consumer products, even the most common, are possibilities.

CONCLUSION

This paper has argued that the issues raised in the 1970s over the imbalance of communication-cultural flows among nations are by no means dead in the present decade. In fact, faced with growth in new technologies and exports of software to nurture them, the international cultural market will become increasingly important and the issues of cultural integrity even more acute. For this reason, it is time to reexamine the assumptions of the different positions in the debate on cultural exchange and cultural dependency. The position taken in this paper is one that places more emphasis on the economic structures of cultural production called the cultural industries' approach. Although it does not contradict the more common cultural imperialism and cultural dependency perspectives, it stresses the importance of the interaction of the industrialization process in cultural creation and exchange of products.

From the perspective of these theories concerning the cultural creation and exchange of such products as television programs, films, musical recordings, etc., the use of national case studies emerges as an important step in a research strategy. Instead of trying to create a theory suited to all countries and having arguments raised about the generalizability of results and the validity of the theory, the study of the growth and impact of cultural industries within each country is more appropriate. Brazil is used as an example because it in many ways seems to have escaped the most obvious forms of cultural imperialism. Taken within its own context and historical circumstances, however, the growth of television in Brazil shows the elements of great structural similarity and presumably similar cultural consequences as the dominant U.S. commercial television model. This case illustrates as well that much greater detailed analyses need to be done in each country to trace the structural constraints and consequences of the specific communication systems on their populations. The 1980s may well be characterized by such country studies through groups of local scholars and communicators who have more than mere academic interests in confirming a theoretical position. Rather, it is hoped that such evidence gathered in a national context may be used by national groups for the creation of better strategies for combatting the negative consequences of the cultural industries whether these consequences flow from internal or external sources.

REFERENCES

Arendt, H. (1961). "Society and Culture." *In* N. Jacobs (Ed.), *Cultural for the Millions?* Princeton, NJ: Van Nostrand.

Bell, D. (1975). *The Cultural Contradictions of Capitalism.* New York: Basic Books.

Beltrán, L. R. (1976). "TV Etchings in the Minds of Latin Americans: Conservatism, Materialism and Conformism." Paper prepared for 10th General Assembly of the International Association of Mass Communication Research, University of Leicester, UK.

Beltrán, L. R., and Fox, E. (1979). "Latin America and the United States: Flaws in the Free Flow of Information." *In* K. Nordenstreng and H. Schiller (Eds.), *National Sovereignty and International Communication.* Norwood, NJ: Ablex.

Cardoso, H. (1971). "Teoria da Dependencia ou analises concretas de situacoes de dependencia?" *Estudos Cebrap,* Vol. 1. Sao Paulo.

Cardoso, F. H., and Faletto, E. (1979). *Dependency and Development in Latin America.* Berkeley, CA: University of California Press.

Chronicle of International Communication. (1981). February, Washington, DC.

Council of Europe. (1980). *The State's Role vis-à-vis the Culture Industries.* Strasbourg, France: Council of Europe.

Cruise-O'Brien, R. (1976). "Professionalism in Broadcasting: Comparative Study in Algeria and Senegal." Institute of Development Studies, University of Sussex, Brighton, UK (mimeo).

Cruise-O'Brien, R., and Helleiner, G. (1982). "The Political Economy of Information in a Changing International Economic Order." *In* M. Jussawalla and D. Lamberton (Eds.), *Communication Economics and Development.* Honolulu, HI: Pergamon and East–West Center.

Donner, J. (1980). "European Film Policy: Major Issues Regarding the Development of Film Production and Systems of Public Intervention." *In The State's Role vis-a-vis the Culture Industries.* Strasbourg, France: Council of Europe.

dos Santos, T. (1974). *Dependencia Economica y Cambio Revolucionario en America Latina.* Buenos Aires: Ed. Viejo Topo.

Enzenberger, H. M. (1964). *Einzelheiten I Bewusstseins-Industrie.* Frankfurt au Main: Suhrkamp Verlag.

Fejes, F. (1980). "The Growth of Multinational Advertising Agencies in Latin America." *Journal of Communication 30*(4), 36–49.

Flichy, P. (1979). *MacLuhan à Wall Street, Economie des Systemes Audio-visuels.* Grenoble, France: Presse universitaire.

Golding, P. (1977). "Media Professionalism in the Third World: The Transfer of an Ideology." *In* J. Curran, J. Gurevitch, and M. Wollacott (Eds.), *Mass Communication and Society.* Beverly Hills, CA: Sage Publications.

Gutierrez, F., and Schement, J. (1981). "Problems of Ownership and Control of Spanish-Language Media in the U.S.: National and International Policy Concerns." *In* E. McAnany, J. Schnitman and N. Janus (Eds.), *Communication and Social Structure: Critical Studies in Mass Media Research.* New York: Praeger.

Guback, T. (1971). "Film and Cultural Pluralism." *Journal of Aesthetic Education 5,* (2), 35–51.

Guback, T. (1974). "Film as International Business." *Journal of Communication 24,* (1), 90–101.

Hall, S. (1980). "Cultural Studies: Two Paradigms." *Media, Culture and Society 2,* 57–72.

Jacobson, R. (1979). "Satellite Business Systems and the Concept of the Dispersed Enterprise: An End to National Sovereignty?" *Media, Culture and Society 1,* 235–253.

Janus, N., and Roncagliolo, R. (1979). "Advertising, Mass Media and Dependency." *Development Dialogue 1,* 81–97.

Janus, N. (1981). "Advertising and the Mass Media in the Era of the Global Corporations." *In* E. McAnany, J. Schnitman and N. Janus (Eds.), *Communication and Social Structure: Critical Studies in Mass Media Research.* New York: Praeger.

Johnson, R. (1982). "State Policy toward the Film Industry in Brazil." Paper prepared for the Latin American Studies Association meeting, Washington, DC.

Katz, E. (1979). "Cultural Continuity and Change: Role of the Media." *In* K. Nordenstreng and H. Schiller (Eds.), *National Sovereignty and International Communication.* Norwood, NJ: Ablex.

Katz, E., and Wedell, G. (1977). *Broadcasting in the Third World: Promise and Performance.* Cambridge, MA: Harvard University Press.

Lee, C. C. (1980). *Media Imperialism Reconsidered: The Homogenizing of Television Culture.* Beverly Hills, CA: Sage Publications.

Lerner, D. (1963). "Toward a Communication Theory of Modernization." *In* L. Pye (Ed.), *Communication and Political Development.* Princeton, NJ: Princeton University Press.

Mahan, E. (1982). "Commercial Broadcast Regulation: Structures and Processes in Mexico and the United States." Unpublished dissertation, University of Texas at Austin.

Mattelart, A. (1973). *Agresión Desde Espacio: Cultura, Nepalm en la Era de los Satelites.* Buenos Aires: Siglo Veintiuno.

Mattos, S. (1982a). *The Impact of the 1964 Revolution on Brazilian Television.* San Antonio: Klingesmith.

Mattos, S. (1982b). "Domestic and Foreign Advertising in Television and Mass Media Growth: A Case Study of Brazil" Unpublished dissertation, University of Texas at Austin.

Murdock, G. and Golding, P. "Capitalism, Communications and Class Relations." *In* J. Curran, J. Gurevitch and M. Wollacott (Eds.), *Mass Communication and Society.* Beverly Hills, CA: Sage Publications.

Nordenstreng, K., and Varis, T. (1974). *Television Traffic—A One-Way Street?* Reports and Papers on Mass Communication #70. Paris: UNESCO.

Pool, I. (1977). "The Changing Flow of Television." *Journal of Communication 27* (2), 139–149.

Pool, I. (1979). "Direct Broadcast Satellites and the Integrity of National Cultures." *In* K. Nordenstreng and H. Schiller (Eds.), *National Sovereignty and International Communication.* Norwood, NJ: Ablex.

Read, W. (1976). *America's Mass Media Merchants.* Baltimore, MD: Johns Hopkins University Press.

Sainsbury, P. (1980). "Possibilities for Joint European Action to Shape the International Market Forces: Alternative Strategies for Government Intervention." *In The State's Role vis-a-vis the Culture Industries.* Strasbourg, France: Council of Europe.

Salinas, R. and Paldan, L. (1974). "Culture in the Process of Dependent Development; Theoretical Perspectives." *In* K. Nordenstreng and H. Schiller (Eds.), *National Sovereignty and International Communication.* Norwood, NJ: Ablex.

Sarti, I. (1981). "Communication and Cultural Dependency: A Misconception." *In* E. McAnany, J. Schnitman and N. Janus (Eds.), *Communication and Social Structure: Critical Studies in Mass Media Research.* New York: Praeger.

Sauvant, K. (1979). "Sociocultural Emancipation." *In* K. Nordenstreng and H. Schiller (Eds.), *National Sovereignty and International Communication.* Norwood, NJ: Ablex.

Schiller, H. (1976). *Communication and Cultural Domination.* White Plains, NY: International Arts and Sciences.

Schiller, H. (1981). *Who Knows? Information in the Age of the Fortune 500.* Norwood, NJ: Ablex.

Smith, A. (1980). *The Geopolitics of Information: How Western Culture Dominates the World.* New York: Oxford.

Straubhaar, J. (1981). "The Transformation of Cultural Dependence: The Decline of American Influence on the Brazilian Television Industry." Unpublished dissertation, Tufts University.

Tunstall, J. (1977). *The Media are America: Anglo-American Media in the World.* New York: Columbia University Press.

UNESCO (MacBride Commission Report). (1980). *Many Voices One World.* New York: Unipub.

Valdez, A. (1981). "The Economic Context of U.S. Children's Television: Parameters of Reform?" *In* E. McAnany, J. Schnitman and N. Janus (Eds.), *Communication and Social Structure: Critical Studies in Mass Media Research.* New York: Praeger.

Vignolle, J. P. (1980). "International Concentration of Distribution, Vitality of National Cultural Production and the Role of the Authorities: The Situation in France." *In State's Role vis-à-vis the Culture Industries.* Strasburg: France: Council of Europe.

Wells, A. (1972). *Picture-Tube Imperialism? The Impact of US Television on Latin America.* New York: Orbis Books.

Section III

EUROPE

10

Twenty-Three Guidelines for a Political Debate on Communication in Europe

Armand Mattelart and Jean-Marie Piemme
(translated by David Buxton)

After an initial appraisal in *Télévision, enjeux sans frontières* (Presses Universitaires de Grenoble, 1980),[1] we have carried out, at the request of the Département Audiovisuel du ministère de la Communauté Francaise in Belgium, a study aiming at setting out alternatives in the field of both established and new media.

The following text is made up of a series of guidelines that fix the general framework of the study and define a number of perspectives that are developed in the analysis.

1. The Very Nature of Information has Changed

During the last decade, and particularly since the so-called energy crisis, the production of information has ceased to be restricted to the journalistic sphere. In the near future, the information sector will be called upon to make itself relevant to increasingly numerous spheres of society. Information has become a basic resource (some would say a new form of raw material, a new energy source) for the management of society. It includes the rules, prohibitions, knowledge, and know-how that condition and irrigate all human activity. More concretely, the concept of information now covers areas as diverse as the contents of databanks (scientific, technical, financial, social, military, civil, etc.); so-called cultural

---

[1] See also Mattelart and Piemme, 1980; 1982.

information, comprising fiction (films, television series, dispatches, magazines, advertising, inquiries, educational series, scientific populari- zation, etc.) produced by what are now called the culture industries; and, all the theoretical and practical knowledge linked to the mastery of tech- nology (know-how, patents, management, engineering, planning, train- ing, etc.).

2. The Information Industry Has Become a Leading Economic Sector

In the advanced capitalist countries, information, understood in the above sense, has become a powerful economic motor. It it increasingly a party in the production of a country's wealth. In the United States, for example, the information industry has for several years been responsible for over half of the gross national product, and an increasing number of people are now employed in this sector. The information industry is found at the con- vergence of the new technologies of production, storage, and distribution such as computers, satellites, cables, optical fibers, television, telephone, videodiscs, and videotape recorders. The advent of these technologies and the globalization of information systems cannot be understood without mentioning the second wind of a model of development and growth whose validity is now no more questioned than it was in preceding decades.

3. One Medium Displaces Another

In every communication system, one medium is hegemonic in relation to the others. It marks out the framework in which they are inscribed. The dominance of a new medium necessarily forces the others to redefine the field of their autonomy and dependence. The history of the first modern communication technologies (railways, telegraph, telephone, etc.) should be re-interpreted with this factor in mind. Today, it is important to recog- nize the nature of the dominant medium and to pinpoint the areas where it exercises its influence. A new medium isn't simply added to established ones, but rather helps them re-form themselves into a new configuration qualitatively different from the sum of the effects of each medium. Thus, the arrival of the computer, rather than purely and simply adding itself to television, defines, through their convergence, a new stage of technologi- cal rationality.

4. The Information Industry is Transversing Sectors Previously Independent of the Industry

At the end of the 1960s, the transformation of the cinema and television industry heralded the restructuring of the culture industries, which since has only accentuated. Powerful conglomerates have reunited previously dispersed industrial activities: manufacturers of input media are more and more interested in the production of programs, and they are discovering that they can regroup other types of industrial production around them. From Warner—once taken over by a plumbing and funeral parlor firm, and today a flourishing multimedia enterprise in which films, television series, books, electronic games, toys, etc. all coexist—to the interest shown by Exxon in office computers and information systems and the links of IBM to the satellite, without forgetting the advances made by the American telecommunications giant AT&T towards cable television, we are today witnessing a vast process of concentration and diversification. In the search for new forms of capital accumulation, this model seems to be slowly gaining ground in Europe where, on a smaller scale, the same efforts at concentration and diversification are taking place. The merger between the satellites and armaments firm, Matra, with the fifth biggest publishing multinational (Hachette) is a convincing example of this.

5. The Information Industry is Transforming the Traditional Concept of Culture

The development of a cultural policy is directly confronted with the multiple effects of the products and the functioning of the information industry. In the domain of entertainment, education, adult education and retraining and cultural action and creation, the information industry proposes models and a mode of production and consumption which forces former models to either redefine themselves or collapse. Thus, if they are not reduced to being gadgets as television was in its time, the introduction of computers in schools necessarily leads to a complete revision of existing pedagogical models, even for courses which do not use them. Similarly, the existence of performance arts today can no longer fulfill the same functions that they had done prior to the mass broadcasting of television.

6. An Information Industry to Politically Administer the Crisis

Nobody can any longer deny that an information industry exists. However, Americans also speak of an "information society." A new mythology is infiltrating in this slide from one concept to another, bringing former labels like "mass society," "the leisure society," and "the consumer society" back into fashion. The principal effect of these labels is to mask the real rather than to explain it. These "concepts" have the serious defect of obscuring how it is that a new phase of advanced capitalism is constituted, both in its rupture and its continuity. The idea of an "information society" (sometimes called "communication society") hinders understanding of the political function that the development of new communication technologies is called upon to play in the restructuring of the political and cultural apparatuses of the world capitalist system in the installation of a new power bloc. Notably, it does not allow one to understand the role played by the new technologies in the production of a consensus and the advent of new mechanisms of social control. The impact of this formidable development of the information industry cannot be reduced to a relationship between industrialists, commodities and consumers. More profoundly, it affects the relationship between the state and the citizen: the introduction of the law of value in the most diverse domains completes the atomizing process of the commoditization of civil society.

7. Internationalization is Threatening Cultural Identities

More and more countries are questioning their particularity when faced with the process of internationalization. Evidence can be found in situations as diverse as the claims of Third World countries for a new world information order, the latest French protests against the hegemony of American cinema within France, and the anxiety arising from the fact that 90 percent of all French databanks are American and only stock information of potential economic and political profitability. Faced with internationalization, several governments along with certain groups have put forward a claim for cultural identity. However, if one is not careful, cultural identity can become a jumbled, catch-all concept. By using this notion lightly, one always runs the risk of turning it into an open house in which the nationalist demands of a certain Right coexist with legitimate resistance to the colonization process. Internationalization proceeds according to the existing power relations within different sectors of the information industry. From this point of view, there are two fundamentally different types of internationalization. On the one hand, there is the export of a product from one country only and which thus constitutes a hegemonic industry (for example, the world domination of American cinema); on the other hand, one must take into account internationalization through the interiorization of production and distribution norms and models leading to a nationally-produced commodity which, however, corresponds in every way, to a transnational logic. By making this distinction between two types of internationalization, one avoids the trap of a rigid and chauvinist use of the concept of Americanization and one prevents demands for autonomy foundering into a simpleminded, gut-level anti-Americanism.

8. The New Information System Corresponds to New Relations Between Nations

The possibility of the production and distribution of information as a commodity has become one more element of segregation between peoples.

From now on, there are data-rich and data-poor countries. To the extent that some countries have it at their disposal, and others do not, information has become a fundamental weapon in the military-economic strategy of defense and attack. Information also becomes a central element in security policy. In the new international division of labor, the grey-matter favors the setting up of "soft" systems of international domination. The anxiety of Third World countries faced with transborder data flows is the most recent illustration of this. However, much wider issues, which concern the whole of the productive apparatus, are at stake. Already some Third World countries are anxious over the possible consequences of repatriation of certain key industries installed in the Third World for reasons of economic convenience (for example, better political conditions for the exploitation of the workforce) to their home countries owing to the automation of certain sectors of the industry.

9. The New Information Systems are Reformulating the Distribution of the World of Work

The new information systems have been called upon to transform in depth the production process and thus, the composition of the workforce. They are challenging the factory as the visible center of production and as the privileged site of the formation of working-class consciousness, which the factory has held ever since the constitution of large production units in the 19th century. The information industries favor the accession of a stratum of technicians in the construction of new sites of power and the rearrangement of the sociological distribution of the old working-class. The new information systems thus constitute a challenge for contemporary forms of resistance to the capitalist development process and they force the workers' movement to an effort of social imagination.

10. The Cultural Industries are also Vectors of Privatization

Cultural industries are a part of the information sector. Contrary to definitions that confine them to the economic sphere, contrary to tautological definitions that simply see cultural industries as industries producing cultural goods with industrial technology, we would define them as channels for the commoditization of sectors (culture, religion, education, etc.) that have hitherto remained outside the commodity circuit and thus little affected by the law of value. This process opens the door to the progressive privatization of the state sectors which have up until now been oriented by the norms of public service. One cannot therefore reduce the relation between the state and the cultural industries to a confrontation between two distinct adversaries. In the present phase of transnationalization being carried out by the cultural industries, the capitalist state is very much involved in the progressive stripping of its own functions. Only the social contradictions circulating through the state apparatus, and localized resistance within civil society, constitute a check on the tendency to privatization and allow us to pose the question of the social base of alternatives.

11. The New Information Systems Put the Question of Social Creativity on the Agenda

The new communication systems are contemporaneous with a profound crisis of the whole model of development of our societies and the alternative models that were developed toward the end of the nineteenth and the beginning of the twentieth century. Only the sterility of both the capitalist and the alternative models of structural change has enabled one to imagine that new technologies carry, in their very technicity, a solution to these crises. Besides, a social revolution through technology does not seem to be imminent. This feeling is becoming more and more widespread with the profound divorce between technological sophistication and the models (forms, content) to which it is supposed to correspond. In this light, the absence of reflection on the pedagogical models and goals that ought to accompany technological development are particularly felt. Similarly, the margin of real creation, which breaks with the dominant mode of the imaginary and reconstitution of the real, runs the risk of being submitted to an incessant process of remakes in which the old is perpetually recast in the fashion of the moment.

12. Is the Model of Development of Transnational Capital Suitable for Belgium?

In this, and the following two sections, we will consider the particular case of Belgium. The Belgian industrial production apparatus is essentially centered in sectors that are in crisis. Today, Belgium is paying the consequences of a policy which opened its gates to multinational firms. Its electronic and telecommunications industry was developed under the aegis of foreign firms (Philips, Siemens, ITT, etc.), and it is therefore vulnerable to the restructuring, on a worldwide scale that these firms carry out. Leaving aside several exceptions, Belgium's own productive capacity in the information sector is extremely weak. One might add that this weakness is extremely unequally distributed between the two linguistic communities: in tne telecommunications industries, for example, 73.2 percent of the employment is concentrated in Flanders, 22.1 percent in the Brussels region and only 4.7 percent in Wallonia. In addition, multinational firms have often used Belgian territory for managing their European, if not global, affairs. Brussels has thus become the center of a network of world banking information (the SWIFT[2] network) which links the principal international banks. Too often, Belgium has served as a center for operations that do not necessarily coincide with a model of development corresponding with its long-term needs. The inevitability of this externally-oriented model of development appears less so if one analyses in retrospect the lost chances by the government and the trade unions for strategic negotiation with transnational capital.

13. Culturally, Belgium is Becoming More and More Dependent

Belgium is particularly dependent on foreign cultural production, American and French, for the French-speaking part of the country. Cinema, television, and especially certain domains like fiction, records, and books are essentially dominated by foreign firms. Up until recently, the state took practically no account of these sectors as domains of production, being content to dispense limited aid without this really constituting a stage in a concerted plan of development. The smallness of the forecasted budgets scarcely allows for the exploitation of the offers of cultural creation which come from certain sectors of the Francophone community or to stimulate initiative in areas where it is lacking. The historical accumulation of dependence combined with the stagnation of its own productive apparatuses is preventing the Francophone community from setting itself up as an autonomous pole of cultural growth. It is also forcing creators into exile, or reducing them to silence or slow death through exhaustion.

14. Transnationalization is Making the Public Monopoly Paradoxical

With the development of cable television since 1970, the main center of mass cultural production (the RTBF, Radio-Télévision Belge Francophone) finds itself subjected to sharp competition from foreign television. Through this situation, Belgium is foreshadowing what could happen to other European countries once direct-broadcasting satellites have allowed the overflowing of the frontiers of the nation-state and new technologies like the videodisc have vastly increased the choice of programs. There is thus a paradox evident in maintaining a form of protectionism in the production of the televisual image at the very time when choice is becoming more and

---

[2] The international bank wire operated by the Society for Worldwide Interbank Telecommunications.

more vast. The consequence of this paradox is to make monopoly unsuitable as an instrument for realizing and guaranteeing public service. Not only has the monopoly become incapable of assuring the maintenance of a real cultural identity for favoring an idea of public interest, but one could go so far as to say that it is today preventing the emergence of forms of resistance to the transnational commercial thrust.

15. Pragmatism is Not a Policy

Apart from a few limited circles which have made it their main preoccupation, the paradigms conveyed by the information industry and its new developments, are far from being the object of public debate and far from imposing their urgency on various socio-political decision-making centers in most countries. Too many projects for the introduction of new communications technologies are drawn up in terms of a pragmatism in which their cultural and social consequences are all but ignored. The case of cable TV in Belgium, which has developed in the total absence of theoretical reflection and placed the authorities in a *fait accompli* situation, could very well repeat itself with the avalanche of new technologies. Even the new experiments that are rich in alternatives and original in relation to those being carried out in Europe, have not given rise to a real process of theoretical accumulation for want of being sufficiently analyzed according to adequate concepts. Without a detour through theoretical reflection, there is little possibility of extricating the long-term tendencies implicated in these experiments. Without this necessarily thankless theoretical "detour", it is equally impossible to sort out superficial effects from those carrying the germs of another model of communication. By treating communication as a series of problems which demand only immediate practical solutions, and, in short, to remain within a practico-empirical discourse, one contributes to the reproduction of the spontaneous ideology of issue groups which think through their actions without taking into account the general structure of the terrain in which they operate. Thus, the extremely harmful division between those who think that only new forms of communication supported by new technologies constitute the real alternative and those who continue to wait for an alternative simply as an effect of the contradictions of large-scale apparatuses is perpetuated.

16. Communication Alternatives Are Linked With the Production of New Social Forms

Discussion and research on communication alternatives should not be limited to discourses of communicators whether they be practicioners or experts in mass-mediology. The communication phenomenon affects the roots of the social organization, which must, however, be understood in terms of the relations of power and not in terms of communicability or non-communicability. Communication models do not explain society; rather, it is the social structure which explains communication models. Thus, the difficulty in finding alternative forms of communications is linked to the difficulty the great historical forces struggling against capitalism have in producing new forms of relations within their own organizations and, on a wider scale, within the overall social formation.

17. Technological Progress Does Not Necessarily Mean Social Progress

To the extent that one cannot purely and simply assimilate social progress to technological progress (only a capitalist logic thinks that one can automatically be assimilated to the other), communication alternatives must take into account the efforts of various groups in the advanced countries and in the Third World to draw up a model of development which is not linked to the productivist ideology entrenched in both the East and West. It is not a question of denying the existence of technology or of living with the nostalgia of a pre-technological purity now lost, but of situating technology differently within other forms of social relations. This means that all research imprisoned within a technological patriotism ("The Americans have got culture industries, why can't we have them?") only reproduces, often as a poor relation, the main themes of the productivist model. The development of capitalist competition and the production of alternatives are not to be confused.

18. New Technologies Are Accentuaing the Social Division of Labor

The intensive use of new information technology in offices, factories, places of entertainment and everyday life, etc., confirms the importance of a new social actor: the corps of technicians, executives, engineers, cultural managers, experts, etc. Its emergence raises the thorny issue of the social division of labor which has weighed heavily on the whole history of the workers' movement, particularly since 1917. The use of new technology within the terms of productivist ideology runs the risk of increasing still more this social division of labor. As with all rising groups, the one composed of the users of new technologies could very well make out that the sum of its particular interests represent some sort of truth for the whole social body. One cannot think out alternatives separate from an analysis of the role of a particular group's interests in its relation with other groups and classes.

19. The New Technologies are Attacking Traditional Partitions

One of the main difficulties in thinking up alternatives today is that efforts of transformation often come up against the private hunting groups of administrative domains. One can often find striking examples within the very ministeries of a government: that of Education, for example, finds it hard to tolerate the intervention by their colleagues from the Ministry of Culture within their fiefdom and the Ministry of Economics or Telecommunications tend not to accept any interference by cultural or communications experts in their sector. One of the undeniable effects of the development of the new technologies has been to reshuffle these compartmentalizations to the extent that no overall policy of communication can be envisaged today without proceeding from a decompartmentalization of the various state departments. However, in order that this indispensable decompartmentalization of the state apparatus is not limited to a restructuring with a view to the profitable reception of the new technologies, it must go hand in hand with a similar decompartmentalization of those sectors fighting for an alternative. A capitalist state will have all the more chance of proposing an alternative in the terms of the logic of transnational redeployment as long as unions, for example, have not destroyed the barriers between certain professional sectors on the one hand, and between struggles in manufacturing and in everyday life on the other.

20. Decentalization is a Site of Confrontation

Whereas the process of transnationalization operates in favor of an increasingly accentuated economic concentration, the legitimation of all forms of power emanating from the center is being more and more called into question. Decentralization has become a major necessity for the apparatuses of the center in order to compensate for this loss of legitimacy. At the same time, we are seeing a series of pressures from many sectors for increasing decentralization allowing various groups and society as a whole to develop their potential for greater democracy. Contrary to existing hypotheses that see the taking of the state apparatus as the first, indispensable step for the institution of a democracy which goes beyond mere formalism, it is increasingly accepted today that the construction of a popular hegemony that is both a necessary instrument in the transformation of the nature of the state and a guarantee against possible backlash from the state apparatus is an essential precondition for this enlarged notion of democracy. It is important, therefore, to clearly distinguish the movement towards decentralization, when it looms to consolidate a faltering, centralized power, from an idea of decentralization as a constituent element of popular hegemony. For this reason, demands for the return to the "local", the renaissance of "popular culture," and the celebration of "closeness" cannot automatically be seen as progressive struggles. The forms and contents of these demands are the site of confrontations at once theoretical and practical. The development of a policy for new technologies cannot be detached from the experience of democratic relations in everyday life. It cannot be dissociated from the large-scale debate which has only just begun on the political functioning of civil society.

21. Pluralism Does Not Guarantee Plurality

The plurality of the groups making up civil society and the diversity of their interests demolishes a strictly juridico-political and, more often than not, formal conception of pluralism as the doctrinaire foundation of the public service. This confrontation between plurality and pluralism has been the guiding principle behind numerous experiments seeking to establish themselves on the periphery of the audiovisual apparatus (community television, free radios, communal computer terminals, etc.). It is important today to revise the idea of public service in order to better take into account this plurality. In the absence of a re-examination of the public service, the dynamic of commercial and private interests will appear as the most suitable medium for this demand of expression. This new definition of the public service implies a different distribution of the relations between centralized media and cultural institutions and peripheral experiments (free radio, community TV, etc.). These latter must not simply "rejuvenate" the formulas of the old audiovisual system that would include the "strokes of inspiration" from the periphery in its practices, but radically transform the nature of the communication system in order to abolish the center-periphery relation in favor of a balanced proliferation of media for social creativity.

22. An Alternative Implies A Different Idea of Consumption

Communication alternatives not only imply a different production policy, but also another type of relationship to the product. A communication policy must embrace the field of communication by reducing as much as possible the encounter between the individual consumer and industrial strategies. It is significant that consumer organizations, parents' organizations and teachers' groups are worried over the way audiovisual means shape the social collectivity and they see in the critique of the form and content of audiovisual media an essential step in the search for alternative paths. A change in the status of the consumer, which would use this as the point of departure for the demand of something different and not as an element in the reproduction of the same, supposes that the mode of evaluation of demand and "taste" is not left to the rationality of audience ratings or the techniques of "need discovery," dear to marketing specialists. It is somewhat paradoxical that this sort of measure unifies the practices of the public service and commercial systems. In the face of private cultural industries, particularly in the face of those which are transnational, it is necessary to develop collective mechanisms of access to products which are in themselves potentially capable of favoring a different way of consuming existing products (borrowing instead of buying is only one example among others), but, even more importantly, liable to give rise to the production of different products. It is desirable from this perspective that it is to define or to specify the function of institutions such as media or video libraries, documentation centers, databanks, etc. In addition, it would be desirable for the public authorities to support distribution or broadcasting channels which market alternative products that through their very nature call for another mode of consumption.

23. Transnationalization Calls for a Policy of Production Slots

As the industries situated in countries with restricted domestic markets find it impossible to compete with transnational firms, and as the models conveyed by these firms are politically undesirable, the construction of an alternative must necessarily begin from a few, limited options which are specific to each country. These must, however, be well defined. Their specificity does not simply consist in occupying an economic free slot in which they could be competitive. It is rather a question of finding this specificity in the production of slots with which the transnational model cannot compete, either for profit reasons, or because these slots crash headlong into its rationality and ideological bedrock. The specific product, in the sense we have just given it, becomes important when one takes into consideration the place that certain impoverished countries run the risk of occupying in the new international division of labor, firstly at a continental level, then at a world level: the greater their specificity, the lesser the probable risk of sub-contracting imposed by the more favored countries. For countries that do not have very strong possibilities of manufacturing hardware at their disposal, particularly as international debates indicate in the computer field, it appears that one of the better solutions is to work in the production of software oriented toward balanced socio-economic development. This option offers the advantage of potentially using an often-unemployed reservoir of grey matter. However, one must avoid seeing a miracle remedy in this strategy for the relations of force at both the continental and world levels are necessarily reproduced in the software as well as in the hardware field.

REFERENCES

Mattelart, A., and Piemme, J. M. (1980). ''New Means of Communication: New Questions for the Left.'' *Media, Culture, and Society (I)*2, 321–338.

Mattelart, A., and Piemme, J. M. (1982). *In Cultural Industries: A Challenge for the Future of Culture*. Paris: UNESCO.

11

Media Control in France: Conflict Between Political and Economic Rationale

Patrice Flichy
(translated by Brigitte Trevedic)

The question of control over the media is posed very differently in the U.S. than it is in Europe. This contextual difference explains the controversies that have developed between European and American critical researchers. One of the most recent controversies is undoubtedly the one that has grown out of Dallas Smythe's theses (1977) in which the audience is said to constitute the merchandise form of all communication products in contemporary capitalism. If this theory correctly underlines the central position occupied by advertising mechanisms in the working of the media, it nonetheless completely ignores the political role of the media. The "flow media" ("media de flot") (television, press) function along two different rationales. If, on the one hand, they strive to maximize their audience, on the other hand, they try to reinforce the "social link," to insure the visibility of power. These two economic and political rationales are always present in the media, but their intersection will be different depending upon whether they involve the public or the private sector. Contrary to the U.S., the media in Europe belong to both of these sectors. The question of control must thus be studied separately in the private sector and in the public sector. Finally, one must take into consideration technological developments: the new forms of media that are just being born are greatly disrupting the present systems of control.

THE INDUSTRIAL RESTRUCTURINGS
IN THE PRIVATE SECTOR:
CREATION OF MULTIMEDIA GROUPS

The capitalist countries are now experiencing in the field of communication an important restructuring phase that is manifested through the emergence of large multimedia conglomerates. This new form of concentration appeared in the U.S. in the 1970s, and in Europe shortly thereafter. In France, it came in the 1980s. Even if the signs of this multimedia concentration are evident, in order to be able to assert that it is an important transformation, it is necessary to determine whether similar transformations have occurred before. Phenomena of horizontal concentration have already taken place in media of similar content. In the 1930s, two large American groups, RCA and CBS, took control of two large record firms: Victor Records and Columbia. Similarly, the press has invested heavily in radio and television stations. This press-television connection has been very strong in the U.S. In 1950, 42 percent of the TV stations were controlled by the press; it has decreased so that the press, today, controls only 28 percent of the stations (Sterling, 1979, p. 93). Until the 1960s, horizontal concentration in the American media occurred within the framework of the following groupings of neighboring media: sound media; radio and record; audiovisual media: television and cinema (it is known that Hollywood firms are the main supplier of fiction for the American television); journalistic activities (press, radio and television).

The transformation that has evolved in the 1960s and the 1970s has been the result of the decision by large media groups to invest in the cultural industries sector, of which they had no know-how. This is how Warner implanted itself in the recorded music market as early as 1958; CBS and RCA in the market of book publishing at the end of the 1960s; Time Inc. in the cable and pay-television markets. In this manner, these firms became huge multimedia conglomerates that are active in three, four or five media.

These different forms of horizontal concentration between media do not only correspond to the financial logic inherent in conglomerate structure. The objective is also to launch multimedia operations, as is exemplified in the simultaneous release of a film, a book, or a record entitled "Star Wars." These products, spin-offs of a film or a broadcast, often receive huge audiences as they benefit from the success of the first product. Thus, the book that followed the broadcasting of the series "Holocaust" in the U.S. sold more than one-and-a-half million copies. Similarly, the record sound track from the film "Saturday Night Fever" broke all music publishing records with a world sale of thirty million copies. The multimedia release of cultural products allows for a spin-off phenomenon from which each particular medium benefits.

In France, the field of culture and communication, essentially made up of single-product enterprises remained for a long time outside of the movements of industrial restructuring. In the 1970s, one saw a first wave of concentration but it was limited to internal branch concentration. In the field of cinema, three large movie-theater networks (Gaumont-Pathé, U.G.C., and Parafrance) were forming and were slowly gaining control of the whole business. Similarly, the Hersant group was forging its empire in the daily French press.

At the end of 1980, one saw a new type of concentration when the electronic group Matra (which shares control of the radio station Europe I with the French state) bought Hachette, the first French publishing group. Matra-Hachette-Europe I thus formed the first French media group. Would this financial operation correspond to a simple juxtaposition of different types of cultural industries, the group becoming a kind of large conglomerate, or on the contrary, would a synergy emerge from this regrouping?

It is certain that the managers of the group wished to make the best use of the regrouping of media and the connection between equipment and programming. First of all, the connection between radio and press: the chief editor of Europe I also became the editor of a newspaper of the Hachette group. Radio also could provide advertising for book publishing. Nevertheless, if such a liaison seems possible for some books with a large circulation, one could hardly imagine fine literature publicized in such a way.

In fact, if the synergy between cultural products was so efficient, the record firm of Europe I (Disc'AZ), which greatly benefited from the help of its mother-firm, should have obtained a larger portion of the French market than its actual 5 percent. Nevertheless, the new group has increased possibilities of being active in the new media market of the 1980s. To prepare a satellite TV channel, the group can make use of the television experience of Télé Monte-Carlo (a subsidiary of Europe I). Even if this station has a very limited area of distribution in France, it has, on the contrary, an important audience in Italy. Hachette also has two subsidiaries: Télé-Hachette which specializes in production; and Channel 80, which is a technical video services firm. These two subsidiaries are a firm base for the development of a television production sector. Theoretically, this activity will be able to take hold of the editorial character of Hachette. But in fact, when one knows that commercial television tends to decrease the production of fiction, one realizes that, in this case as well, the synergy is more illusionary than effective.

As to satellites, some analysts have underlined the group's future activity in the two aspects of the audiovisual industry: construction of spacecraft, and the production of programs. But, in fact, Matra is participating in the satellite's project (Telecom 1) and not in the direct television's project (TDF 1). True, these are neighboring technologies, but even if Matra was present in this second project, the industrial synergy would be nearly nonexistent: the selling of the satellite technology would not involve the selling of programs and vice-versa. On the other hand, the situation is very different in the case of videotext, because the idea of the terminals must take into account their forecasted use. Moreover, a firm's ability to simultaneously provide the consumers with terminals and corresponding databanks creates an important commercial advantage; and while Matra builds terminals, Hachette's encyclopedical nature unquestionably provides precious capital for the creation of general public databanks.

In conclusion, if the purchasing of Hachette by Matra caused several potentially fertile industrial regroupings (videotext, press-radio relations), the synergy created by this deal was also overestimated. Above all, it was a very clever financial coup: with a very small investment, Matra bought possibilities of important developments at a price that was evidently undervalued on the stock exchange.

The decision taken by the French government during the Fall of 1981, to nationalize 51 percent of Matra has greatly altered the situation. Indeed, only the Matra group is nationalized, Hachette will remain a private group and the participation of Matra in Europe I will be transferred to the Hachette group.

Parallel to the effort to build a large multimedia group around Matra-Hachette, another group, Havas-CLT is quietly forcing itself upon another base of the French media industry. Havas is the largest advertising group in Europe, as well as being the second largest stockholder (after a Belgium financial group) in the Compagnie Luxembourgeoise de Télédiffusion (CLT) which manages a television (Télé-Lux) and a radio station (RTL). RTL has a large audience in the northern half of France. Besides these financial links, there are tight industrial ties between Havas and CLT: Information et Publicité, a subsidiary of Havas, manages advertising on RTL and is, as a consequence, interested in the Luxembourg station's new projects—especially those concerning a possible direct television satellite. Besides its links with CLT, Havas controls the primary French technical press group (Compagnie Européenne de Publication). In 1979, Havas took control of the Editions Nathan. It also has varied interests in the cinema industry.

The Compagnie Luxembourgeoise de Télédiffusion, which controls different firms in television production (Télé-Union, Vidéo-Téléfrance), technical video services (VCI), and animated films (DIC), is interested in the publishing industry as well. It is the major stockholder of the TV magazine "Téléstar" and it owns 42 percent of a regional daily newspaper and

15 percent of the magazine "Actuel"—"Actuel" is one of the largest successes of the new French press.

The majority of the Havas' capital has belonged to the French government since World War II. Under the presidency of Giscard d'Estaing, the government permitted the group to develop this multimedia strategy; the present government has not really defined the orientation that it wants to give to Havas.

Besides these two large bases of the media industry (made up of a radio, press and book publishing partnership), one finds other smaller diversification attempts.

Gaumont, the largest company in the cinema industry and moreover vertically integrated from production to movie theaters, has been trying to diversify for several years. When Nicolas de Seydoux bought the firm in 1975, he first wanted to place the company on an international level, particularly through investment in Italy, the only European country other from France to have hold on a sizeable cinema industry. Gaumont also came to the U.S. and with other French partners create Téléfrance, which offers three hours of French programming each week on the American cable networks. Very recently, Gaumont has created a common subsidiary with Columbia.

The group has adopted a strategy promoting high quality films and has tried to diversify its activities with a simultaneous intervention in other media. After having been compelled to entrust CBS with the production of the music for the film "Don Giovanni", Gaumont decided to intervene in the production of classical music; it has thus bought 75 percent of the firm Erato. The remaining capital of Erato belongs to RCA, with which Gaumont is also associated in the promotion of video cassettes. To be able to keep for itself a reservoir of scripts, the Nicolas de Seydoux group decided to intervene in the book publishing industry as well. It bought the majority of Ramsay capital and created a subsidiary with the principal publisher of fine French literature, Gallimard. At the end of 1981, Gaumont took control of one of the large French news magazines: "Le Point".

An Inevitable Concentration?

Many commentators on the Matra-Hachette deal have underlined the fact that this operation would provide France with an important base in the media industry and with a good position to compete internationally. The managers of Matra would like to create "une CBS à l' européeanne" (*Les Echos*, December 10, 1980). As one can see, the model followed by these large multimedia groups comes directly from overseas. If creating a large industrial group of international dimension is not a subject of criticism in itself, one wonders if such a model is necessary in the field of culture and communication. By importing this type of cultural industry model (multinational and multimedia groups) from the U.S., one imports not only an economic, but also a cultural, model. In large conglomerates of this kind, a single logic is dominant: quicker and quicker product turnover. And whereas time is an important dimension in all cultural creations—indeed, a work of art does not always immediately find public acceptance—on the contrary, the logic of large industrial groups is to achieve immediate profitability, which imposes another type of demand on cultural products. In other respects, the multimedia groups' strategy of launching the same cultural product in different forms (book, record, videocassette) obviously decreases the possibilities of creation.

Most of the economists that have studied the cultural industries have noticed that these industries were based on a complex dual structure, which associated large oligopolistic groups and small firms. Whereas the former could possibly smother the latter, they did not do so because the small firms were playing a very innovative role in, and at the end were insuring the continuity of the whole communication branch. The arrival of large multimedia groups put an end to this equilibrium. The development of new technologies will cause a stagnation, perhaps a recession, in several sectors of the cultural industries, for it is certain that the firms linked to large groups will have the financial means to invest in new domains and thus endeavour upon total or partial reconversions; on the contrary, the independents will not have this possibility. The fear of being marginalized seems very strong for small publishers like Jean-Pierre Ramsay who was calling for the union of independent publishers in the December 19, 1980, issue of the "Nouvelles Litteraires", but who two months later, decided to join the Gaumont group.

The media concentration we now see, only follows the concentration in the press that took place a few years ago, and that might endanger freedom of expression. If one is tempted to believe that these large conglomerates will decentralize their editorial decisions, the firing of the editorial staff of *L'Express* (which had bent slightly towards Mitterand's side in the second round of the May 1981 presidential election) reminds us that, in the end, the owner owns the editorial power. In a period of political struggle, he may even sacrifice some of his economic interest to utilize his newspaper as a political tool.

STATE CONTROL

Information

Thus, under certain circumstances, political rationale can replace an economic rationale in the private media. Political rationale on the contrary imposes itself in the French radio-television domain. The model of the media as a public service had been defined in France since the Liberation. Y. de la Haye and B. Miege (1982) have shown, contrary to what one may believe, that this model is not very far from the conception of freedom of the press as it was defined at the end of the nineteenth century. The 1881 press law was the starting point of an important development and diversification in French newspapers. Nonetheless, this legal status did not prevent journalists from being pressured by economic power. In their attempt to move the press away from the marketplace, the French Socialists of the Front Populaire (1936) tried to introduce legislation to define a noncommercial space for the press where ideological debates could flourish. This humanist proposition, mainly inspired by Léon Blum, remained an important reference for decision makers who concerned themselves with the information domain at the time of the Liberation. The public monopoly of radio-television, as it was defined in 1945, belongs to two traditions: first, the technical monopoly over telecommunications—most of which dates from the 1837 laws on the electrical telegraph: second, the "public monopoly". The public service monopoly is not an end but a means. It allows for the provision of objective information that is not dependent upon pressure issued by different social forces. The state, obviously not a referee of political struggles but a federation of the complex interest of the classes that possess the political power, has rapidly transformed the public service of radio-television into a subordinate system.

In answer to a Representative's question, the Minister of Information of the Fourth Republic declared "The French broadcasting system is continuously involved in politics in defending the national interest of France. The government believes that it is the true representative of the nation, since it is supported by a majority of the National Assembly and that it has the duty to express the wishes of the nation" (quoted by de Tarle). As A. de Tarle (1979) notices, this total dependence of radio-television vis-à-vis political power, has been calmed by the permanent instability of the governments of the Fourth Republic. In the end, each political party returning to power, was able to influence the orientation of radio-television.

With the birth of the Fifth Republic, the palliative introduced by the changes of governments disappeared because the Right has reigned for twenty-three years. Television, for President Pompidou, was "The Voice of France". As J. Thibau (1973) has expressed, information was dealt with in order to reintroduce facts so as to fit with official truths. This operation was done through daily meetings held under the authority of the Minister of Information and during which it was decided which themes would or would not be spoken of during the news broadcasts.

It was probably in May 1968 that the effect of such a system of control over information appeared most clearly to the public. For a few days, television did not report on the student demonstrations that were front page headlines in the press and widely commented on by peripheral radio stations (Europe I and RTL). After that episode, the obvious governmental control over televised information became impossible lest the TV screen lose all of its credibility in matters of information.[2] Thus, in 1969, the first government of President Pompidou suppressed the Ministry of Information and throughout the 1970s, control over information by political power became more discrete. The 1974 reform made by President Giscard d'Estaing which aimed at dissolving the "Office de la Radio Television Francaise" (ORTF) in order to introduce competition between the three television channels, should have involved a liberalization of information. But, in fact, the government intervened directly in the nomination of the directors of the information of each channel. Thus, the main change between the 1960s and the 1970s was that the government no longer controlled the release of daily information but instead, chose journalists sympathetic to its political beliefs. If this evolution did not cause a true and real liberalization of information, it did alter its presentation. Otherwise, due to several presidential campaigns (1965, 1969, and 1974) during which all candidates were provided with equal airtime to present their programs, it became impossible to prevent opposition leaders from appearing on broadcast as was done before 1965.

The new law pertaining to the audiovisual field, which the Socialist government brought to the floor of Parliament in April 1982, is, in some way, a return to the spirit of the Liberation and to Léon Blum's theories of freedom of information. The public service of radio-television is now under the auspices of a "Haute Autorité" that will be responsible for guaranteeing the freedom of the stations. On the 1st of April, Prime Minister Pierre Mauroy indicated at a press conference that "our worry is to protect radio and television from all influences" and he pointed out that these influences were not only governmental but also economic influences. One can see that the goal of this law is to achieve complete freedom of information.

In fact, because the majority of the "Haute Autorité" members are nominated by the government and because this new body has no financial authority, it corresponds less to the actual emergence of the "Fourth Power" than to the creation of a larger distance between the power of the State and public radio-television.

Television as a Cultural and Entertainment Tool

Television is known to be a complex medium in which information is but a single element. Entertainment is probably television's major function, yet,

---

[2] A poll made after the May 1968 events and quoted by A. de Tarle (1979) shows that 86 percent of the surveyed persons thought that televised information should be independent from the government.

paradoxically, this part of television's activity is rarely accounted for by political thought. From this perspective, the Socialist government is not very different from its forerunners. In this domain as in the domain of information, it is necessary to briefly recall history to understand the present stakes.

Until 1968, French television was financed entirely by the fees paid by those who had television sets. These revenues were not linked to the size of the audience (which therefore was not measured). The allocation of resources among the different programs was not made according to market considerations, but according to the specifications of a cultural project. During the first twenty years of French television, the program directors had assigned goals of cultural democratization. The most valued programs were dramas; they were supposed to provide the public with access to great works of occidental art. Given such a perspective, the directors held an important artistic power and the direction was towards a "télévision de la création."

To start such a project, French television provided itself with an important production tool. It tended to integrate activities of program production, establishing a broadcasting network covering the whole country (including remote rural areas).

Because the "Office de la Radio-Télévision Francaise" (ORTF) was conceived as a branch of the State apparatus, it had to be able to provide for all of television's functions. The "Office" thus became a true vertically integrated cultural industry.[3] To fulfill the missions of a large public cultural service, French television like other European television, had slowly changed. The dynamic of this change from the primitive practices to the industrial planning of the 1970s would deeply modify programming.

This transformation has been effected over several years. At the beginning, there was a desire, independent of the programming people, to create a second and third channel on 625 lines UHF (the first channel being on 819 lines VHF) and to develop color television. On one hand, the promoter of these developments was the French electronic industry, which saw in them the possibility to find new markets from both a professional and a consumer equipment standpoint; on the other hand, there were the ORTF engineers. These new developments having been granted by the government, forced the ORTF to make investments that seemed difficult to finance only through the television set-fees. Thus, the government gave in to the pressures from advertisers who wanted to use this new medium, and it decided in 1968 to introduce advertising on television. The "Office" thus found complementary revenues. At the same time, to answer the advertisers' and managers' request, audience polls were systematized. These had been done only several times each year, but, in 1968, they be-

---

[3] See Beaud, et al. (1981) on the analysis of television as a cultural industry.

came daily measures. These two moves completely changed the programming principles. Moreover, the growing importance of the production tool necessitated industrial planning of equipment and work force. Also, to better control the production costs, analytical accounting and management control were introduced.

At the end of the 1950s and the beginning of the 1960s, the mobilization of intellectual resources was of prime importance, for the whole institution was organized around a cultural project. Ten years later, the situation had radically changed. The creative activity is integrated with the production apparatus. This technico-institutional complex normalized production. To control such a diversified whole, the manager, who, little by little, took over the programming person's position, became tied to programming schedules. It is in this way that content and style are distributed through time and space. It is also the way to attract and retain a public. But the programming schedules also allowed for production planning and for the organization of the tasks' division.

The increased importance of rating results and the necessity to optimize the utilization of the production tools have caused a stiffening of the programming schedules. The comfort provided by forecasting encourages the reproduction of the same product lines. The space for innovation thus shrunk. Innovation involves changes in planning; it also means taking important risks (uncertain audience, unforeseen political reactions).

The planning necessities do not only impose a fixity of programming schedules. They also involve anticipation of style and content through explicit or implicit preestablished norms. This premeditation of programs is expressed by a television producer's words to a weekly magazine: "notions for fiction scripts could very well be given to research firms which could then produce the scripts depending upon a precise set of needs and rules" (*Telerama,* January 14, 1981).

Finally, television with its entertainment function, has moved away from the initial idea of a public service geared toward cultural democratization and has become the most elaborate model of the cultural industries. The public nature of French television did not succeed in foreseeing the evolution that was first started by the institution itself.

As French television adopted management methods and programming techniques, it was brought closer to commercial television. It went from one rational mode to another; economic logic was thus substituted for political logic.

Centralization and Localism

The French political system is considered by most political scientists to be one of the most centralized of all of the Western democracies. Radio and television do not seem to provide an exception. Whereas before the war, radio service was organized around regional radio stations, it was reorganized at the Liberation in a centralized way: radio, like television, was to provide the same programs to all French people. Moreover, the third television channel, the so-called regional channel created in 1973, only offers three-and-a-half hours of regional broadcasting per week, outside of the national programming. Thus, the case seems clear: the French State is hypercentralized and radio and television are organized in the same manner. To remain at this level of analysis would be to ignore one of the two bases of the relays that the central power can use at the local level. If these relays do not exist as far as radio and television are concerned, we shall see that they do indeed exist in the field of the press.

To understand the meaning of the centralization of radio that was accomplished at the Liberation, one must place oneself in the context of that period. Before the war, there were two types of radio stations: private stations and the PTT stations—those have been little by little organized into a network "àl'américaine." At the Liberation, the private stations were sequestered, their owners in some cases, having been disgraced for collaborating with the Germans. It was thus necessary in 1945 to restructure all radio activity, for radio was becoming a mass medium.[4] One kept the idea of creating a large public service like the transportation (railroad) or energy networks (electricity, gas). The concept that prevailed in these last domains came from the principle of equality between users of the services; in other words, the same service for everybody at the same price. This desire to suppress regional inequalities has allowed the establishment of a network that provides television to all French people; even in isolated rural areas. But as the programming became more uniform, the central power was able to diffuse its views to every corner of the country.

Nonetheless, regional media had not disappeared. During the last thirty years, through some kind of inverse symmetry effect, regional press has appeared to be particularly dynamic. It proved much more resistant to television competition than did the national press.[5] As has already been noticed by J. Attali and Y. Stourdze (1977) pertaining to telephone, it seems that far from wanting to smother local power, the central State delegated some tasks to the local elites. It comforts the local elites, and, at the same time, it gives a larger base to the central power in providing for local relays. Contrary to the telephone for which the central power has granted, in terms of financing, explicit delegated authority to local communities, the

---

[4] Radio development has been much slower in France than in other European countries. In 1936, France had only 60 radio sets for 1000 inhabitants, whereas Germany had 105, the U.S. had 153, and Great Britain had 158.

[5] From 1970 to 1977, the regional press readership did not change, but the national press readership decreased 41 percent. (Quoted in Aglietta, 1978).

press has a more implicit agreement. Thus, whereas in 1968 the government had decided to introduce advertising on television despite pressures from the national press, a few years later it created the third television channel but it did not grant any advertising resources to this channel so as not to displease the regional press. Similarly, was blocked cable television in the mid-70s and local radio at the end of the Giscard d'Estaing presidency.

Because there were conflicts between the government and regional press, especially during the Gaullist period, one wonders what was the basis of this implicit agreement between the two partners. At the National Assembly in 1965, De Gaulle's Minister of Information, Alain Peyrefitte, declared that television should counterbalance the influence of the press, which was to a great extent against the government.[6] The paradox resides in the fact that the government never used the electronic media that it controlled to counterbalance the hostile attitude of the press. At first sight, this can be explained by B. Prunieres' analysis (1969) that shows that the regional dailies are, in fact, depoliticized although they explicitly claim to belong to ideological families or to political parties; the State would thus encourage the regional press because it is apolitical. But this explanation is still insufficient. If it allows us to understand why the State used radio-television to compete with the national press (which is explicitly political) rather than with the regional press, it does not explain the links that exist between the central information and the local apparatus. It is precisely this question that L. Quere (1982) has analyzed in a recent article. He shows that the regional daily newspaper is very often linked to modernizing currents within the local communities and "became not really the expression of a regional elite of change that has established the possibility of market economy development and of participation in the national institutions." These regional elites need a specific medium to fulfill their central power's relay function. The Jacobin State, thus, would not benefit from trying to reduce the role of this medium.

NEW TECHNOLOGIES, NEW CONTROLS

The 1837 law governing the electrical telegraph instituted a jail punishment for "anyone who will emit without authorization signals from one place to another, either with telegraphical instruments, *or by any other means.*" This text expresses one of the great principles of communication law in France for the last century-and-a-half: not only does the State have a

---

[6] Official Journal, National Assembly debate, April 30, 1965, as quoted in de Tarle (1979).

monopoly on technical systems, but it also has a monopoly on technical systems to be invented.

This strong defense of the monopoly against technical innovations that could threaten it, characterizes very well the attitude of the French administration during the last ten years. During the last half of the 1970s, the government has thwarted the development of cable television and FM radio, as well as many other systems. For the political power, it was a matter of avoiding the birth of a plurality of radio and television information sources. But, the new techniques do not only question the information monopoly. They also largely change the rapports between the media. The new media will be a competitor of the older one; they will create audience deplacements; they will also change the conditions of program production, particularly the production of full-length films in the cinema industry.

For twenty years, television has been taking advantage of its dominant position; it has imposed low prices on the films of cinema producers. This attitude has been harmful to the "Seventh Art" (cinema), particularly since French television has always used films in its programming and these films have attracted sizeable audiences. It is obvious that the potential appearance of pay-television would question the conditions of the domination of television over cinema. The arrival on the market of new film bidders would necessarily make prices rise.

Forms of employment and working conditions in the audiovisual field will be largely transformed by the coming of new technologies. Presently, the radio-television workers that belong to the public sector have complete employment security whereas the workers in the private sector (that is, mainly in cinema) are for the most part intermittent workers. The new technologies will question the separation between television and cinema, and will eventually make this separation of employment forms impossible.

The equilibrium between central and local powers that we have previously analyzed will also be changed. The satellite raises the question of a television network covering only the national territory: indeed, with direct television satellite, the national space will slowly melt into the European space. At the other end of the spectrum, there is a rebirth of the local space with FM radio (free radio stations) and cable television; there is also greater autonomy in the private space with the advent of the video player. The national radio-television that was created within a national and homogeneous space, is confronted by a widening and a dissolving of this very space.

Facing such a potential destabilization, the government like the labor unions, had a very reserved attitude vis-à-vis the new technologies. The labor unions were denouncing any technical system or any measure that could question the existence of the monopoly. Thus, for example, the labor unions CGT and CFDT declared themselves against the free radios; but at the same time, some of their members opposed their trade unions by launching free radios in Longwy (Radio S.O.S. Employment, Radio-Lorraine-Coeur d'acier), in Nantes, and in Belfort. The labor unions' position of defense of the monopoly could be summarized by the following axiom—monopoly: public service: quality of programming.

Finally, this position is not very far from the governmental stand. President Giscard d'Estaing declared, in 1976, to a television weekly magazine (*Tele Sept Jours,* February 7, 1976): "I believe that we should now pose the question to know whether we should multiply to the infinity communication and information means. The danger is indeed that the information means will eventually destroy each other. . . . The three television channels have not as yet reached their full developments. One should thus wait for the full use of the present communication means before asking ourselves the question." He pointed out a little further: "Cable television, understood as a supplemental local communication means, is not a priority."

In 1977 and 1978, two decrees defined the utilization of cable: cable could only be used to relay the French channels to the scarce "zones d'ombres"; and the foreign channels only in areas where they were normally received through broadcasting. A 1978 law specified the framework of the monopoly in order to clarify the prohibition on free radio stations.

THE TECHNICAL LOGIC

As the government was trying to prevent the different social forces from entering the radio-television monopoly and in doing so stopping the growth of new technologies, it was taking voluntary measures for the industrial developments of some new technical systems. In 1979, the government announced the decisions to organize the following experiments: an experiment for a general public interactive videotex in 2,500 households at Velizy, a Parisian suburb; an experiment for the electronic phone book in the department of Ile-et-Vilaine; a direct television satellite to begin in 1984 in cooperation with Germany; an optical fiber network for 1,500 subscribers in Biarritz. All these decisions were part of a global political scheme, a scheme that chooses telematics and space as the two most advanced technologies in which France could occupy an important world position.

No political software scheme corresponds to the political choices in the hardware domain. For example, in the case of the three circuits that will be provided by the direct television satellite, the government has planned to transmit the two first television channels on two of the circuits; the use of the third circuit has yet to be defined. Therefore, when the decision was made to launch a satellite, the only forecasted use was to provide the two first channels to the 1 to 2 percent of the French people who do not normally receive television signals.

The decision to employ electronic phone books stems from a similar logic. The administration uses its strength to impose a videotex terminal on the consumer as a substitute for ordinary "paper" phone books. The PTT's bet is that once the consumer is accustomed to his electronic phone book, he would use his terminal for other videotex services as well.

This strategy was set in the framework of an alliance between the State and the large companies of the electronic field. At first sight, it appeared to be very efficient: when a public research laboratory (CNET, CNES)[7] discovered something of importance, it was very quickly implemented in order to better exploit the technological advancement and to improve the position of the French industry on the world level. In launching a direct television satellite before the U.S., France—with Ariane—took an important step in the space industry market, and can hope to attract a part of the international satellite launching business, especially in the Third World.

To be able to widely export one's technology, one must first be capable of implanting oneself in one's own national market. If the software part of these new technical systems is not developed, as was seen in the government of Giscard d'Estaing, it is because the government was hostile to the development of the new media. A top technology that has not succeeded in establishing itself on the marketplace—this is the syndrome that afflicted the Concorde.

This political scheme of engineer-conceived networks without any thought of programming projects, was strongly attacked by the press, particularly during the Parliamentary session of the Fall 1980. The press suspected the PTT administration of wanting to compete in the field of classified advertisements through the use of videotex and the electronic phone book. The press feared that the promoters of the network would create a new centralized medium. The government compromised by creating a special commission to monitor telematics experiments. This confrontation between the PTT and the press has divided the journalistic profession: the owners of the press who are most open to technical progress are participating in the Velizy experiment and are preparing other experiments; others are still trying to pressure the government.

This conflict with the press caused the Giscardian government in the last months of its existence, to interest itself in the software of these new technologies. To do that, it helped large private groups to facilitate their intervention in the new media. It is exactly in this way that the government helped along the repurchase of Hachette by Matra (see p. 227). The new

---

[7] CNET: Centre National d'Etudes des Telecommunications.
CNES: Centre National d'Etudes Spaciales.

group, with interests in the daily regional press ("Les Dernieres Nouvelles d'Alsace"), was ready to develop videotex experiments. Moreover, the government was thinking very seriously of entrusting this group with the third satellite circuit. The State, as was seen, controls the majority of Havas which in turn has numerous links with the Compagnie Luxembourgeoise de Télédiffusion. The government had thus another possible partner which it could ask to intervene in the field of the new media. One seemed to favor the maintenance of the public monopoly in the radio-television field with the participation of private monopolies in the new media market. However, this last point was not very clear for the law remained very restrictive.

THE NEW SOCIALIST AUDIOVISUAL LAW

The new audiovisual law recently passed by the Socialist government radically changes the role of the State in communication matters. This law maintains the technical monopoly on the networks that will be built either by the State itself or by other entities having the State's authorization. The monopoly on programming is abolished and entities other than the State are permitted to program networks. More precisely, systems such as interactive videotex or pay-television (télévision à la demande") through optical fibers—i.e., the user only receives the programes that he has asked for— are under a set of regulations based on a preliminary notification.[8] Local FM radio and cable television are under another set of regulations: the license. This kind of license is delivered by the "Haute Autorité". Finally, the State guards the possibility of granting licenses for any other technical systems, especially satellite systems. The bearer of a license can finance the proposed service through advertising; however, advertising revenues will not be able to exceed 80 percent of the total system's revenues. The same person or the same firm will not be permitted to obtain more than one license or even to direct or manage more than one company having such a license. This last clause is aimed at preventing the formation of networks.

In fact, this law allows the State to maintain its monopoly over the classic national radio-television industry while allowing other entities to enter the market of new media programming, especially at the local level. Once the main legal obstacle to the development of new media is overcome, it remains to be seen what entities will be granted authorizations and what kind of programs these new forms of media will offer. Conceivably, for reasons of economic efficiency, the large multimedia groups that

---

[8] A provisional regime of licensing will nevertheless be maintained until 1985.

are presently forming will be granted special privileges. In this case, the new audiovisual law will have simply provided the large monopolistic groups with the legal framework, which they were lacking, to develop their new activities. Moreover, these groups might employ a large amount of foreign programming. The present programming of a station like Télé-Luxembourg, for example, which consists of 58 percent foreign programming (Souchon, 1982) gives an indication of the eventual content of the new private television channels.

In the event that new forms of media succeed in acquiring a public, the large investment needed to create new networks might lead to a situation which favors penetration by American media. Indeed, the necessity of being able to have cheap and attractive programs when beginning a new communication system, will probably encourage the buying of American programs.

At present, it is difficult to say if the Socialist government will know how to resist this development. Nevertheless, the decisions made by the Minister of Culture, recently announced in the field of cinema, shows that the government is sensitive to these problems. The government indicated that it will consider limiting large oligopolistic intervention in the cinema industry, and that it will assist French movie-production. It is certain that the relative strength of this industry, as compared to other European cinemas, constitutes a precious trump card that France can play to develop national audiovisual program production for the new media systems.

CONCLUSION

The French radio-television network has been organized since the Liberation as a branch of the State apparatus, working primarily along the lines of political rationale. Information was completely controlled by the government. The programs, on the other hand, were part of the framework of a project of cultural democratization that the power structure of this period perceived as a component of the economic growth of the 1950s and 1960s. The introduction of advertising, audience ratings and heightened management methods, has slowly altered the logic of the workings of television moving to primarily an economic logic, at the exclusion of the informational domain. A very similar evolution also exists with new technologies. In the face of the capitalist logic of the large electronic industry groups and the help of the PTT Administration, the political logic has slowly been chipped away. By the 1980s, audiovisual communication had become a sector where economic rationale was largely dominant; political logic only imposing itself in the narrow meaning of the information sector.

The authors of the new audiovisual law underscore the fact that independence of radio-television vis-à-vis political and economic powers must be legally guaranteed. We have seen that independence vis-à-vis political power will not be absolute; as to the independence vis-à-vis economic power, if it signifies developing an audiovisual production sector that is no longer controlled by the logic of the ratings, it is encouraging. On the other hand, if it means forgetting that radio-television belongs more and more to the strategies of an economic framework, it is idealistic and in the end, it will allow the electronic industry and the large multimedia groups to be autonomous. To differ from the previous systems of control over communication, the new Socialist form of control will have to be tailored to recent media developments.

REFERENCES

Aglietta, J. (1978). "Les Publics de la Presse Quotidienne Francaise et Leur Evolution." Paper presented to a conference on "Les Nouveaux Developpments de la Press Ecrite, Parlée et Télévisée," Foundation Nationale des Politiques, Paris, November.

Attali, J., and Stourdze, Y. (1977). "The Slow Death of Monologue in French Society." *In* I. de Sola Pool (Ed.), *The Social Impact of the Telephone.* Cambridge, MA: MIT Press.

Beaud, P., Flichy, P., and Sauvage, M. (1981). *Television as a Cultural Industry.* Multiple Copy. Paris: UNESCO.

de la Haye, Y., and Miege, B. (1982). "Les Socialistes Francais aux Prises Avec la Question des Medias." *Raison Presente,* No. 61.

de Tarle, A. (1979). "The Monopoly That Won't Divide." *In* A. Smith (Ed.), *Television and Political Life.* London: MacMillan.

Prunieres, B. (1969). *La Presse Sans Politique. Etude Systematique de la Presse Lue dans le Calvados.* Paris: L.G.D.G.

Quere, L. (1982). "Le Paradoxe d'une Presse Sans Politique." *Raison Presente,* No. 61.

Smythe, D. (1977). "Communications: Blind Spot of Western Marxism." *Canadian Journal of Political and Social Theory 1*(3), 1–28.

Souchon, M. (1982). *Trois Semaines de Television: Une Comparison Internationale.* Paris: UNESCO.

Sterling, C. H. (1979). "Television and Radio Broadcasting." *In* B. M. Compaine (Ed.), *Who Owns the Media?* White Plains, NY: Knowledge Industry Publications.

Thibau, J. (1973). *La Television le Pouvoir et Argent.* Paris: Ed. Calmann Levy.

12

The Commercialization of Culture—Perspectives and Precautions

Morten Giersing

INTRODUCTION

In the field of the electronic media, the Scandinavian welfare-state societies can accurately be thought of as advanced societies. The total commercialization, not least of all in the USA, can be considered a *completed* evolution comparable with, for instance, the private hospital system.

The new media—satellites, cable and video—can nevertheless mean that the Scandinavian route will turn out to be a blind alley rather than a short cut. The new media will, if they are not regulated soon and through international agreement, send the "Scandinavian model" of media back to square one—in a game where the American development is *the* development. From a Scandinavian point of view the new media can mean not just a violent increase in the effect of *foreign culture,* but an additional commercialization of the media system previously unseen in this area. A retrospective look back from the start of the third millennium at these small, but advanced, cultural societies could indicate a development which would be described as a commercial cultural revolution.

Seen from the American viewpoint this process would be a *dejà vu.* But if one could imagine that American television had been dominated mostly by educational television since the fifties and then, in just five years, had succumbed to thoroughly commercial TV networks then the contours of the possible revolution are plain.

Whether this development is to be seen as not just being a possibility for Scandinavia, but as a realistic probability is due to more than just

243

the new media's potential. It is related to the effect of the lengthy economic crisis which makes old capitalistic ideas fashionable. It is not so much that these ideas can exhibit results—in fact they indicate in the American and British variants a real decline. It is because, as the carriers of welfare state politics, the Social Democratic parties can't manage any more. Both Norway and Denmark now feature bourgeois administrations. Confidence in the welfare state model, and in its related media system, is shaken. This is related once again to the content of these media policies. As an extrapolation of BBC's traditions they have, on the one hand, kept the public service free of commercial influence and have maintained educational (in the broadest sense of the word) program policies. But, on the other hand, they have not brought this program policy into a democratic harmony with the wishes of the population groups. Programs have certainly been made *for* people, but seldom on the basis of people's *own* requirements.

This is why the welfare state can be—with a degree of truth—experienced as a paternalistic society. Resistance to the possible commercialization of the TV medium in Scandinavia is therefore less advanced than it had been. In fact, public opinion polls claim that two-thirds of the population actually want it: even though we have to bear in mind that those questioned don't actually know what commercial television is.

In this situation, where many politicians view the new media, and their shaking up of the media structure, as unavoidable, and, where a large number of the population, in reaction to the paternalism exhibited by the public broadcasting corporations, welcome commercialization, the climate for regulation and alternative models is worse than one might have expected in countries which have near world record living standards and educational levels.

In the following pages, I will dash from one new medium to the next and then do the same thing once more. The first analysis will be to put the imminent commercial development and its consequences into focus as seen from a Scandinavian point of view. In the second analysis, I will point out the chances for precautionary actions and the positive uses to which the new media can be put. This is quite naturally limited to the special Scandinavian conditions, but, hopefully, it has relevance elsewhere.

PERSPECTIVES

Commercial Television

The real nature of commercial television is exemplified most typically in the developments in American television where the commercial interests have had particularly free rein. Television is not implicitly commercial because it is in private ownership, but its commercial aspect is due to its being a medium for advertisements.

Television has, until now, been a medium with national coverage which has meant that the advertisers have been interested in obtaining the highest number of viewers. The principles for program policies have been based on the lowest common denominator, which attempts to combine the needs of many different viewer groups.

In addition, the advertisers' own direct influence comes into play: programs must not be in conflict with the advertising message, and they should preferably provide for the advertisement a supportive environment. This influence also takes place through a lowest common denominator principle: there are many different advertisers and the program must harmonize with the *compromised* sum of all advertising interests. The "free competition," therefore, leads to a situation in the television medium where there is great uniformity rather than great variation. American television has evolved a multitude of programs but very *few* program types. Commercial television reduces programming to a medium where the consciousness of the viewer can be exposed to the advertiser's *message* or *massage*.

There is a tendency towards this situation in all television supported by advertising revenue, but it is most clearly present when several advertising-supported television stations compete because the common denominator principle becomes quite unavoidable. If Station A doesn't take commercial needs very seriously then advertising revenue will go over to Station B, which will quickly put station A back on the right path. This situation, which can be termed *competing commercial television,* has determined American television since its inception and it is this situation, which because of the transnational television satellites, can revolutionize the development of the media in Western Europe.

At this stage I want to introduce two other circumstances to which I will return later. From the *viewers* point of view, the *weakness* of the lowest common denominator program output is that it cannot meet his or her needs in an optimal manner because the output additionally has to satisfy the needs of viewers who have quite other requirements as well as the advertisers. But the *strength* of the common denominator programs lies in the fact that they always necessarily must satisfy *some* needs, however few and incomplete these may be, which is not the case in a public service television. Public service can very well supply a product which nobody is interested in "buying." The drawback for the viewer is, in a way, a drawback for the advertiser as well. Advertisers in the present commercial television system have great difficulties in reaching a defined target group with reference to both financial considerations and program environment.

The new media provide the opportunity for a distinct rationalization of the commercial interest.

Satellites

Even though the exact plans undergo continual change, there can be little doubt but that at least West Germany, France and Great Britain around the middle of the eighties will put up their own satellites for direct trans- mission. These satellites originate within a commercial strategy: television reception is already satisfactory in these countries. The mainstream of European thought is that one must develop satellite technology not least in relation to future export to the Third World. As a direct consequence, there is a great deal of uncertainty about what these satellites will trans- mit. It is reasonable to suppose that they will transmit the programs that they already send from ground transmitters. But it is conceivable that they will transmit special programs produced for an external market, for in- stance films and sport. Various kinds of pay television have been men- tioned as well. But let us look at the situation where they restrict themselves to further distribution of programs already produced and transmitted, even though they undoubtedly must sent out more in order to justify the project for taxpayers.

In this situation the British commercial television will, for example, reach out to most of Europe because of spillover. For the very first time in Europe there will be the already-mentioned situation of competing com- mercial television stations. A whole series of British television programs will be attractive, for example, to West German viewers which will mean a drift of advertising to ITV. This will, in part, be due to characteristics of British television but also because the regulation of advertising in Britain is more liberal than in the West German counterpart. This competitive situa- tion will, of course, be made much keener if one or more satellites are directly utilized for a commercial European program sent, for instance, in English, German, and French on the audio side. Plans involving such an initiative exist at the moment at Radio Luxembourg and in a collaboration between Swiss newspapers and Britich commercial television. But one or more of the larger nations can, at some stage, enter this sphere of activity.

The new competitive situation will, as a tendency, mean that *all* Western European television organizations must introduce advertising in order to give the domestic advertiser a chance against the multinational advertiser *and* they must liberalize their regulation of advertising so that it matches the regulation of the most liberal country. This will in practice mean that the resultant regulation will not be discernibly different from the (absent) American-type regulation. It is not just the commercial structure which will ape the USA—the content itself will be largely American because of the well known pricing mechanisms in the international television market where American programs can be sold at dumping prices. *Dallas,* which costs around $500,000 per episode to produce, can be bought by Danmarks Radio for $1,000. A corresponding Danish dramatic production (heaven preserve us!) would cost about $300,000 to produce.

The *Belgian* experience during the past few years can provide a preview of the meaning of direct broadcast satellites. Belgium was one of the few countries outside Scandinavia that did not have commercial television. But they did have neighbors with considerable television output. Belgium experienced a tremendous development of cable television based on local privately-owned receiving antennae. These cables distributed the foreign advertising as well. Belgium—the only country until now—tried to stop this activity. The transmission of advertising through the private cable was forbidden since it would undermine the Belgian ban on advertising on television. Because of the European Economic Community there had to be a special court action because of the relationship with common European legislation. Belgium won these law suits but found that the ban could not be carried out in practice. Cable nets continued to spread the foreign advertising and Belgian advertisers gave revenue to the foreign stations, especially to the strongly commercial Radio Luxembourg television. Belgians saw more and more foreign television and less and less of their national television. Belgian television had apparently only one alternative: if one wanted to maintain a national television station then the ban on advertising had to be ended, with hopes that the additional finance would be sufficient to produce more attractive television. And this is what they have done. Only time will tell whether this more attractive television will be dominated by imported British and American programs. But this seems unlikely, and not a very Belgian solution.

The satellite situation in Europe has become even more confused with the announcement of regular TV-services on the *ECS-satellites,* which will be the first ordinary communication satellites of the Eutelsat co-operation set up by the tele-communication authorities in Western Europe. The long planned satellite collaboration, hoping to become the European counterpart of the US-dominated Intelsat, was mainly aiming at ordinary telecommunication traffic. But inspired by the many satellite plans, and the commercial interest in the test satellite OTS, Eutelsat suddenly announced the spare satellite of the first couple open for booking by parties interested in TV-distribution. To be launched by mid-1983, the ECS-satellites will be operational long before the first DBS-satellites, planned for 1986, but will, of course, as 'weak' communication satellites, not allow the small dish reception made possible by the DBS-system. The many places already cabled and the densely populated areas easily cabled will, however, not experience the big difference between ECS and DBS as long as the box delivers the right mix of Lucille Ball, Gunsmoke and Dallas. Around 30 consortia have applied for broadcasting facilities on ECS-1 and ECS-2 and it seems quite certain that several of the supposedly 10 transponders available will be allocated to plain commercial companies without any national authorization to broadcast in ordinary ways. Whereas the DBS-system, being allocated to nations and not companies, at least is open to regulation, the ECS-system, managed by common carrier organizations, seems much more sacrosanct and indefeasible once allowed. Just as Comsat in the USA may arrive with its DBS-possibilities in a market already covered by weaker satellites, the ECS-satellites of Eutelsat may render the plans of national DBS-systems in Europe obsolete. At any rate the programming offered on ECS, first sponsored by commercials and later perhaps organized as pay-TV as well, may determine the later use and regulation of the direct channels.

Cable

As the Belgian example indicates, the prime motivator in Europe for the establishment of neighborhood receiving aerials has been the possibility of receiving other countries' television programs. Cable developments have been particularly common near borders where the normal radio wave transmission has been strong enough to ensure acceptable reception quality. Small countries with large neighbors, like Holland, Belgium, and Denmark, have been particularly at risk in this development. This is because their geographical size makes most of the country in a border area and because their national television production, qualitatively and quantitatively, must be considered weak as compared with their large neighbors. In Denmark, less "surrounded" than either Holland or Belgium, the situation today is such that approximately 50 percent of all households are connected to neighborhood aerials that facilitate reception of West German and/or Swedish television. This compares with 55 and 65 percent for Holland and Belgium, respectively. Cable development could have been even more extensive if it wasn't for the legislation concerning copyright which restricts the establishment of cables to these areas that "naturally" receive neighboring countries' television. One is not allowed to use cable transmission into areas which are outside the range of the neighboring countries' transmission.

When the copyright problems are solved, or when satellites are in place, whichever comes first, the establishment of cable links will receive a new boost, and, at the same time, all densely-populated areas in Denmark will be served by cable in a very short time.

Up until now the establishing of cable links to neighborhood aerials has been an affair for private enterprise. On the one hand, the State has not wished to encourage this import of culture—which is anyway under a copyright cloud—but on the other hand, wouldn't forbid it. Cable installations have again only been used for enhanced reception of foreign television—not for pay-TV. In other words, the problem has been underestimated and, in practice, no one has had any idea what to do about the problem. Most installations have been established as cooperatives within distinct residential units. In larger installations—those covering a whole community or town—the private company remains the owner of the equipment which is then leased to the users. In some areas in Denmark the local county authorities have become the owners.

There is usually a service agreement between the cooperative and the private company, and it is the regular servicing which provides the economic interest for the company. But it is obvious that in the long term there are a number of other perspectives related to neighborhood receivers —the possibility of pay-TV, commercial local television, etc. These seem likely developments when we examine the ownership of the largest cable installer and owner in Denmark, *STOFA*. Fifty percent of the company is owned by Danish media conglomerates while the remainder is owned by the American corporation, Cox Communications.

The present private ownership of cable networks will perhaps be a crucial argument for the private utilization of networks for pay-TV and for advertising-supported local TV. The fact that it was cable corporations that had invested in England was an argument for their permission to run a trial period of two years with pay-TV which would give them a certain return on their investment. When Europe is overrun with ten to twenty satellite channels—and the majority of them will be with advertising—it will also be impossible to make an argument for the continued ban on the commercial use of the nets. And those who will be able to use these new opportunities will most naturally be the established media conglomerates; not least of all the monopolies of the press who can additionally argue that their situation will be threatened if they are not allowed access to the new media. In the smaller cultural regions there will be difficulties in filling out these new opportunities with indigenous products because television in its present form uses so many resources. The purchase of suitable programs from the larger nations, especially the USA and Britain, will play a major part for both the national distributor to the cable net as well as the national television in a large part of Western Europe. Cable systems, *both* as distributors of satellite programs *and* as original distributors, will be the network which can realize commercialization and foreign cultural reorganization of leisure time.

But there is, however, some doubt as to whether the present chaotic evolution of cable will be allowed to continue. The new cable technology has, in several countries, led to plans for a new telephone system. This is the so-called integrated wideband net which, through the use of fiber optics and digital transmission, can communicate everything from telephone conversations and data to the videophone and vast numbers of television programs. The national telephone companies envisage this kind of network as a guarantee that they will continue to remain in business. The national cable and electronic industries dream, along with a large part of the rest of private enterprise, of all the possibilities. In the short term, there can arise a conflict between those who have invested in the chaotic development of cable—often small private entrepreneurs—and those who either explicitly or implicitly can get a license to print money in a system both centrally planned and built. These types of conflicts of interest usually have a solution, but they can lead to *delay* which in the short term can lead to the still-birth of the dream of an integrated network. If satellites are put up first this will mean that small, differentiated cable installations will blossom up overnight and require heavy investment that will create both financial and political problems for those who want the integrated network. A speedy decision in favor of an integrated network with public accountability will both halt the present chaotic piecemeal development, raise money and, not least of all, be able to marshal the average viewer's wish to see more foreign television so that a total network can be constructed which can be used for much *more* than watching television. But these other uses cannot be used as bait.

While cable installations in Western Europe have nearly always been used for *basic cable,* the USA (still hoping to be the land of the future) a long time ago started *pay cable.* The few exceptions in Europe are the previously mentioned British experimental period with pay-TV and a pay-TV net in Helsinki, which, interestingly enough, has recently been taken over by Finland's largest newspaper.

From the viewer's point of view, pay-TV in the USA has been motivated by the wish to escape advertising. I think it reasonable to assume that this freedom, judged a dangerous development from the advertiser's view will prove to be a transitional stage. When American distributors of pay-TV buy secondhand television programs, they benefit in the same way as do Western European countries because the show has already been paid for once and is therefore cheap. The second, and more important, content of pay-TV's programs today, feature films, are analagous: they, too, are secondhand goods. They have first earned money in the national and international markets. The third supply is made up of their own productions. Quite naturally, these cost a good deal of money, and they make up the smallest part of pay-TV transmissions.

If one considers it likely that pay-TV in the long run will become the dominating form of distribution in the USA, then pay-TV without advertising will cease. If the pay-TV companies themselves should have to pay all basic costs which are today paid for by advertising and cinema-goers, this would result in a prohibitive license fee for many current and potential users. Pay-TV, when considered as programs without advertising available through subscription or through payment for individual programs, is a sham and is not able to carry the real costs of production. A combination of rental payments and advertising revenue pay-TV is a possibility for the future of TV in the USA just in the same way as is a pure advertising revenue cable-TV system.

Cable television, as opposed to network television, gives opportunities for *target population* advertising. Through satellite distribution and/or through transmission in wide-band cables, which allow 20 to 40 television channels, it will be possible to differentiate the television public into suitable target groups. Television advertising won't have to restrict itself to programs seen by a mass public, but instead, it can follow the programs produced for specific target groups in terms of those who drive a Ford as compared with those who drive a Cadillac. The advertising's "wrapping" —that is, the program—can, in this way, attract the right viewer group more effectively and the advertisement's own style can be adjusted to the target group. This transition which broadcast media will undergo is equivalent to the change from family to specialized magazines. From a critical view point, this means a greater intimacy in the commercial organization of population group's consciousness.

This process has already begun and it is due to cable nets ability to offer audience differentiation on a social class basis in their present form. Cable nets match residential areas which, as is well-known, are, to a great degree, divided into social classes. The diverse classes and groups in American society may, via satellite or via wideband cables, be assembled into autonomous target groups—everyone of which is sufficient for a special television production because they are sufficient enough to warrant a special—and therefore effective—advertising influence.

This fragmentation will require the development of *target oriented television software*, with which Hollywood has limited experience.

Video

In the same way as pay-TV, video differs from ordinary television in being a narrowcast medium. In the present situation video as pay-TV is without the suitable software, i.e. target oriented software matching the qualities of the medium. Hollywood's enormous stocks of old television series just cannot be distributed in the new way. Television series are produced as lowest common denominator goods, and only with few exceptions can they stand a video showing. Up until now only two things have been successfully offered on video. The special mixture of porno and extreme violence, existing for long as a special type of film production, and the Hollywood feature film, which has itself become a more and more specialized product as the cinema evolves as a narrow medium. Neither of these program types have been able to establish sales in Scandinavia; video-programs are only rented for a day or two.

In spite of a lack of content, sales of machines are booming, not least of all in Scandinavia, where Sweden is on the way to becoming the world's largest per capita video market. In a recent Swedish study, research showed that video, so far, is not used as a new medium, but as a time-delayed replay of ordinary television programs. A specific group of the population, the young men living in the big cities, however, has a different pattern: they use the machines several hours a week and mainly for rented programs.

When we look at video today we must bear in mind that we are also in a *transitional stage*. The medium has not yet received its message because the culture industry has not reorganized its production to match narrowcast TV. This explains why video *disc* players have not been a success—they can only replay and not record which puts them completely at the mercy of adequate software. But this will come at some time in the '80s. Media conglomerates have prepared themselves for this development through their buying up, in the '60s and '70s, of publishers with the necessary expertise.

The transitional stage means that critics should not just grapple with the porno and violence with which children, through the video wave, are just now inundated. Violence and porno make up a completely distorted percentage of the market compared with actual needs because there is a lack of other types of software. As the video market becomes monopolized by the culture industry, the organizations will clear away these items from the selection available. Violence and porno will be relegated to those quarters where they were once only available on super 8 film.

The real risk is the commercialization that video will induce. A few more areas of individual leisure will be decided by the offerings of the cultural industry, while the programming which must be varied, the public broadcasting stations and the public libraries, will diminish in importance.

Viewdata

Viewdata, a system, which, via the telephone, puts the television screen in direct contact with a computer and where the user can obtain various information—for a price—was first developed in Britain (Prestel). It has more or less been put into operation in Canada, France, and Western Germany. At the moment, the majority of Western European countries are investing considerable sums in experiments with this strange medium. I am not going to give the phenomenon much space here since it is in my view, in its present form, still-born as an ordinary consumer medium. The sales curve in Britain seems to confirm this harsh evaluation.

I touch on the medium for two distinct reasons. First of all, it shows a medium where the *integration of information and advertising* is almost complete—a situation which is also becoming pronounced in the printed media. For instance, American Express appeared as an advertiser in the Financial Times' section of the Prestel Computer. But they soon found out that it was smarter to function as an independent supplier of information —with data about the destination's currency and, quite naturally, with the absolutely essential travellers checks. This sort of combination is called, in newspapers, concealed advertising.

The second reason for touching on the subject is that it is a medium undergoing transition. Even though in Europe the medium is said to be the latest result of technological progress, it is in fact dependent on old technologies, that is, the telephone and the television. But when the existing traditional telephone cable is replaced by optical wideband cables then viewdata will no longer be restricted to tedious data printouts, but will be able to send moving pictures like all the other commercial pay-TV distributors.

Taking *this* into consideration viewdata becomes a very interesting proposition rather than a runt. In the Scandinavian situation, where television advertising is not allowed, and where its existence would cause the end of a number of newspapers and magazines, it is understandable why viewdata receives a lot of interest. It will not just act as a Trojan horse, introducing advertising before anyone discovers it, but it will provide a suitable *organizational form*. With the Danish telephone company as the common carrier of the viewdata system, media capital, without any great investment, will quietly be able to find suitable methods of collaboration and put the squeeze on those who don't fit. They won't have to take bits of each other and they won't have to fight a commercial television station, which would take up a very sizeable chunk of their advertising turnover.

The odd Trojan horse could very well turn out to be a dark horse in the stakes concerned with the commercialization of—at least—Scandinavian television.

AT THE FINISHING POST

Seen from a Scandinavian point-of-view, the new media's prospective is a clear commercialization of that part of the media structure which is publically "owned" and non-commercial and which, not least in the future, will be the most important. It is also that part of the media structure furthest removed from non-professional production. Many people can write an article: only a few can produce a television program. It is also that component of the media which the educational system mostly neglects. Most people learn to read and some are able to exhibit analytical skills concerned with what they are reading, but very few people have the necessary foundation for a critical contact with visual media.

The possible revolution will be characterized by increased cultural imports. There is a maxim that every time a smaller cultural area extends its television output then it will expand its *import* of television programs because the imported product is 200 to 300 times cheaper than domestic production. This is also very likely to be the case in the video market, pay-TV, and even for the extended television output which the public television corporations will attempt as a counter-measure.

Cultural imports will, of course, be without competition on satellite television; here the American programs will dominate as they do in video and in pay-TV. In Western Europe, the mean percentage of total output which has been produced by the transmitting company is at the most around 50 percent. This means that only about half of the satellite output will actually originate in that country. The dominating exporter to all countries is the USA. Additionally, a greater part of the European production has American origins due to the imitation of American series (as the United States is the most lucrative market, for instance, for British productions) and the more direct reason that European production apparatus is American-owned (the Gulf & Western purchase of EMI is a current example). *And* at least half of the ten biggest advertising bureaus in Europe are American subsidiaries.

PRECAUTIONS

My point of departure here is the regulation of the new media and the more positive perspectives that I can glimpse in the light of the Scandinavian situation surrounding the new technology. First of all, I don't think that television in itself is an evil—even though one must admit that the American evolution has done what it could to ensure this viewpoint. It is not so much the medium but its content and use which can be alternatively good or bad. I don't share the Western European media criticism which for a long time had the basic assumption that television, in particular, was a nasty discovery which degenerated everything—including the culture which media critics like other intelligentsia consume—that is, the inherited bourgeois culture. Instead of attempting to distinguish between sheep and goat in the total culture, the whole culture has been perceived collectively. At best, the culture has been perceived as communicated to those without cultural background. The *book,* in particular, has been explicitly exhalted as being more or less *the* medium. The intellectual has become accustomed to it. But the book is, in fact, very restricted in the use of senses as compared with, for example, the sound track, the picture, and the colors of TV. Walter Benjamin has written of the special aura of the book where the self has to create the accompanying moods and pictures while television provides the lot, but in a specified way for all viewers. One has, with a greater or lesser degree of openness, made an a priori distinction between Art, basically that which is already institutionalized, and Pop culture, which covers just about everything which the non-intellectual consumes. This is, among other things, an extension of Adorno and Horkheimer.

There are, of course, good reasons for this "we know best" attitude towards culture which has additionally colored official cultural policies since the second World War, including the programs of the public broadcasting corporations. There was a paternal wish to bring Art and Culture to the people, no matter what the people said about it. They wanted to inform and to keep people oriented. But this has taken place on the basis of the dominating classes' premises rather the premises of the people. This program policy has meant that there *has been* a degree of cultural democratization which *has* undoubtedly *raised* the level of general knowledge. Compared with the commercial development, it must, naturally, be defended. But it has *also* led to an understandable degree of aversion among a large proportion of the population against this paternalistic attitude. Programs have been directed towards or have involved, experts and politicians rather than the man in the street. If the commercial challenge is to be met, then an absolute requirement is a genuine democratizing of the public broadcasting corporations. If they don't understand that they have to produce using the *viewers'* premises instead of the *cultural elites'* premises, which are those premises operative at the moment because the producers belong to this elite, then they won't be able to compete against the commercial offerings. This is because the commercial program, in spite of its paucity, must naturally fulfil the needs of the viewers—without them it is no money-spinner. A democratic utilization of the television medium must not only battle against the imminent commercialization, but must additionally fight against the established public broadcasting corporations if it is to have any sort of contact with the people.

Democratic Television

The commercial challenge is not just commercialization, but for most countries it means a greatly increased importation of culture. The visual culture area is dominated to a much more extreme degree than the printed media, by the culture industry's few multinational centers. Counter-measures should be a restriction on the commercial takeover of the electronic media and a strengthening of national television production.

The democratic use of the television medium must have the principle of *all-sidedness* as a prime requirement. This is not just political all-sidedness but it is also the variation that is required in relation to the different population groups' different and distinct informational and cultural premises and felt needs. Recognition of these *differences* will encounter resistance because it conjures up visions of a class society. But there are numerous studies of information and culture gaps in society which will provide evidence substantiating such an argument. It has received recognition in Danish cultural life: one has begun to speak about cultural democracy (support to grass root's cultural activity) as a possible alternative to making culture democratic (selling Art to the people).

The principle of all-sidedness means that we must produce *different* programs made for *different* population groups (in terms of gender, age, social class and interests) based on these groups *own* premises. The more a production is *aimed* at a particular target group, the greater the *use* it has for the individual.

But the principle of all-sidedness must in addition be thought of as meaning all-sidedness in regards to the actual producers. The greatest possible number of individuals and groups should be given production facilities. Both cable and video offer opportunities for this variation, as well as providing the chance for greater commercialization. But before I look more closely at these media's possibilities, we must consider satellites where one can identify any sort of positive side only with a great deal of fantasy.

Regulation of Satellite Television

In view of the financial interests involved in plans for satellites, and of the industrial political views of the Western European governments related to the sector, a considerable degree of fantasy is required to even believe in the possibility of regulation.

The chance for regulation is, however, due to the myopic industrial political motivation for the satellite projects. The use to which these satellites are going to be put has not yet been seriously discussed; there have only been few attempts at assessing the political and communication (political, in particular) consequences in the inter-European assemblies (Council of Europe and the EEC). But these questions will emerge more frequently as we approach the launching around the middle of the '80s. Such questions as:

- What will the political and cultural effect be on, for example, England receiving German television, and France receiving English television?
- What will be the effect on all countries receiving commercial television from, say Luxembourg, well-packed with cheap American programs?
- What will happen when competition for the Western European national media is financed by advertising money?

This last point is particularly complicated because a movement in advertising money will at the same time both strengthen the foreign influence and weaken the national media. The problem will evolve at various tempi:

- Is it possible to accept that some countries which either have no advertising on television (Denmark, Sweden and Norway), or a fiercely regulated version (like West Germany), are subject to competition from other countries (like, for instance Britain) which have a much more liberal advertising code (for instance, advertising within the individual programs)?
- If there is *no* regulation will this mean that the most liberal country (i.e., Luxembourg or, perhaps, England) will lay down the norms which others will follow in order not to create a distortion of the competitive situation. Can one allow a marketplace with free competition? This situation would attack the foundations of the national television and government regulation of the medium with which people spend most time. Western European television would be wide open for the international American culture industry.
- If there is regulation, for instance, in some form of compromise between a strict and lax regulative legislation, then there will still be commercial television imposed on certain countries against their will and there will exist inter-European competition for advertising revenue. This will mean financial insecurity for the national media and particularly for national television. Competition will nominally take place without any kind of handicap: but, in practice, certain countries will have a considerable advantage because of language and cultural conditions, and they will be much stronger in this "fair" competition. Dare one open up for even this regulated competition?

If satellite television is "switched on" in Europe, a very unpredictable confusion of political and cultural influence will arise. At the same time, the start of advertising on satellite transmissions will create a considerable risk for national media, which is to a great extent, financed through advertising. Until the opposite can be shown to be the case, it seems realistic to expect that a well-prepared and well-argued presentation of these problems in international fora will both worry national governments and national capitals so much that they will hinder advertising on satellites. A certain apprehension can be detected. West German Social Democrats have spoken out strongly against the Luxembourg satellite which has been offered financial backing from West German newspaper interests. England's strategy, even with Mrs. Thatcher at the reins, is, at present, limited to sending advertising-free BBC programs via satellite. And in France, most interests in the field are now state affairs as a result of nationalization. But the Mitterand government, which also has a large part of the shares of Radio Luxembourg, is yet to decide whether it will fight commercials on satellites or, on the contrary, go for the lion's share of the European market for transnational TV.

The unknown factor in the regulation as well as the overall development of DBS in Western Europe is the unforeseen use of ordinary communication satellites for regular TV-broadcasts. Allocated to nationally unauthorized TV-companies, the first satellites in the ECS-system, to be launched in 1983, will offer several all-commercial programs, surely beyond any kind of national regulation. However the question remains, will the national governments allow *reception* of these signals—risking not only unfair competition against national stations, but endangering the whole concept of DBS, which will not be operationable until 1986?

Since the unregulated use of satellites will undermine the so far carefully planned use of television in Western Europe, one can argue the rationale of a continued, necessarily inter-European regulation. But even presupposing that this regulation will be wished by a majority of European nations, which is not to be taken for granted, one may doubt they can agree on a common policy in time. Without regulation, however, Western Europe is facing the well known American state of affairs, competing commercial television, which all European politicans say they want to avoid.

Regulation of Cable

The development of cable networks can in most Western European countries, with some difference in the time-tables, run along two different lines. The first is a continuation of the ongoing private installation of cables, which is the cheapest in the short term since the economic optimum is reached with some 50–100 households. Alternatively, we might find a regulated public installation in which the national PTT or public telephone companies provides a wideband net in part using the existing systems based on neighborhood aerials. This second system would be more expensive in the short term and would need legislation and financial backing. It is the first alternative that will "emerge" as soon as satellites are in operation. I won't raise here the national economic argument which can be used to justify the public alternative in the long term. I will just state that, in my opinion, it is only the public system which gives the *opportunity* for the regulation of the *use* of the net.

The private nets are today subject to considerable restrictions in most countries. But, in a situation where satellites transmit a large number of programs, and where the video market offers interesting software, who is going to stop pirate enterprise in the private net—and with which arguments? Will it be possible to prevent the private nets being linked to a larger net—and with which arguments? The only argument which can be used at the moment to hinder this link-up are based on matters of copyright. When this problem is solved, can a ban be maintained?

A public net, by contrast, presents an opportunity for regulating access. This regulation can match the national media, communications and cultural policies. It would be optimal in Denmark to forbid transmission of advertising, demand a fixed percentage of national production for the various suppliers and ensure capacity in the net for noncommercial programs.

The outlook of an integrated net with an almost unlimited capacity can, for the uninitiated, appear to be something of a nightmare. All sorts of monitoring, control, and direction can happen—home and workplace can be connected and individuals can be totally isolated. An integrated net can result in, not just the same kind of commercial organization that the chaotic development will lead to, but it can, in many observers' views, bring about a centrally-controlled data hell. But one should remember two things during this nightmare. The first is that all data communication can take place in the existing telephone net, with perhaps minor modifications. It is only picture transmission which demands the capacity of wideband which will be provided cheaply through optical fibers. The second point is, that if a public cable transmission net doesn't get established then a widespread private wideband net will arise which, although likely not to be complete in its coverage, will be an alternative to the public telephone net. One can mention here the American deregulation wave in the field of telecommunications and corresponding plans in England. Finally, as noted already, a decision about public widebands is necessary because the possibility for making private nets must be stopped *before* satellites are in action.

The Utilization of Cable: Media Workshops

A public net with space for a considerable number of television programs provides opportunities for local production sites and for *more* than just local distribution. Thoughts and experiments with decentralized television media have, until now, been concentrated on the *immediacy* which a distinct local-oriented program production could use. It is an open question whether this reliance on the limited "geographical" common factor is reasonable. Our private interests and wishes relate much more to our social class membership, gender, age, and education rather than to where we presently live. The production which emanated from local organizations, grass roots movements, mutual cultural interests, etc., but which could be distributed not just to the local society but to *interested groups in the rest of society*—would have considerably more meaning and impact. A group of women in a distinct local society could reach interested women over the whole country. An amateur theater group could come in contact with interested parties in the whole nation. Educational centers could establish "open universities."

A nationwide wideband net will allow this kind of distribution to either the individual households or to places where people meet and this would enhance tape recording and further distribution. The most obvious "center" in Scandinavia would be the Public Library which could act as a production site with technical expertise available and as a meeting place and a distribution center for videotapes. While the existing experiments with local television have had to compete with professional television, this flexible distribution form would allow those with interest to choose both the time and the place for looking at these "amateur" programs. In a society where the video recorder has spread to most homes, programs could be distributed to the individual households. This could even be during the night when the net is not being used for other purposes. This model of production would also allow groups to get away from the present experimental production where programs are made continuously and which quickly sap resources. Groups would be able to produce once a week or once a year depending on needs.

A public wideband net could be kept free of advertising but hardly free of private pay-TV in its various forms, and it is an open question whether it would be an advantage. A public net would also allow the public broadcasting organizations to supplement their output with pay-TV programs and to supplement their revenue at the same time. The pay-TV market should not only be of benefit to private corporations. Since there will be considerable industrial political interests involved in the establishment of a national wideband net, it will be reasonable to match their wishes with a demand that the local production and distribution centers (one in every distinct area) must be linked to any permission given to the establishment of the net. The tradition in Europe surrounding the education of the working man, which ensured the foundation of the public library system, ought to be able to maintain democracy in the picture medium cultural area.

Video and Public Service

In this way video could be a meaningful part of the distribution system in relation to "alternative" production. But the alternative production can only be part of a counterweight balancing the commercialization of video.

As a form of distribution, video is a threat for public service institutions. In national markets video means that there will be other purchasers and importers of programs than just the national broadcasting organizations. Both national and international programs could be reserved for the video market. This will sabotage the whole concept of the public service— certain programs will be restricted to those who have the financial resources to pay for them.

In terms of national economies, the distribution of video programs through private household video machines is extremely costly compared with the radio wave transmission of the public service institution. But a ban on video machines is unthinkable! The alternative to this must be that the public broadcasting organizations enter the video market themselves— both as distributors of their own programs *and* as buyers of domestic and foreign programs with special reference to video distribution. It would be sensible to establish a joint venture with public libraries which, through purchase of video recordings in the same way as book purchases, could have a balancing effect on the market.

By going into the video market, the public broadcasting organizations could ensure a balanced supply in the video market *and* could ensure the broadcast of a desired program in the traditional way. As is the case with pay-TV, it is important that public service institutions get their share of the considerable sums which will be invested in the video market. The public broadcasting corporations must get out of the "transmitted TV" side-branch, and into the mainstream of "TV" if they are to survive both financially and in terms of presenters of culture.

The public broadcasting corporations' competitiveness is good compared with both pay-TV and video. Because of their charters, which stipulate that they must produce balanced programming, they have a much greater experience in making minority programs than do commercial television stations. They have long traditions of "narrow programs" for distinct interest groups: from nature films to stamps, from chamber music to opera.

The great danger is that the public corporations don't realize this and, because of external competition they think they have to compete with Hollywood-type entertainment programs. The last few years developments in Danish television, for instance, indicate this danger very well. Danmarks Radio has put a greater emphasis on Light Entertainment and Sport—and imported series—in its program policies because one third of the Danish population can see the same things on West German television. Taking such a course of action will be suicidal for smaller broadcasting organizations. I think that one both *can* and *must* battle against commercial television with television that people are in some way able to *use*. But if the solution of combatting American programs in satellite TV, video TV, and cable TV becomes a matter of transmitting more American programs *oneself,* in order to keep the viewers one has now, then one might as well give up. Cultural independence is not just a question of national language sub-titles in Anglosaxon programs.

AT THE FINISHING POST

The central element in this attempt to counterbalance the foreign cultural and commercial invasion is not very original. This was a strengthening of the national production, in part through the auspices of the public broadcasting corporations, and in part through the local media workshops. In relation to the first, I have considered it vital to stress that a public service will only be able to survive if it is able to establish real cultural democracy in its program policies. Only by producing different programs aimed at societies' distinct groups will it be able to build up a consumer utility which can compete against the commercial offerings which will also be aimed at particular groups. The starting conditions are such that the public corporations have a certain experience with production aimed at specific groups and that, in the long-run, they have an advantage over the commercial organizations in that they don't have to nurse advertisers' needs.

The second point I have thought essential to stress related to decentralized production. I feel that geographic commonality, which has been the motivation until now, is not enough in itself. There has only been limited success in the many national experiments with local television and radio. There are many reasons, including the simple economic factor, but it is also due to the one-sided reliance on an audience which is only defined geographically. The more important factors are social class, gender, and age. One of the few experiments which has worked—the Reading, PA.

trial in the USA—was such an experiment: the provision of television for the elderly.

The foundation of media workshops, suitably equipped with technical and personnel resources, available to all the local societies' citizens and interest groups will give rise to genuinely original productions. These won't interest everyone, but will very strongly interest those groups who have the same perceived situation. It is crucial that these media workshops have a distribution side which extends beyond the local society so that sufficiently large receiver groups are available. Wideband nets will be a suitable distribution system because they can transmit to, for instance, libraries, where productions can be viewed or loaned on video as well as being the source of special arrangments, and they can also transmit to the individual households.

I don't believe that a critical attitude towards the new media and its technology is acceptable if this doesn't, at the same time, see that some of this technology is part of a better society—perhaps even as a prerequisite for a better society. The new media provide an opportunity for a real democratizing of freedom of expression and of cultural life in general.

Rather than reject it out of hand and revert to privatized self-sufficiency, we should use its possibilities. Perhaps again, if we must be self-sufficient, if we must use the earth's ecology correctly, if we shall avoid a whole world full of restrictions and requirements, we will need to have easy access to considerable databanks so that we can, in a decentralized way, control these complex processes.

A last remark. Both the commercial challenge and the democratic response make it necessary that the total educational system accepts that the visual culture is not just a curious appendage to the culture of the written word. A critical relationship to the stream of pictures in our society and practical skills in the use of the picture media must receive a more important position in the educational process than they have today. But taking everything into account, shouldn't it be possible to make sure that all this can lead to something other than a commercial revolution in culture?

13

The "Privatization" of British Communications

Graham Murdock

INTRODUCTION

The present Conservative Government in Britain came to power in May 1979 pledging to roll back the boundaries of the State and to restore market competition. This remains the central plank of their economic policy. As the Chancellor of the Exchequer, Sir Geoffrey Howe, recently told party members, their policies are guided by the basic principle "that state ownership and control should be displaced or supplemented wherever sensibly possible, by the discipline and pressures of the market place and by some degree of private ownership."[1] This process of "privatization", as it is usually called, is already well underway within the communications industries, where it has been pursued in a variety of ways.

The two most publicized moves have involved selling shares in nationalized companies back to private investors and ending The Post Office's historic monopoly over the supply of telecommunications equipment and services and opening up selected areas of activity to private contractors. Less obvious, but equally important, is the impact that intensified competition and restrictions on public funding have had on British Telecom and on the BBC. Here we are not talking about a *transfer* of ownership and allocative control from the State to corporate enterprise, but about a subtle *transformation* within the public sector itself in which notions of public service are being jettisoned in favor of criteria of profitability and market success. And last, but certainly not least, there is the "privatization by default"

[1] Quoted in Riddell, 1982, p. 7.

265

that is occuring in the key areas of cable and satellite technology, where the Government is encouraging rapid expansion while insisting that the financial backing comes entirely from private sources and making no provision to establish a public sector in either industry.

This paper details the way these various forms of "privatization" have been pursued so far, highlights some of their consequences, and points to some of the contradictions that are beginning to emerge around them.

DENATIONALIZATION TO DATE

The nationalized companies have been the first and most obvious target for the government's "privatization" policies. They came in promising to sell back the shares to private investors as quickly as possible, but things have proceeded rather more slowly than many people expected. The long awaited disposal of 51 percent of Britoil, the major North Sea oil concern, had to wait until November 1982 and the plans to sell off British Airways had to be shelved when the company incurred serious losses, though some of the more buoyant divisions are being sold off. In June 1982, for example, the government invited bids for International Aeradio which makes air traffic control systems and manages airports in the Third World, and has made consistent profits since its foundation in 1947. The following month, it also announced that it had "unfrozen" the shares of Ferranti, a leading defense and electronics company. The government had originally placed the public shares (acquired in 1974) with private investors in 1980 on the condition that they did not re-sell them. This restriction was lifted in July 1982, leaving shareholders free to buy and sell in the normal way, and it is widely thought that a takeover bid may be in the offing, particularly since Ferranti's defense interests look even more enticing now that the equipment lost in the Falklands War is due to be replaced. The likeliest bidder is GEC (General Electric Company) whose current cash reserves of around £800 million are just about double the likely asking price. As well as returning Ferranti to the private sector however, the government has also denationalized two other important communications concerns: British Aerospace and Cable and Wireless.

British Aerospace was the first to go when half the shares were sold off early in 1981 for around £150 million. The group, which was formed in 1977 to bring together the various nationalized aerospace and aviation concerns, currently ranks as the fourth largest aerospace company in the Western world with important interests in civil and military aircraft, missiles, and satellites. It is the prime contractor for the European Space Agency's major L-Sat project (L for Large) which will carry both television channels and business communications facilities, and it is a partner (along with Ferranti, Avica, and the Midland Bank) in the British consortium which holds a 2.4 percent share in Arianespace, the company formed to develop the Ariane rocket which is providing the launch facilities for the ESA satellite programme. In addition, British Aerospace has important stakes in the burgeoning privately financed satellite sector. Together with Ferranti, Barclays Bank and Guiness Mahon, it was a prime backer of Satellite Television Ltd. (SATV) which successfully started Europe's first transnational commercial television service in April 1982. This uses the ESA's experimental Orbital Test Satellite to provide an English language channel which is relayed to a total of some 20,000 households in Finland, Norway, and Malta via community receiving dishes. Also, BA has recently gone into partnership with GEC and British Telecom to form United Satellites which has been asked to build Britain's own Direct Broadcasting Satellite.

The other major communications company to be denationalized to date is Cable and Wireless. This was originally formed in 1929 to bring together the telecommunications and cabling activities of companies operating in different parts of the then Empire. It was nationalized in 1949 but the bulk of its interests remained in laying and maintaining submarine cables and in operating telecommunications networks in overseas countries. More than three-quarters of its business still comes from franchises in these areas, the largest being in Hong Kong and Bahrain. Cable and Wireless installs a public telecommunications systems at its own expense and in return gets a share of the operating revenues. These activities continue to be very buoyant and in the financial year to the end of March 1981, the company made pre-tax profits of £62 million. Consequently, it proved a vary attractive proposition to private investors and when 49 percent of the shares were put up for sale at the end of 1981, the offer was oversubscribed six times and raised £224 million. Although Cable and Wireless' historic strength lies in its overseas operations it has recently declared its intention of moving into the British telecommunications market to take advantage of the recent relaxation of the State's monopoly on provision. And in February 1982, it made an important breakthrough when the government announced that it was awarding a 25 year license to the alternative telecommunications system proposed by the consortium which Cable and Wireless has formed with British Petroleum and Barclays Merchant Bank. This "Mercury" system, as it is called, aims to cream off some of the lucrative business traffic from the British Telecom network by providing advanced voice, data, and teleconferencing facilities. These services will be carried on a figure-of-eight optical fibre loop linking London to six major provincial cities using the "wayleaves" (or rights of way) alongside British Rail's existing tracks, thereby cutting costs and heading off environmental objections. This initiative is one of the first substantial outcomes of the more general "liberalization" of telecommunications set in motion by the British Telecommunications Act of 1981.

THE RE-MAKING OF BRITISH TELECOM

The Act did two main things. First, it split the British Post Office into two self-contained operations. The Post Office continued to deal with mail, while telecommunications services became the province of the re-named, British Telecom. And secondly, it ended the State's monopoly over the provision of services in both areas and opened them up to commercial competition. As a result, there are now several private mail concerns competing with the Post Office for a share of the money-spinning business trade, including Priority Mail, a joint venture between Western Union Corporation and English China Clays. The situation in the telecommunications sector is rather more complex, however, since "liberalization" is proceeding along three separate dimensions; equipment supply, the licensing of alternative networks, and the provision of "value-added" services.

One important area of equipment supply where competition is gathering momentum is the market for private automatic branch exchanges (PABX's) which provide the hub of a company's in-house telephone system. Until recently, British Telecom had a monopoly on the provision of systems offering under one hundred extensions. This has now lapsed, and since trade sources estimate that this sector of the PABX market will be worth around £60 million by the beginning of 1984, the large transnational suppliers like ITT have been quick to move in. However, the likely pattern of competition is already apparent in the longer-running battle over the supply of telephones themselves.

British Telecom's monopoly in this area ended in the Autumn of 1981 when seven models were cleared for open sale through any retailer. Most of these were drawn from the gimmick range (such as the "Mickey Mouse" and "Snoopy" phones), but in the summer of 1982 twelve more models were released, including a number of executive styles with strong sales to business users. To many commentators' surprise, British Telecom responded to this increased competition aggressively. They formed a new division, British Telecom Enterprises, and went in for some high powered marketing. They recruited a seven hundred strong sales force to sell telephones and peripherals to the business community, and in June 1982 they started to market phones to domestic users through seventy branches of Boots, the large department store. These moves are indicative of an important re-orientation in British Telecom's activities and operating philosophy. As one financial journalist (Brooks, 1982) put it; "BT is turning itself into a well-run, market-oriented and commercially minded company. Put simply, BT is out-privatizing private industry" (p. 7). But this economic success entails considerable social costs, as we can see if we look at the way that British Telecom has responded to the government's decision to license the rival "Mercury" network.

Traditionally, British Telecom has fulfilled its public service function of trying to bring a phone within the economic reach of every household, by subsidizing the losses on local calls (which are mainly made by domestic subscribers) out of the profits from long distance and international calls, 80 percent of which are paid for by business users. However, in May 1982, BT announced a new tariff structure aimed at phasing out the cross-subsidy to domestic users and massively favoring business. Charges on the one hundred most used trunk routes (which include the routes that "Mercury" will compete for) were cut by 35 percent, and there were substantial reductions on other long distance routes and on Transatlantic calls. After the new charges were announced one of the major banks calculated that its annual phone bill was likely to drop by around 75 percent. But these gains for business have meant losses for domestic consumers in the form of increased rates for local calls and higher installation and rental charges which will take a telephone out of the reach of even more families. It already costs £96 to install a phone and pay the first quarter's rental before any calls are made, and for many semi-skilled and unskilled workers this is almost twice their weekly take-home pay. As a result, five million low income households are currently without a phone and this figure is bound to rise substantially as the new cost structure begins to bite.

A similar shift in favor of business users is also evident in the other main area of "liberalization"—"value-added services" which are provided and paid for on top of the basic telephone service. These include, teleconferencing, "electronic mail," and viewdata services, and it is in this last area that BT's shift of emphasis from public utility to corporate service is most evident.

British Telecom's Prestel service was launched in 1979 as the world's first interactive public viewdata system which allowed subscribers to use the phone network to call up specific "pages" of information from a central computer store for display on specially adapted domestic television sets. The service was originally conceived as a mass public utility with three million subscribers by 1983. But take-up was much slower than expected and by the Spring of 1982 there were still only 17,000 subscribers in all (Post Office Engineering Union, 1982, p. 28). Domestic penetration, the original rationale of the system, was particularly low, the main problem being cost. In addition to buying or renting the necessary receiving equipment, Prestel users have to pay for the calls to the central data store, for the time they are connected to the computer, and for the individual "pages" of information they consume. According to one estimate, for an average domestic user these costs were likely to add up to around £35 a month in 1980 (Young and Grey, 1980), which was well beyond the means of many households and certainly "high enough to prevent Prestel becoming a regularly used source of information in the home" (Winsbury, 1979, p. 46). In the meantime, private viewdata systems like the Stock Exchange's TOPIC share-price information service, had begun to develop in the hope of creaming off some of Prestel's existing and potential business users. In response, BT more or less abandoned its original project of providing a cheap and universally accessible home information service, and set out to make itself more attractive to corporate customers. As Richard Hooper, Prestel's newly appointed director told the press at the beginning of 1981, "our new marketing strategy replaces the shotgun 'all things to all men, women and children' approach with a rifle-shot 'hardsell'."[2] More recently Prestel has made some belated attempts to woo back domestic users with a cheap off-peak service and travel and banking facilities, but the main thrust of its strategy remains the "hard-sell" to business.

The first move in this direction was the introduction of the "Gateway" system which linked the Prestel computer with a range of private data bases to give business users access to a much greater range of information. The latest addition is a link-up with American Express to provide direct access to the airline flight information displayed in the major terminals at Heathrow, Gatwick and Manchester. As well as extending the range of available information, Prestel has also increased the variety of services it offers business users. It now provides electronic funds transfer facilities and an "electronic mail" service which can transmit documents at a rate of 3,500 words a minute (as against 80 words a minute over the standard telex system). And last, but by no means least, it has massively expanded its ability to cater to corporations wanting a secure "in-house" communications system. To this end, in March 1982, Prestel announced that it was increasing the number of "closed user-groups" it could handle from 50 to 32,000, and slashing the basic cost of the service by 90%, from £2,500 a year to £250.

A similar orientation to business users is also evident in other aspects of BT's "value-added" services. In June 1982, for example, the Industry Secretary announced that the government was proposing to license a consortium to be formed by British Telecom (but with at least half the shares held by private investors) to operate an expanded radio telephone service for corporate and institutional users. In addition, British Telecom is a partner (along with British Aerospace and GEC) in the United Satellite consortium which is currently negotiating with IBM to establish an advanced business communication system between Britain and the east coast of

---

[2] Quoted in Stothard, 1981, p. 61.

North America carrying telephone, data, and teleconferencing services. Moreover, BT has already announced a link-up with another American concern, Satellite Business Systems, to allow its customers access to SBS's system in the USA, and it is planning to use one of the European Space Agency's ECS satellites to launch a small dish service, called Satstream, which will provide "electronic mail," data transmission, and teleconferencing facilities for business users throughout Europe by the end of 1983.

But British Telecom's growing commercial orientation and success carries with it a contradiction, since the more profitable it becomes the weaker the established arguments for retaining it within the public sector and the greater the pressures to make it into a fully commercial company. The government has been quick to recognize this and in November 1982 they published a second Telecommunications Bill providing for the sale of five percent of BT's equity and the establishment of a new regulatory Office of Telecommunications. The bill is expected to become law in the Summer of 1983, and with Telecom's net assets currently standing at £8 billion this will be far and away the biggest nationalized concern to be offered for sale so far.

However, the debate over whether or not to de-nationalize British Telecom cannot be properly understood in isolation. It has to be seen as part of the government's overall approach to the development of the "new" television industries which are beginning to emerge around the technologies of satellite and cable.

COMMERCIALIZING THE "NEW" TELEVISION INDUSTRIES: SATELLITE AND CABLE

The present government's enthusiasm for the rapid expansion of commercial satellite and cable services marks a significant break with the thinking that prevailed during the last Labour administration, as we can see if we look at the most important official document on communications policy produced in that period, The Annan Committee's report on *The Future of Broadcasting*.

The committee was appointed in the Spring of 1974 to consider the future shape of broadcasting services, with particular reference to the implications of new technologies. In the event, most of the discussion centered around the allocation of the vacant fourth national television channel so that when the report finally appeared in the Spring of 1977, the discussion of new technologies took up only one chapter out of twenty-nine. But what there was certainly did not please the commercial lobby. The committee did not support "cable services being developed as Pay TV" (p. 220), and they saw no prospect of an early start to Direct Satellite Broadcasting services. "We guess," they said, "that countries in Western Europe will not give a high priority to providing broadcasting satellite services. But we cannot rule out the possibility that there will be a move to launch a service in the next 15 years" (p. 385). This turned out to be a monumental miscalculation. Just two years later, in 1979, France and West Germany announced a joint project to launch national DBS services by 1983, and Radio-Télé-Luxembourg commissioned three feasibility studies to investigate the prospects for a commercial DBS system covering most of Western Europe.

Not surprisingly, many British commentators were worried about the impact these developments might have on the domestic media industries. The Committee on the Film Industry (chaired by the former Labour Prime Minister, Harold Wilson) expressed their concern "as to the effect on the British film industry of this intrusion into the home market of films in English transmitted from outside the United Kingdom" (p. 12). While senior figures in commercial television, like Howard Thomas, talked about an "invasion from Outer Space via Madison Avenue" (1980, p. 16). But others in the communications industries were rather more positive, spurred on by the prospect of rapidly expanding markets for equipment and programming, both at home and abroad, and particularly in the Third World where satellites provide an economical solution to the problem of setting up a national television service. Consequently, they began to lobby hard for an early start to a British DBS system which would stimulate the domestic market and provide a shopwindow for potential overseas customers.

The Conservative Government responded by setting up a Home Office inquiry to investigate the options. It reported in May 1981, recommending an early but modest start with a two channel DBS service by 1986. This decision was strongly endorsed by the Home Secretary whose ministry is formally responsible for satellite developments. He declared that he was "prepared to give serious consideration to the option for as early a start as possible with satellite broadcasting, with perhaps one or two television channels and possibly other information services" (Home Office, 1981, p. 2).

And after considering a number of bids, the government announced that the privately backed United Satellite consortium was to build the satellite, and that the four available radio channels and both television channels would be run by the BBC, but would *not* be financed out of public funds. According to the BBC, the first channel, called "Window on the World" will be supported by a supplementary license fee of around £10 a year levied on everyone buying or renting the necessary receiving equipment. For this viewers will be able to see repeats of the "best" of BBC 1 and 2 and a selection of material from around the world. The second channel will be a straight subscription service using a scrambled signal and costing around £10 a month. This will offer new feature films (possibly within weeks of their theatrical release), full coverage of selected sporting events, and broadcasts of operas, concerts, and dramatic performances. While these proposals pose a considerable problem for established notions of public service broadcasting (as I shall show in more detail later), they are entirely consistent with the way the "new" television industries are becoming "privatized by default" through the government's insistence that developments are financed entirely from private sources. This same trend is also characteristic of the other main area of expansion, cable television.

Cable has a long history in Britain. The first cable system for relaying radio services was installed in 1928, just six years after the BBC first started broadcasting, and by the end of the last War around a million households were receiving their radio over the "wire." But the big expansion came when television transmissions resumed in 1946. Take-up was uneven however. In a number of areas poor signal reception deterred people from buying or renting a television set, while in other place local councils were banning rooftop aerials on environmental grounds. Cable provided a solution to both problems and offered a double income to the cable operators since the major concerns (like Rediffusion and Radio Rentals) were also among the main companies renting receiving sets. As UHF transmissions steadily improved in quality, however, the number of cable subscribers started to drop and the operators began to press for permission to introduce subscription services to bump up their revenues. Despite concerted lobbying, however, the Pilkington Committee on Broadcasting which reported in 1960, argued strongly against any experiment with pay TV (p. 271). But then, to the surprise of many commentators, the recently elected Labour government granted a license to Pay TV Ltd. in 1965, to conduct a home box office experiment using British Relay's cable networks in London and Sheffield. However, when the government refused to extend the project in 1968, it folded. Nor was the incoming Conservative Government much more sympathetic. They granted five licenses for experimental services in 1972, but they were all for non-profit-making community channels. Nevertheless, three of these were backed by the major concerns, Rediffusion, British Relay and EMI (as it then was), in the hope that they could keep a foot in the door and demonstrate their public responsibility. Nonetheless, when a Labour Government was elected again in 1974 it became obvious that they were not going to be allowed to launch full subscription services, and one by one they withdrew their support.

By the time the Thatcher administration came to power in 1979, however, the major cable companies were under pressure. The growth in set rentals brought about by the introduction of color television had begun to level off after the dramatic increases of 1975–80 when the proportion of

TV households with color sets rose from 39 percent to 70 percent.[3] Expansion was continuing with the acquisition of second sets and the boom in the use of videotape recorders, but it was widely felt in the trade that pay-TV would provide a useful extra stimulus. In addition, the cable operators who were also major set manufacturers (notably Thorn-EMI) were worried about the expiration of the patent for Britain's PAL system in 1983 and the further exposure of the domestic equipment market to overseas competition, particularly from Japan. At the same time, corporations like Thorn-EMI and Rediffusion who also have substantial stakes in program provision (through their film and television production interests) were eager to capitalize on the "software" market that pay-TV would open up. As a result, the cable industry began to lobby hard for the rapid extension of subscription services.

The government responded quickly and sympathetically. In November 1980, the Home Secretary announced that he was prepared to consider applications for pay-TV franchises from existing holders of cable licenses, and in March 1981 pilot schemes were authorized in eleven locations, with two further licenses added soon afterwards. These schemes were all commercial ventures offering a selection of recent feature films for an average monthly subscription of around £10. None of them are being run by local authorities, and with the exception of British Telecom's operation in Milton Keynes, none is controlled by a public corporations. However, BT's involvement has made no difference to the service provided, since it is conceived as a profit-making venture and the programming is being supplied by Selec TV who is also servicing the two Phillips operations. Moreover, though several operators have plans for local community services of one kind or another, they are not officially required to provide finance, equipment, or transmission time for them if they don't wish to. It is, in fact, another clear instance of "privatization by default" in which a key area of future communications is being colonized by private capital and market criteria with no attempt to provide for a countervailing public sphere.

The cable companies see the experiments rather differently however. For them, they do not go nearly far enough along the road to "privatization" since they are forbidden to take advertising and the franchises are due to expire in September 1983. The industry's position was very firmly expressed in the *Report on Cable Systems* (1982) which the government commissioned from the Information Technology Advisory Panel it had appointed in June 1981. The Working Group who compiled the Report all had interests in the cable industry and one was a senior executive of Rediffusion, the largest cable operator in the country. Not surprisingly, their

---

[3] Calculated from figures provided in Flach, 1982, Table 1, p. 12.

conclusions endorsed the dominant view in the industry and called on the government;

> to remove the barriers to private investment in cable systems that at present exist, to allow reasonable (though not absolute) freedom for entrepreneurial flair and in so doing give a great stimulus to large parts of the IT industry. (p. 49)

Moreover, they stated "quite categorically" that there was "no need for any public subsidy to cable systems" (p. 47), and that future expansion could be safely left to private investors, providing they were allowed to maximize their profits by taking "overall responsibility for providing cable services, including both the physical infrastructure and the programme material in one area" (p. 41).

The Report was warmly welcomed by the Minister for Industry and Information Technology, Kenneth Baker, who claimed that the "re-wiring" of Britain by the cable industry is essential to the country's economic recovery since it "will not only create jobs, it will create new industries. Just as the railway network did in Victorian times."[4] On closer inspection, however, this analogy with the railways turns out to be rather more double-edged than it looks at first. True, the railway "mania" of the 1840s provides a model of buccaneering enterprise carving out huge opportunities and profits for private business. But the later history supports the case for an integrated public service in the interests of rational planning. And this tension, between the rhetoric of unfettered competition on the one hand and the logic of national planning on the other, has now begun to surface in the debates around the future of cable, as we can see if we look at the evidence presented to the Hunt Inquiry which the government set up to consider the further implications of cable expansion.

"RE-WIRING" THE NATION: CONFLICTING INTERESTS AND POLICIES

The Cable Report's scenario for "re-wiring" the nation has had a mixed reception from the media industries, reflecting the conflicting interests of the different sectors. Not surprisingly, the advertisers are by and large strongly in favor since they see cable as a fairly cheap way of reaching clearly defined (and high spending) social groups (see The Advertising Association, 1982), and they estimate that given the go-ahead, commercial cable could be attracting annual advertising revenues of £120 million by 1995 (at 1980 prices), which is around four percent of the projected total for

---

[4] Quoted in Chamberlain, 1982, p. 51.

the UK industry (Institute of Practitioners in Advertising, 1982, p. 4). The commercial television companies, on the other hand, are rather more cautious since they see cable as a threat to their revenues and audiences and they have called for a much fuller investigation of "the amount and form of advertising to be permitted on Cable and the likely impact on other services funded by advertising" (Independent Television Companies Association, Ltd., 1982, p. 4).

The Independent Broadcasting Authority (which is the official body charged with regulating commercial television and radio) has gone even further and urged that cable services should be financed solely from subscriptions to prevent "unfair" competition for advertising revenue (1982, p. 7). The BBC, too, is less than enthusiastic, despite the fact that its Enterprises division is currently providing the programming for Visionhire's cable operation in central and south London. However, as we shall see presently, their major interest in new technology lies with DBS and they see the social inequalities produced by commercial cable as a fundamental break with the principles of public service on which their operations ostensibly rest. As they told the Hunt Inquiry:

> A novel kind of inequality may be introduced into the broadcasting system when ability to pay for services relates to the economic status of whole communities or suburbs. Wideband cable is not likely to make economic sense outside the larger cities and towns, or even the more affluent suburbs of some cities. So yet another shadow of social divisiveness may fall across our communities...If cable becomes symbolic of what Mayfair can have but Brixton cannot, what Metropolitan Man may enjoy but Rural Man is denied, then one more social tension will be generated in an uneasy age. (1982, pp. 4–5)

This argument against an exclusively private sector approach is strongly supported by the Post Office Engineering Union (1982a) who represent around half of British Telecom's workers, and it forms the jumping-off point for their alternative plan. "What Britain needs," they argue, "is one integrated communications system carrying the whole range of telecommunications and broadcasting services in a single set of ducts on a single fibre optic cable" (p. 32). An exclusively private sector approach will never achieve this since operators will only be interested in the more lucrative markets. Consequently, to achieve full national coverage and to avoid the wasteful duplication of facilities, they recommend that "British Telecom should, provide, install, and maintain the cable for all the cable systems in this country" (POEU, 1982b, p. 3).

BT's case is backed up by its technical expertise and superiority. Whereas the commercial cable companies are proposing to extend the existing co-axial cable network, British Telecom is planning to use advanced fibre optic technology, and in June 1982 they launched a two-year feasibility study to iron out the technical problems with an integrated broadband system. This FibreVision project, based on Milton Keynes, is small in scale (only eighteen households) and restricted to relaying conventional broadcast signals plus the subscription service and Prestel (which is being provided free for the purposes of the study), but it contains two important innovations. Firstly, it replaces the normal tree and branch pattern of cabling with a star network which connects the user to a central switching point and allows a wider range of interactive services to be provided more cheaply. And secondly, it simplifies the equipment that users need by building most of the necessary electronic "intelligence" into the cable system itself. FibreVision is British Telecom's prototype for the national cable system of the future where they would operate the system itself, but apart from selected "value-added" services, the "software" would "be provided by the widest possible range of public and private operations" (Post Office Engineering Union, 1982b, p. 2). This division of responsibilities already operates within the Prestel system with British Telecom acting as a common carrier for a variety of Information Providers, ranging from nationalized industries and governmental agencies to commercial data companies and citizen's advice organizations like the Consumers' Association.

British Telecom's plan is widely supported within the Labour Movement and has attracted some program providers (most notably SelecTV) who see it as offering them better opportunities than a system where the major cable operators would also act as the main "software" sellers. More surprisingly, it is also backed by the Centre for Policy Studies (1982), a Conservative Party think-tank, who are strongly in favor of a scenario in which "BT or a consortium of BT and private interests would provide the means of transmission and have the role of common carrier and a range of other information providers would supply everything else" (para. 2.3). This endorsement, which is clearly at odds with the rhetoric of free competition, is indicative of an important split in Conservative policies towards communications in general and information technology in particular.

Although the government is pledged to stimulate national economic recovery through private enterprise and market forces, the term, "national," is rather more significant than it first appears. It implies not only the revival of domestic demand but also the strengthening of Britain's competitive position in world markets, a point that was strongly underlined in a recent report (1981) by the National Enterprise Board (the main organization for channeling public money into industry). This began by arguing that information technology (broadly defined) is the world's fastest growing economic sector and that between 1980 and 1985 the global market for equipment and service is expected to more or less double, from £54 billion to £105 billion (at constant prices). But it went on to show that Britain is currently in a weak position to take advantage of this expansion since domestic companies have been losing ground rapidly to overseas manufacturers in both the international and home markets, the most spectacular example being videocassette recorders where Japanese firms have taken the lion's share of British sales. To counteract this decline, the NEB advocates state intervention to support companies which have a chance of achieving a meaningful share of world markets in high technology products. However, they concede that since only a handful of firms are in this position, this would mean backing the established market leaders or large corporations (such as British Petroleum) who want to move into information technology. This policy of sponsoring the megafirms is also backed by a recent report on the state of the electronics industry from the National Economic Development Office which argues strongly that;

> Public sector resources will need to be concentrated on individual firms (or groups of firms for joint projects) who are likely to be able to build up internationally competitive positions. (1981, p. 21)

This argument is further strengthened by the fact that similar policies are also being pursued by Britain's two main European competitors, West Germany and France, with the same end in view. Nevertheless, this thrust generates an interesting contradiction between the rhetoric of free competition and minimal state intervention, and the economic logic of sponsored monopoly. Even so, there are clear signs that this logic is being pursued in various ways.

The government is still backing the information technology ventures which the last Labour administration supported through the National Enterprise Board (which has now been renamed The British Technology Group). The most important of these initiatives is the "microchip" manufacturer, INMOS, which has received almost £100 million of Government money so far, in the hope that it will make a major impact on the international market for advanced semiconductors with its 64–K D-Ram unit launched in July 1982. Up until recently, the government also made important interventions through its procurement policies which tended to favor British firms when awarding contracts for work needed by Government departments or public organizations. However, a 1981 EEC directive now makes this preferential treatment much more difficult by insisting that foreign companies are invited to tender for all public contracts, and the American firms of Burroughs and IBM are currently testing the strength of this rule in the courts, alleging that ICL (Britain's only significant computer maker) was unfairly favored by recent contract decisions. In its regulatory and licensing roles, however, the government still has considerable powers of positive discrimination and the recent franchises awarded to "Mercury" and United Satellites show a clear tendency to favor major British corporations. Both consortia involve leading IT companies (GEC,

British Aerospace, and Cable and Wireless), major banks (Barclays and Rothschilds), and in the case of "Mercury," one of the very largest companies in the economy, British Petroleum.

At the time of writing, the final decision on cable expansion has not been announced. But it is already clear that British Telecom will play a central role in "re-wiring" the nation through its participation to consortia bidding for local franchises. The award of the first two DBS channels to the BBC also suggests that the government sees the corporation as a potential world beater in the international market for satellite "software." But to understand this, we need to look more closely at what has been happening to the BBC over the last few years.

THE ENTERPRISING BBC: THE TRANSFORMATION OF PUBLIC BROADCASTING

The BBC has been in severe financial difficulties for some time. Whereas in the late sixties it cost around £15,000 to produce a 90 minute single play, it now takes £150,000, a ten-fold jump in just over a decade (see Sutton, 1981). Increases in other areas are less spectacular but still substantial. Over the same period, however, the BBC's real income has steadily dropped as the revenue derived from the compulsory license fee has fallen further and further behind the rate of inflation. And the situation is getting worse. Over the next few years, the BBC has to replace the color video equipment which was installed in the sixties and is now coming to the end of its useful life, and invest in the new generation of electronic cameras and digital editing facilities. In addition, the introduction of the second commercial television channel (Channel Four), the launching of breakfast-time TV, and the growth of the video, cable, and satellite industries is pushing up the price of creative labor, program ideas, and feature films (which up until now have provided a reasonably cheap schedule-filler). To meet these demands, the corporation calculated that the annual license fee for a color set would need to be raised from £34 to £54, but political realism led them to pitch for £50 (see Sandles, 1981). In the event, they got £46, which was already nowhere near enough to cover projected costs, particularly since increasing numbers of people had been defaulting on their license payments. This shortfall has had the effect of intensifying the BBC's search for alternative sources of income through its enterprises division.

This started modestly enough in 1960 when the corporation set up a Television Enterprises section to handle overseas program sales and product merchandising from popular shows like *Dr. Who*. In 1968, this merged with the equivalent radio department to take on the production and sale of records as well, and by the end of the 1975 financial year, the revamped division, renamed, BBC Enterprises, was achieving a total turnover of £5 million. Then in May 1979, the division's formal status was changed. It was registered under the Companies' Act as a limited company, and though it remained a wholly-owned subsidiary of the BBC, it was given more freedom to operate independently as a commercial venture. The impact showed up rapidly in the annual figures. Whereas in 1980 turnover stood at £9.6 million, a year later it had jumped to £15.6 million, reflecting the division's more aggressive stance.[5] Not everyone has welcomed this development however. A number of Third World countries, for example, have begun to complain that the new competitive pricing policy puts BBC programs out of their reach. But as the Controller of BBC 2, Brian Wenham has explained (1981) this is inevitable.

> BBC Enterprises now takes a consciously more aggressive sales posture, so much so that poorer countries used to gentle treatment wonder openly whether the institution they seek to emulate has not lost something of its missionary and tutorial position . . . the answer is that it has, for hard-nosed commercial reasons. (p. 39)

As we shall see, this abandonment of the "tutorial" stance towards the Third World is part of a more general retreat from paternalism. But the BBC's new aggressive export policy is not confined to developing countries, it has also made an impact on the world's most lucrative market for television programming, the USA.

Up until recently, BBC programs were mainly distributed through the Public Broadcasting System, which was good for the corporation's critical reputation but not for its revenues. It made some impact on the network market when CBS screened the second run of *The Six Wives of Henry VIII* in its 1971–72 season, but it was still known mainly for its costume dramas and prestige documentary series such as, *The Ascent of Man*. However, the cult success of *Monty Python's Flying Circus* and Thames Television's surprise hit with *The Benny Hill Show,* suggested that there was growing interest in British entertainment shows, and the BBC determined to capitalize on it. Accordingly, it terminated its long-standing distribution agreement with Time-Life and looked around for alternative outlets. The breakthrough came in June 1982, when BBC Enterprises announced a ten-year deal to provide up to 40 percent of the programming for the new Rockefeller-backed Entertainment Channel. As Bryon Parkin, Enterprises Managing Director, explained at the time, the potential payoffs for the BBC are enormous, since not only can

---

[5] Figures taken from the last Annual Report and Accounts of BBC Enterprises Limited deposited in Companies House, London.

American audiences (now) enjoy a much wider range of BBC programmes. What is more, The Entertainment Channel acts as a showcase for our programmes with PBS and the commercial stations. We
hope to get two bites at the cherry.[6]

In addition to increasing program sales to the USA, the BBC is also
hoping to make substantial profits from video "software" and subscription
television. The first of these areas gathered momentum in 1978 when BBC
Enterprises established its Home Video Department to market cassettes
and discs of BBC programs, while the second took off in earnest in March
1982 when the government approved the BBC's plans for two DBS channels, following a change in the terms of the corporation's charter in 1981,
to allow it to participate in cable and satellite services.

The BBC justifies these moves by arguing that the revenues they produce will help to maintain the diversity and quality of the service offered
to ordinary license payers in an era of escalating production costs. As Robin
Scott, one of the BBC's senior executives, has explained;

These new ventures (or adventures) into profit-making activities
must be seen to be, and must actually be, extensions of the public
broadcaster's mission. They must be more than self supporting. They
must be profitable enough to finance the development of programme
services at all levels to the direct viewer. (Scott, 1980, p. 17)

But others are less convinced, and see these moves as marking a significant break from the defining tenets of public service broadcasting.

The first, and simplest of these is the principle that every license
payer should have equal access to the whole of the BBC's output if they so
choose. This was firmly established by the BBC's original Director General, Lord Reith, in the corporation's first ever annual report in 1928,[7] and
it was strongly endorsed in the BBC's recent evidence to the Hunt Inquiry,
where they claim that public broadcasting expressly

precludes elitism. There is a healthy indiscriminateness about it. It is
not directed at one class or income group. All citizens have the right
of equal access to the BBC's service of information, education and
entertainment provided they are prepared to pay their license fees.
(BBC, 1981, p. 1)

But if this is so, doesn't the introduction of DBS subscription services violate this principle? According to the BBC the answer is "no." On the contrary, it argues:

It was the appeal of their universality—the ability of everyone from
Brighton to the Butt of Lewis to acquire additional services firstly by

---

[6] Quoted in Hodges, 1982, p. 19.
[7] On this point, see Swann, 1980, pp. 6ff.

the acquisition of a receiving dish and if he so chose, by the payment of a subscription—that attracted the BBC to DBS in the first instance. The ability to pay a little more offers all viewers the enrichment of their choice without the unwelcome social divisiveness that cable must produce.

On closer inspection, however, the "little more" to be paid, turns out to be quite a lot. In addition to buying or renting the necessary receiving equipment, subscribers would have to pay at least £130 a year to obtain both channels, and this is well beyond the pockets of most families living on low incomes or state benefits, and with unemployment running at three million, this is a sizeable section of the population. Consequently, as Brian Wenham (1982) has conceded; "from the point of view of 'citizen as viewer' . . . we have to assume that broadcasting's third age could see deepening divisions between those who have access to the new and those who have no such access" (p. 8). In fact, the poor may well be disenfranchised twice over; once by their inability to pay for the new services, and once again by the reduced diversity of mainstream programming brought about by the combination of increased competition for audiences and mounting political pressures.

Historically, the BBC has opposed the commercial sector's celebration of the audience's sovereign right to be entertained, with an ideology of authorship which insists on the producers' right to express themselves. This is the other main defining principle of public service broadcasting. Indeed, according to Robin Scott, "the public broadcaster must stand or fall on his record in the encouragement of authorship" (1980, p. 18). So, where commercial production sets out to give the public what it appears to want (as measured by the ratings), or what advertisers are prepared to subsidize, public service broadcasting aims to give them what they "need" as defined by the creative personnel and intellectual mandarins. As the 1928 annual report put it, the BBC set out to "give the public something slightly better than it now thinks it likes." This project necessarily involved a paternalistic, even patronizing stance towards the audience, an assumption that "we" know what's best for "you." But, as the BBC told the Pilkington Committee in 1960, they "held it to be an important part of their responsibility to "give a lead" to public taste, in literature and the arts and elsewhere. There was in this a risk of paternalism, but it was a risk of which they were conscious and which they must accept (pp. 37–38). As a consequence, public broadcasting has traditionally centered around a thoroughly bourgeois public sphere opposed to both the populism of the market and the more critical, combative currents within popular culture. These elements were never completely excluded, however, and they have maintained a constant though marginalized presence through the work of radical playwrights and documentary-makers whom the ideology of authorship has given a license to provoke.[8]

However, this space is now beginning to close as mounting competition pushes prime-time output more and more towards populist programming which can mobilize the broadest possible audience. This means more use of commercially successful formats, a greater tendency to work with the images and assumptions that are already most firmly embedded in popular consciousness, and less willingness to take risks with innovative and radical shows which may offend or bore sections of the potential audience. These pressures are not in themselves new of course. They are indicative of a more or less permanent tension between the commercial and the "cultural," the acceptable and the agitational, which goes back to the beginnings of the BBC's operations.

The corporation started out in 1922 as the British Broadcasting Company, a private consortium formed by the leading equipment manufacturers (at the government's urging) as a monopoly supplier of programming to help promote the sale of receiving sets. John Reith was appointed Managing Director; a dour, humourless, Scottish Calvinist, who felt he had a mission to turn what had begun as a business into a cultural crusade.[9] Consequently, when the company was turned into a public corporation in 1926 (following the recommendations of The Crawford Committee) Reith's desire to "elevate" the masses was given full reign. But the corporation never quite shrugged off its commercial origins. Moreover, because it remained a monopoly supplier it was obliged to provide something for everyone, which meant catering to existing tastes as well as trying to elevate them. Serving the public by entertaining them was therefore built into the original definition of public service and, as Reith explained in his 1928 report: "Let there be no idea that this category is one given grudgingly and under pressure. . . To provide relaxation is no less positive an element of policy than any other."[10] For some time, these twin aims of entertainment and education were pursued together through the policy of "mixed" programming, whereby variety shows on the main channel would be followed by classical recitals in the hope that "people would turn on to Tommy Handley (a popular comedian) and then by accident hear Beethoven" (Trethowan, 1970, p. 5). In this way, the programmers hoped to encourage listeners to "progress smoothly from the known to the unknown, from 'Grand Hotel' to Beethoven, and perhaps, even from Beethoven to Schoenberg" (Gillard, 1964, p. 7). This policy was abandoned after the last War

---

[8] I have developed this point in Murdock, 1980.

[9] On the BBC under Reith, see Curran and Seaton, 1981, Chapter 8.

[10] Quoted in Scannel and Cardiff, 1982, p. 178.

when the success of Radio Luxemburg and the BBC's own audience research had revealed a hugh unsatisfied demand for more entertainment, and a new mass-channel, The Light Programme, was set up "to provide a service for those who are in the mood for entertainment and relaxation," as the BBC's publicity put it.[11] Then, when the "pirate" radio stations of the mid-sixties discovered the new youth audience, The Light Programme was revamped again and relaunched as Radio 1, with programming based around the "Top 40" play lists, interspersed with talk shows and phone-ins built around the personalities of the new disc jockeys, many of whom were bought in from the "pirates."

A similar process of accommodation to commercial styles and formats can also be traced in television, where competition from the independent companies from the late 1950s onwards, has gradually forced the main channel, BBC 1, to match like against like and embrace the game show and other "American" formats it once despised. These concessions to commercialism are deftly brought within the rubric of public service broadcasting by evoking Reith's original argument that providing good professional entertainment also counts as a service to the public. However, as the IBA's John Thompson (1981) has recognized, by ignoring the other main tenets of the original concept, this revised definition conveniently qualifies all forms of commercial broadcasting for the title of "public service" since in a market system "unless over a significant period the output is serving the public, making itself useful, offering interest and diversion, it can neither grow nor flourish...nor even survive" (p. 16).

As a number of recent commentators (Ehrenberg and Barwise, 1982) have pointed out, the monetary pressures on the BBC to concentrate on "yet more 'Top Twenty' type programmes" (p. 6) are now increasing significantly, as competition from home video, cable services and the Fourth Channel make it more and more difficult for the corporation to hang on to the audience share it needs to justify its continued claim to the compulsory license. And as the Director General Designate, Alasdair Milne, has explained; "if (they) were to fall consistently below 45 percent of the audience in total on the BBC side, (they) would be in trouble" (Milne, 1981, p. 8). As well as these indirect effects of competition, however, commercial criteria have recently entered in the BBC's programming more directly through the rise of sponsorship.

Corporate sponsorship of the arts and sports has grown rapidly in Britain over the last five years, spearheaded by the tobacco firms, the oil companies, and the major banks. The cigarette manufacturers see it as a way round the current ban on direct television advertising, while the banks and oil companies are mainly concerned with improving their images and defusing criticisms of their excess profits and spoilation of the

---

[11] For a fuller account of this shift in policy, see Katz, 1980.

environment. At the same time, escalating production costs and severe cutbacks in public funding have encouraged many arts organizations to look for sponsorship money to supplement their income, and in June 1982, the general image of corporate support got a useful polishing when the National Theatre (which had previously turned down several lucrative offers of business money) signed a three year deal with Imperial Tobacco, worth £240,000. For most sponsors, however, the maximum returns in terms of publicity and public awareness only come if the events they support are televised. For some time, however, the BBC refused to mention the sponsors of the events they screened, either in the credits or in the *Radio Times'* program listings. This has now changed for several reasons. In the first place, it proved impossible to keep the advertisements that festooned sporting grounds out of shot, which made the rationale for refusing to name the sponsor more and more of a ritual gesture. Secondly, this technical breach was underscored by hard economics. The BBC was able to cut its program expenses by offering less to promoters of events who received "a contribution towards the cost" from advertisers, but, in return for this subsidy, the sponsors demanded the right to reasonable acknowledgement in the broadcasts themselves and in the program listings, and this is now accepted. Hence, when the BBC televised Sir William Walton's 80th birthday concert from the Royal Festival Hall in March 1982, the words "concert and exhibition sponsored by The Observer" appeared as a full screen credit, which led one senior broadcaster to remark that sponsorship finally "became legitimate at the BBC that night" (Thomas, 1982, p. 7).

Recently, however, this commercial push towards populist programming which marginalizes dissent and celebrates the commonsense solidarities of consumerism, community, and nationhood, has been reinforced by more overtly political pressures on the BBC's coverage of contentious issues. These have been increasing for some time (most notably with regard to the coverage of the situation in Northern Ireland and to the debates around nuclear disarmament and defense), but they reached a new pitch of intensity during the Falkland's War in the Spring of 1982.

The attacks began in earnest after Britain suffered its first serious loss when the destroyer, HMS Sheffield, was sunk on May 4. From then on, pressures on the media to help the war effort and bolster morale mounted rapidly, and given its unique position as *the* national public broadcasting organization, the BBC was particularly vulnerable. As Alasdair Milne later remarked; "I always thought the Government would turn on us. Once there were losses and the Government came under pressure they would be likely to turn on the media, and the BBC in particular."[12] Conservative critics objected strongly to the BBC's use of the term, "the British," in-

---

[12] Quoted in Pocock, 1982, p. 7.

stead of "we," despite the fact that this convention had been observed throughout the Second World War. As Milne explained; "We always spoke of 'the British' then—one reason is that if you start talking about 'our troops' and 'our ships', then it is natural to speak of 'our policy' when you mean the present Government's policy and then our objectivity would no longer be credible" (p. 7). But it was precisely this attempt to remain detached that critics most objected to. As Mrs. Thatcher told the House of Commons (Parliamentary Debates (Hansard), 1982b) on May 6

> Many people are very concerned indeed that the case for our British forces is not being put over fully and effectively. I understand that there are times when it seems that we and the Argentines are being treated almost as equals and almost on a neutral basis. I understand that there are occasions when some commentators will say that the Argentines did something and then "the British" did something. I can only say that if this is so it gives offence and causes great emotion among many people. (col. 279)

Five days later, on May 11, she returned to this theme again, this time, singling out the BBC for particular censure.

> I know how strongly many people feel that the case for our country is not being put with sufficient vigour on certain—I do not say all—BBC programmes. The chairman of the BBC has assured us that the BBC is not neutral on this point and I hope that his words will be heeded by the many who have responsibilities for standing up for our task force, our boys, our people and the cause of democracy...It is our pride that we have no censorship. That is the essence of a free country. But we expect the case for freedom to be put by those who are responsible for doing so. (Parliamentary Debates (Hansard), 1982b, cols. 598–599)

Four days after this outburst, the Minister for Defense Procurement, Lord Trenchard, attacked a BBC radio story about the delay in fitting the Sea Wolf anti-missile-missile to British warships. Although the report did not suggest that the Sheffield could have been equipped in this way, he nevertheless felt that listeners might be left with the impression that the ship could have been saved, and this he said was "good neither for the morale of the forces in the task force, nor, let it be said, for the widows of the gallant men who died on HMS Sheffield" (Parliamentary Debates (Hansard), 1982a, col. 416). As the BBC's Head of Radio, Dick Francis, saw it, however, even if Trenchard was right "it (was) not the BBC's role to boost British troops' morale or to rally the British people to the flag" adding that "the widow of Portsmouth is no different from the widow of Buenos Aires" (Pocock, 1982, p. 7). The government, however, disagreed, and on May 19, they invoked Clause 19 of the BBC's Charter and took over one of the Corporation's External Services transmitters on Ascension Island to establish their own radio station, Radio Atlantico del Sur, under the direct control of the Secretary of State for Defence, John Nott. This was the first time the government's right to commandeer BBC transmitters had been used since the last War.

The BBC for its part, objected strongly to these moves and called for an inquiry into the administration's actions during the Falklands' crisis. But a number of people, both inside and outside the corporation, are convinced that the government's loss of confidence in the BBC will generate continued pressure and lead to even more caution in the coverage of contentious issues.

CONCLUSION: THE DISAPPEARING PUBLIC SPHERE?

This paper has had the modest aim of outlining the main trends in the British communications industries since the Conservative election victory in the Spring of 1979. More particularly, I have tried to show how recent developments have tipped the already unequal balance between the public and private sectors even further in favor of the leading corporations and has seriously weakened the countervailing power of the public sphere, at both the economic and ideological levels.

However, I would like to add that this shift should not be seen as the exclusive product of Conservative Party policies. These have simply accelerated the more general underlying movement towards a "privatized" communications system based on production commanded by the large corporations and consumption built around the domesticated audience. This movement, which has been gathering momentum steadily since the end of the last War, entails the disappearance of the public sphere in the double sense that public organizations play a less and less important role in organizing core areas of production, and consumers progressively withdraw from participation in collective forms of leisure and social life. Taken together, these trends mark the emergence of a new and "higher" form of Monopoly Capitalism, characterized by the extended reach of the megacorporations and the further rationalization of consumption. The "new" television industries (of video, telematics, cable and satellite) are central to this emerging social formation. Not only do they turn more and more information and leisure facilities into commodities for sale at a price, but they use the domestic television set to deliver them to consumers in the comfort and isolation of their own homes.

Put like this, it is all too easy to lapse into the pessimism which sees this movement as an unstoppable juggernaut. But trends are not necessarily destinies, and as well as colonizing new areas of social and imaginative life for capital, these shifts are also producing new contradictions which may generate new kinds of struggles in the spheres of both production and consumption.[13]

By making access to information and entertainment goods more and more dependent on ability to pay, for example, the "new" communications industries certainly tighten the existing relation between cultural and economic power. But what happens to those who are dispossessed by the commercial "enclosure" of information and priced out of the market for the new forms of managed demand and participation? Will they develop a new culture of "information poverty," a culture of resignation? Or will they create new forms of expression and resistance based on low cost media? The recent growth of community media, alternative recording and film making, and working class publishing in Britain, suggest that this second option might not be entirely beyond the bounds of possibility.[14] At the moment though, these initiatives are fragmented and financially precarious. But could they be strengthened and linked together to create a genuinely popular public sphere that would break with the populism of the market and the paternalism of the existing public institutions, to develop a new kind of communications system? If so, how might it be financed, organized and controlled? And what role should or could the Labour Movement play in promoting forms of expression generated by movements among women, young people, and ethnic minorities, which have only a tangential relation to traditional socialist and trade union organizations? These are large issues and they deserve to be discussed at length, but they will have to wait now for another occasion.

REFERENCES

The Advertising Association. (1982). "Submission to the Inquiry Into Cable Expansion and Broadcasting Policy." (May 26).

BBC. (1982). "The BBC's Evidence to the Hunt Committee." (May).

Brooks, R. (1982). "Telecom's Private Line." *The Sunday Times* (May 9), 54.

Centre for Policy Studies. (1982). "Evidence to the Home Office Inquiry into Cable Expansion and Broadcasting Policy." (April).

Chamberlain, M. (1982). "How a Tory Government is Backing a British Revolution." *Marketing Week* (May 7), 51.

The Committee on Broadcasting (The Pilkington Committee). (1960). *Report.* Cmnd. 32262. London: HMSO.

---

[13] The emerging contradictions in the sphere of production are interestingly discussed in Schiller, 1981, and Lipietz, 1982.

[14] See, for example, Morley and Worpole, 1982, and Partridge, 1982.

The Committee on the Future of Broadcasting (The Annan Committee). (1977). *Report.* Cmnd. 6753. London: HMSO.

Curran, J., and Seaton, J. (1981). *Power Without Responsibility.* London: Fontana.

Ehrenberg, A. S. C., and Barwise, T. P. (1982). "Submission to the Inquiry into Cable Expansion and Broadcasting Policy." London Business School, (May).

Flach, D. (1982). "Celestial Broadcasting—or Just a Researcher's Seventh Heaven." *Journal of Advertising 1* (1), 12.

Gillard, F. (1964). *Sound Radio in the Television Age.* London: BBC Publications.

Hodges, A. (1982). "BBC Wins a US Cable Showcase." *Screen International* (June 12), 19.

Home Office (U.K.). (1981). *Direct Broadcasting by Satellite: Report of a Home Office Study.* London: HMSO.

Independent Broadcasting Authority. (1982). "Evidence to the Inquiry into Cable Expansion and Broadcasting Policy." (May), 7.

Independent Television Companies Association, Ltd. (1982). "Cable and the Future Development of Broadcasting." (May 28), 4.

Information Technology Advisory Panel. (1982). *Cable Systems: A Report.* London: HMSO.

Institute of Practicioners in Advertising. (1982). "Submission to the Inquiry into Cable Expansion and Broadcasting Policy." (May 28), 4.

Interim Action Committee on the Film Industry (The Wilson Committee). (1980). *Third Report: Statistics, Technological, Developments and Cable Television.* Cmnd. 7855. London: HMSO.

Katz, R. S. (1980). "Public Patronage, Music and the BBC." *Journal of Broadcasting 24*(2), 241–252.

Lipietz, A. (1982). "Towards Global Fordism?" *New Left Review 132* (March–April), 33–47.

Milne, A. (1981). "What Changes in British TV in the '80s?" *Combroad 52* (July–September), 8.

Morley, D., and Worpole, K. (Eds.). (1982). *The Republic of Letters: Working Class Writing and Local Publishing.* London: Comedia Publishing Group.

Murdock, G. (1980). "Authorship and Organisation." *Screen Education 35* (Summer), 19–34.

National Economic Development Office. (1982). *Policy for the UK Electronics Industry.* London: NEDO.

National Enterprise Board. (1981). *A Strategy for Information Technology.* London: NEB.

Parliamentary Debates (Hansard). (1982a). *House of Lords Official Report.* Vol. 438, No. 88 (May 14), column 416.

Parliamentary Debates (Hansard). (1982b). *House of Commons Official Report.* Vol. 23, No. 113 (May 11), columns 598–599.

Parliamentary Debates (Hansard). (1982c). *House of Commons Official Report.* Vol. 23, No. 110 (May 6), column 279.

Partridge, S. (1982). *Not the BBC/IBA: The Case for Community Radio.* London: Comedia Publishing Group.

Pocock, T. (1982). "Putting the Truth Before Popularity." *The Standard* (May 12).

Post Office Engineering Union (POEU). (1982a). "The Cabling of Britain." (May 24). London: POEU.

Post Office Engineering Union (POEU). (1982b)."The Submission of the Post Office Engineering Union to the Hunt Inquiry into Cable Expansion and Broadcasting Policy." (June 3).

Riddell, P. (1982). "Howe Aims to Draw in Tentacles of the State." *Financial Times* (July 5), 7.

Sandles, A. (1981). "The Money Programmes." *Financial Times* (November 10), 19.

Scannell, P., and Cardiff, D. (1982). "Serving the Nation: Public Service Broadcasting before the War." *In* B. Waites et al. (Eds.), *Popular Culture: Past and Present.* London: Croom Helm.

Schiller, H. I. (1981). *Who Knows: Information in the Age of the Fortune 500.* Norwood, NJ: Ablex Publishing Corporation.

Scott, R. (1980). "Public Broadcasting: The Changing Media Scene." *Intermedia 8*(6), 17.

Stothard, P. (1981). "Why Instant Information is Slow to Catch On." *The Sunday Times* (January 25), 61.

Sutton, S. (1981). "Spend, Spend, Spend: The Dramatic Rise of Production Costs." *Journal of the Royal Television Society* (March–April).

Swann, Sir M. (1980). "Financing the Concept of Public Service Broadcasting." *Journal of the Royal Television Society* (May–June), pp. 6ff.

Thomas, H. (1982). "The Financier Takes a Little Credit." *Financial TImes* (June 29), 27.

Thomas, H. (1980). "Commercial Challenge of Transatlantic Satellite TV." *Journal of the Royal Television Society* (September/October), 16.

Thompson, J. (1981). "Public Service Broadcasting." *Independent Broadcasting, 28* (March), 16.

Trethowan, I. (1970). *Radio in the Seventies.* London: BBC Publications.

Wenham, B. (1982). "The Third Age of Broadcasting." *The Observer* (March 21), 8.

Wenham, B. (1981). "The BBC Welcomes a New Market." *Intermedia 9* (4), 39.

Winsbury, R. (1979). *The Electronic Bookstall: Push-Button Publishing on Videotex.* London: International Institute of Communications.

Young, I. and Grey, I. (1980). *The Cultural Implications of Videotex Services in the UK.* London: Communications Studies and Planning, Ltd.

Author Index

Subject Index